21

Hiro Mashima

Translated and adapted by William Flanagan
Lettered by AndWorld Design

KC
KODANSHA
COMICS

'ail volume 21 is a work of fiction. Names, characters, places, and incidents
e products of the author's imagination or are used fictitiously. Any
blance to actual events, locales, or persons, living or dead, is entirely
dental.

ansha Comics Trade Paperback Original.

hed in the United States by Kodansha Comics, an imprint of Kodansha
ublishing, LLC, New York.

ation rights for this English edition arranged through Kodansha Ltd.,

ublished in Japan in 2010 by Kodansha Ltd., Tokyo.
'78-1-61262-058-9

d in the United States of America.

kodanshacomics.com

5 4 3 2 1

lator: William Flanagan
ring: AndWorld Design

FROM HIRO MASHIMA

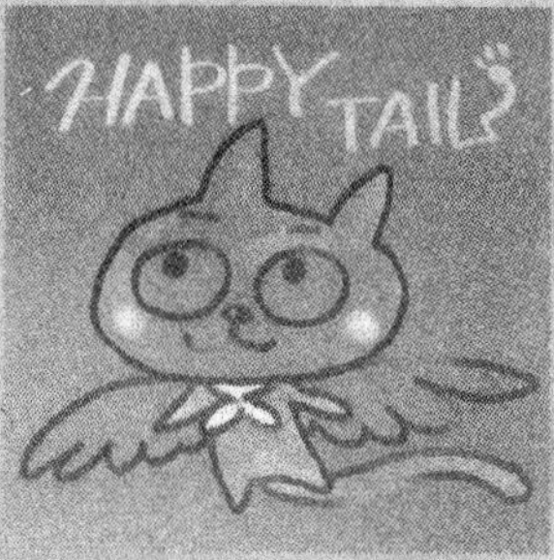
HAPPY TAIL

Wow! At the very same time that this volume 21 comes out in Japan, the fan book called *Fairy Tail Plus* goes on sale too!! It has a short story that never got into the tankobon, a short story drawn just for the book, other manga, stories from behind the scenes, color illustration galleries and more! It's going to be a really fun book!! For all those who would like a more in-depth look at Fairy Tail, I urge you to pick up this book!*

*Fairy Tail Plus is only available in the Japanese language in Japan.

Original Jacket Design: Hisao Ogawa

Contents

Honorifics Explained

Throughout the Kodansha Comics books, you will find Japanese honorifics left intact in the translations. For those not familiar with how the Japanese use honorifics and, more important, how they differ from American honorifics, we present this brief overview.

Politeness has always been a critical facet of Japanese culture. Ever since the feudal era, when Japan was a highly stratified society, use of honorifics—which can be defined as polite speech that indicates relationship or status—has played an essential role in the Japanese language. When addressing someone in Japanese, an honorific usually takes the form of a suffix attached to one's name (example: "Asuna-san"), is used as a title at the end of one's name, or appears in place of the name itself (example: "Negi-sensei," or simply "Sensei!").

Honorifics can be expressions of respect or endearment. In the context of manga and anime, honorifics give insight into the nature of the relationship between characters. Many English translations leave out these important honorifics and therefore distort the feel of the original Japanese. Because Japanese honorifics contain nuances that English honorifics lack, it is our policy at Kodansha Comics not to translate them. Here, instead, is a guide to some of the honorifics you may encounter in Kodansha Comics books.

-san: This is the most common honorific and is equivalent to Mr., Miss, Ms., or Mrs. It is the all-purpose honorific and can be used in any situation where politeness is required.

-sama: This is one level higher than "-san" and is used to confer great respect.

-dono: This comes from the word "tono," which means "lord." It is an even higher level than "-sama" and confers utmost respect.

kun: This suffix is used at the end of boys' names to express familiarity or endearment. It is also sometimes used by men among friends, or when addressing someone younger or of a lower station.

chan: This is used to express endearment, mostly toward girls. It is also used for little boys, pets, and even among lovers. It gives a sense of childish cuteness.

Bozu: This is an informal way to refer to a boy, similar to the English terms "kid" and "squirt."

Sempai/
senpai: This title suggests that the addressee is one's senior in a group or organization. It is most often used in a school setting, where underclassmen refer to their upperclassmen as "sempai." It can also be used in the workplace, such as when a newer employee addresses an employee who has seniority in the company.

Kohai: This is the opposite of "sempai" and is used toward underclassmen in school or newcomers in the workplace. It connotes that the addressee is of a lower station.

sensei: Literally meaning "one who has come before," this title is used for teachers, doctors, or masters of any profession or art.

[blank]: This is usually forgotten in these lists, but it is perhaps the most significant difference between Japanese and English. The lack of honorific means that the speaker has permission to address the person in a very intimate way. Usually, only family, spouses, or very close friends have this kind of permission. Known as yo-bisute, it can be gratifying when someone who has earned the intimacy starts to call one by one's name without an honorific. But when that intimacy hasn't been earned, it can be very insulting.

FAIRY TAIL

フェアリーテイル

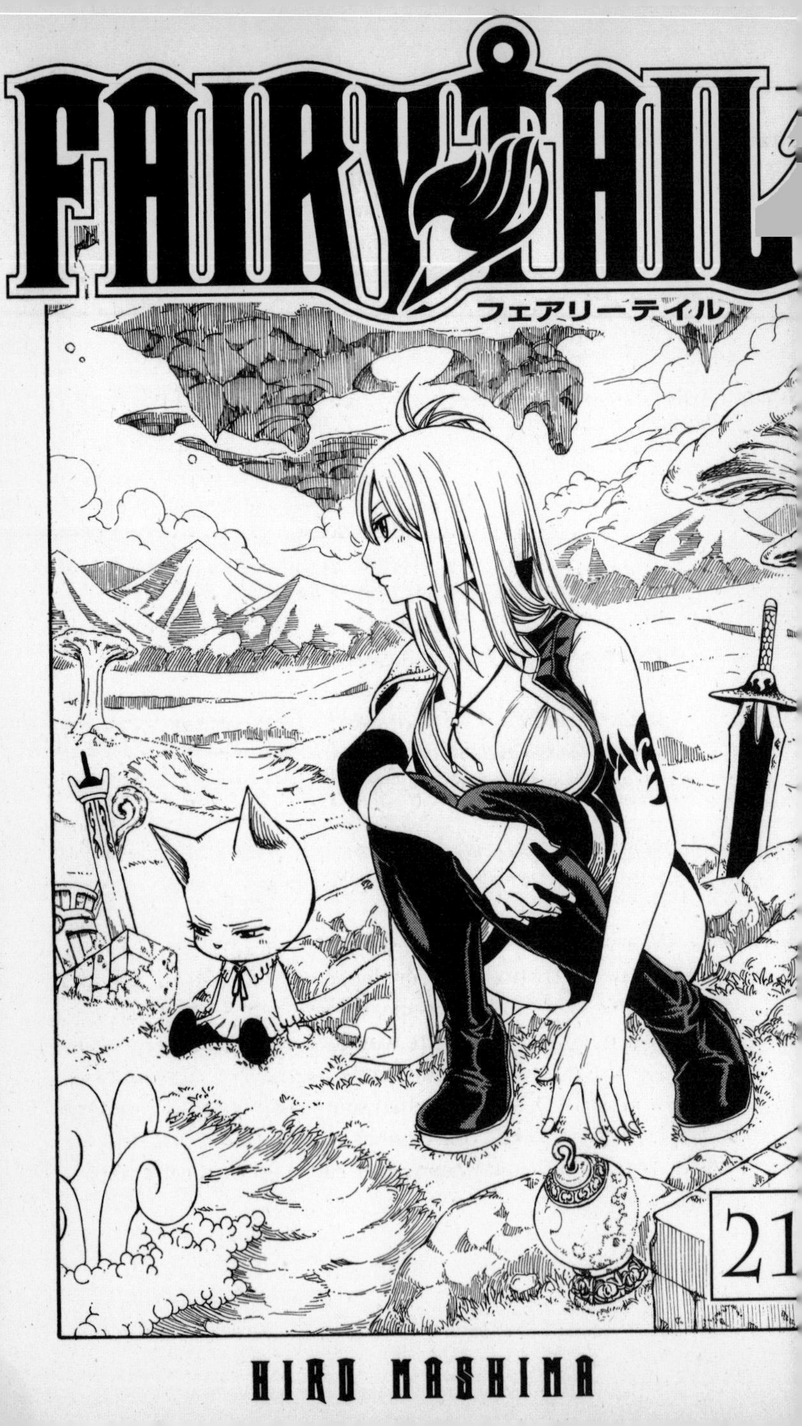
21

HIRO MASHIMA

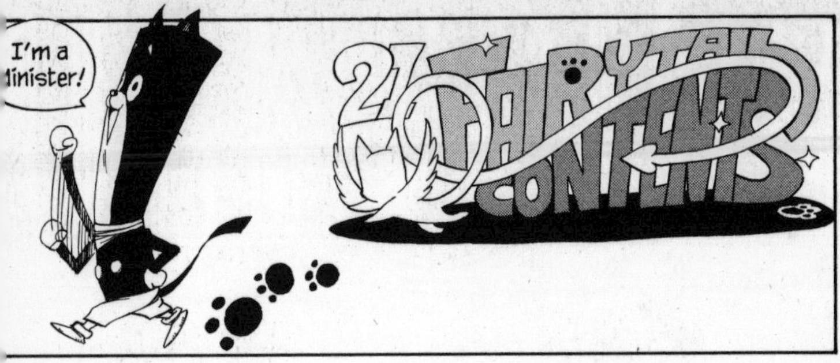
I'm a
inister!
21
FAIRY TAIL
CONTENTS

Published in serial form by Weekly Shōnen Magazine 2010 Volumes 10-18.

FAIRY TAIL

フェアリーテイル

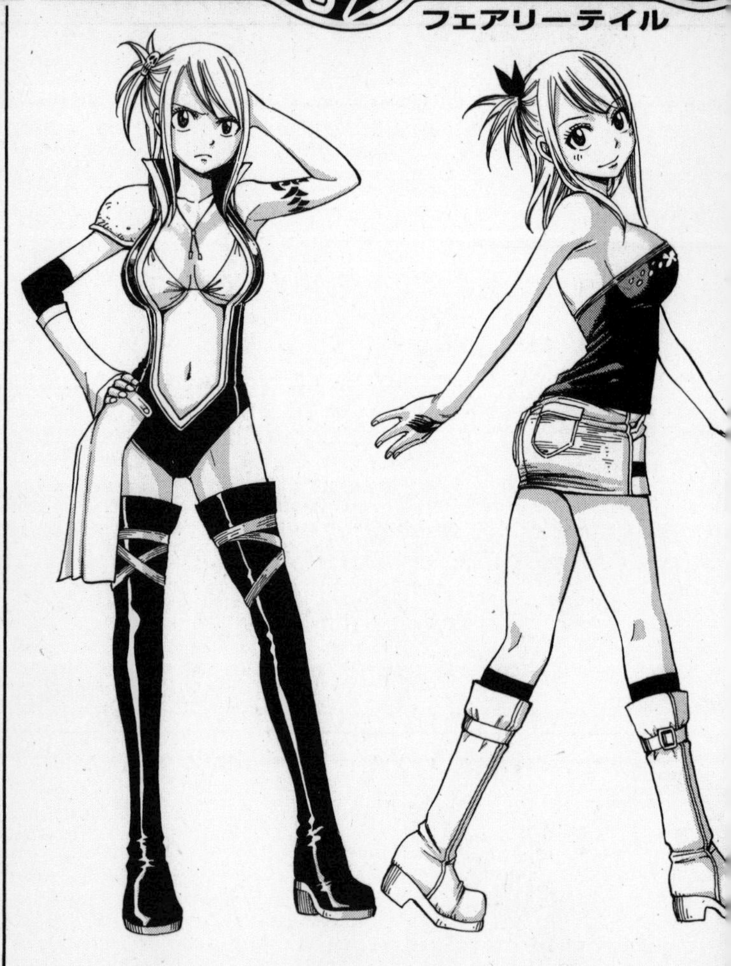

Chapter 170, Fairy Hunting

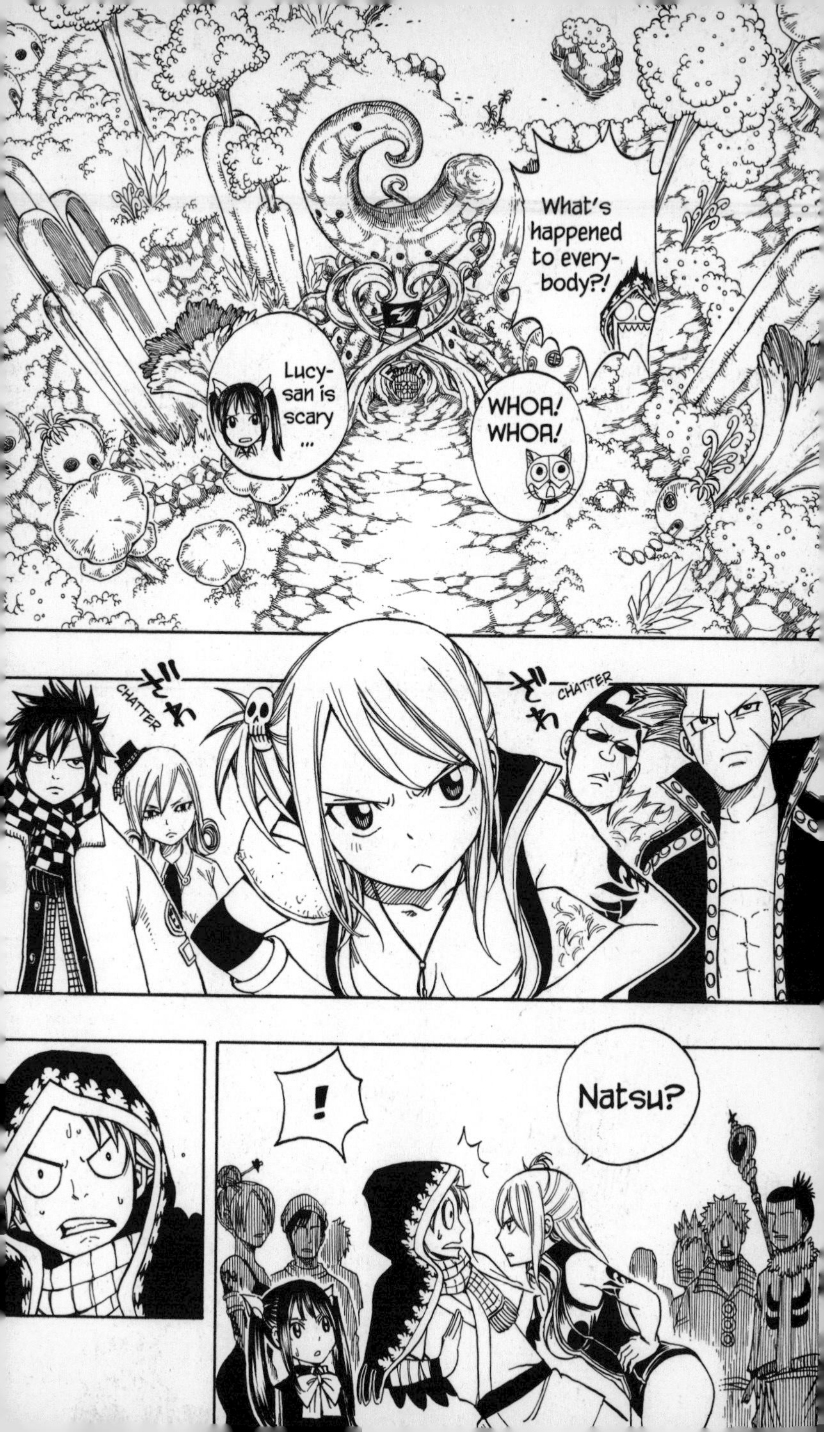

What's happened to every-body?!
WHOA! WHOA!
Lucy-san is scary ...
ざわ CHATTER
ざわ CHATTER
Natsu?
!

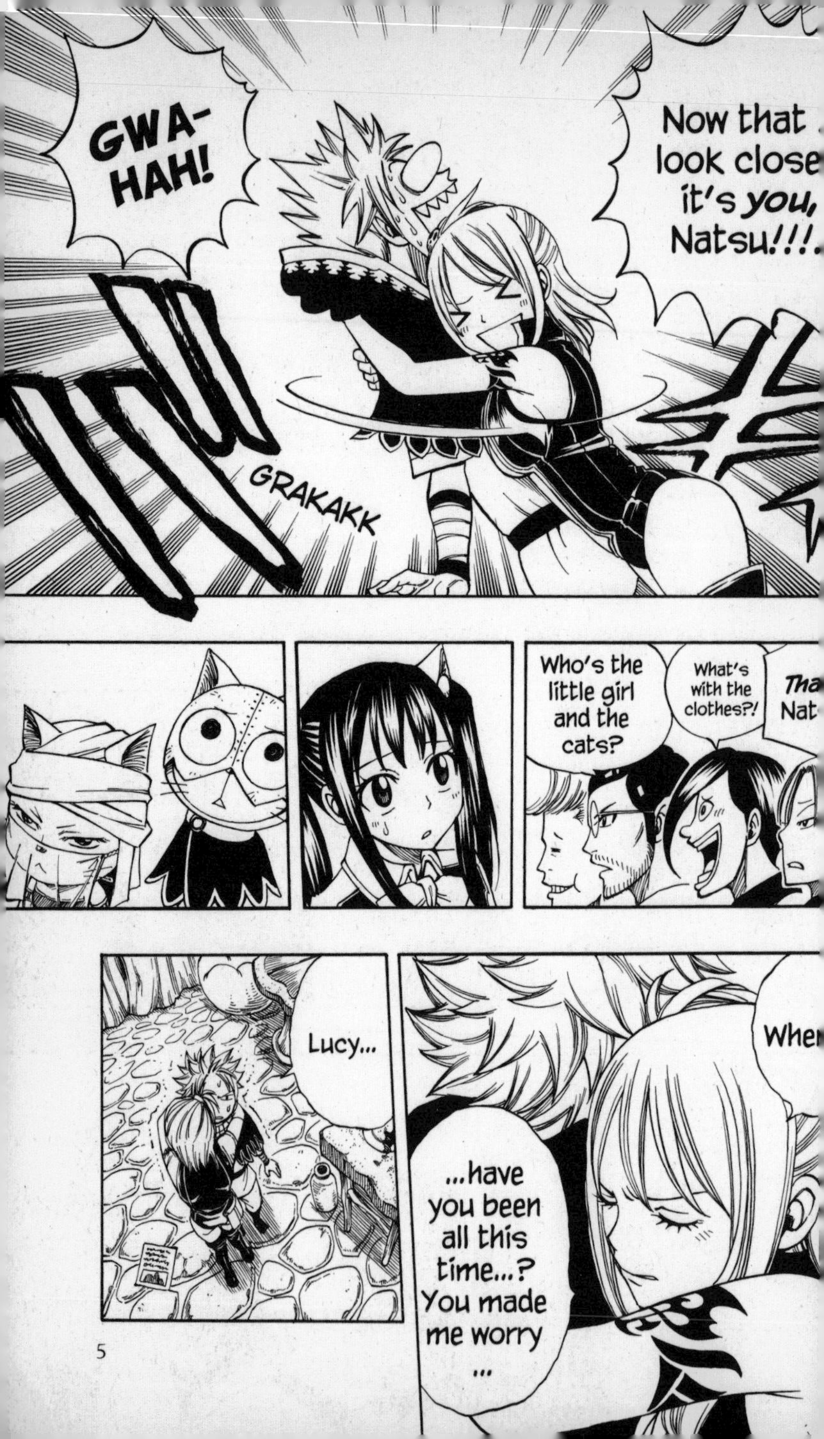

Now that
look close
it's *you*,
Natsu!!!
GWA-HAH!
GRAKAKK
What's with the clothes?!
Who's the little girl and the cats?
...have you been all this time...? You made me worry ...
Lucy...

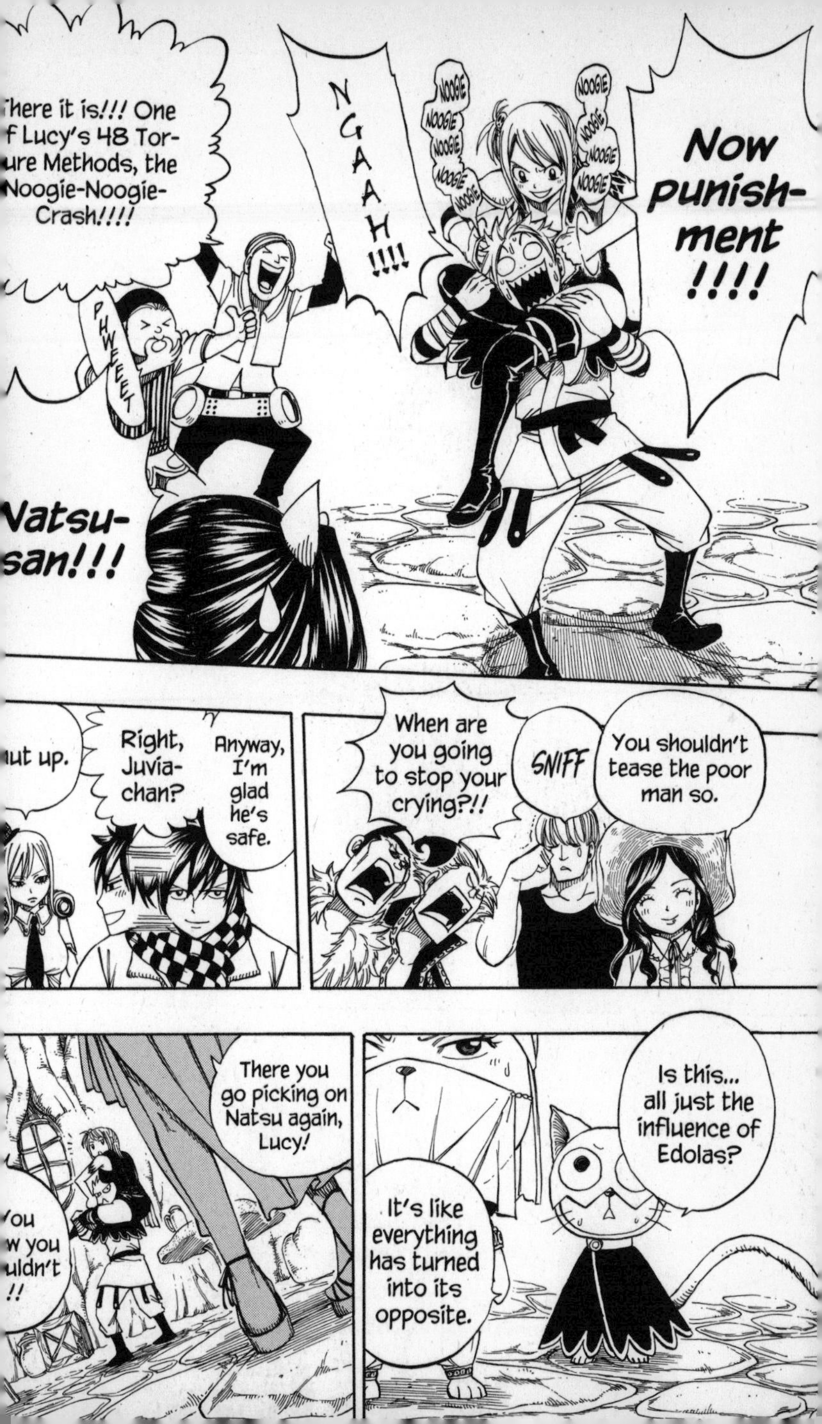
Now punishment!!!!
NOOGIE NOOGIE NOOGIE NOOGIE
NOOGIE NOOGIE NOOGIE NOOGIE NOOGIE
NGAAH!!!!
here it is!!! One f Lucy's 48 Tor-ure Methods, the Noogie-Noogie-Crash!!!!
PHWEEET
Vatsu-san!!!
You shouldn't tease the poor man so.
SNIFF
When are you going to stop your crying?!!
Anyway, I'm glad he's safe.
Right, Juvia-chan?
ut up.
Is this... all just the influence of Edolas?
It's like everything has turned into its opposite.
There you go picking on Natsu again, Lucy!
ou w you uldn't !!

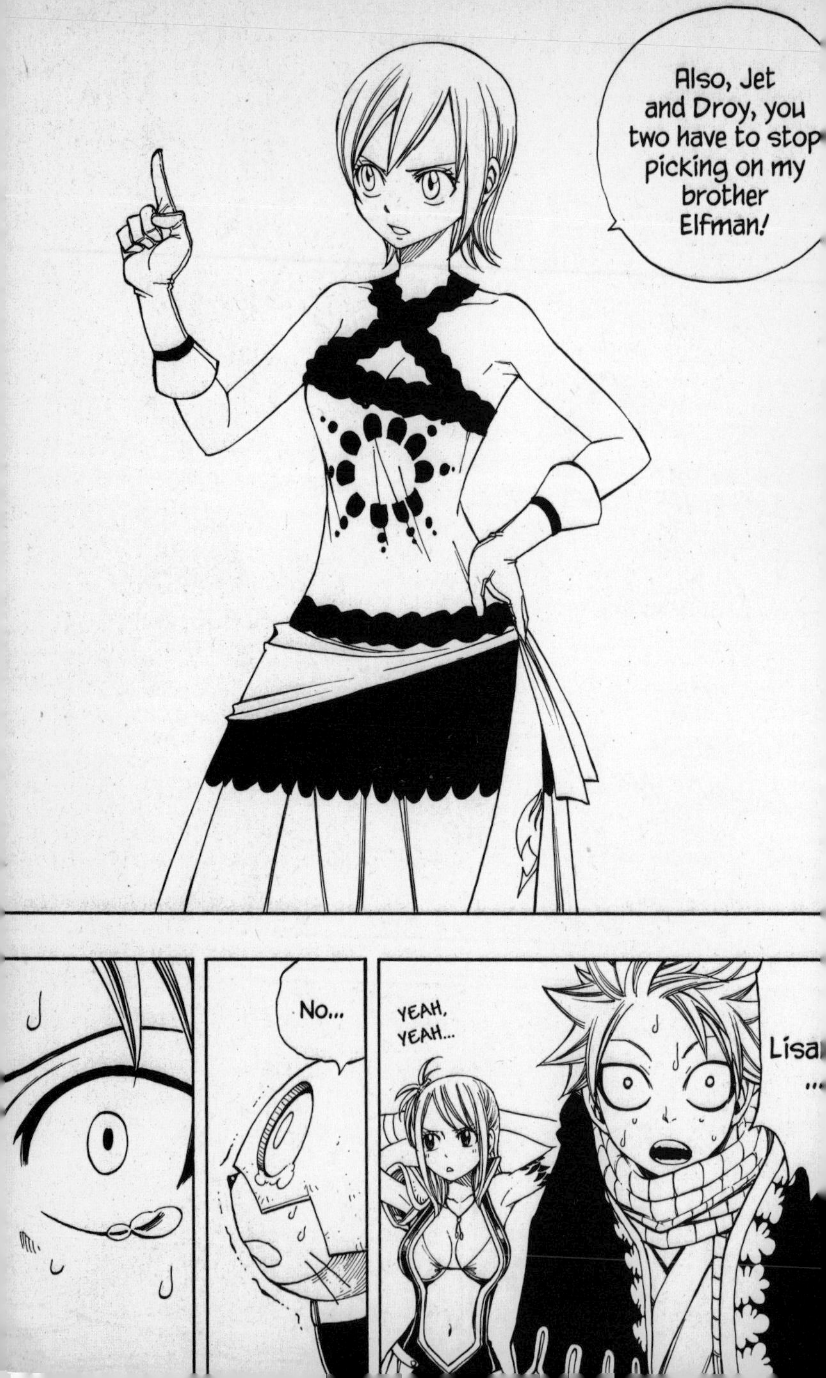
Also, Jet and Droy, you two have to stop picking on my brother Elfman!
Lisa...
YEAH, YEAH...
No...

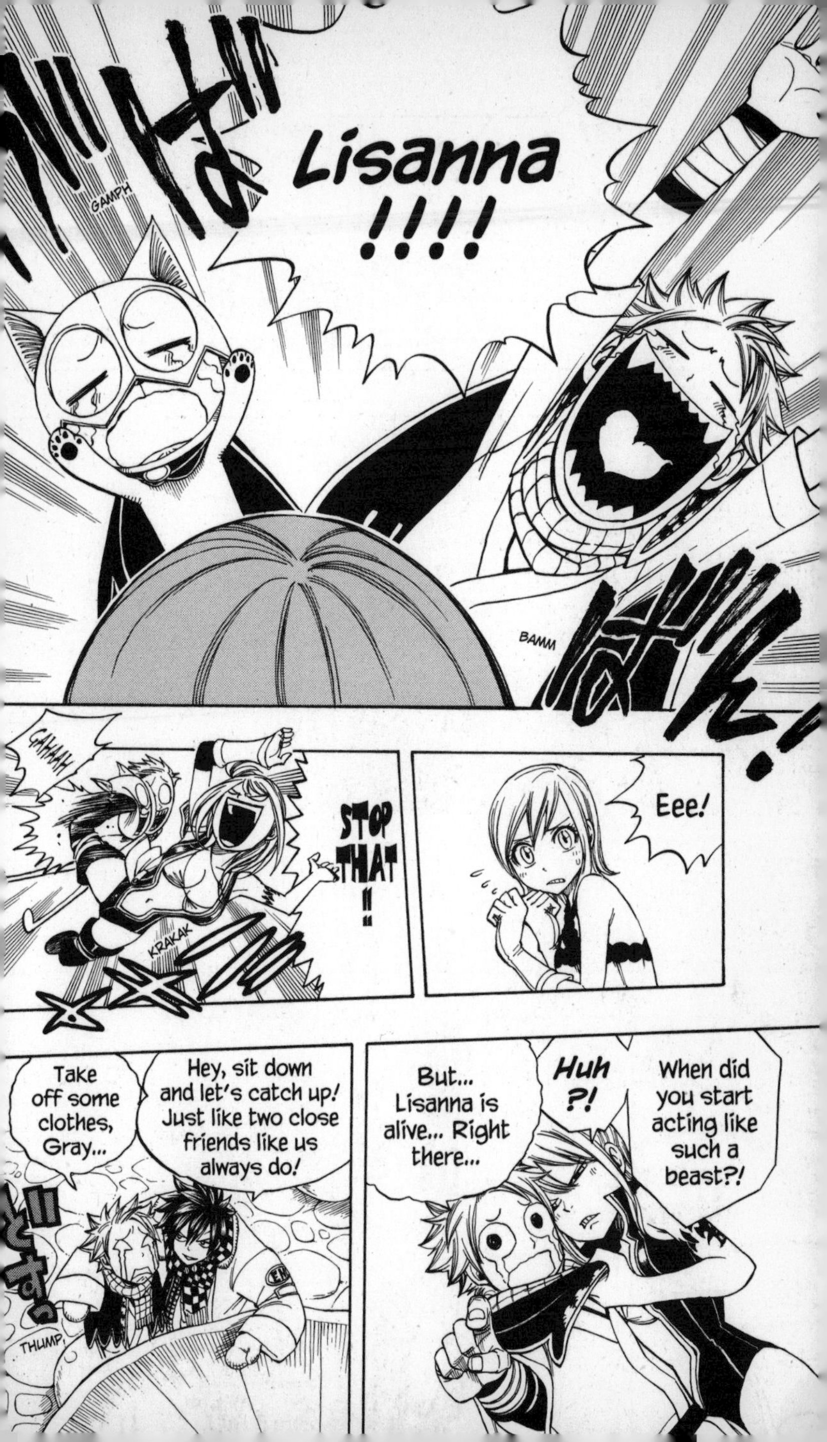
Lisanna !!!!
GAMPH
BAMM
Eee!
STOP THAT !!
GAHAAH
KRAKAK
When did you start acting like such a beast?!
Huh ?!
But... Lisanna is alive... Right there...
Hey, sit down and let's catch up! Just like two close friends like us always do!
Take off some clothes, Gray...
THUMP

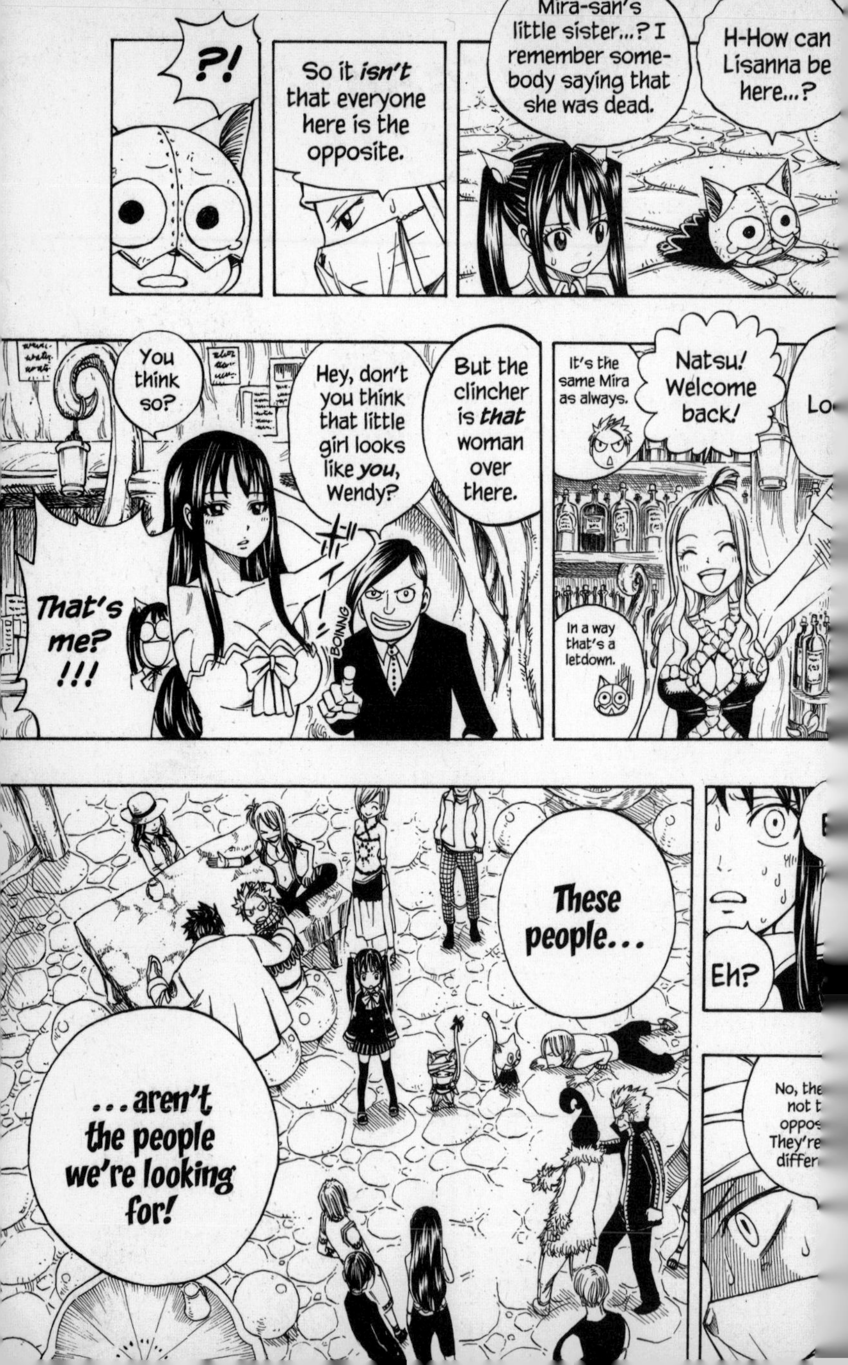
H-How can Lisanna be here...?
Mira-san's little sister...? I remember some-body saying that she was dead.
So it *isn't* that everyone here is the opposite.
?!
Lo
Natsu! Welcome back!
It's the same Mira as always.
In a way that's a letdown.
But the clincher is *that* woman over there.
Hey, don't you think that little girl looks like *you*, Wendy?
You think so?
BOINNG
That's me? !!!
Eh?
No, the
not t
oppos
They're
differ
These people...
...aren't the people we're looking for!

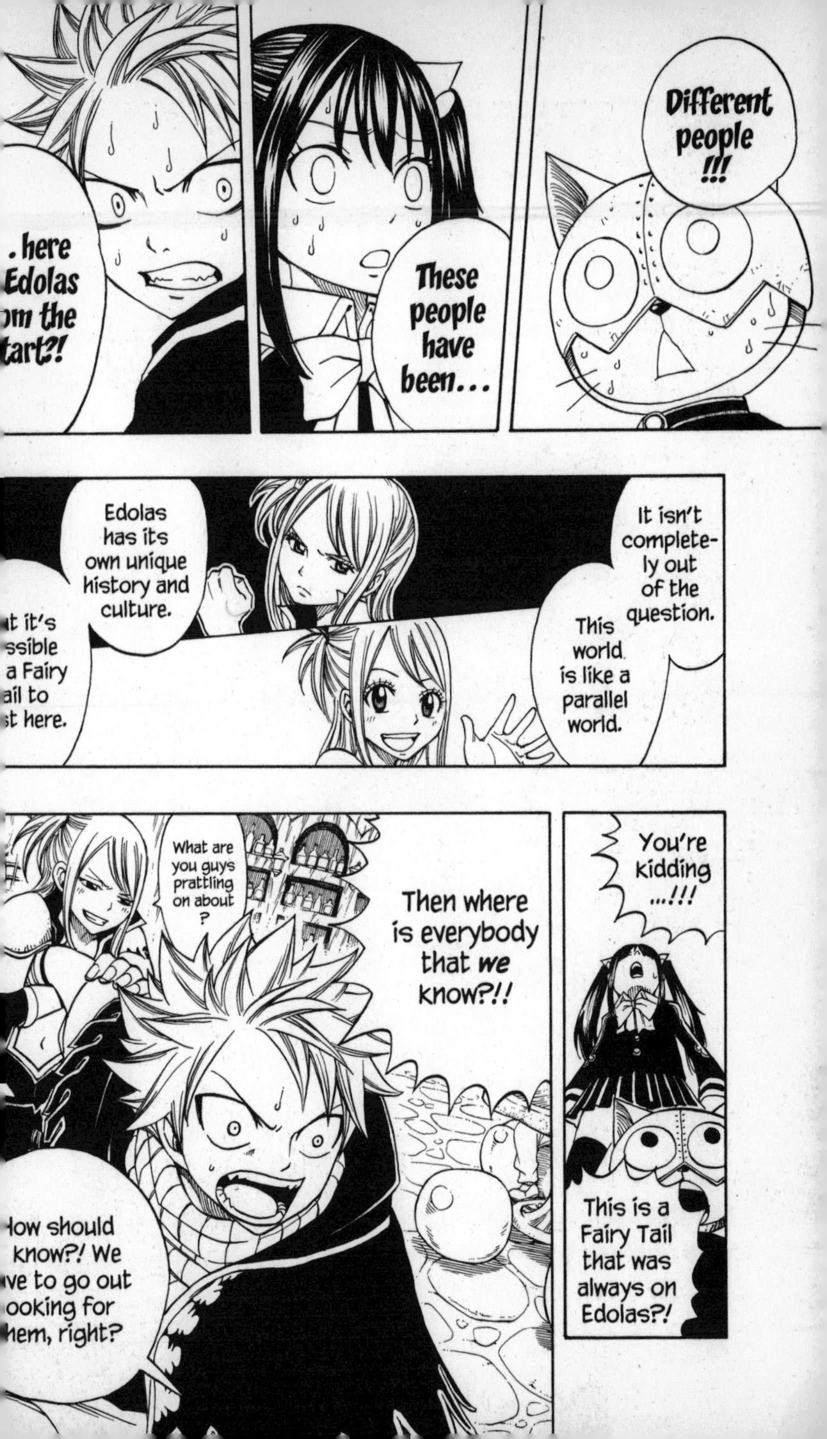

Different people!!!
These people have been...
. here Edolas om the tart?!
It isn't complete-ly out of the question.
This world is like a parallel world.
Edolas has its own unique history and culture.
t it's ssible a Fairy ail to st here.
You're kidding ...!!!
This is a Fairy Tail that was always on Edolas?!
Then where is everybody that we know?!!
What are you guys prattling on about ?
low should know?! We ve to go out ooking for hem, right?

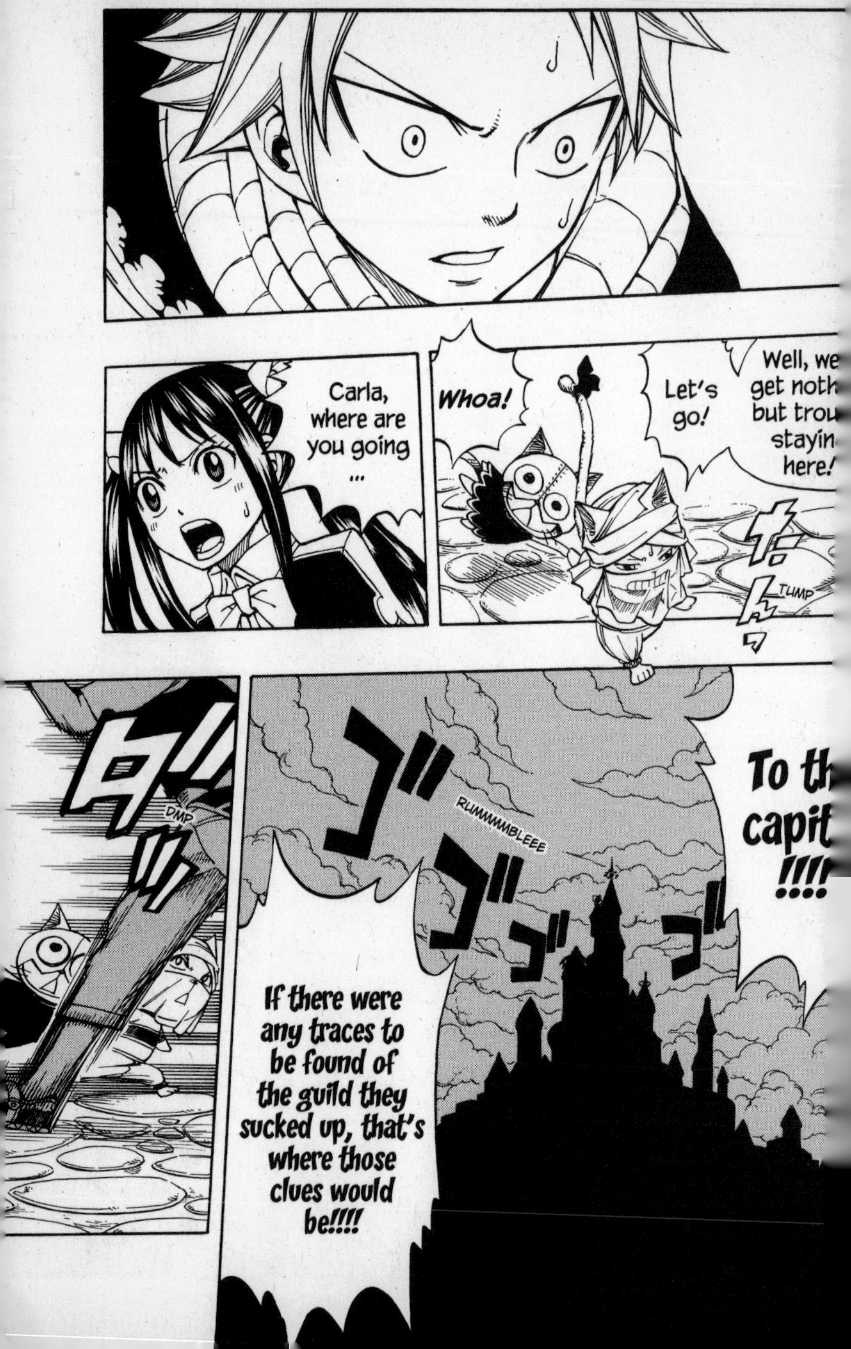

Well, we get noth but trou stayin here!
Let's go!
Whoa!
TUMP
Carla, where are you going ...
To th capit !!!!
RUMMMMBLEEE
If there were any traces to be found of the guild they sucked up, that's where those clues would be!!!!
DMP

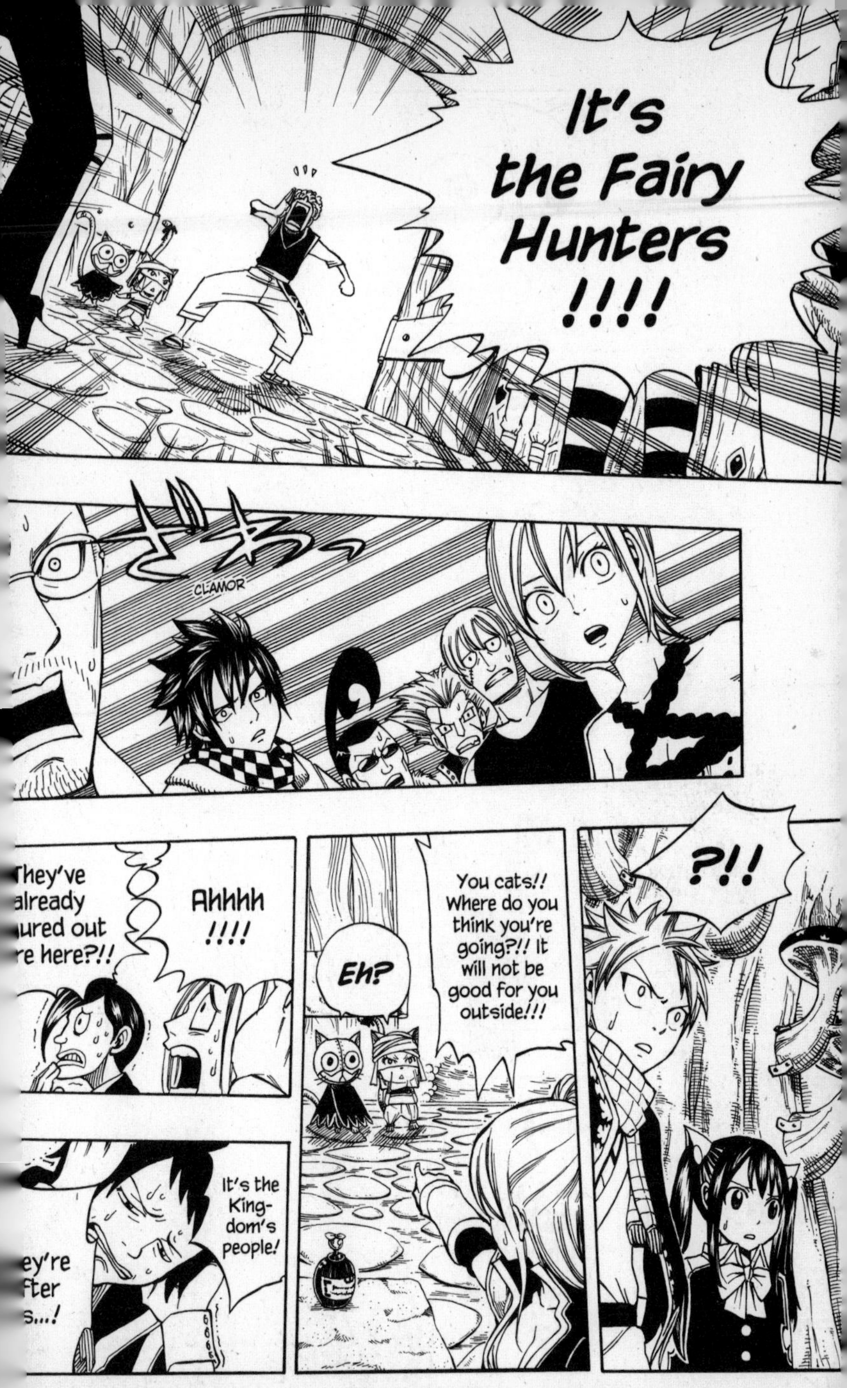

It's the Fairy Hunters !!!!
CLAMOR
?!!
You cats!! Where do you think you're going?!! It will not be good for you outside!!!
Eh?
Ahhhh !!!!
They've already ured out re here?!!
It's the King-dom's people!
ey're fter s...!

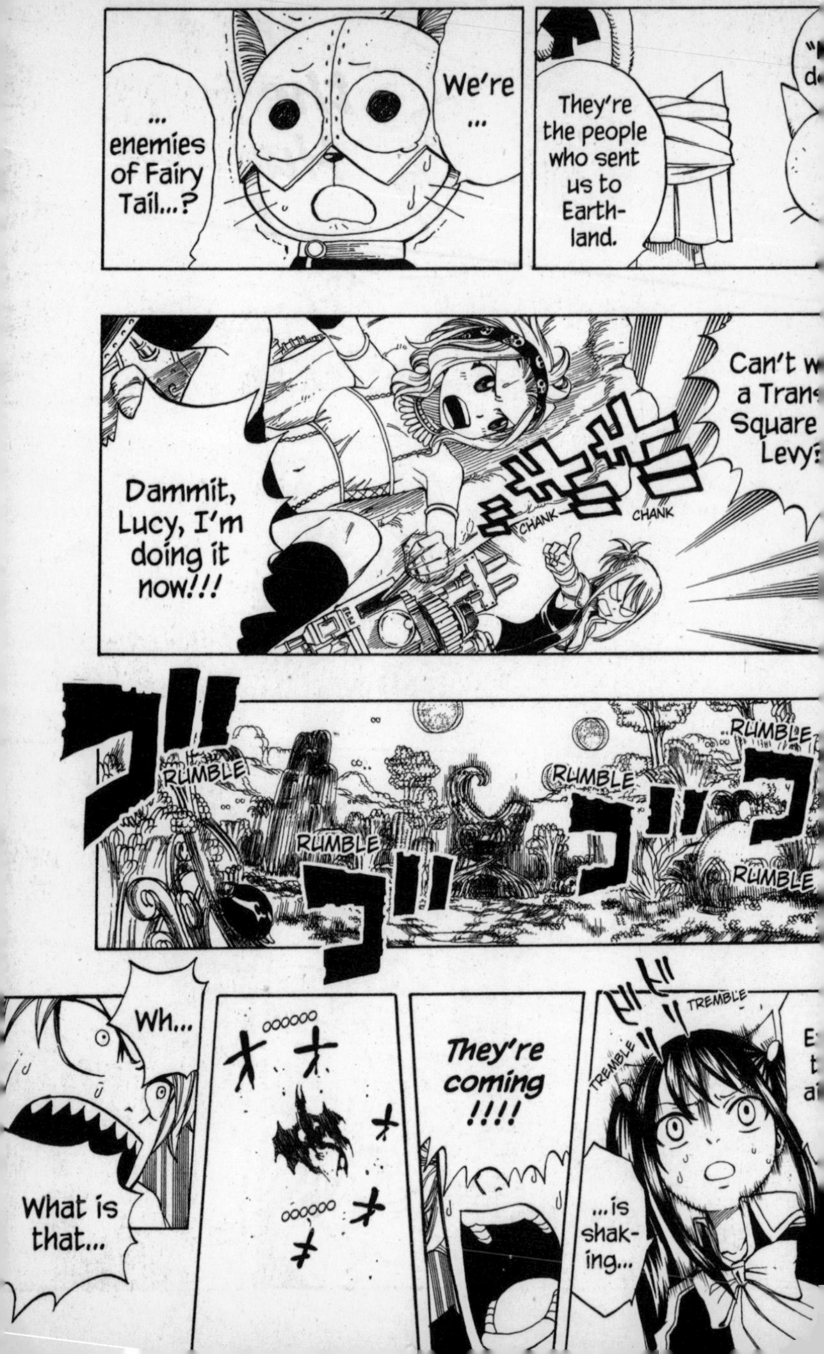
They're the people who sent us to Earth-land.
We're ...
... enemies of Fairy Tail...?
Dammit, Lucy, I'm doing it now!!!
CHANK
CHANK
RUMBLE
RUMBLE
RUMBLE
RUMBLE
RUMBLE
TREMBLE
TREMBLE
...is shak-ing...
They're coming !!!!
oooooo
oooooo
Wh...
What is that...

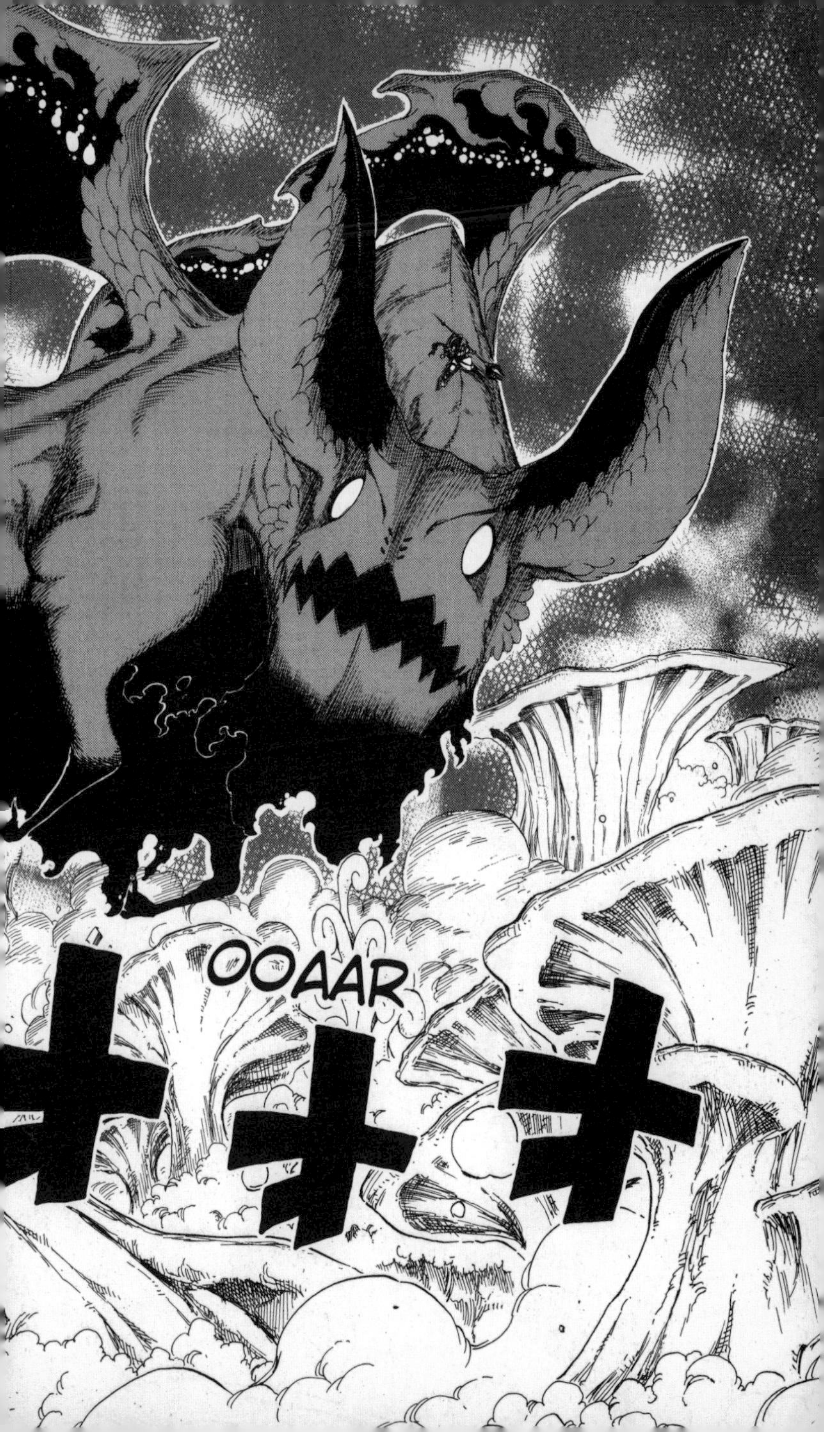
OOAAR

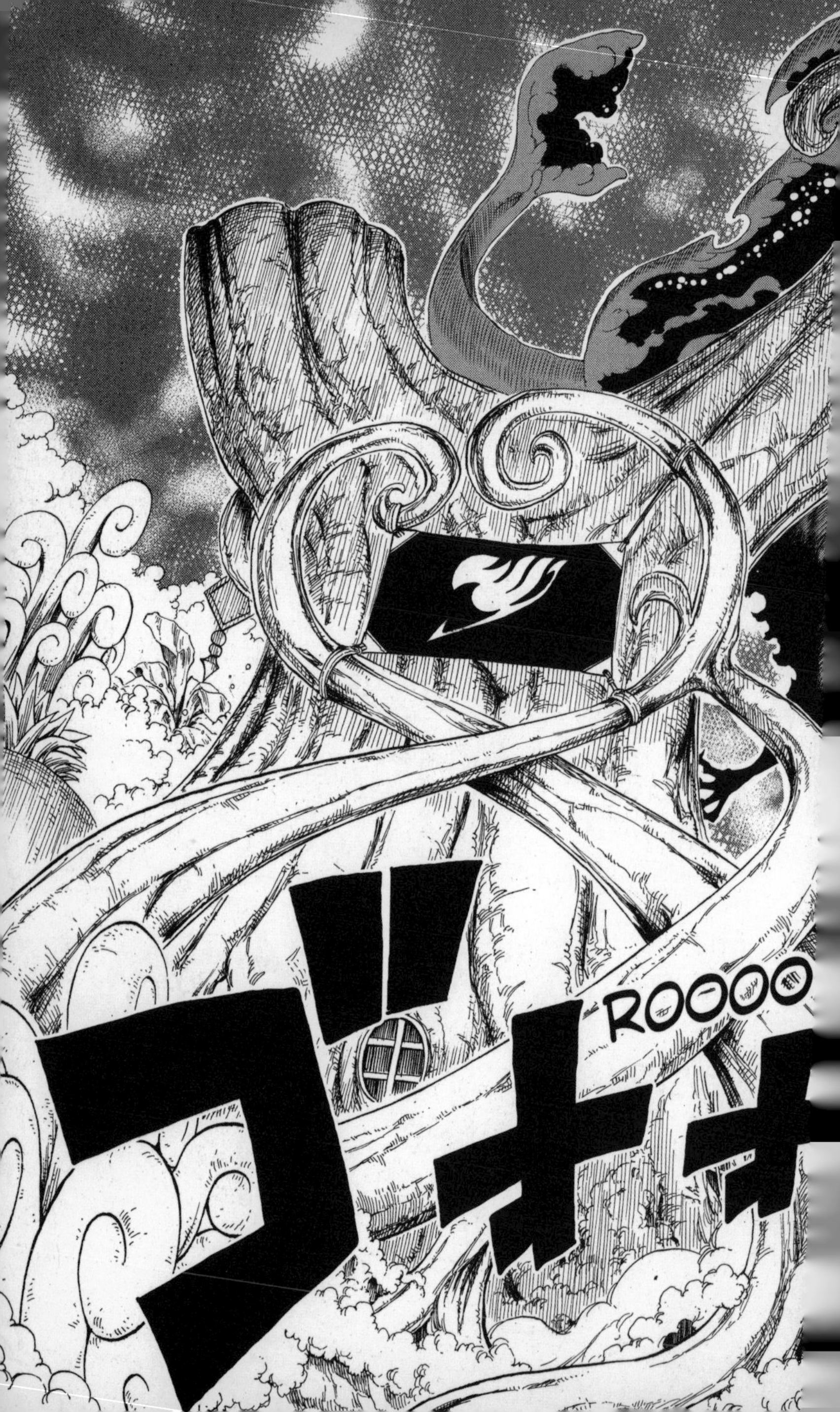
ゴオオ
ROOOO

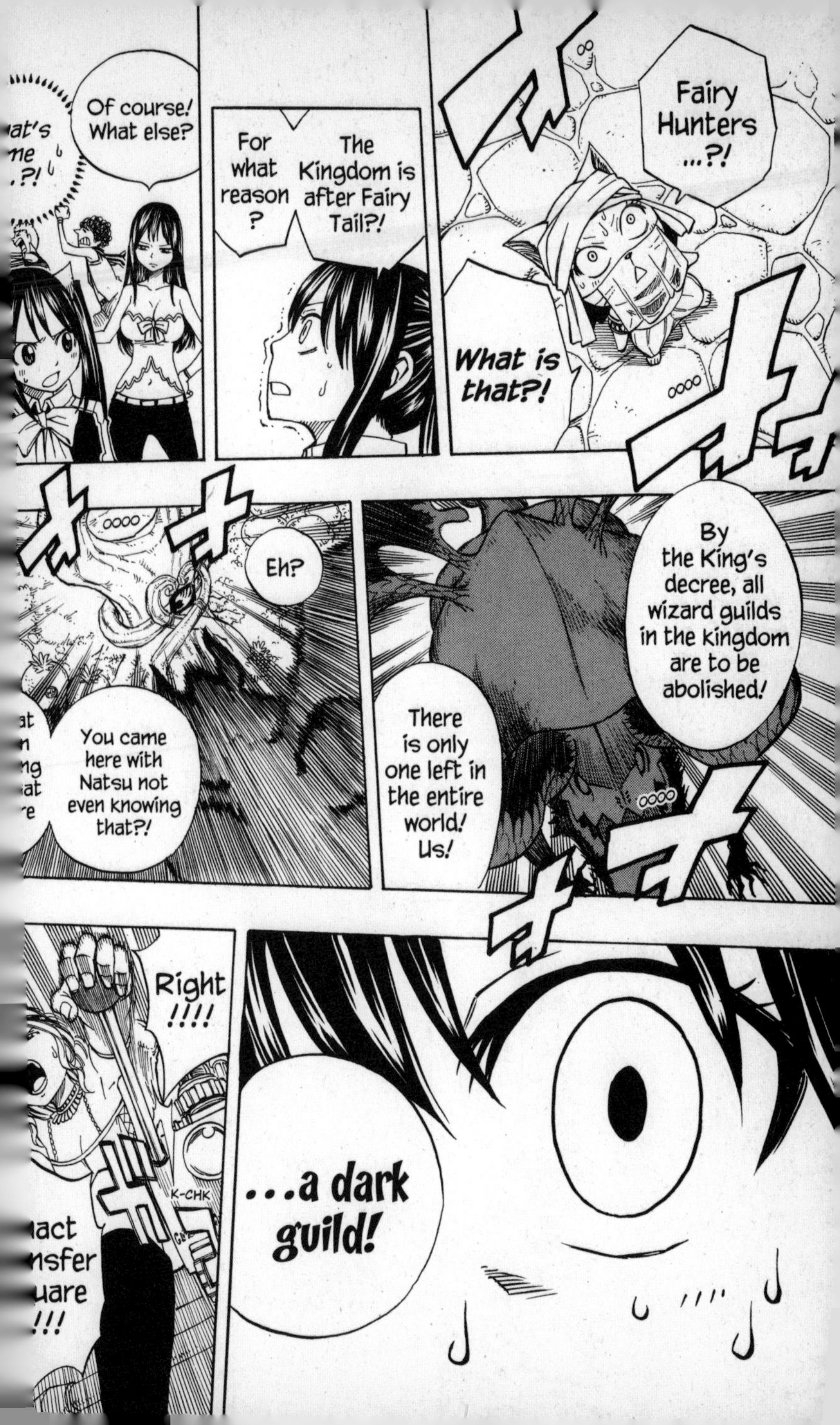
Fairy Hunters ...?!
What is that?!
The Kingdom is after Fairy Tail?!
For what reason?
Of course! What else?
By the King's decree, all wizard guilds in the kingdom are to be abolished!
There is only one left in the entire world! Us!
Eh?
You came here with Natsu not even knowing that?!
...a dark guild!
Right !!!!
K-CHK

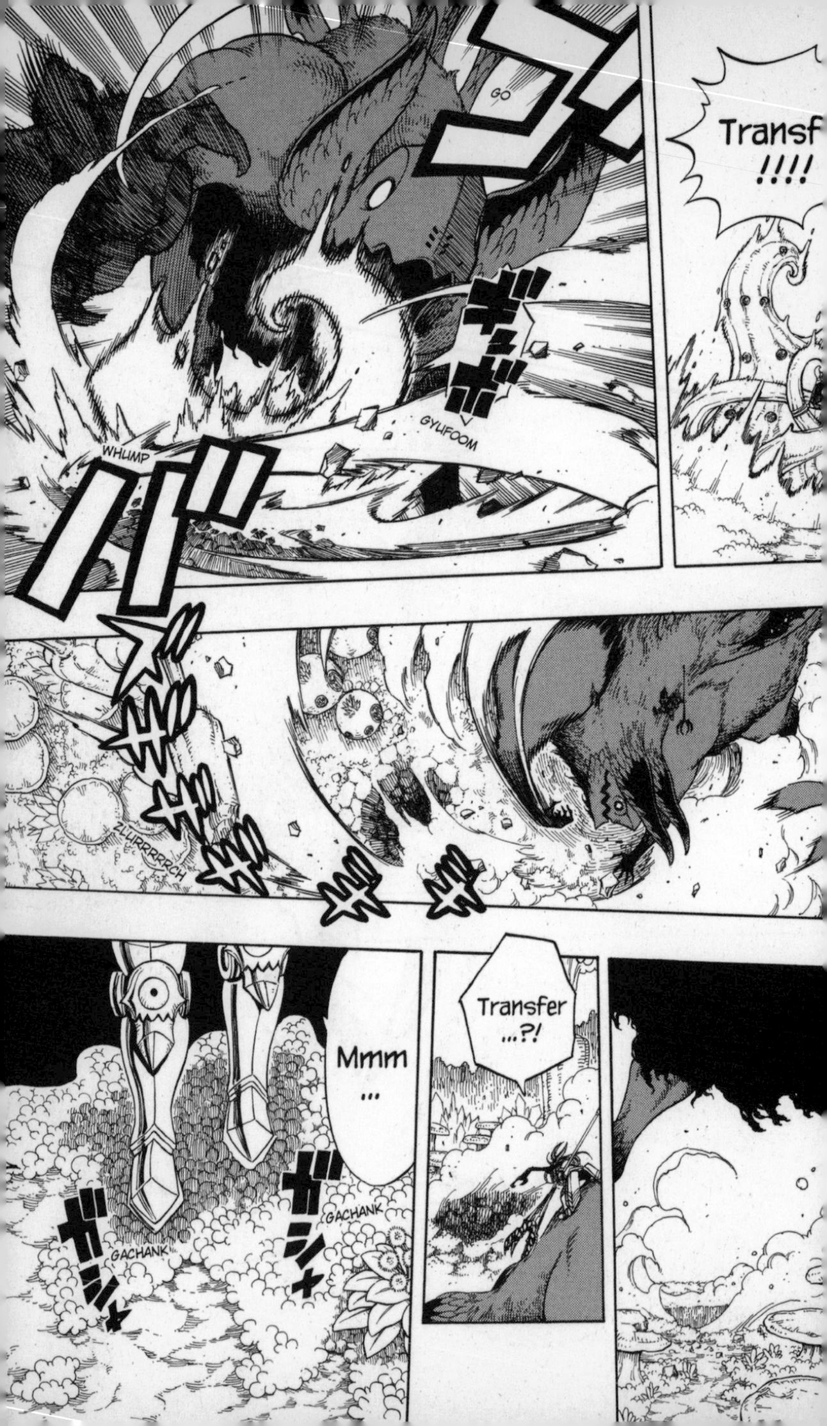
Transf !!!!
GO
GYUFOOM
WHUMP
ZLURRRRRCH
Transfer ...?!
Mmm ...
GACHANK
GACHANK

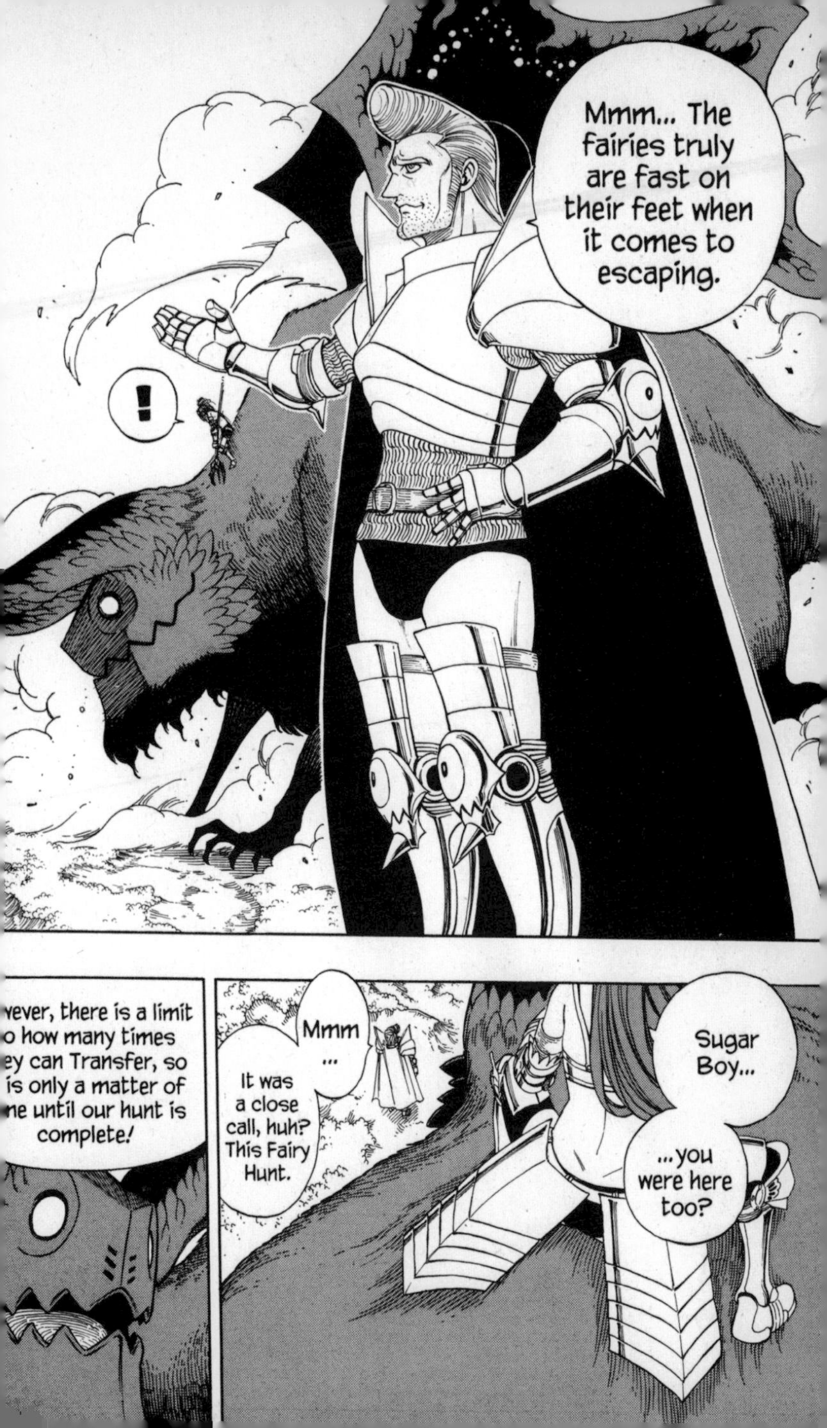
Mmm... The fairies truly are fast on their feet when it comes to escaping.
!
Sugar Boy...
...you were here too?
Mmm ...
It was a close call, huh? This Fairy Hunt.
wever, there is a limit o how many times ey can Transfer, so is only a matter of ne until our hunt is complete!

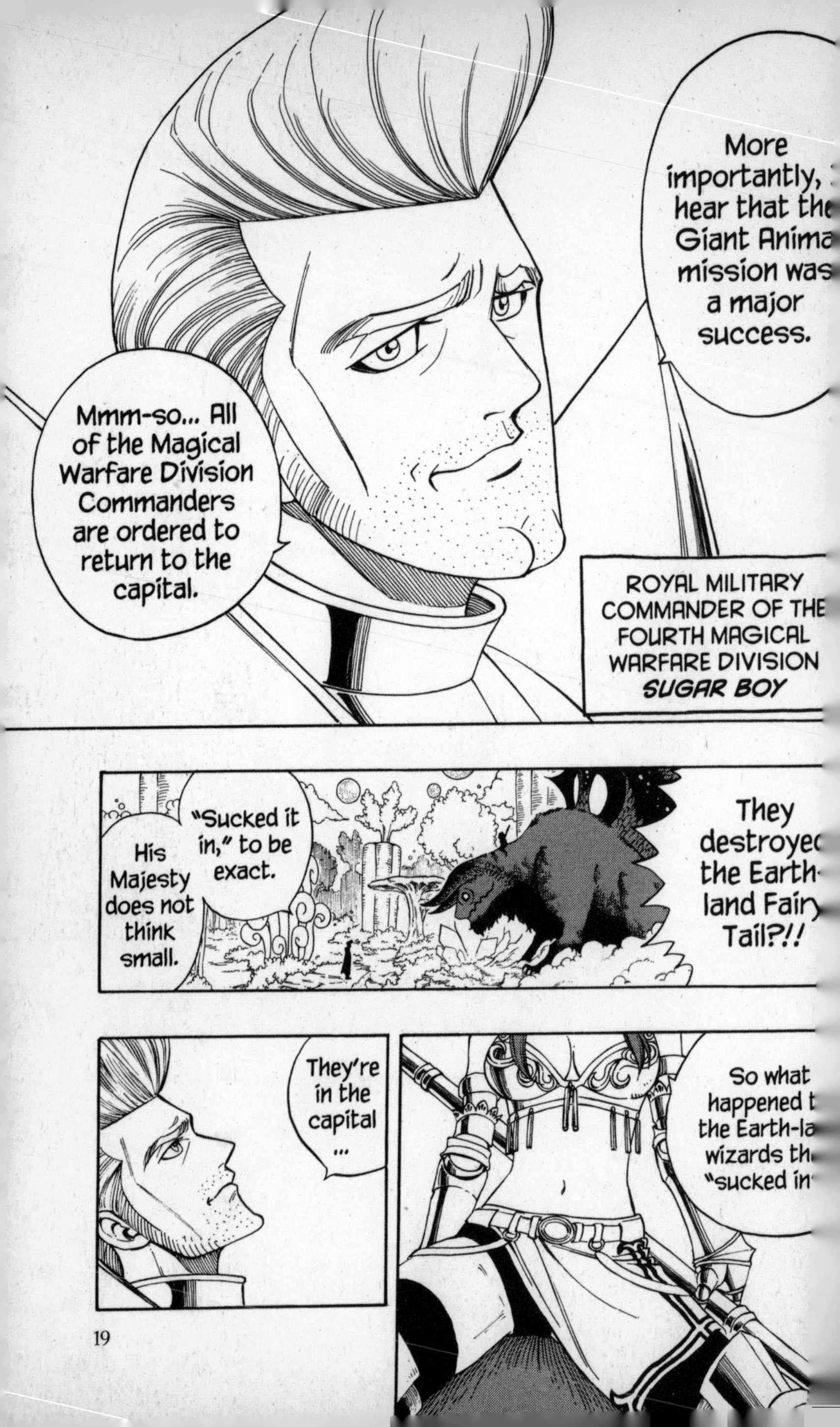

More importantly, hear that th Giant Anima mission was a major success.
ROYAL MILITARY COMMANDER OF THE FOURTH MAGICAL WARFARE DIVISION *SUGAR BOY*
Mmm-so... All of the Magical Warfare Division Commanders are ordered to return to the capital.
They destroye the Earth-land Fair Tail?!!
"Sucked it in," to be exact.
His Majesty does not think small.
So what happened the Earth-la wizards th "sucked in
They're in the capital ...

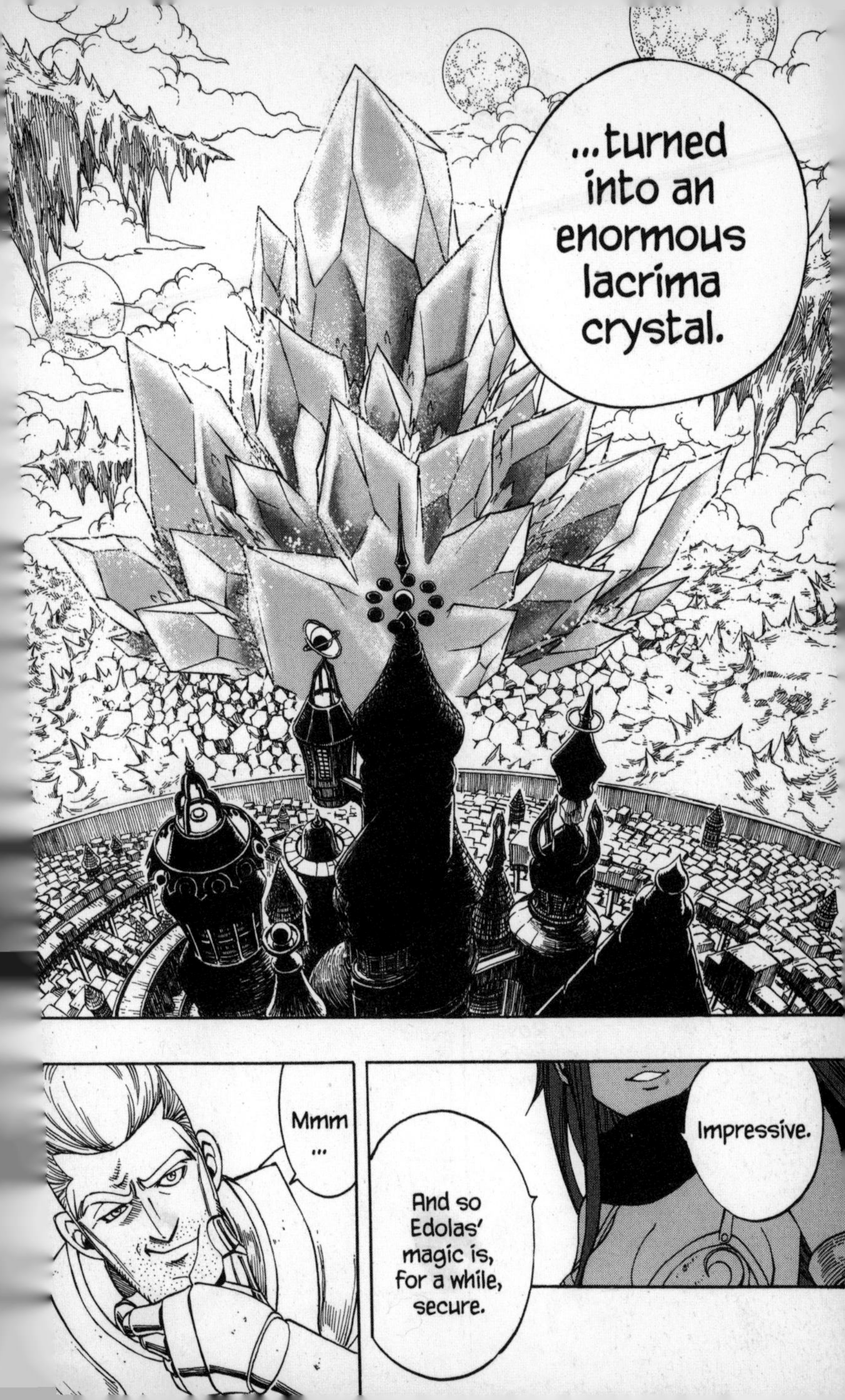
...turned into an enormous lacrima crystal.
Impressive.
And so Edolas' magic is, for a while, secure.
Mmm ...

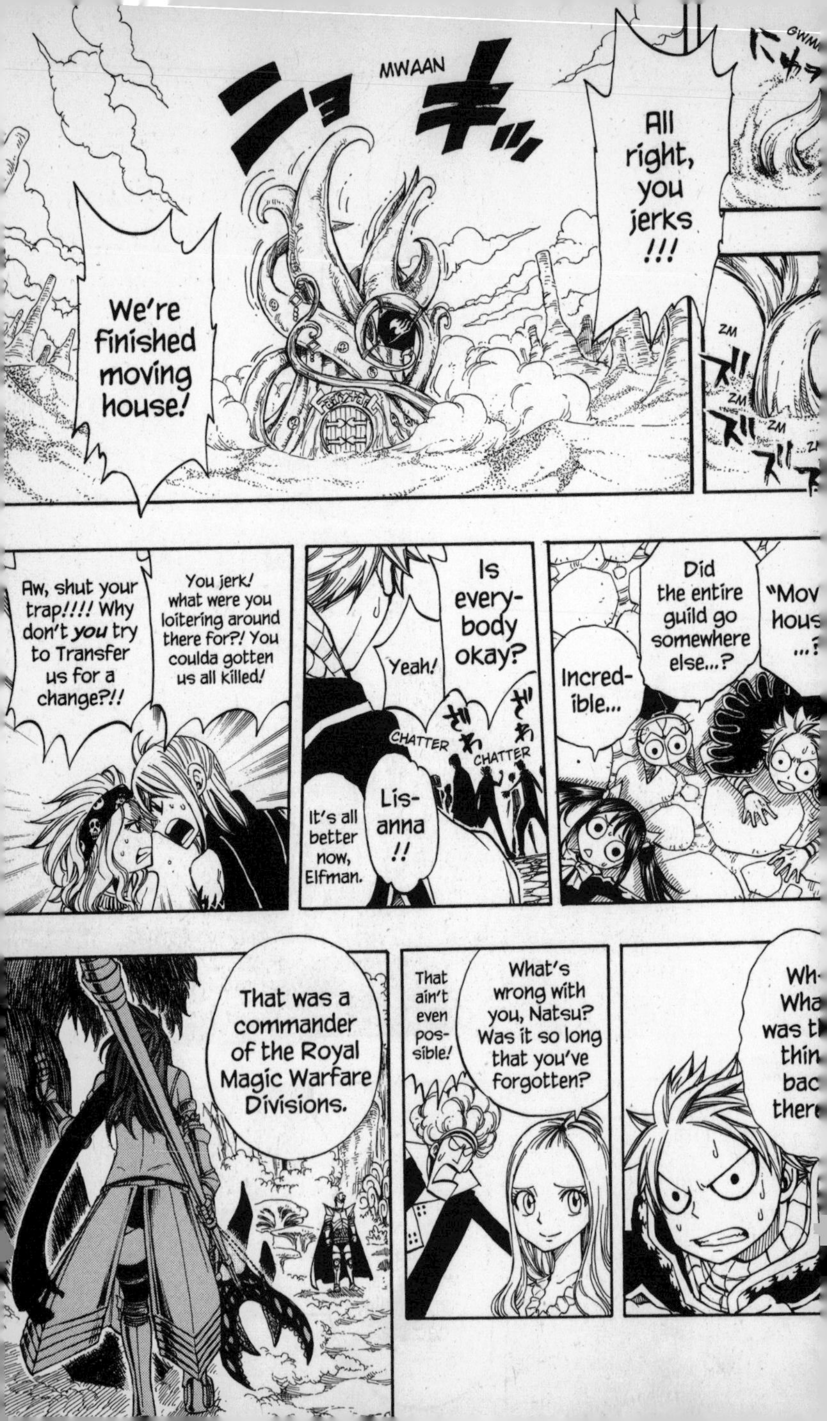
GWMM
ZM
ZM
ZM
All right, you jerks!!!
MWAAN
We're finished moving house!
"Mov hous...?
Did the entire guild go somewhere else...?
Incredible...
Is everybody okay?
Yeah!
CHATTER
CHATTER
Lis-anna!!
It's all better now, Elfman.
You jerk! what were you loitering around there for?! You coulda gotten us all killed!
Aw, shut your trap!!!! Why don't *you* try to Transfer us for a change?!!
Wh- Wha was th thin bac there
What's wrong with you, Natsu? Was it so long that you've forgotten?
That ain't even pos-sible!
That was a commander of the Royal Magic Warfare Divisions.

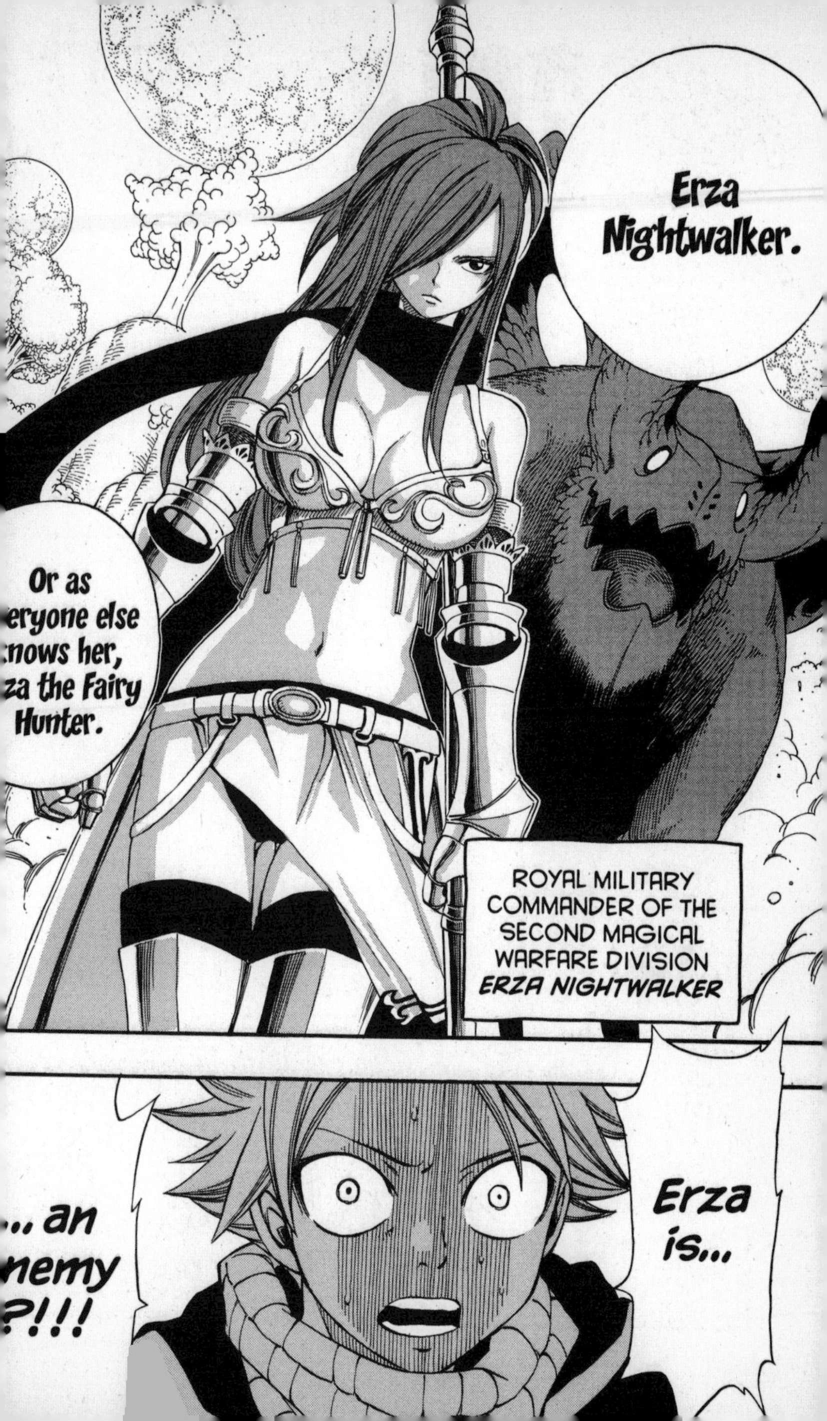
Erza Nightwalker.
Or as
eryone else
nows her,
za the Fairy
Hunter.
ROYAL MILITARY COMMANDER OF THE SECOND MAGICAL WARFARE DIVISION ERZA NIGHTWALKER
Erza is...
... an
nemy
?!!!

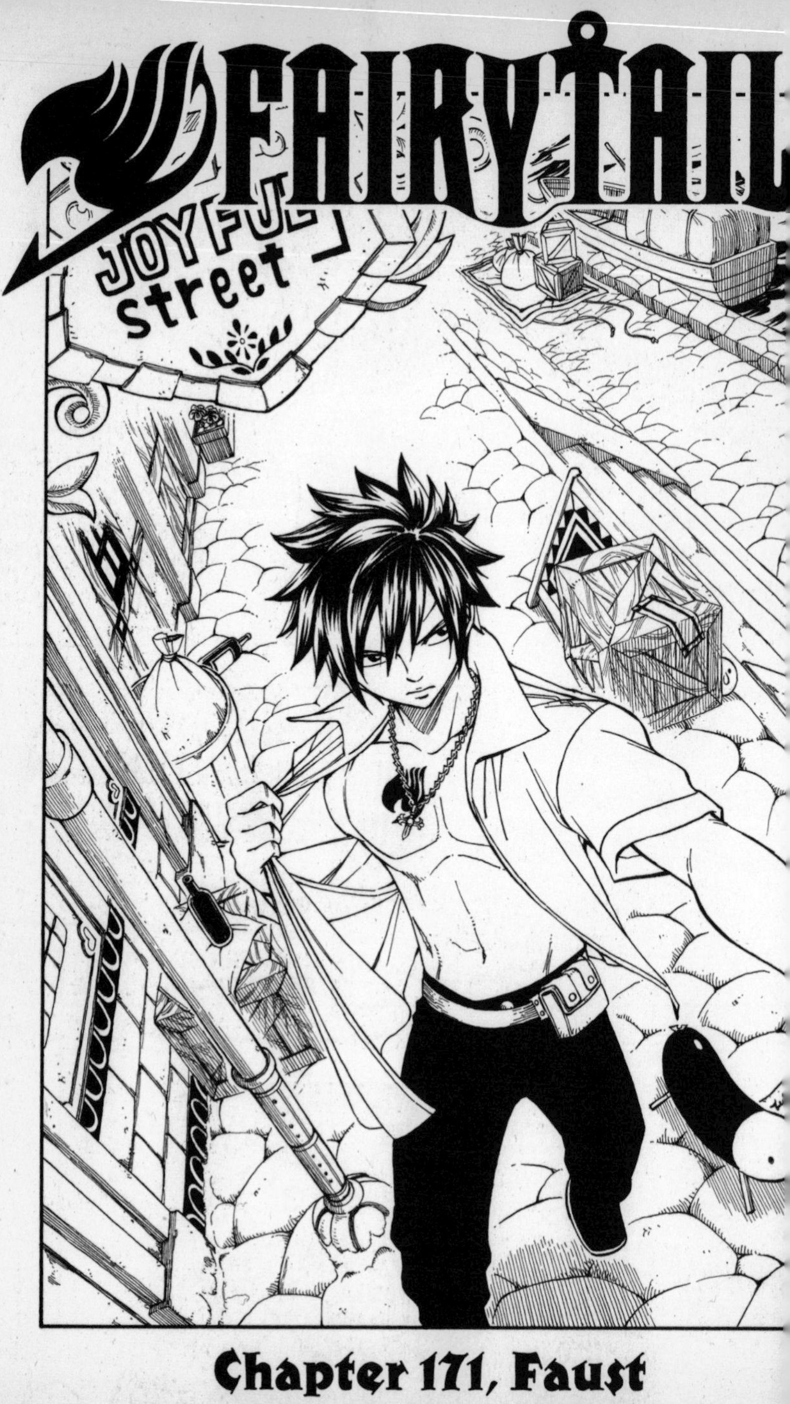
FAIRY TAIL
JOYFUL
street

Chapter 171, Faust

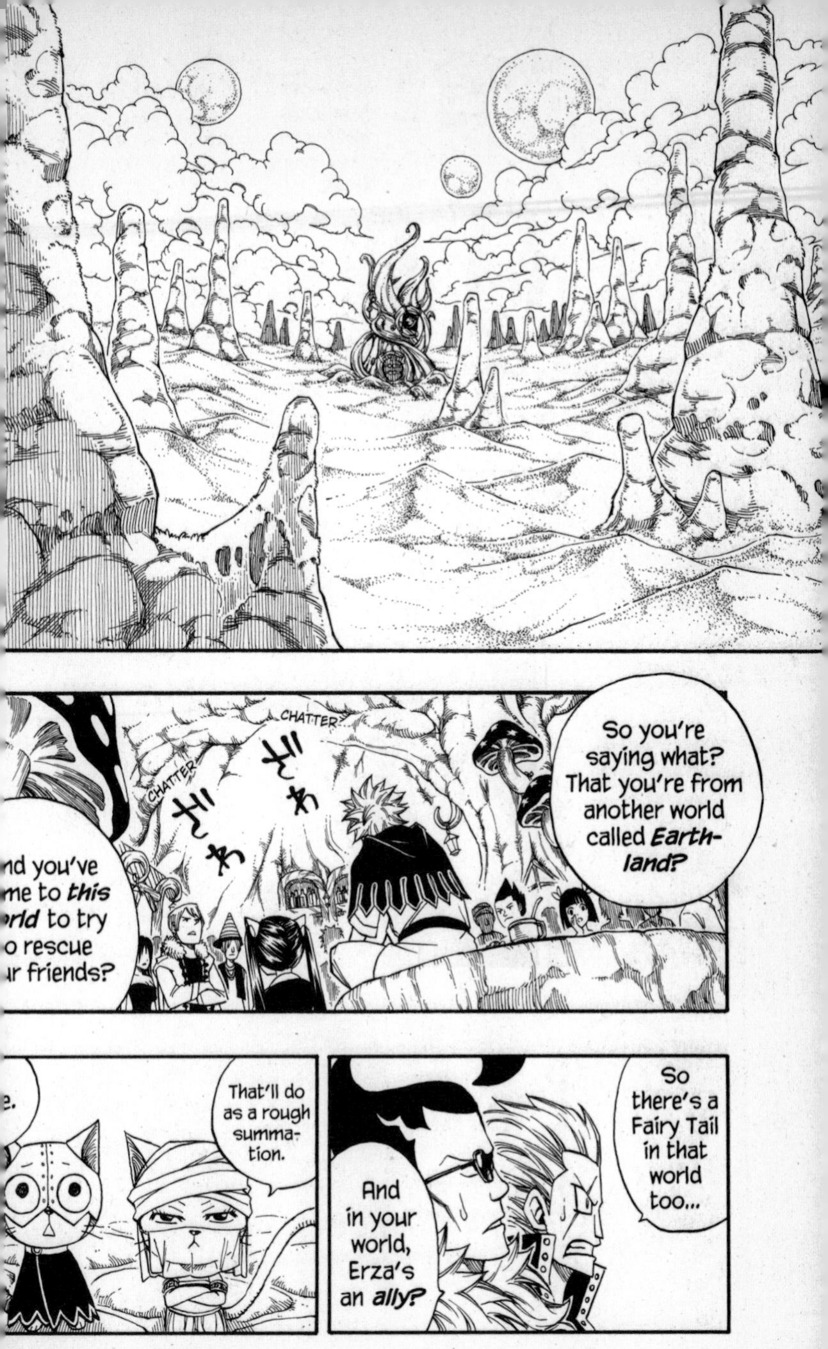

So you're saying what? That you're from another world called *Earth-land?*
CHATTER
CHATTER
ざわ
ざわ
nd you've
me to *this*
rld to try
o rescue
r friends?
So there's a Fairy Tail in that world too...
And in your world, Erza's an *ally?*
That'll do as a rough summa-tion.
e.

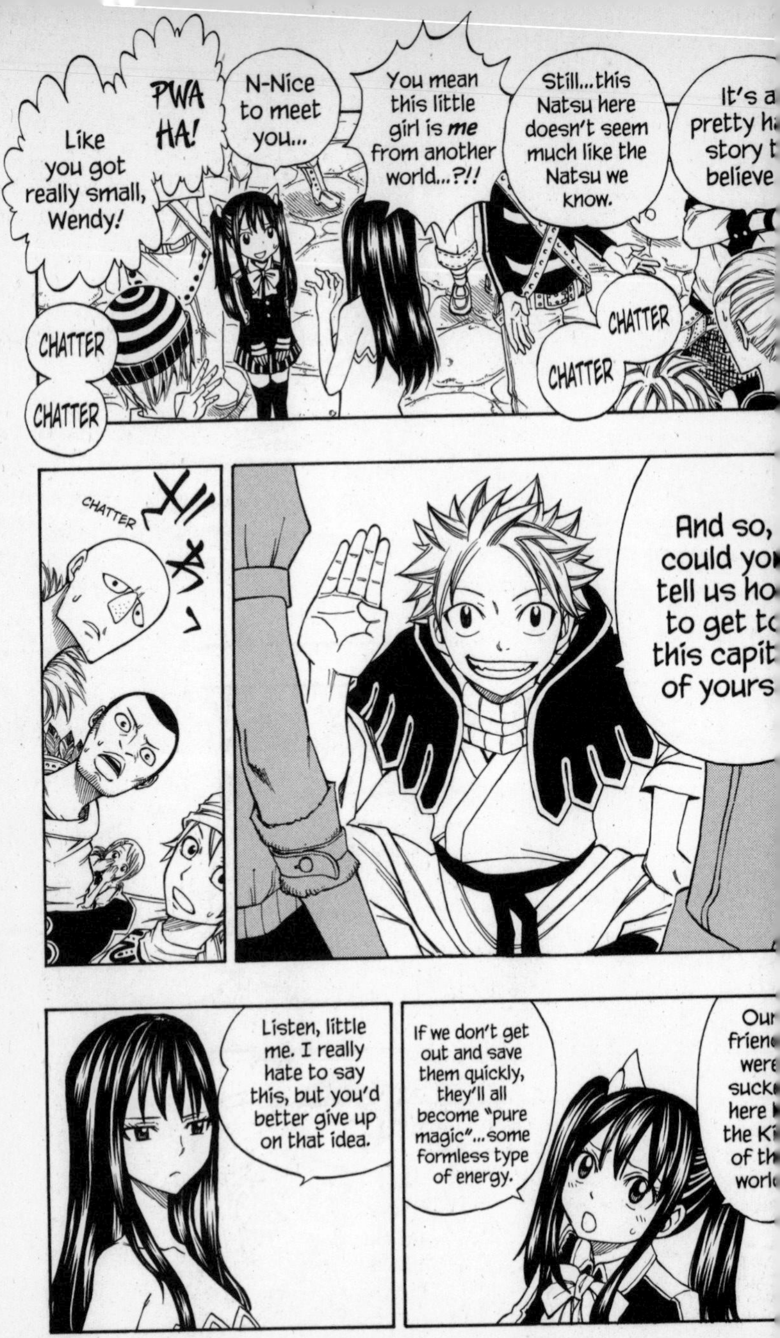
It's a pretty h story t believe
Still...this Natsu here doesn't seem much like the Natsu we know.
You mean this little girl is *me* from another world...?!!
N-Nice to meet you...
PWA HA!
Like you got really small, Wendy!
CHATTER
CHATTER
CHATTER
CHATTER
And so, could yo tell us ho to get t this capit of yours
CHATTER
Our frien were suck here the K of th worl
If we don't get out and save them quickly, they'll all become "pure magic"...some formless type of energy.
Listen, little me. I really hate to say this, but you'd better give up on that idea.

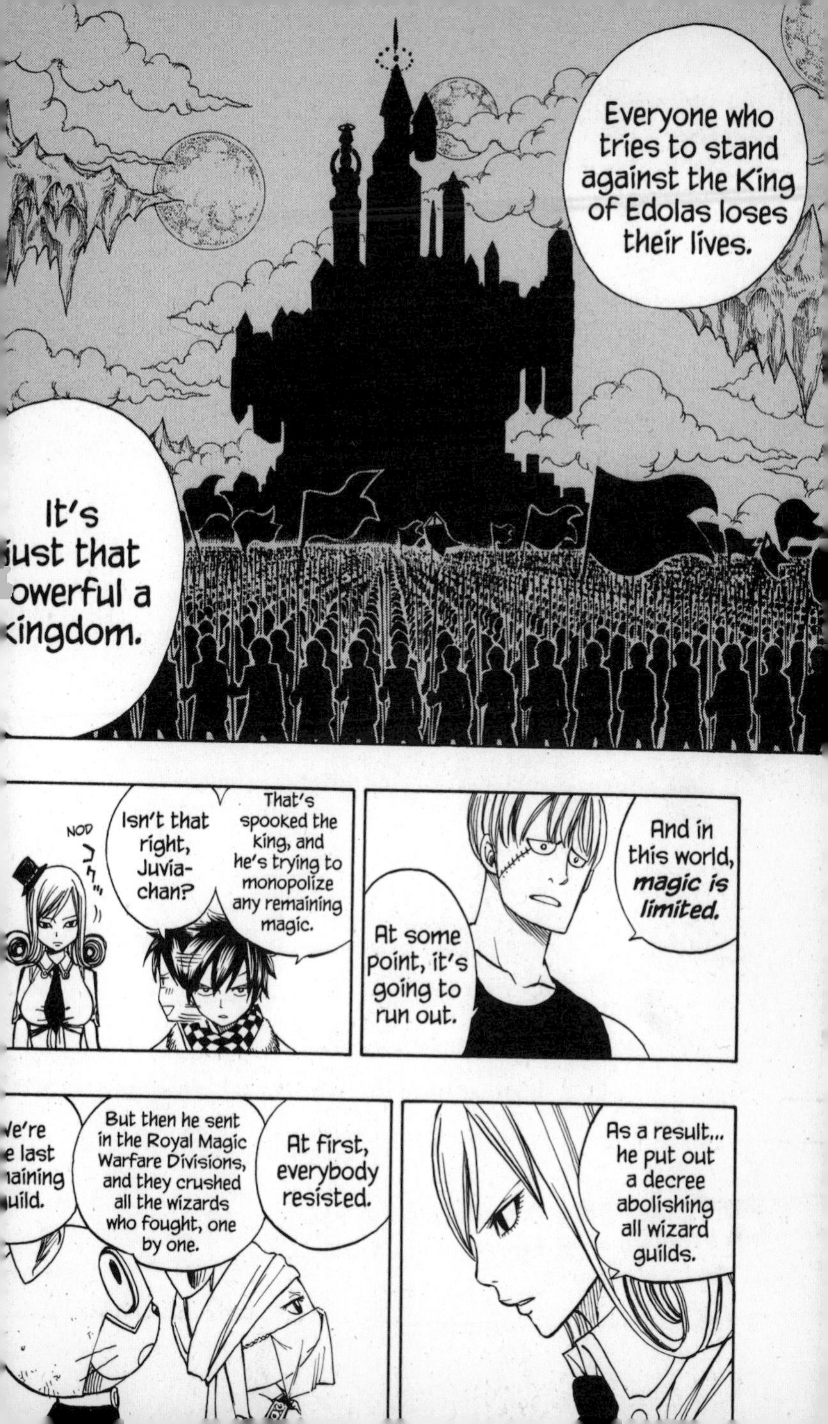
Everyone who tries to stand against the King of Edolas loses their lives.
It's ust that owerful a ingdom.
And in this world, ***magic is limited.***
At some point, it's going to run out.
That's spooked the king, and he's trying to monopolize any remaining magic.
Isn't that right, Juvia-chan?
NOD
As a result... he put out a decree abolishing all wizard guilds.
At first, everybody resisted.
But then he sent in the Royal Magic Warfare Divisions, and they crushed all the wizards who fought, one by one.
e're e last aining uild.

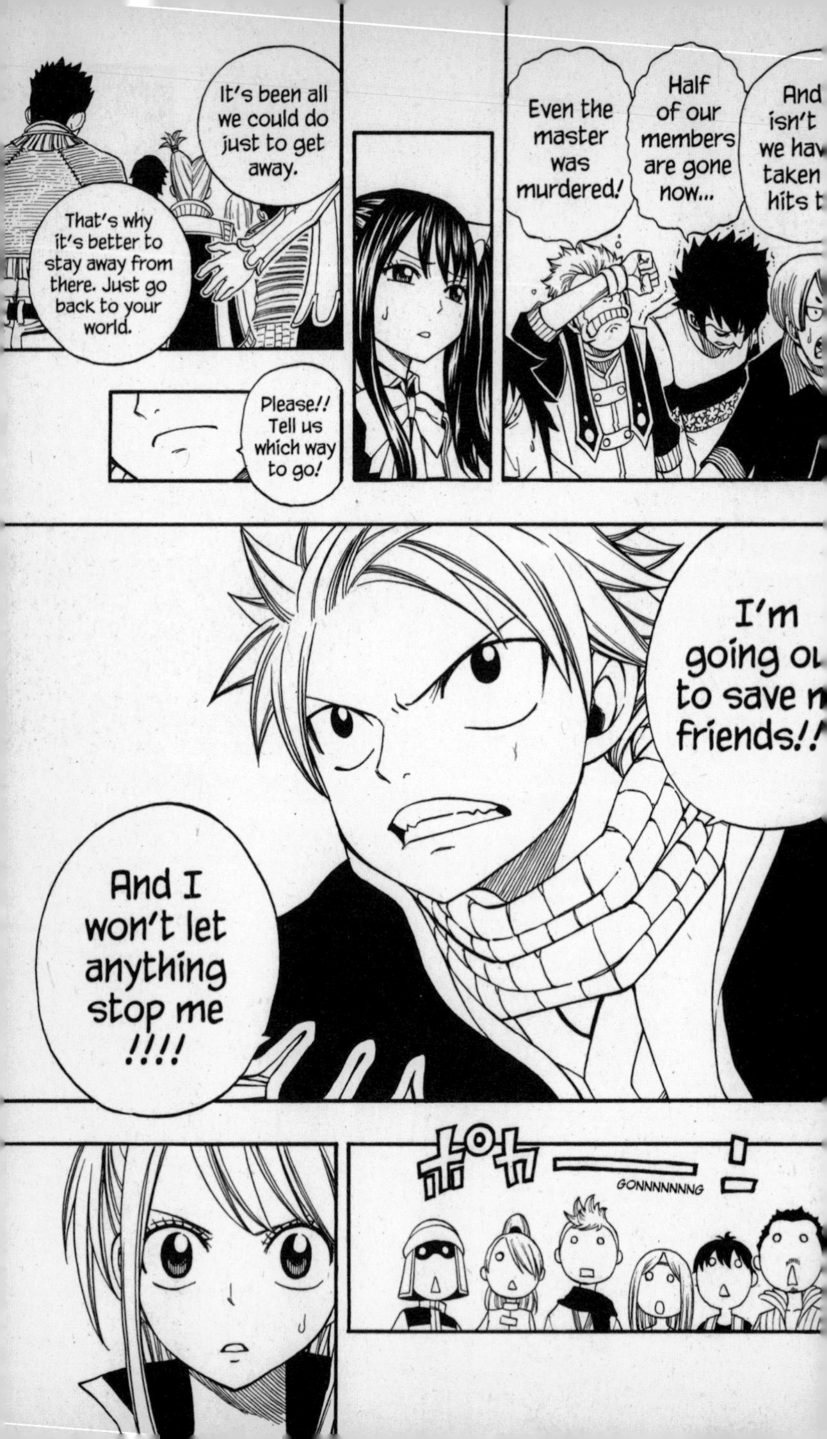
And isn't we hav taken hits t
Half of our members are gone now...
Even the master was murdered!
It's been all we could do just to get away.
That's why it's better to stay away from there. Just go back to your world.
Please!! Tell us which way to go!
I'm going ou to save m friends!!
And I won't let anything stop me !!!!
ポカーン
GONNNNNNNG

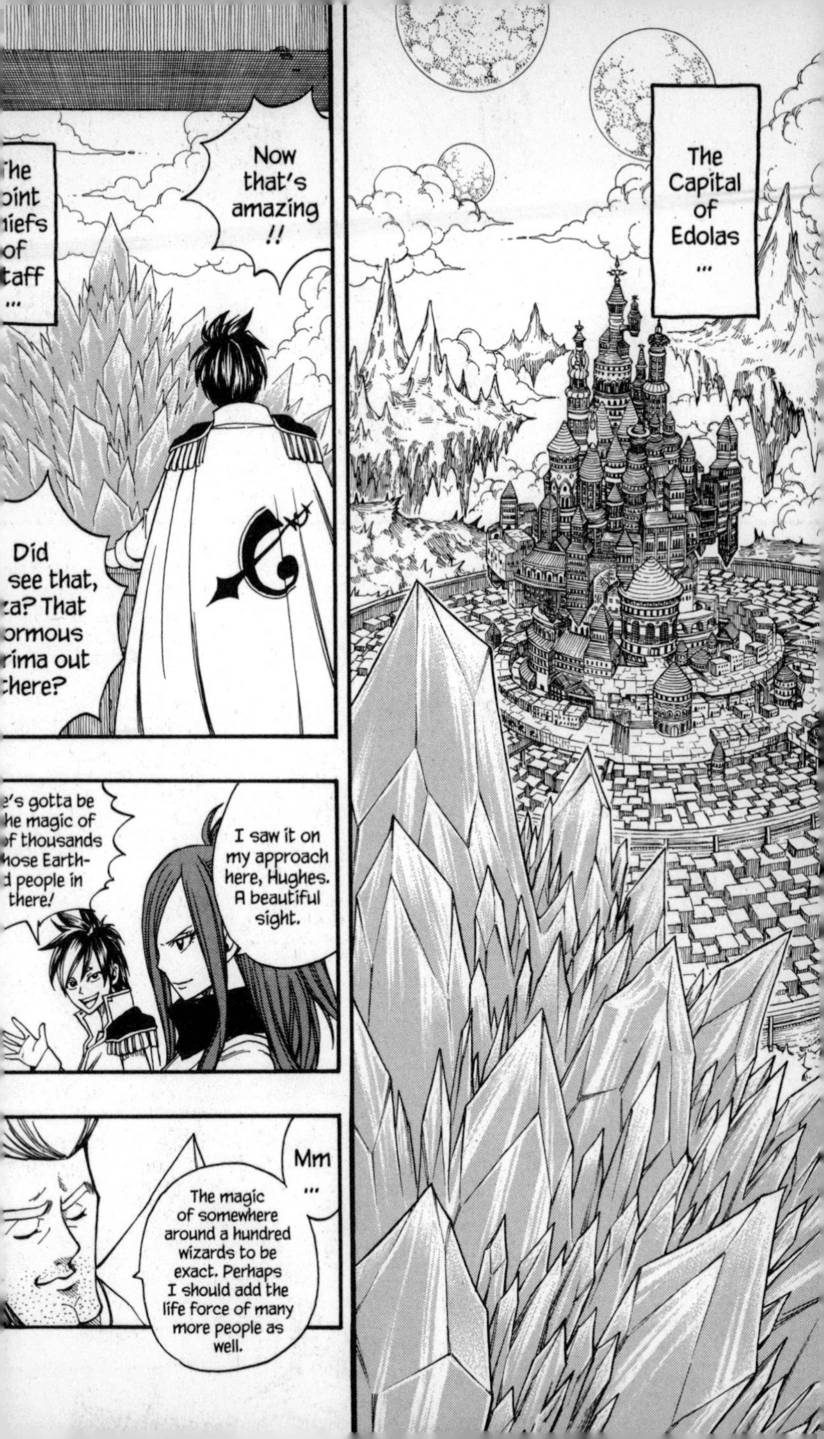
The Capital of Edolas ...
Now that's amazing !!
he oint iefs of taff ...
Did see that, za? That ormous rima out here?
I saw it on my approach here, Hughes. A beautiful sight.
's gotta be he magic of f thousands hose Earth- d people in there!
Mm ...
The magic of somewhere around a hundred wizards to be exact. Perhaps I should add the life force of many more people as well.

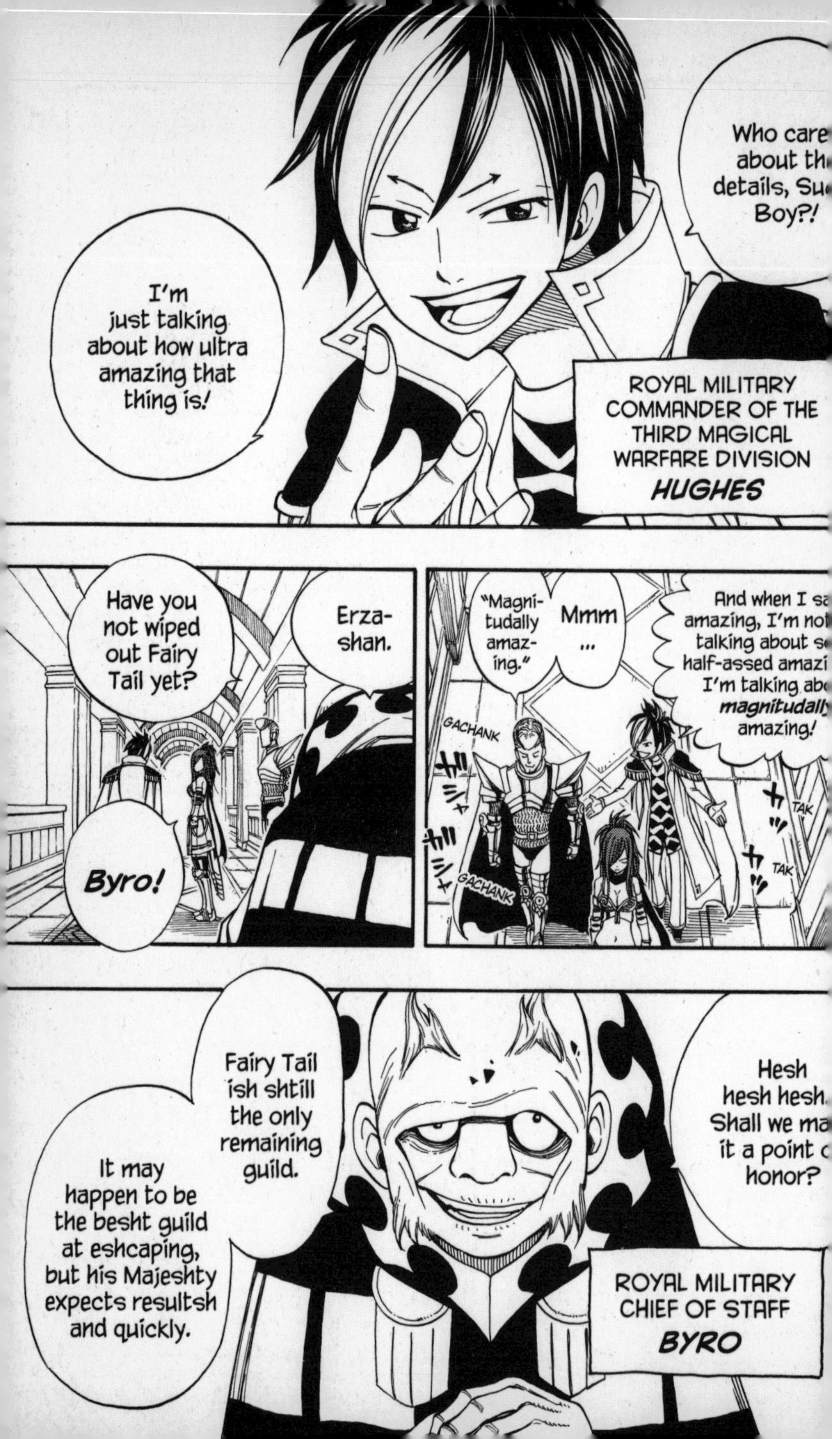

Who care about th details, Su Boy?!
I'm just talking about how ultra amazing that thing is!
ROYAL MILITARY COMMANDER OF THE THIRD MAGICAL WARFARE DIVISION HUGHES
And when I sa amazing, I'm not talking about s half-assed amazi I'm talking ab magnitudall amazing!
Mmm ...
"Magni-tudally amaz-ing."
GACHANK
TAK
TAK
GACHANK
Erza-shan.
Have you not wiped out Fairy Tail yet?
Byro!
Hesh hesh hesh. Shall we ma it a point o honor?
ROYAL MILITARY CHIEF OF STAFF BYRO
Fairy Tail ish shtill the only remaining guild.
It may happen to be the besht guild at eshcaping, but his Majeshty expects resultsh and quickly.

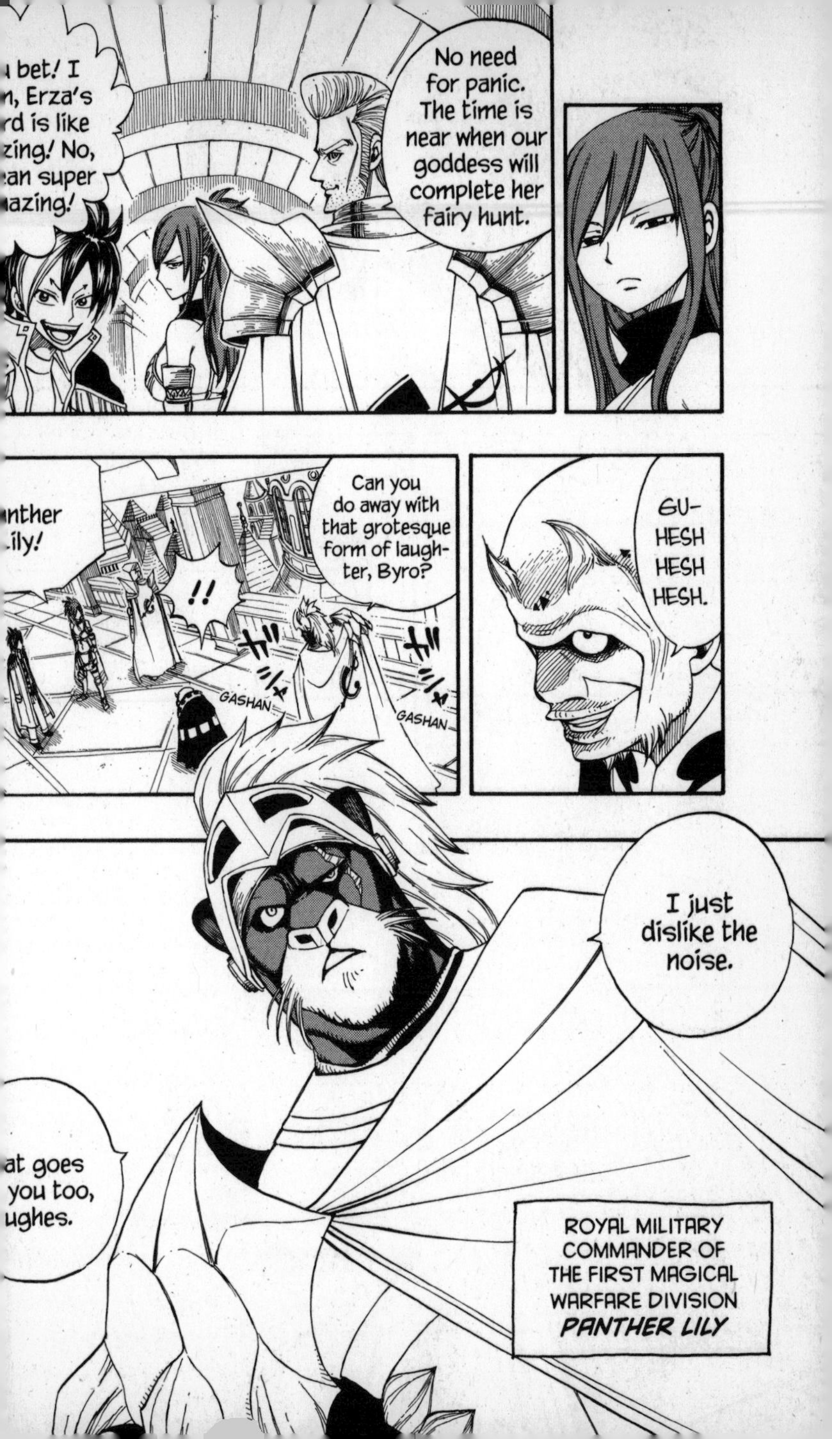
No need for panic. The time is near when our goddess will complete her fairy hunt.
bet! I
, Erza's
rd is like
zing! No,
an super
azing!
GU-HESH HESH HESH.
Can you do away with that grotesque form of laughter, Byro?
nther
ily!
!!
GASHAN
GASHAN
I just dislike the noise.
at goes
you too,
ughes.
ROYAL MILITARY COMMANDER OF THE FIRST MAGICAL WARFARE DIVISION
PANTHER LILY

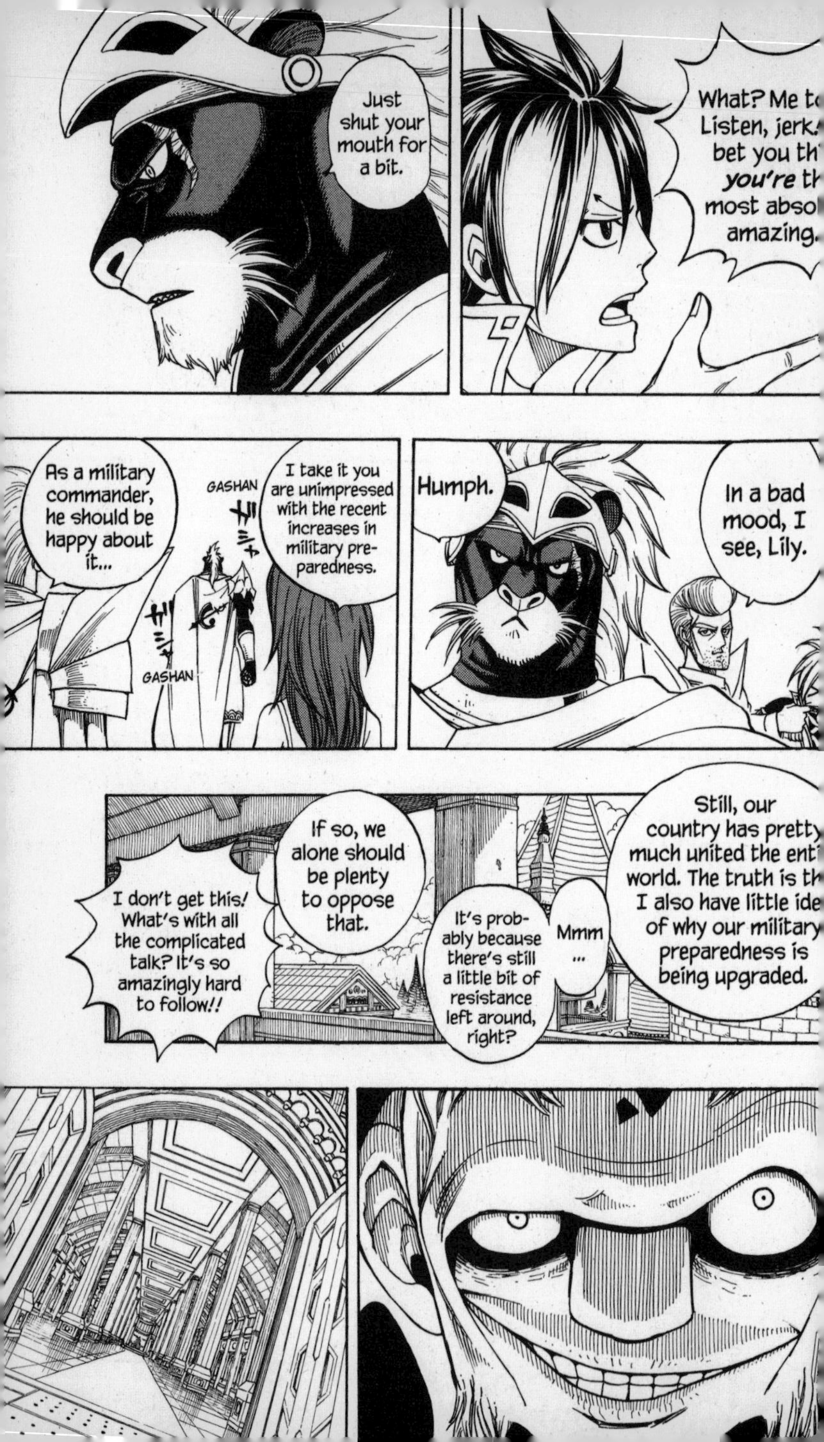
What? Me t
Listen, jerk! I bet you th you're th most abso amazing.
Just shut your mouth for a bit.
In a bad mood, I see, Lily.
Humph.
I take it you are unimpressed with the recent increases in military preparedness.
GASHAN
GASHAN
As a military commander, he should be happy about it...
Still, our country has pretty much united the ent world. The truth is th I also have little ide of why our military preparedness is being upgraded.
Mmm...
It's probably because there's still a little bit of resistance left around, right?
If so, we alone should be plenty to oppose that.
I don't get this! What's with all the complicated talk? It's so amazingly hard to follow!!

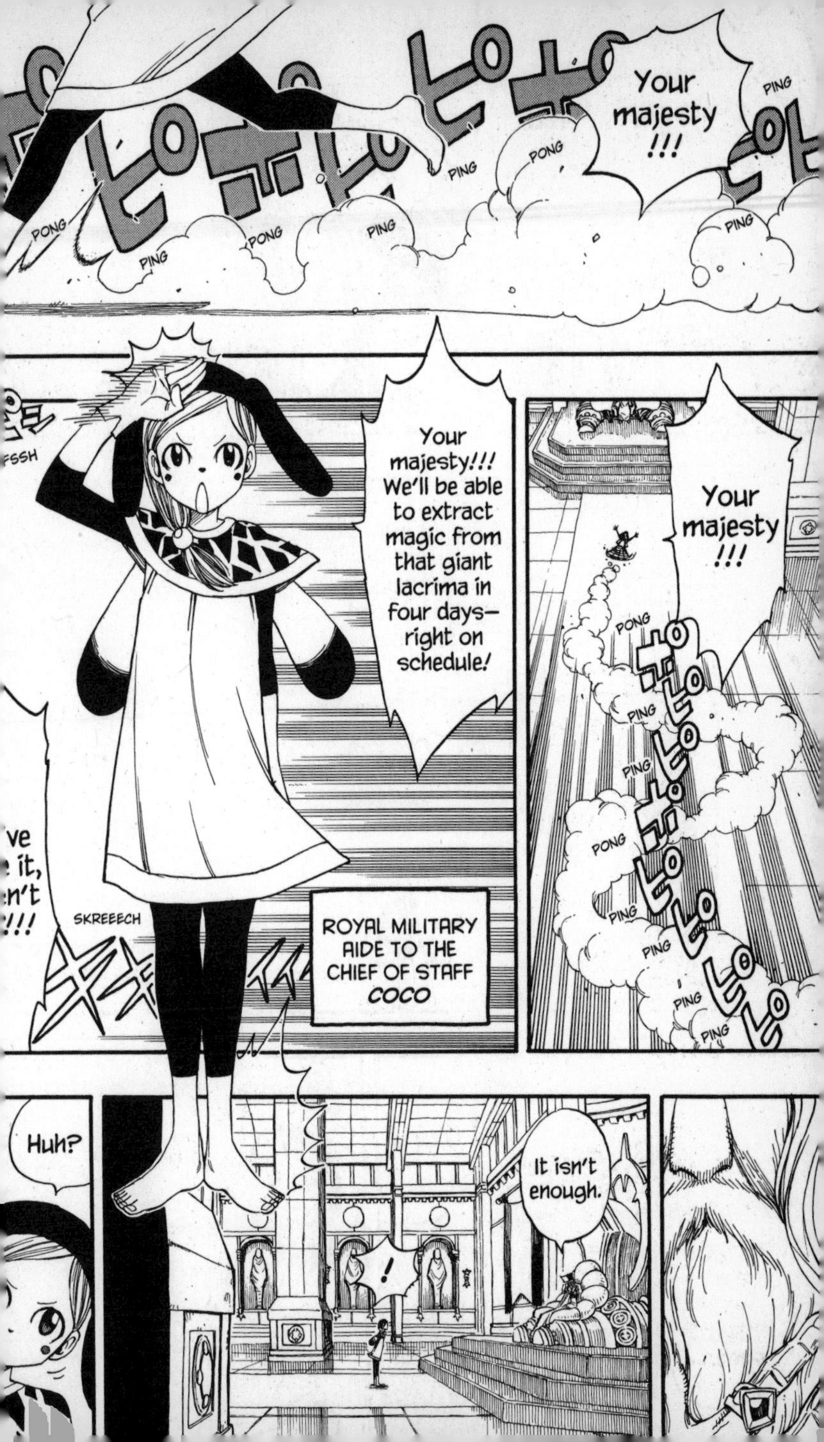
PING
Your majesty !!!
PONG
PING
PING
PONG
PING
PONG
PING
PONG
Your majesty !!!
PONG
PING
PING
PONG
PING
PING
PING
PING
Your majesty!!! We'll be able to extract magic from that giant lacrima in four days—right on schedule!
FSSH
ROYAL MILITARY AIDE TO THE CHIEF OF STAFF COCO
SKREEECH
It isn't enough.
!
Huh?

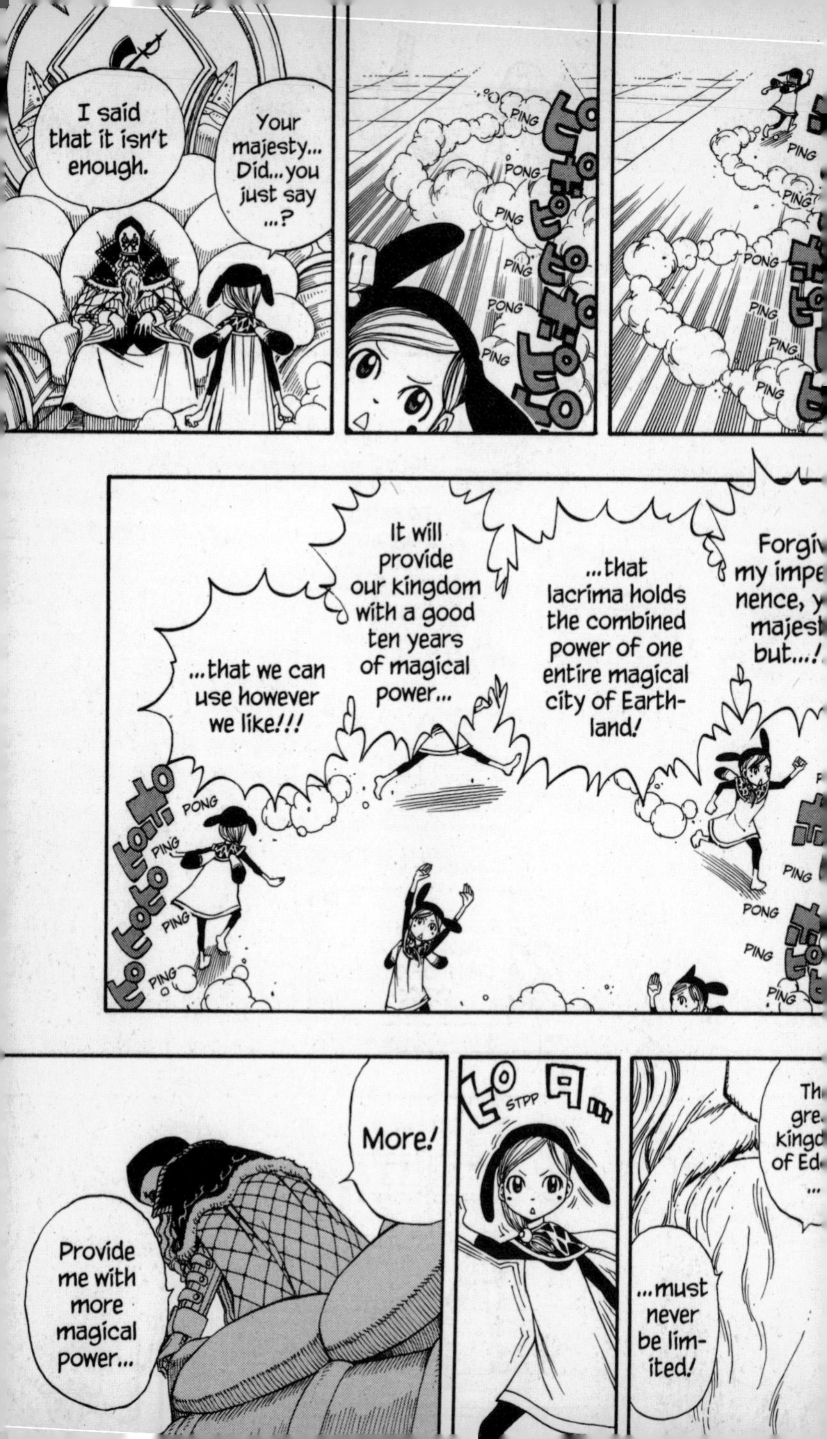
PING
PING
PONG
PING
PING
PING
PING
PONG
PING
PING
PONG
PING
Your majesty... Did...you just say ...?
I said that it isn't enough.
Forgiv my impe nence, y majes but...!
...that lacrima holds the combined power of one entire magical city of Earth-land!
It will provide our kingdom with a good ten years of magical power...
...that we can use however we like!!!
PING
PONG
PING
PING
PONG
PING
PING
PING
Th gre kingd of Ed ...
...must never be lim-ited!
STPP
More!
Provide me with more magical power...

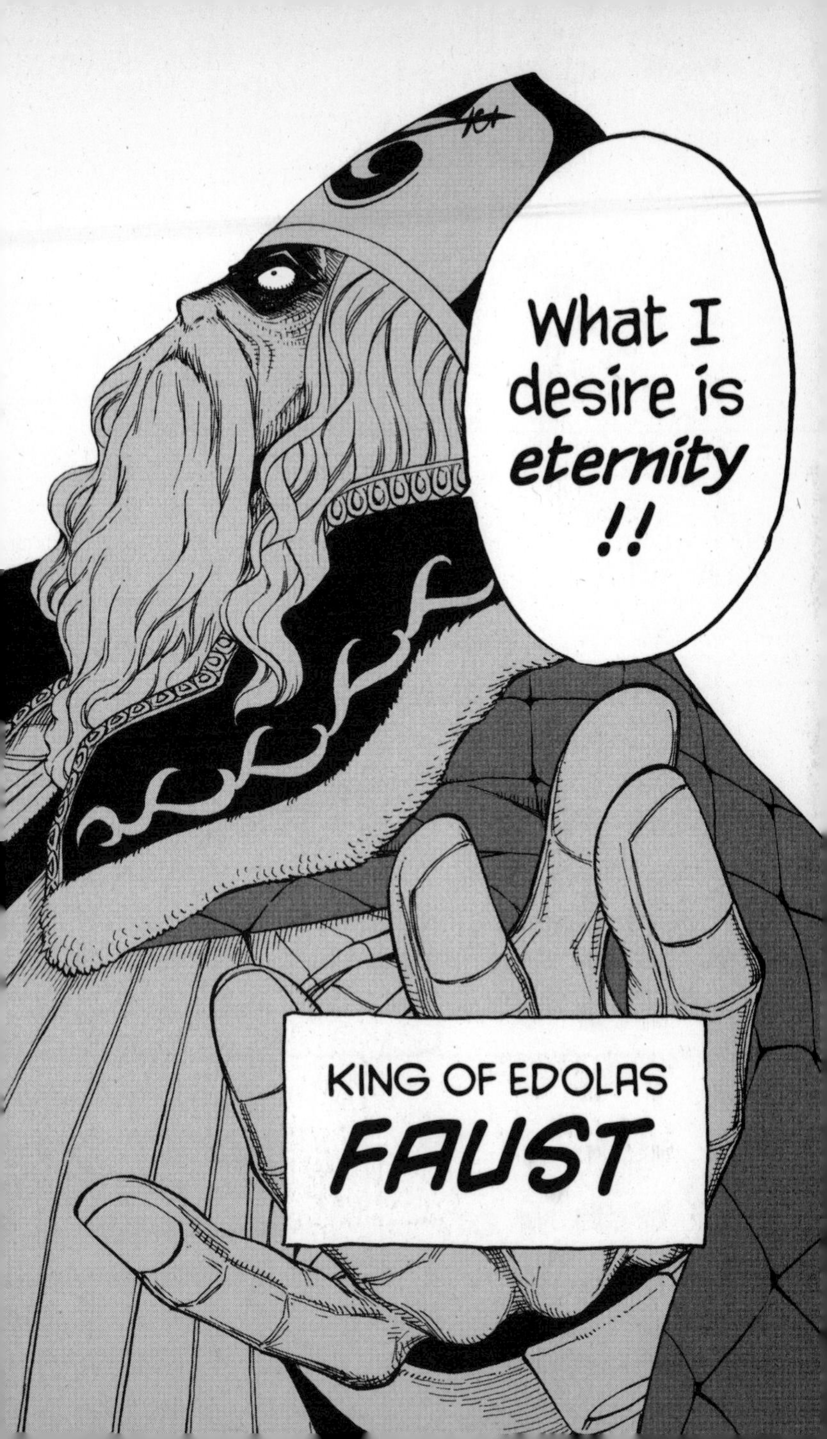
What I desire is eternity !!
KING OF EDOLAS
FAUST

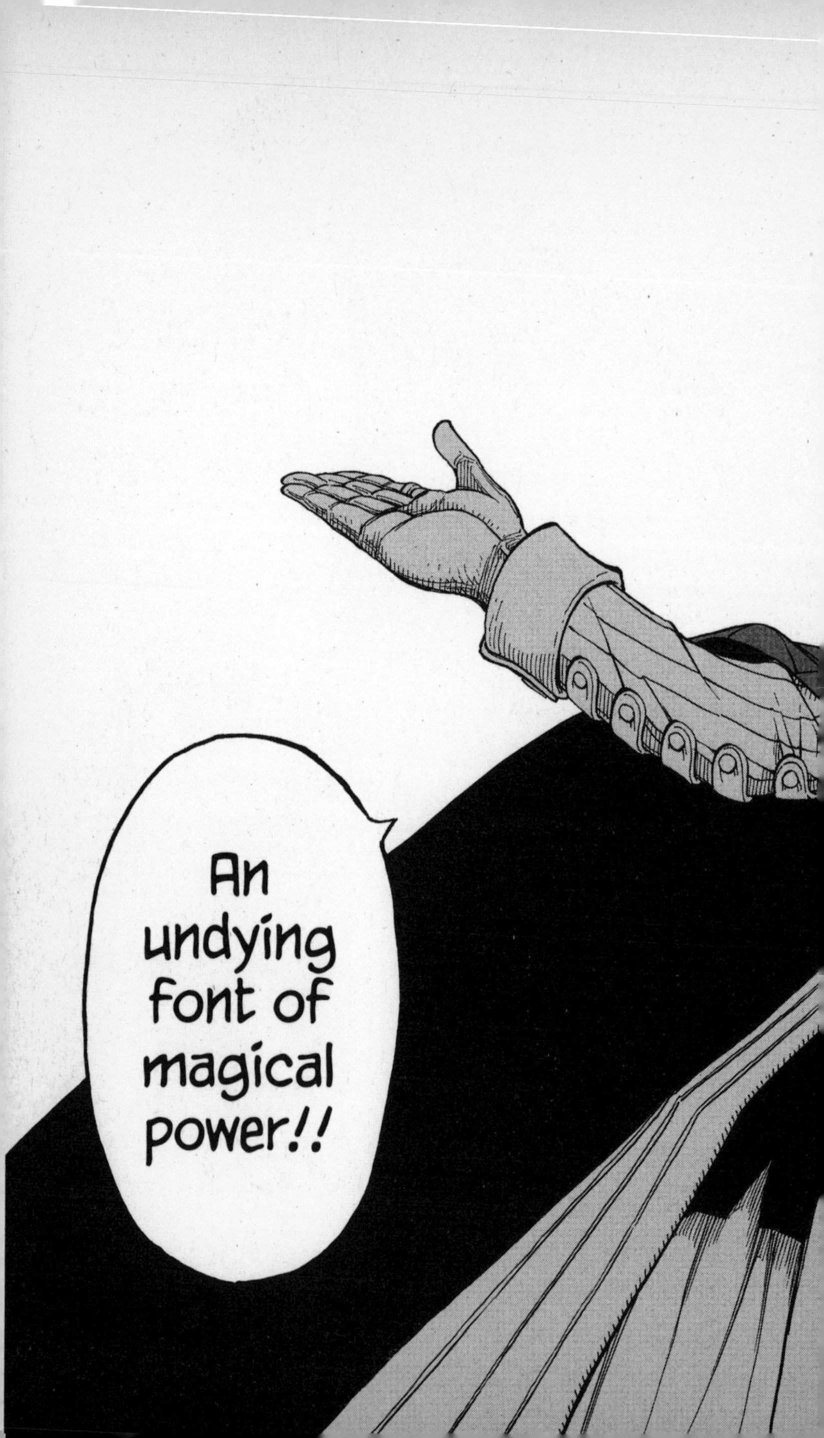
An undying font of magical power!!

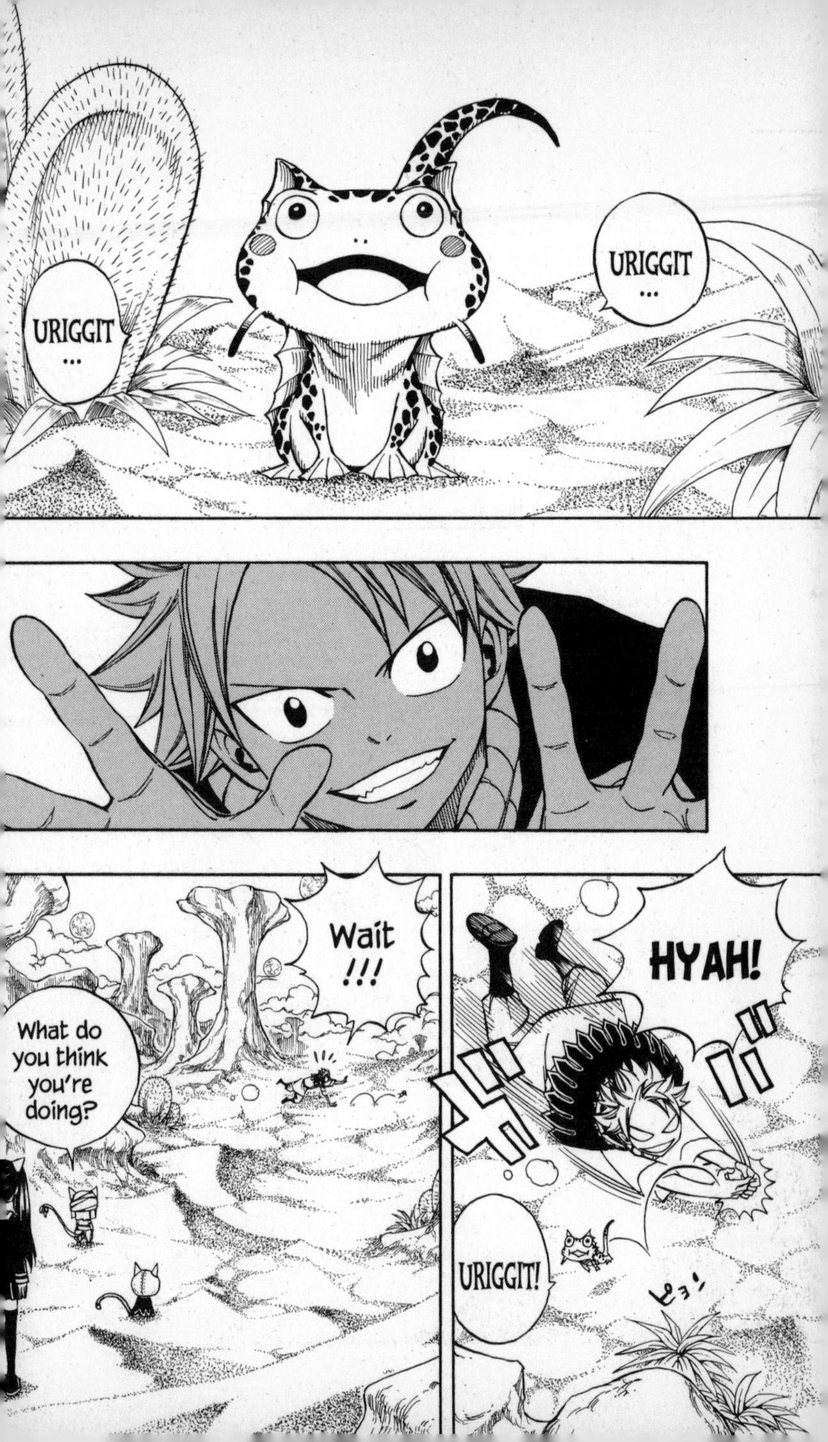
URIGGIT ...
URIGGIT ...
HYAH!
URIGGIT!
Wait!!!
What do you think you're doing?

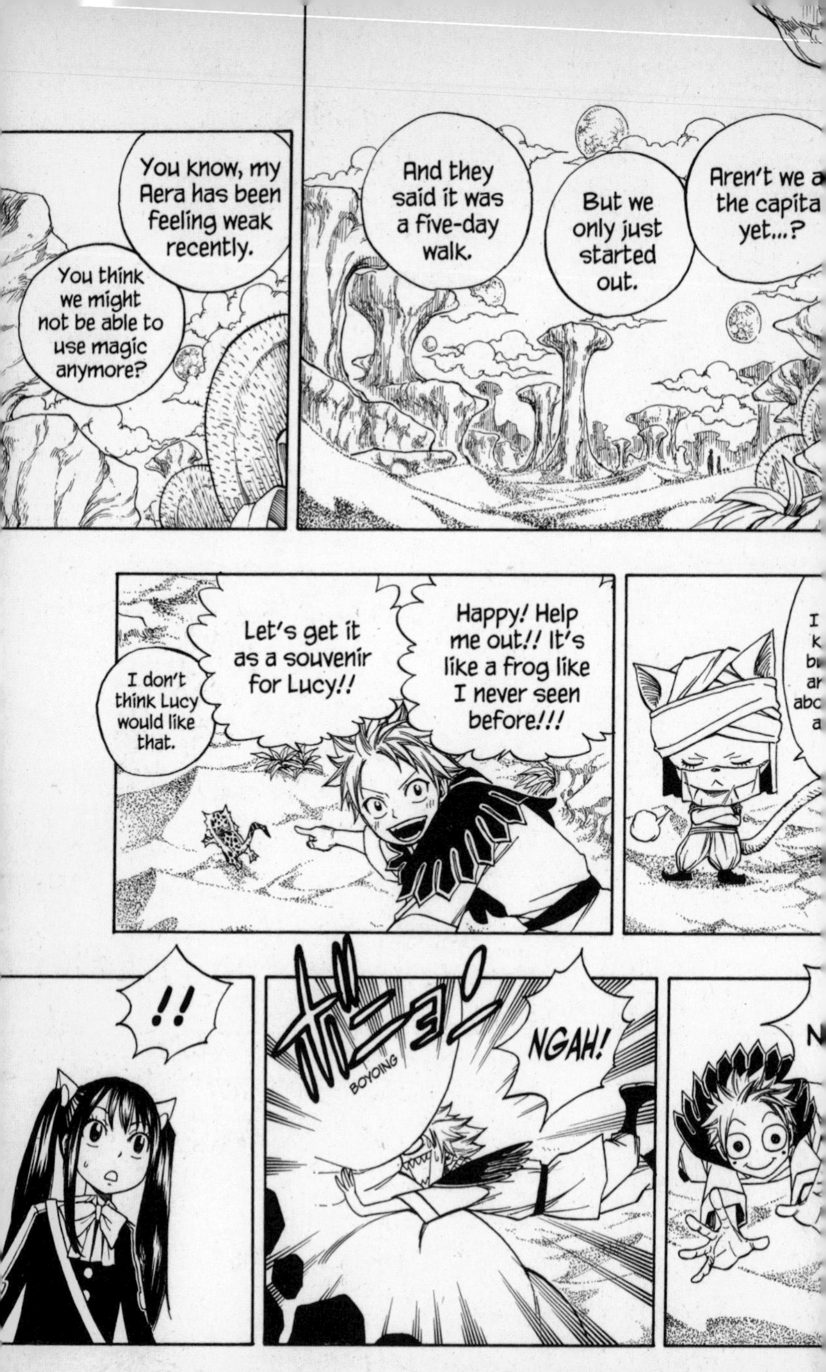

Aren't we a the capita yet...?
But we only just started out.
And they said it was a five-day walk.
You know, my Aera has been feeling weak recently.
You think we might not be able to use magic anymore?
Happy! Help me out!! It's like a frog like I never seen before!!!
Let's get it as a souvenir for Lucy!!
I don't think Lucy would like that.
NGAH!
BOYOING
!!

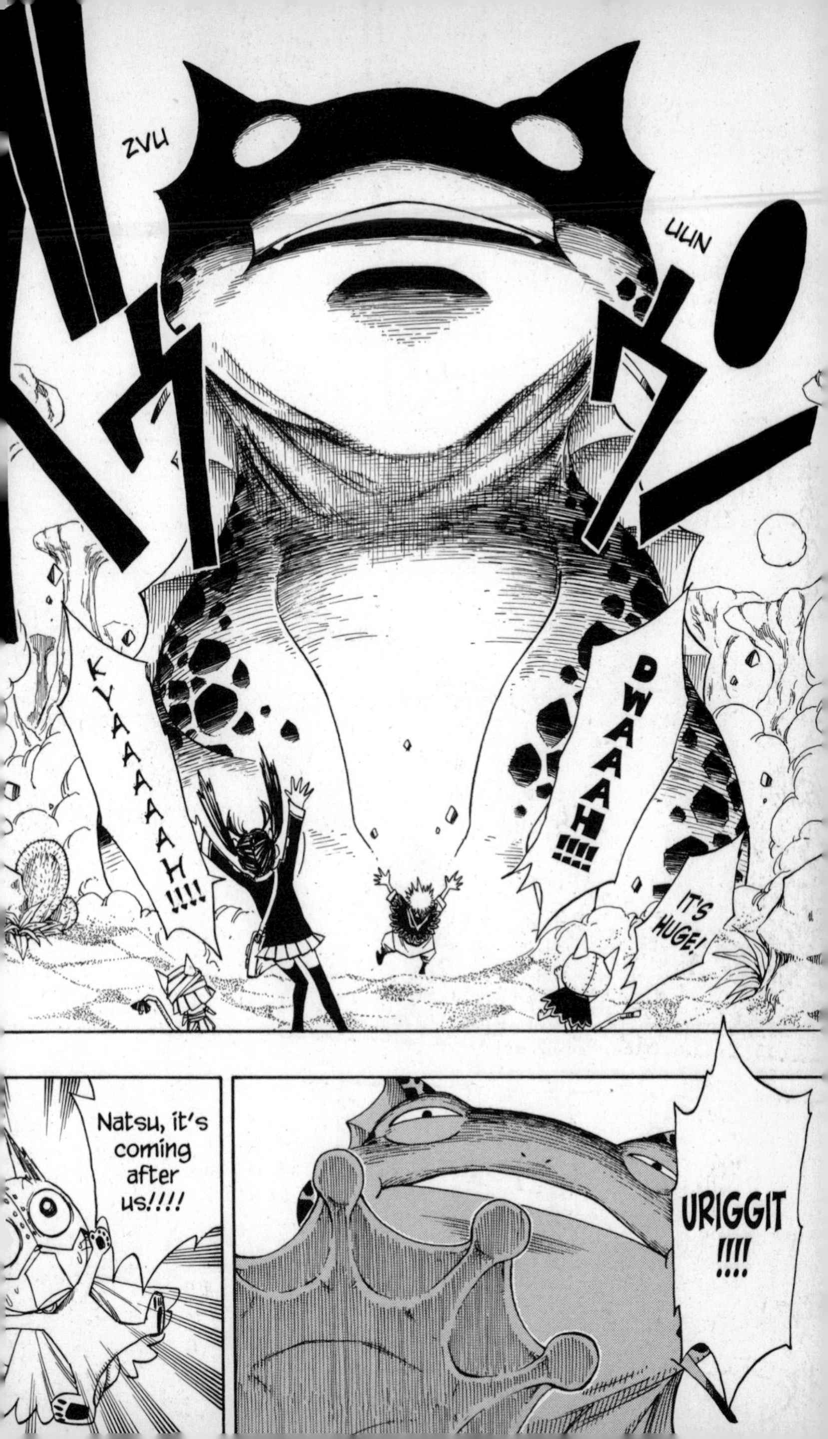
ZVU
UUN
DWAAAAH!!!!
IT'S HUGE!
KYAAAAAH!!!!
URIGGIT!!!!....
Natsu, it's coming after us!!!!

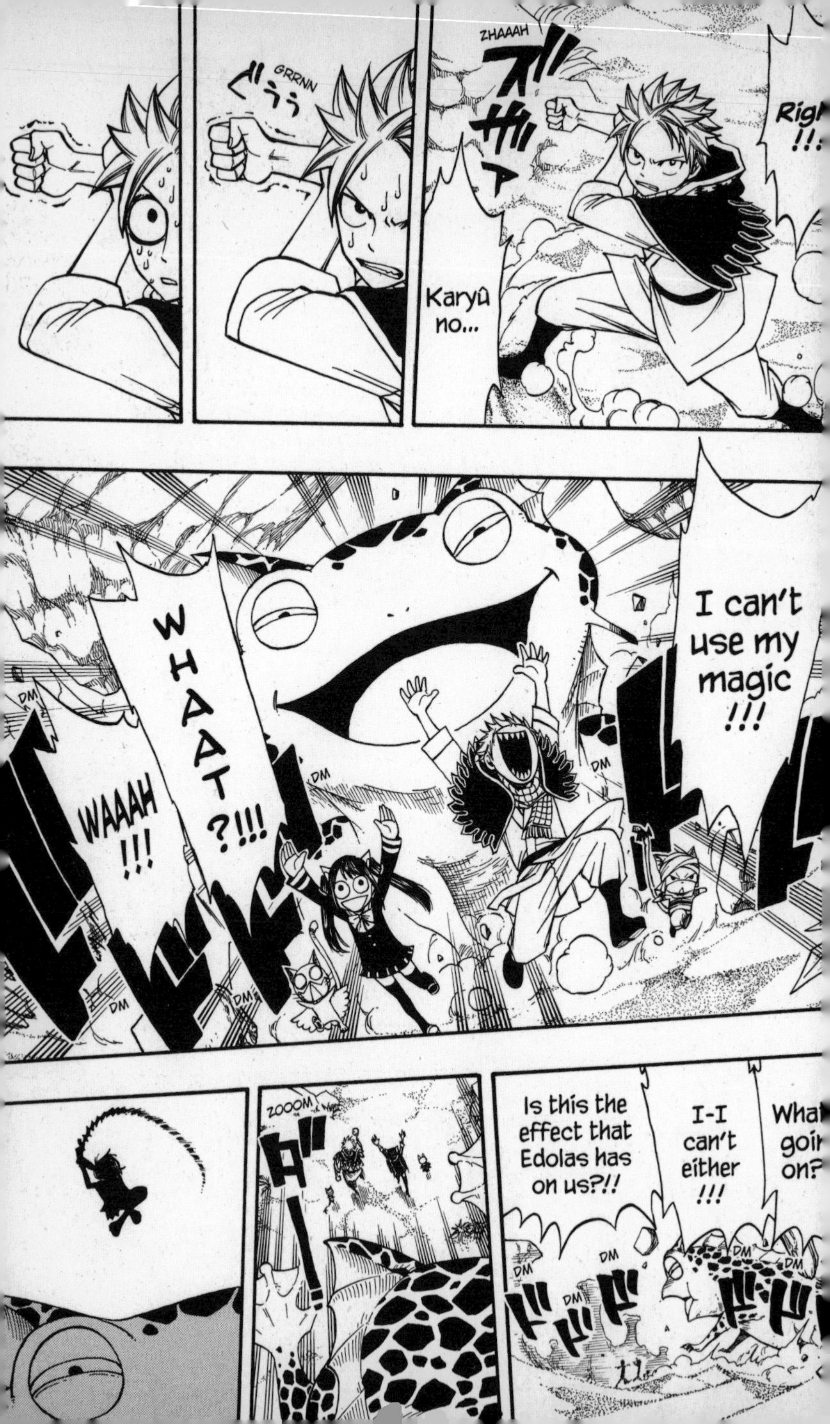

Righ
!!!
ZHAAAH
Karyû no...
GRRNN
I can't use my magic !!!
DM
WHAAT?!!!
WAAAH !!!
DM
DM
DM
Wha goi on?
I-I can't either !!!
Is this the effect that Edolas has on us?!!
DM
DM
DM
DM
ZOOOM

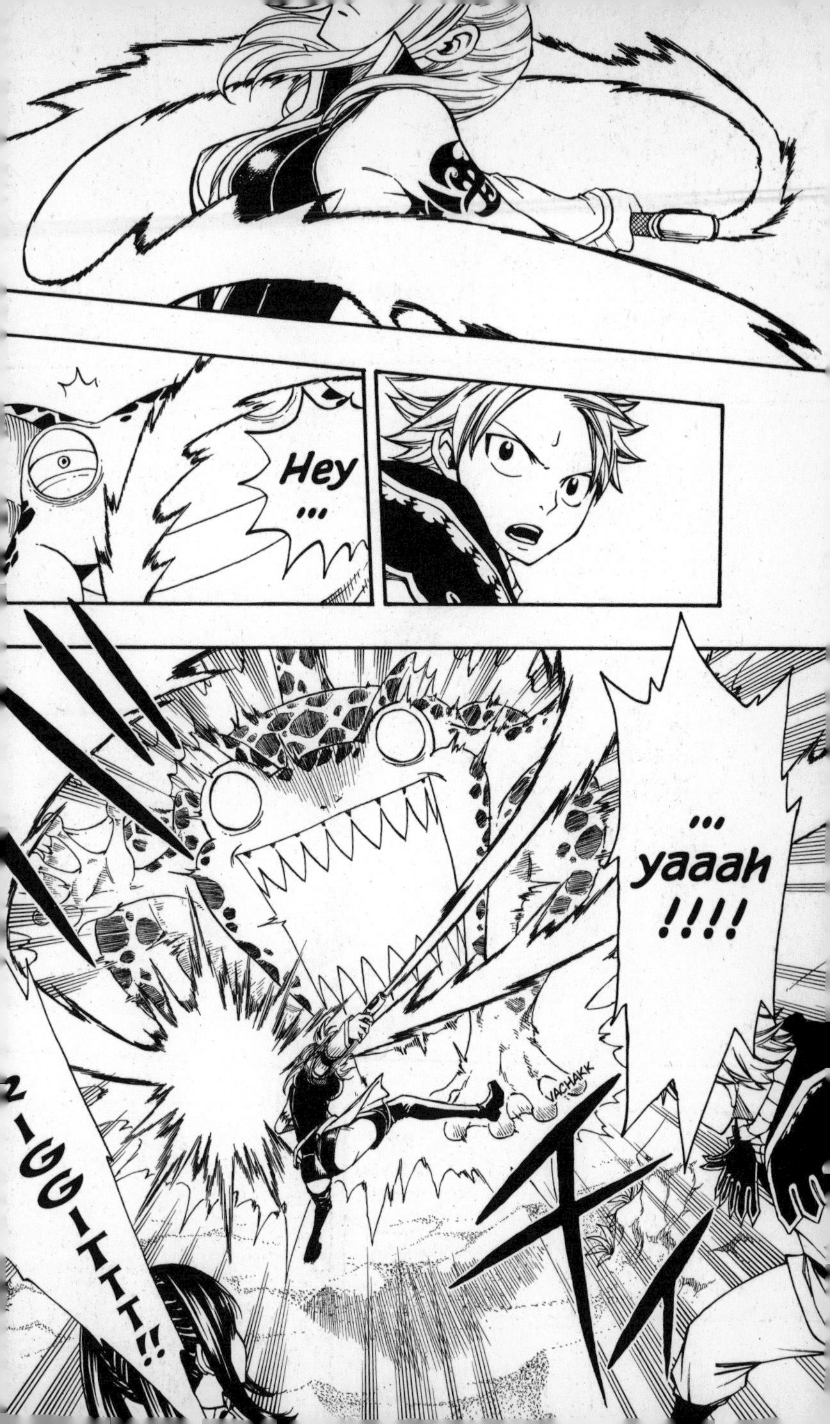
Hey ...
... yaaah !!!!
VACHAKK
ZIGGITTT!!

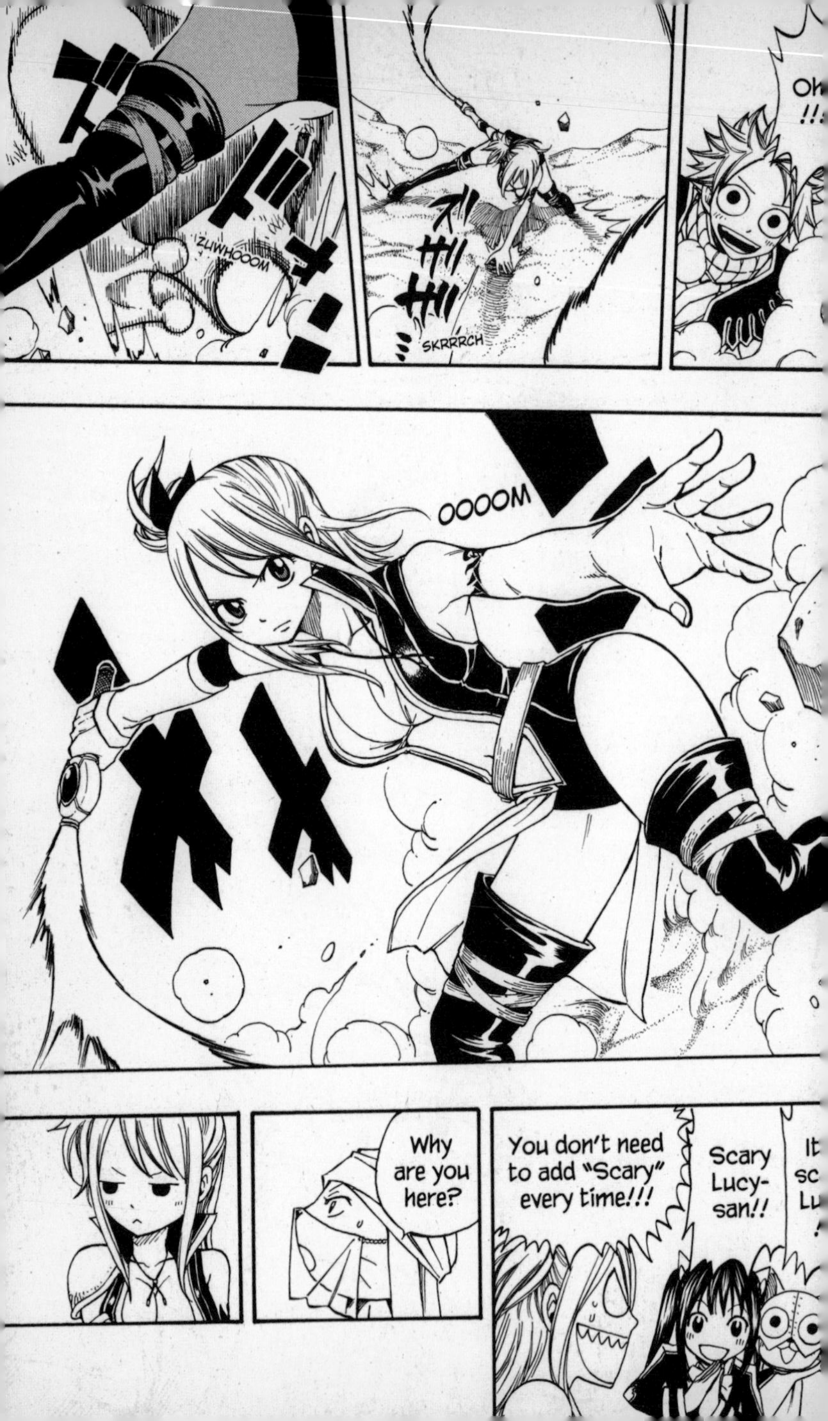
Oh!!
SKRRRCH
ZUWHOOOM
OOOOM
Scary Lucy-san!!
You don't need to add "Scary" every time!!!
Why are you here?

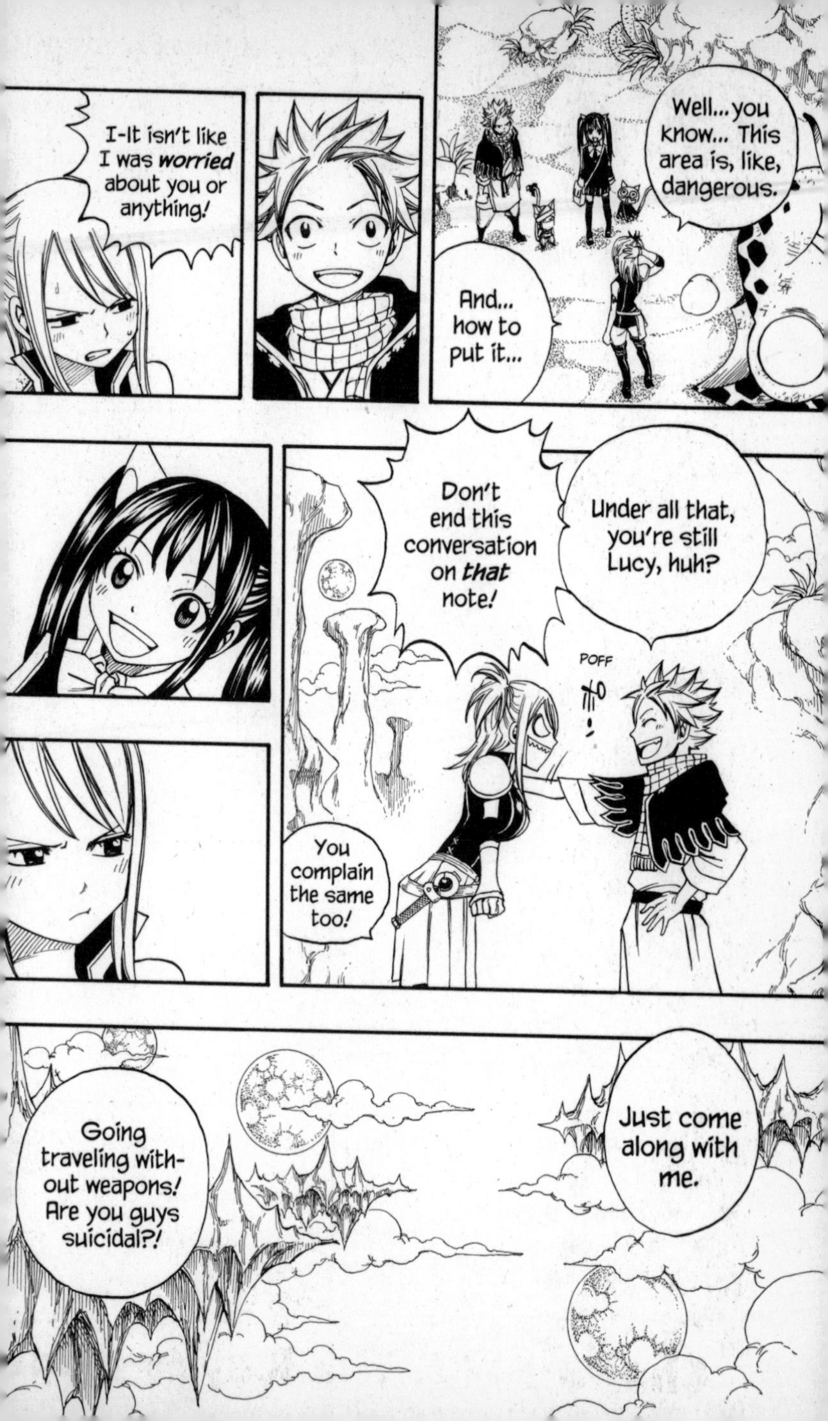

Well...you know... This area is, like, dangerous.
And... how to put it...
I-It isn't like I was *worried* about you or anything!
Under all that, you're still Lucy, huh?
Don't end this conversation on *that* note!
POFF
You complain the same too!
Just come along with me.
Going traveling with-out weapons! Are you guys suicidal?!

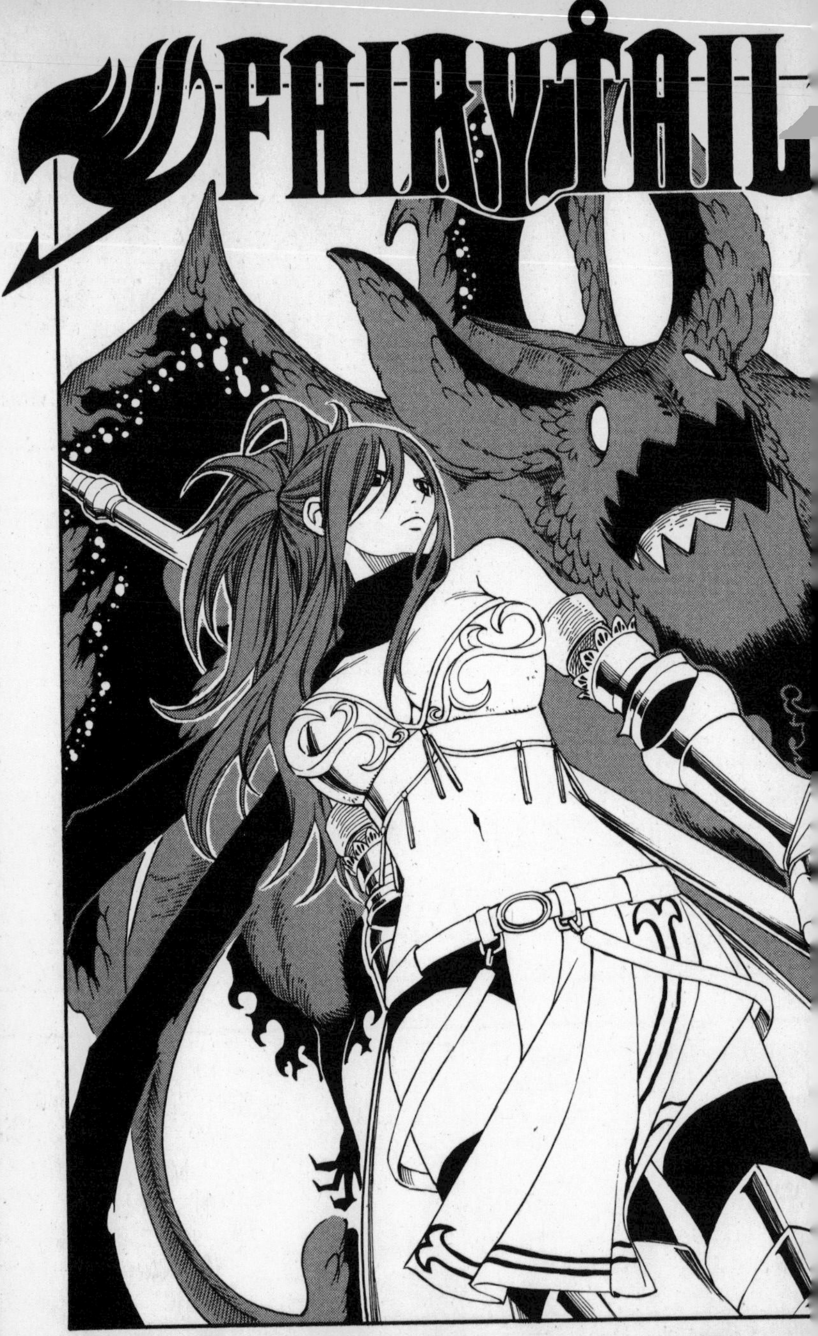
FAIRY TAIL

Chapter 172, The Key to Hope

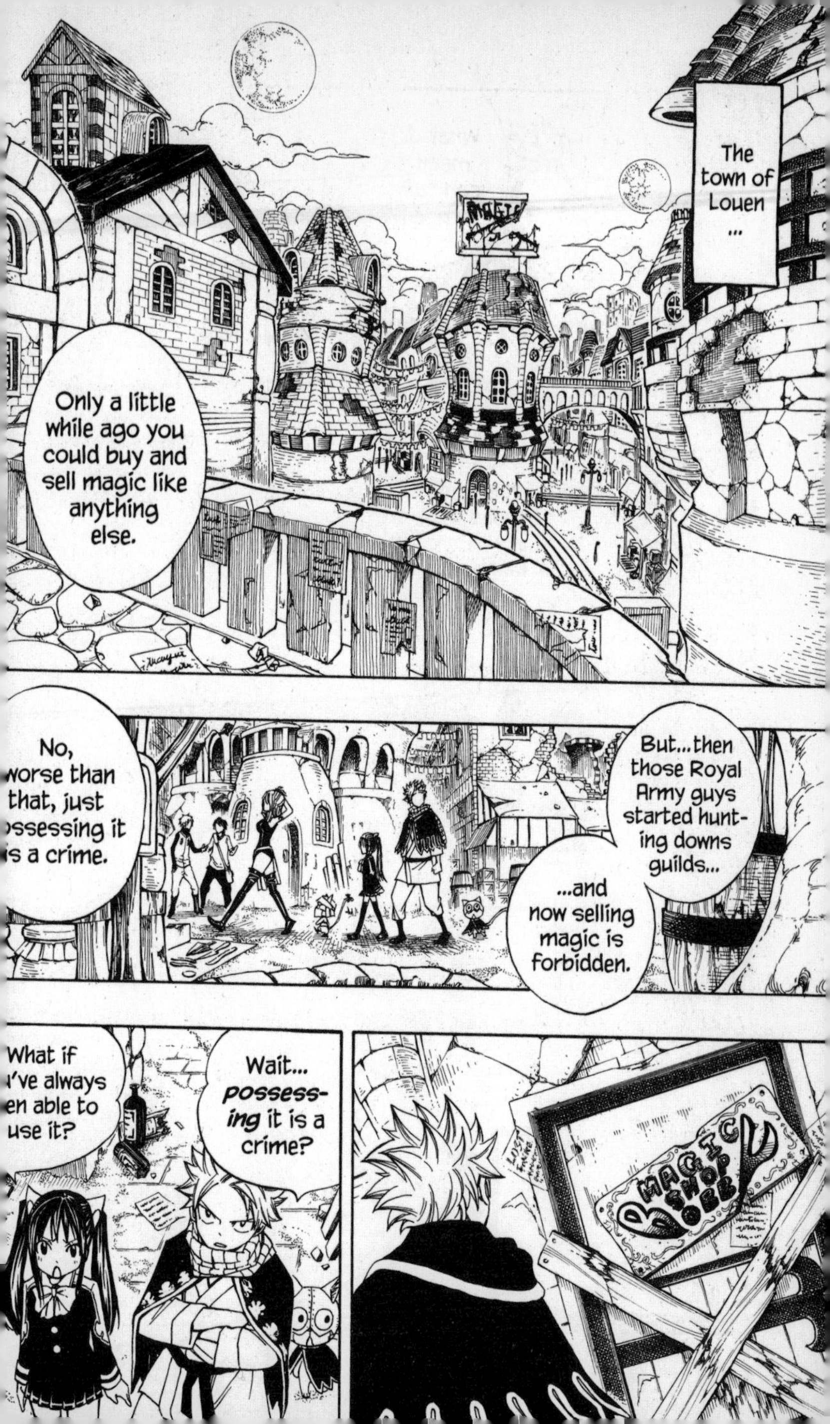
The town of Louen ...
Only a little while ago you could buy and sell magic like anything else.
But...then those Royal Army guys started hunt-ing downs guilds...
...and now selling magic is forbidden.
No, worse than that, just ossessing it s a crime.
MAGIC SHOP
Wait... *possess-ing* it is a crime?
What if 've always en able to use it?

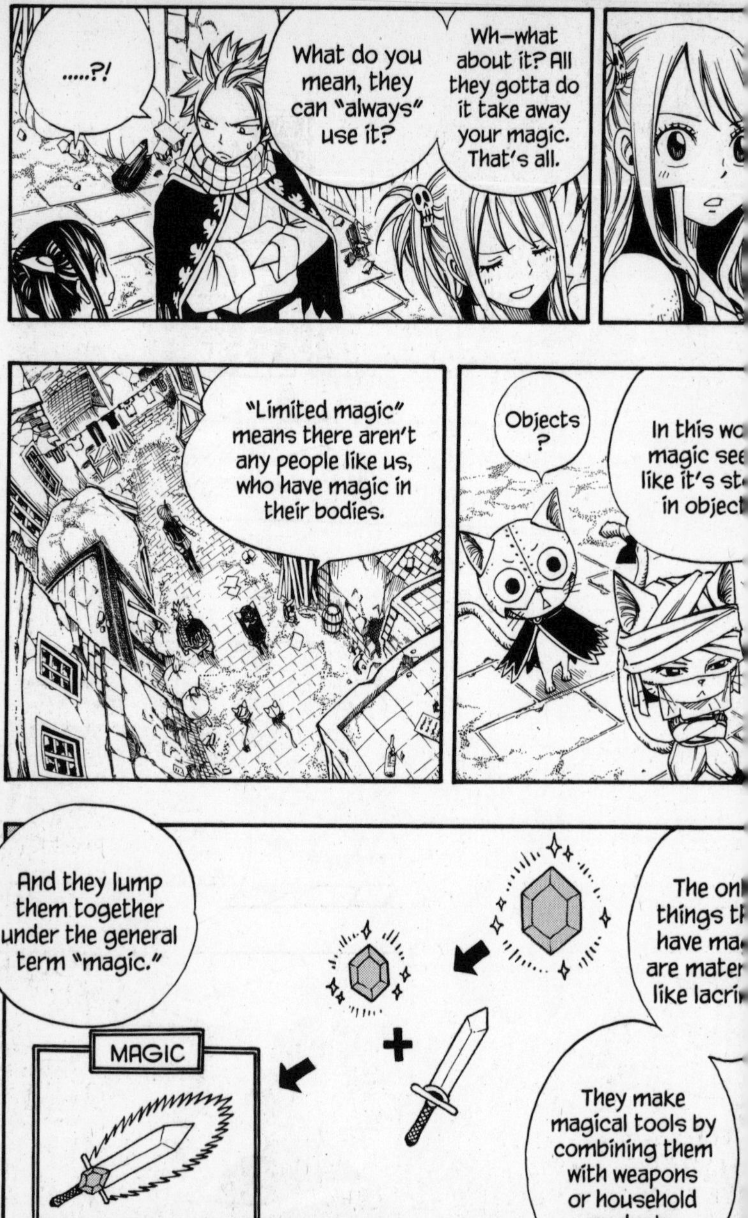
Wh—what about it? All they gotta do it take away your magic. That's all.
What do you mean, they can "always" use it?
.....?!
In this wo magic see like it's st in objec
Objects?
"Limited magic" means there aren't any people like us, who have magic in their bodies.
The onl things th have ma are mater like lacri
They make magical tools by combining them with weapons or household products.
And they lump them together under the general term "magic."
MAGIC

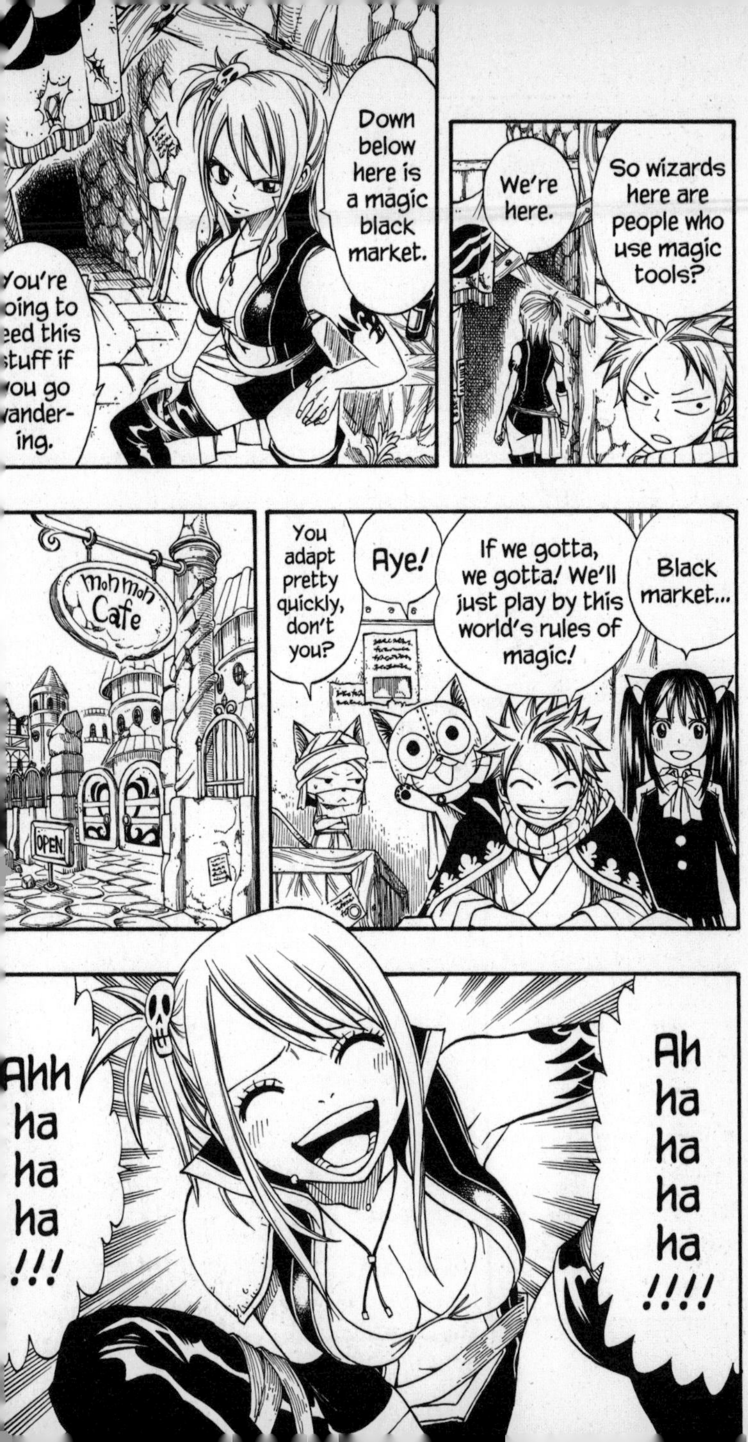

So wizards here are people who use magic tools?
We're here.
Down below here is a magic black market.
You're oing to eed this tuff if ou go vander-ing.
Black market...
If we gotta, we gotta! We'll just play by this world's rules of magic!
Aye!
You adapt pretty quickly, don't you?
moh moh Cafe
OPEN
Ah ha ha ha ha!!!!
Ahh ha ha ha ha!!!

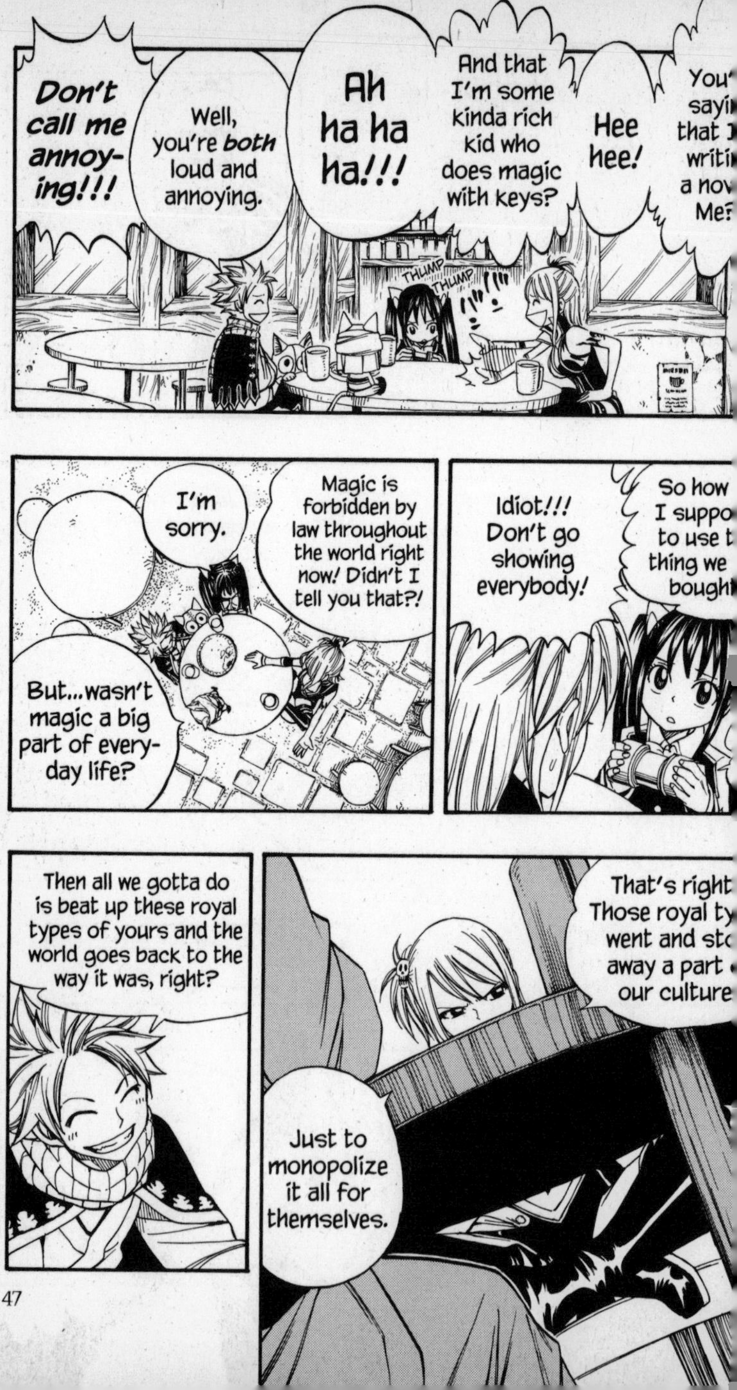
You' sayi that I writi a nov Me?
Hee hee!
And that I'm some kinda rich kid who does magic with keys?
Ah ha ha!!!
Well, you're *both* loud and annoying.
Don't call me annoying!!!
THUMP THUMP
So how I suppo to use t thing we bough
Idiot!!! Don't go showing everybody!
Magic is forbidden by law throughout the world right now! Didn't I tell you that?!
I'm sorry.
But...wasn't magic a big part of everyday life?
That's right Those royal ty went and sto away a part our culture
Just to monopolize it all for themselves.
Then all we gotta do is beat up these royal types of yours and the world goes back to the way it was, right?

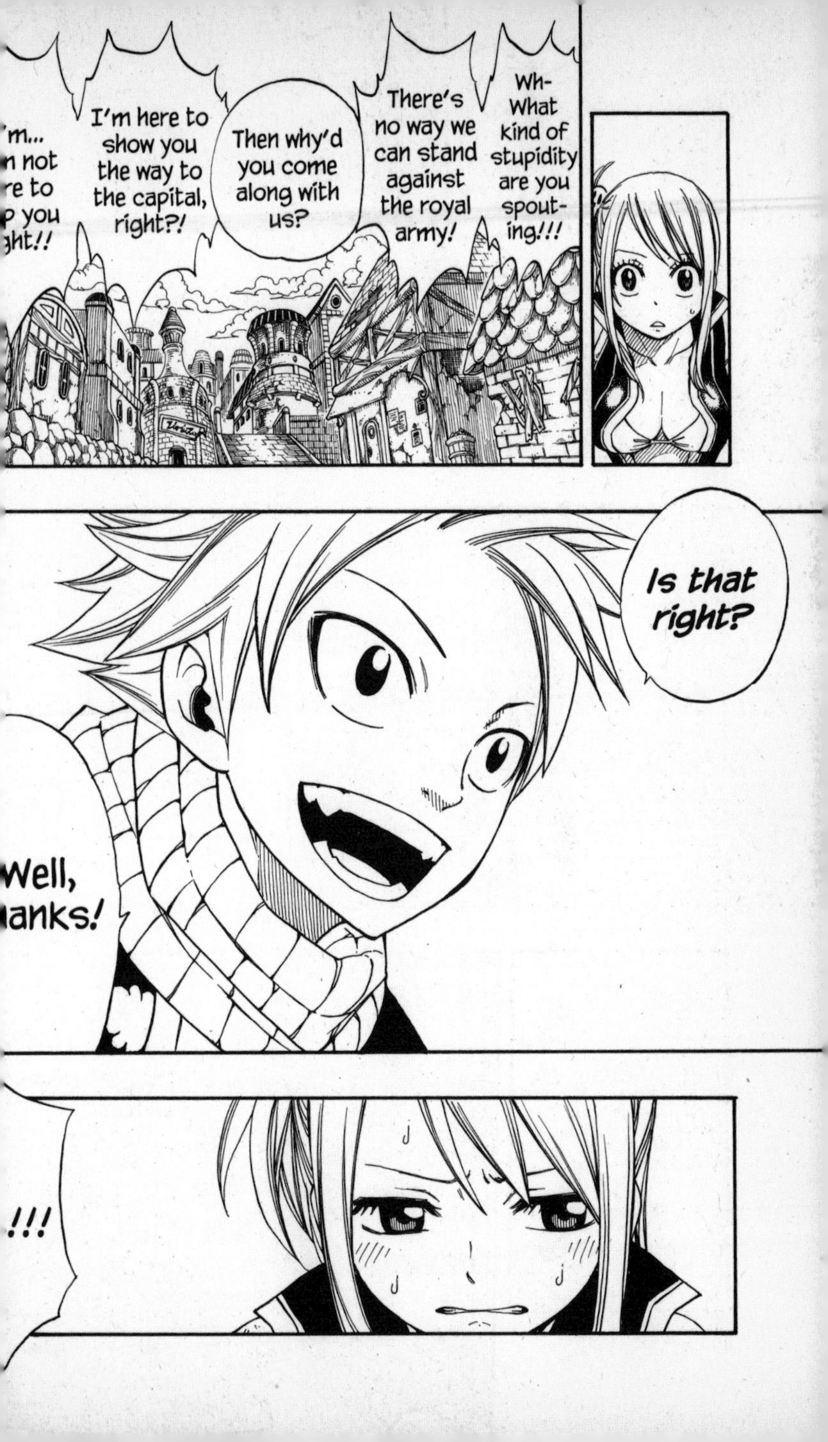
Wh- What kind of stupidity are you spouting!!!
There's no way we can stand against the royal army!
Then why'd you come along with us?
I'm here to show you the way to the capital, right?!
Is that right?
!!!

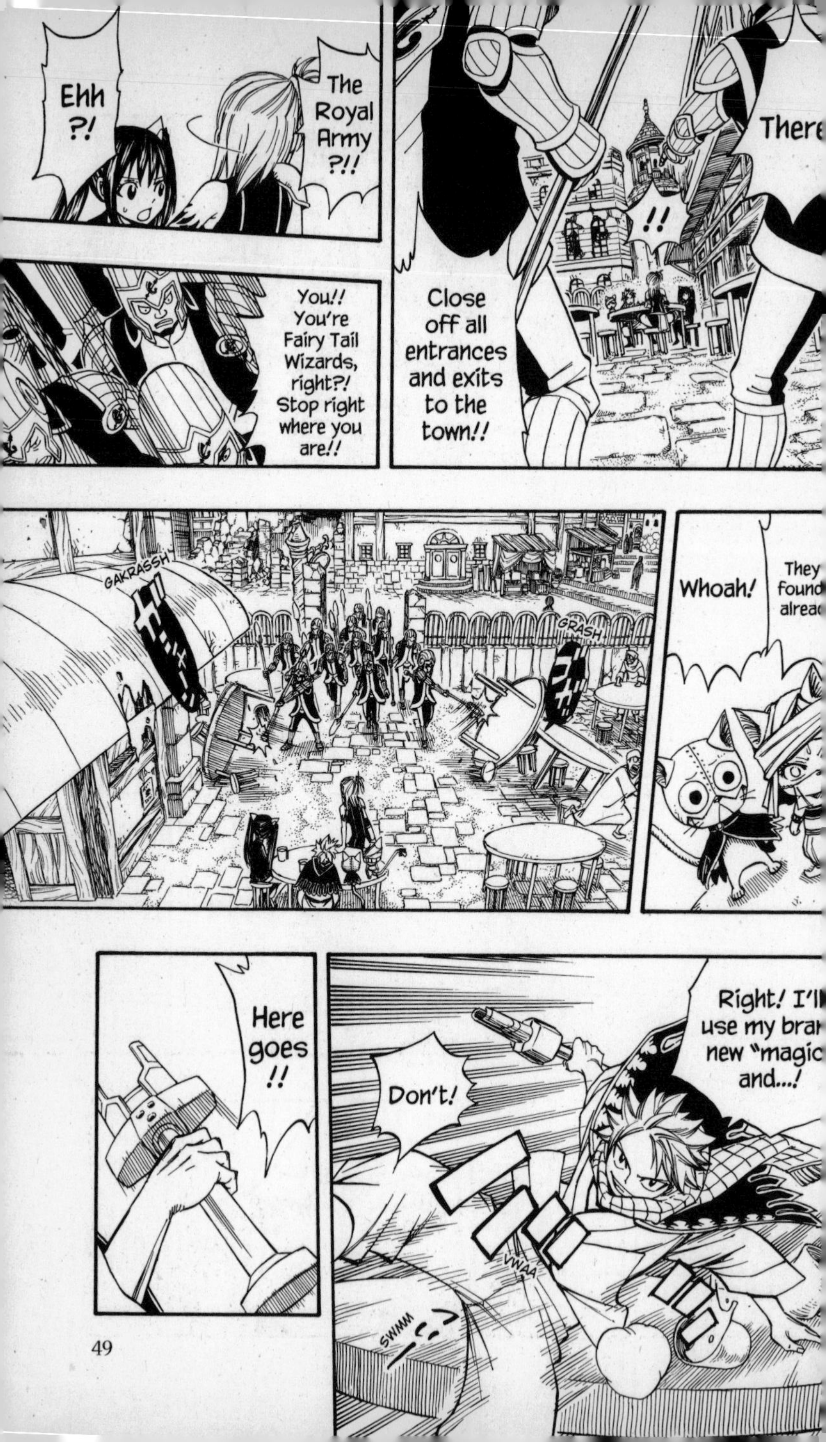

There
!!
Close off all entrances and exits to the town!!
The Royal Army?!!
Ehh?!
You!! You're Fairy Tail Wizards, right?! Stop right where you are!!
They found alread
Whoah!
GRASH
GAKRASSH
Right! I'll use my bran new "magic and...!
Don't!
VWAA
SWMM
Here goes!!

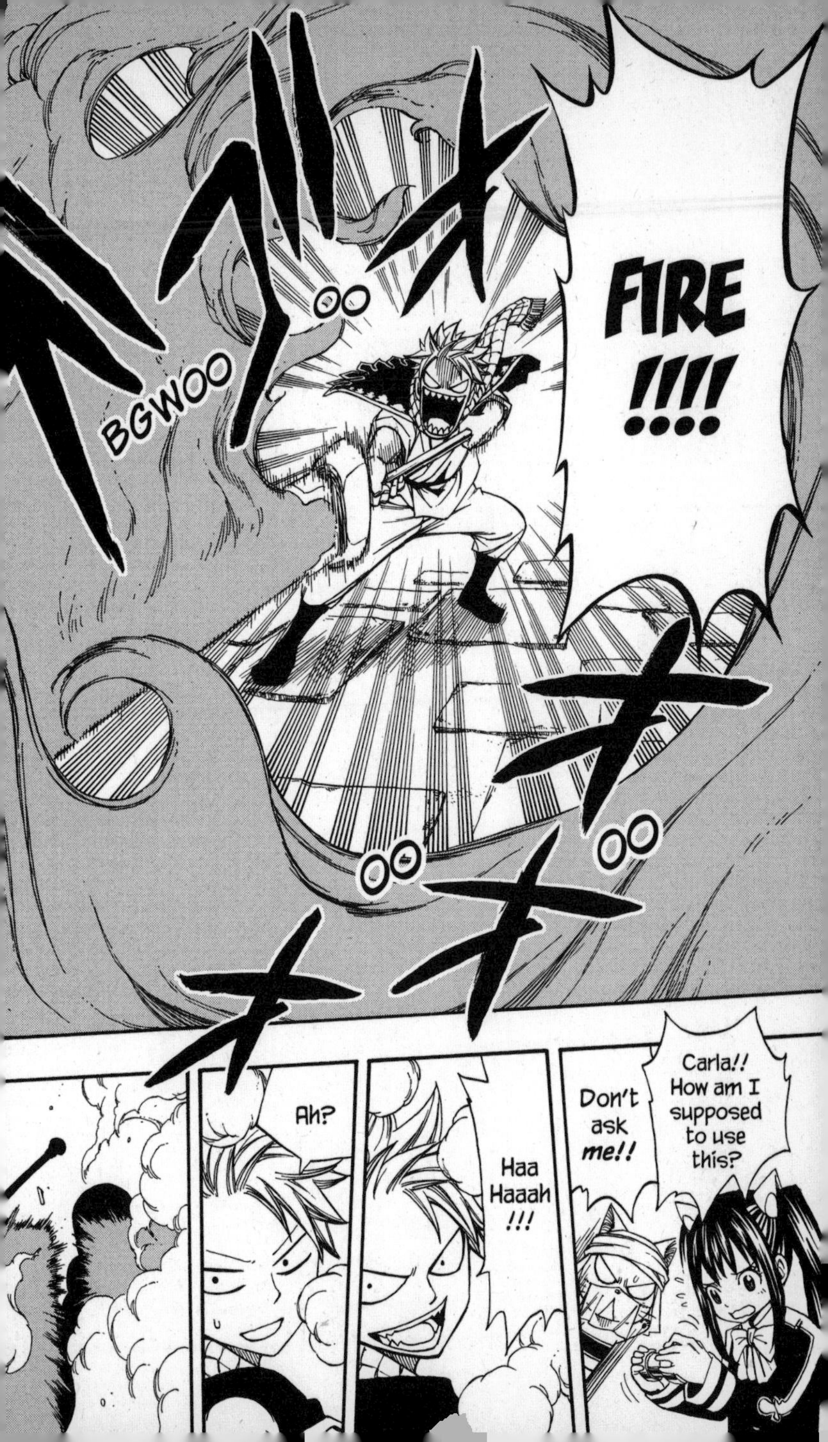
FIRE!!!!
BGWOO
Carla!! How am I supposed to use this?
Don't ask *me!!*
Haa Haaah!!!
Ah?

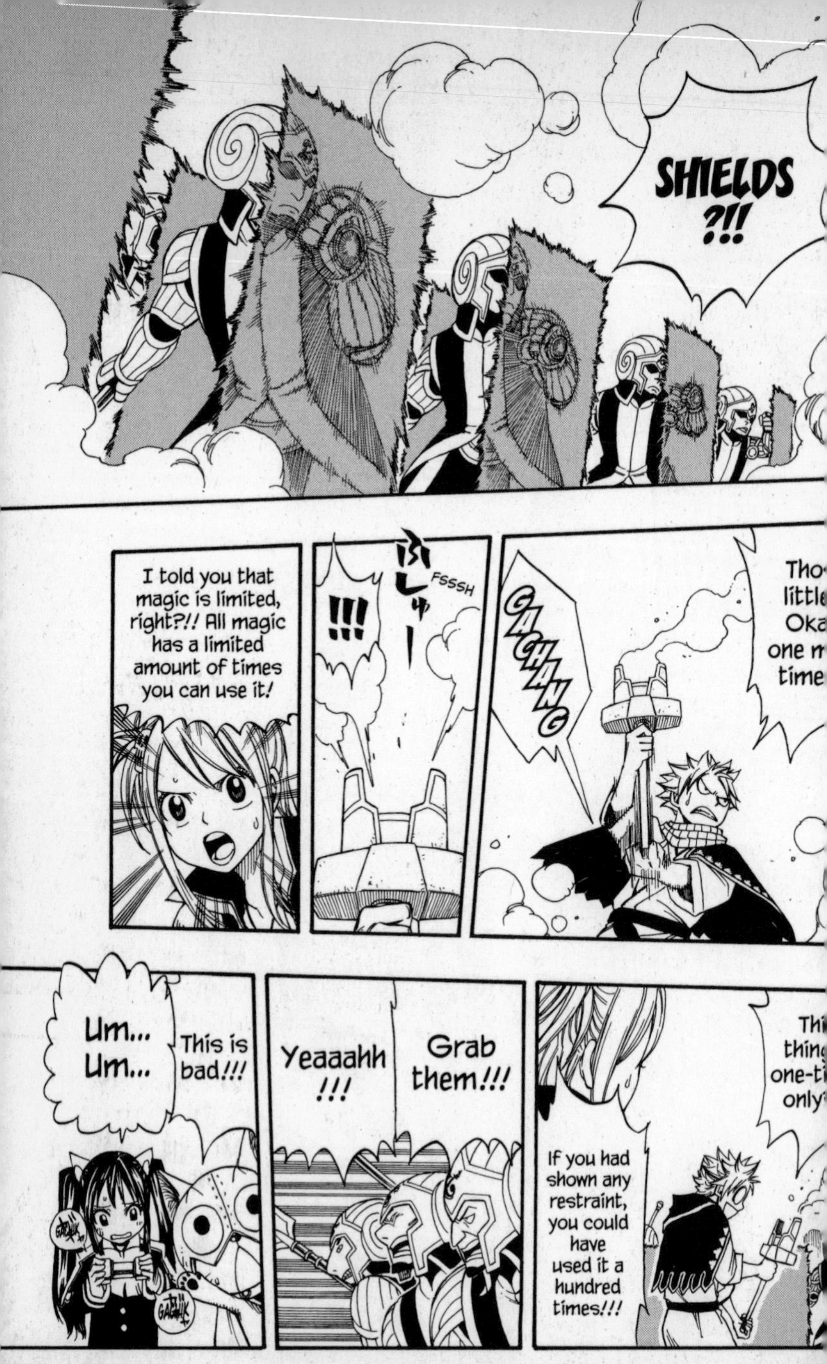
SHIELDS ?!!
Tho little Oka one m time
GACHANG
!!!
ふしゅー
FSSSH
I told you that magic is limited, right?!! All magic has a limited amount of times you can use it!
Thi thing one-ti only
If you had shown any restraint, you could have used it a hundred times!!!
Grab them!!!
Yeaaahh !!!
This is bad!!!
Um... Um...

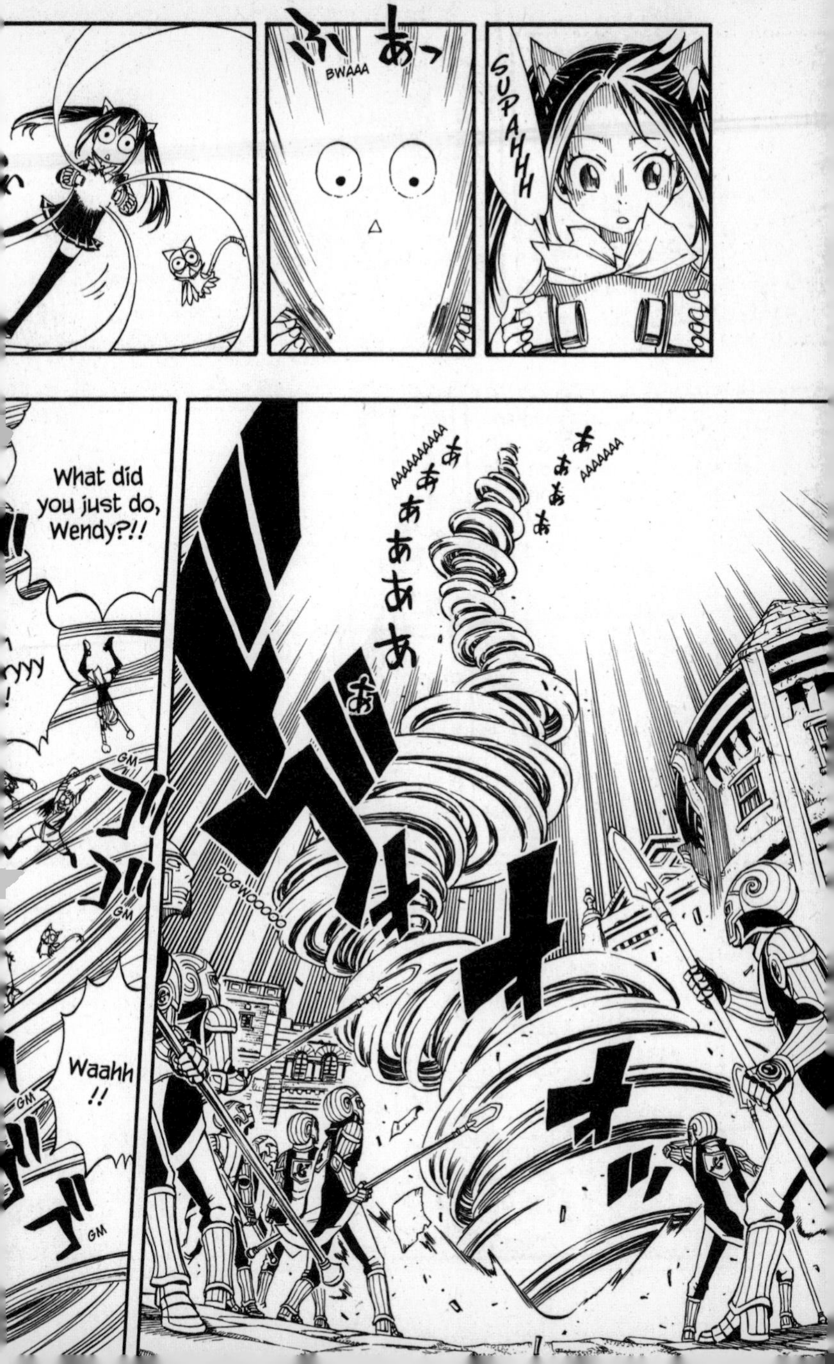
SUPAHHH
ふあっ
BWAAA
ああああああ
AAAAAAAAA
ああああ
AAAAAAA
DOGWOOOOO
What did you just do, Wendy?!!
GM
GM
Waahh!!
GM
GM

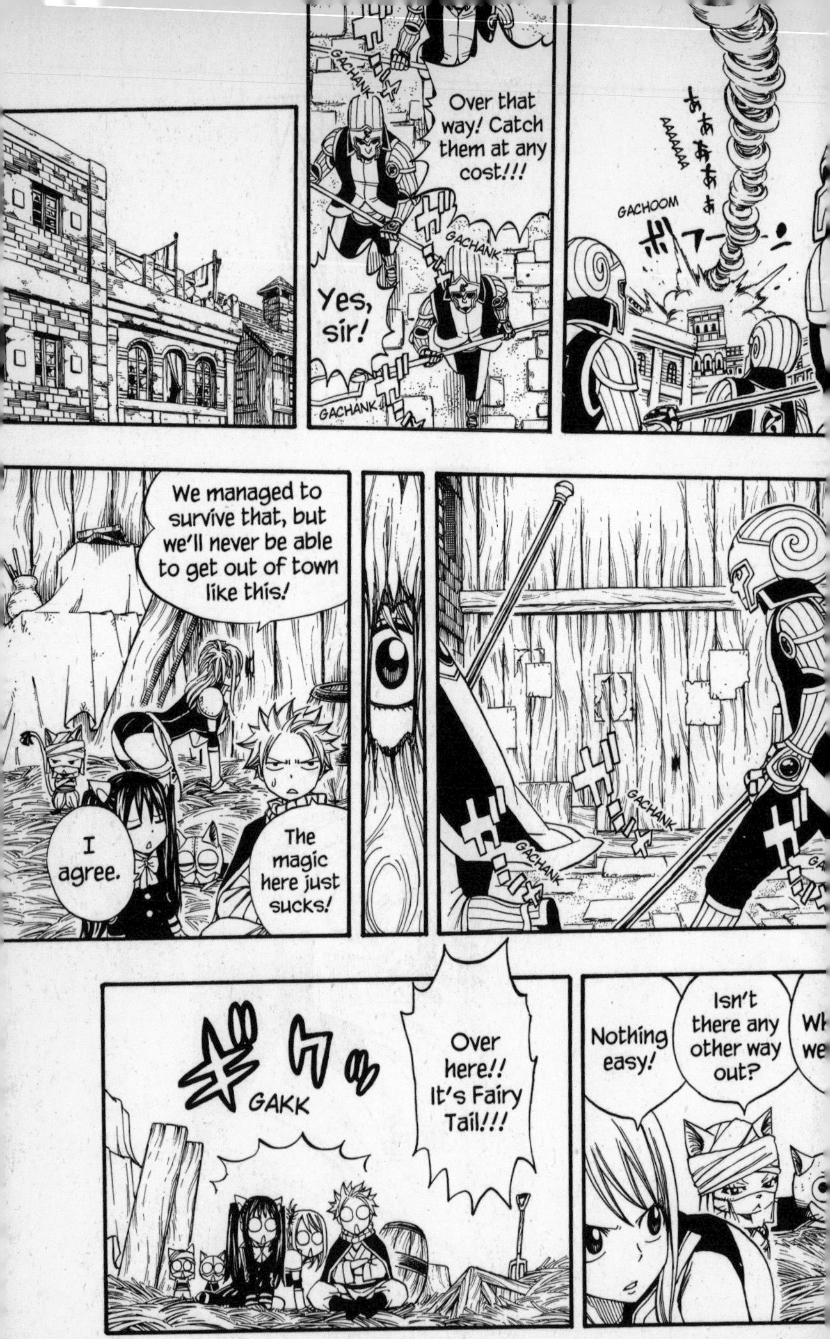
AAAAAAA
GACHOOM
Over that way! Catch them at any cost!!!
GACHANK
GACHANK
Yes, sir!
GACHANK
GACHANK
GACHANK
We managed to survive that, but we'll never be able to get out of town like this!
The magic here just sucks!
I agree.
Isn't there any other way out?
Nothing easy!
Over here!! It's Fairy Tail!!!
GAKK

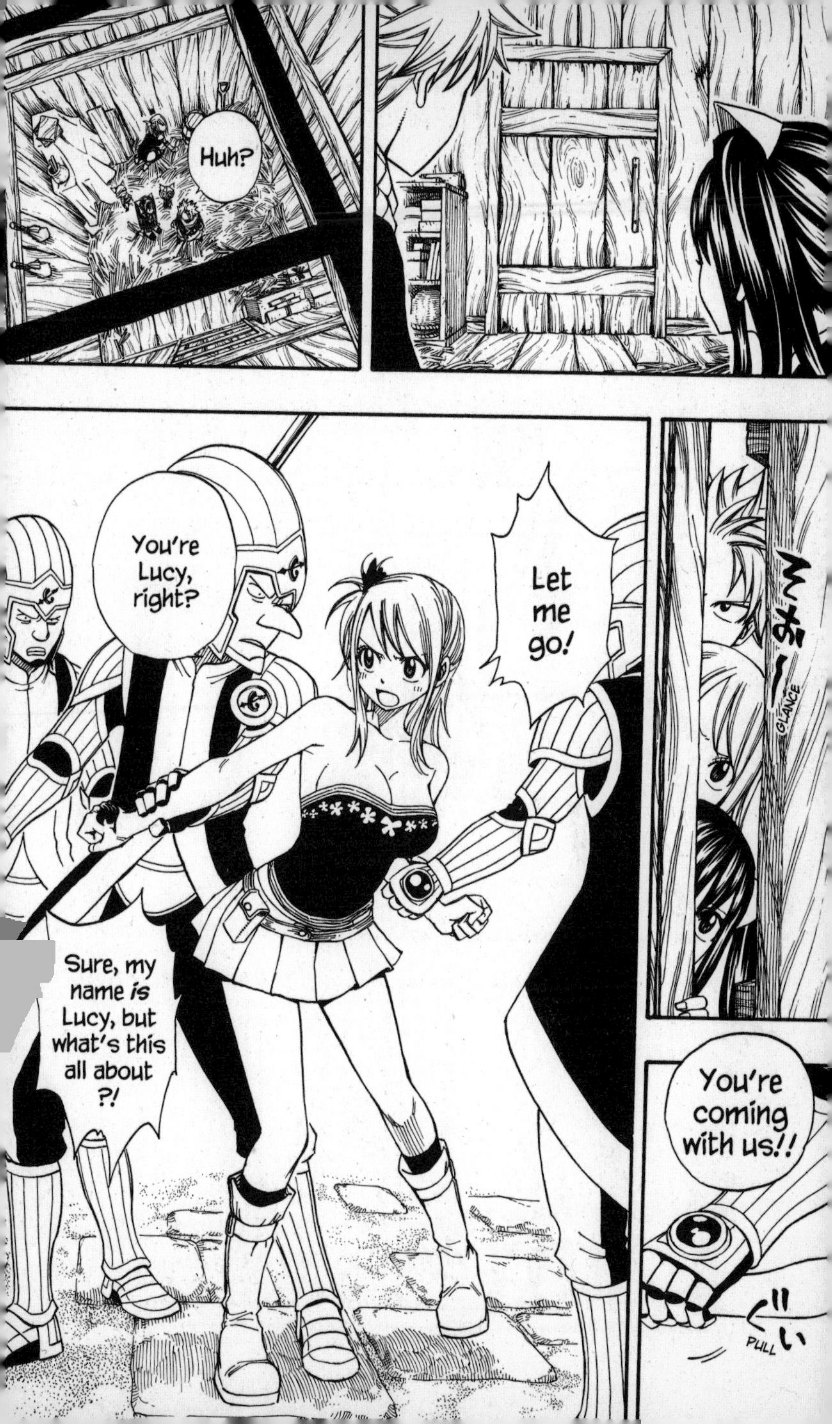
Huh?
GLANCE
You're coming with us!!
PULL
Let me go!
You're Lucy, right?
Sure, my name *is* Lucy, but what's this all about ?!

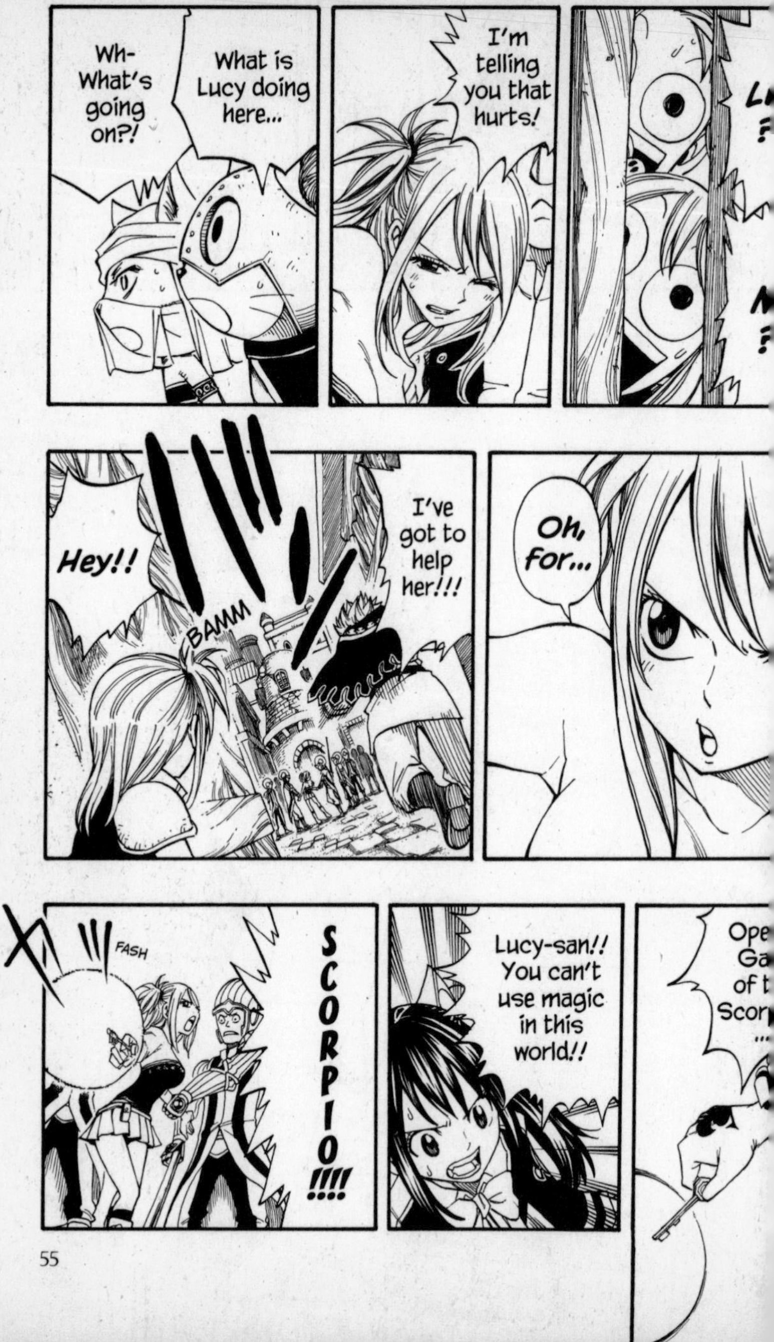
I'm telling you that hurts!
What is Lucy doing here...
Wh- What's going on?!
Oh, for...
I've got to help her!!!
BAMM
Hey!!
Lucy-san!! You can't use magic in this world!!
SCORPIO!!!!
FASH

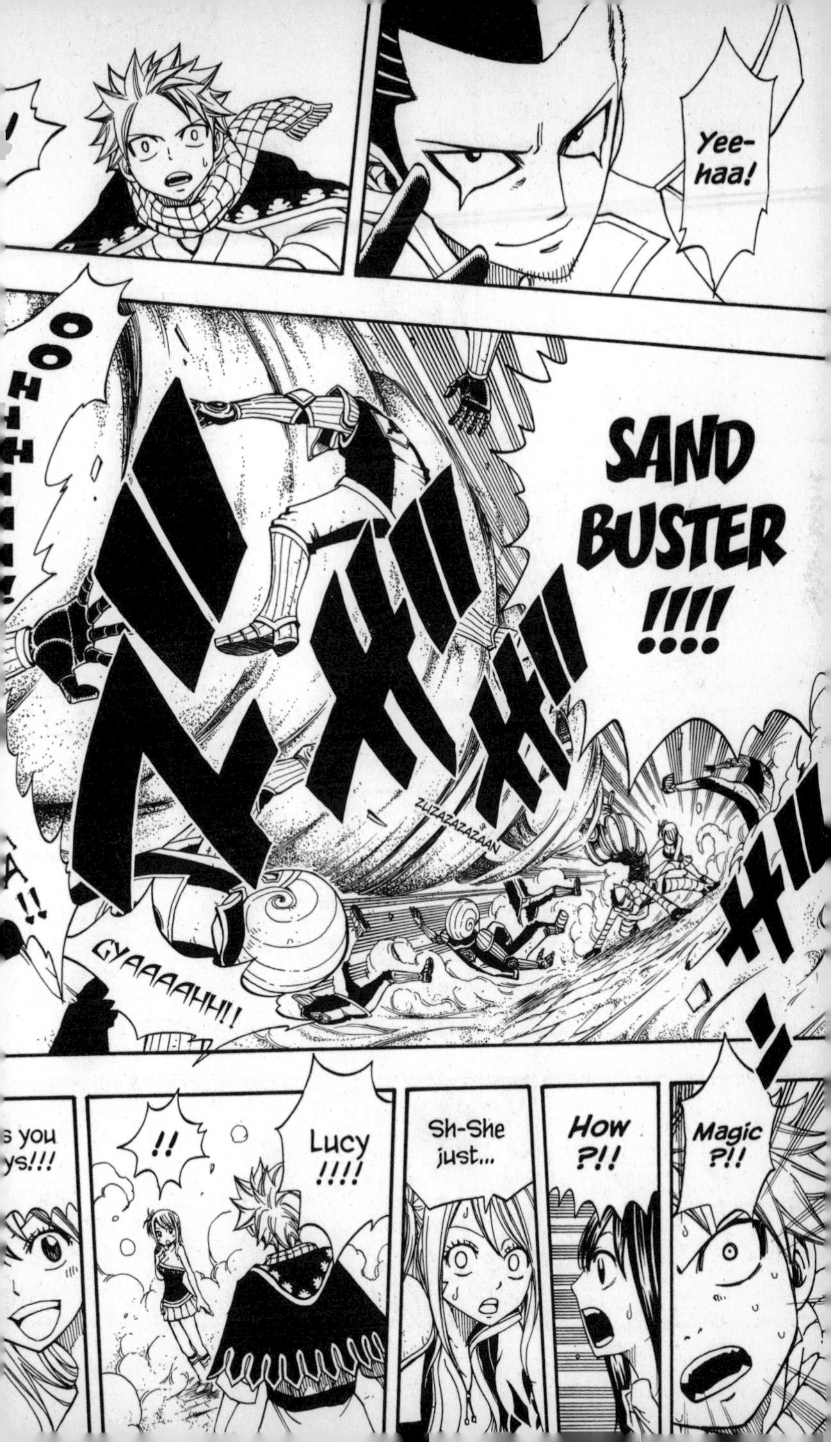
Yee-haa!
SAND BUSTER !!!!
ZUZAZAZAZAAN
GYAAAAAHH!!
Magic ?!!
How ?!!
Sh-She just...
Lucy !!!!
!!

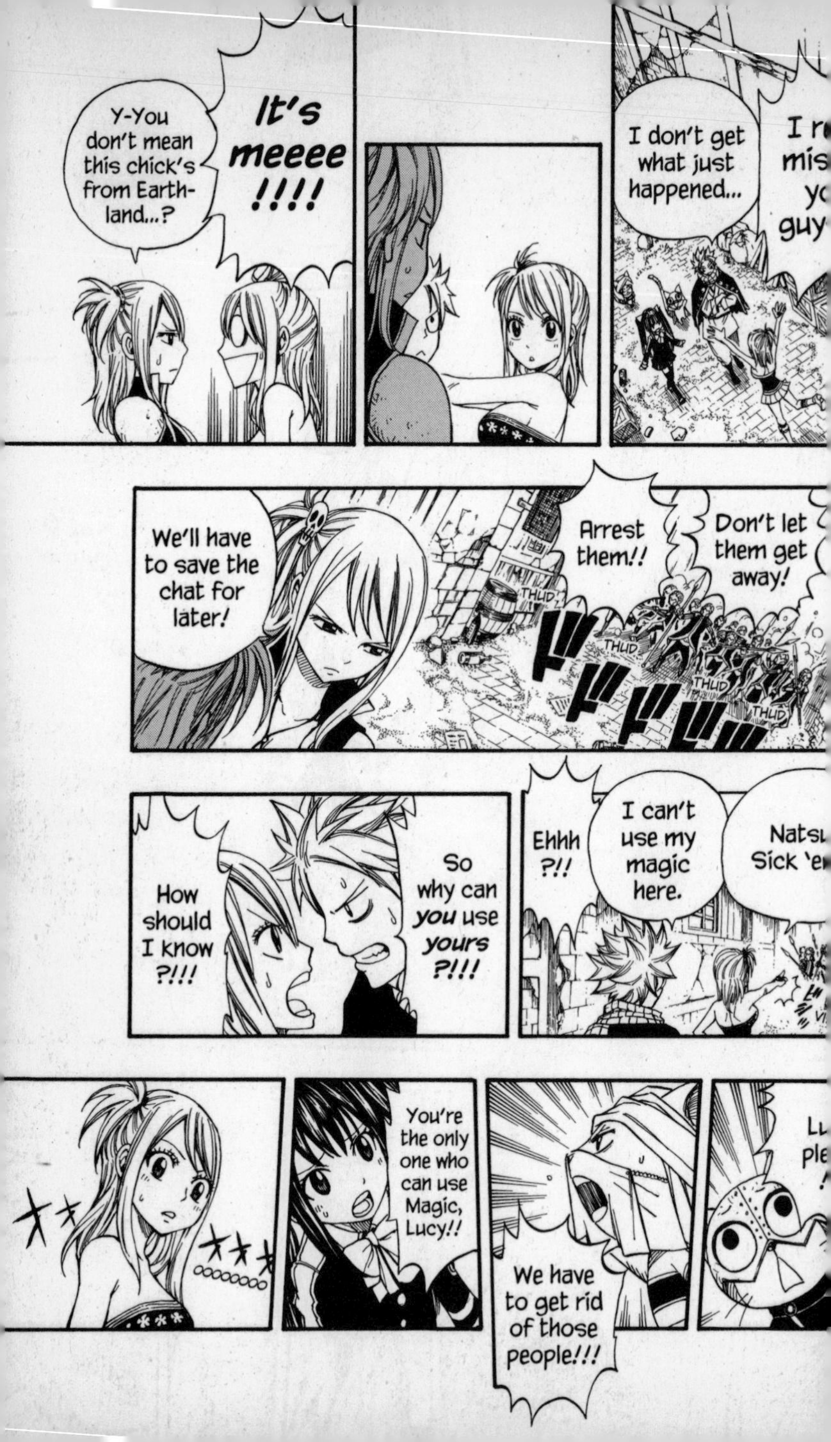

I don't get what just happened...
It's meeeee!!!!
Y-You don't mean this chick's from Earth-land...?
Don't let them get away!
Arrest them!!
THUD
THUD
THUD
THUD
We'll have to save the chat for later!
I can't use my magic here.
Ehhh?!!
So why can you use yours?!!!
How should I know?!!!
We have to get rid of those people!!!
You're the only one who can use Magic, Lucy!!

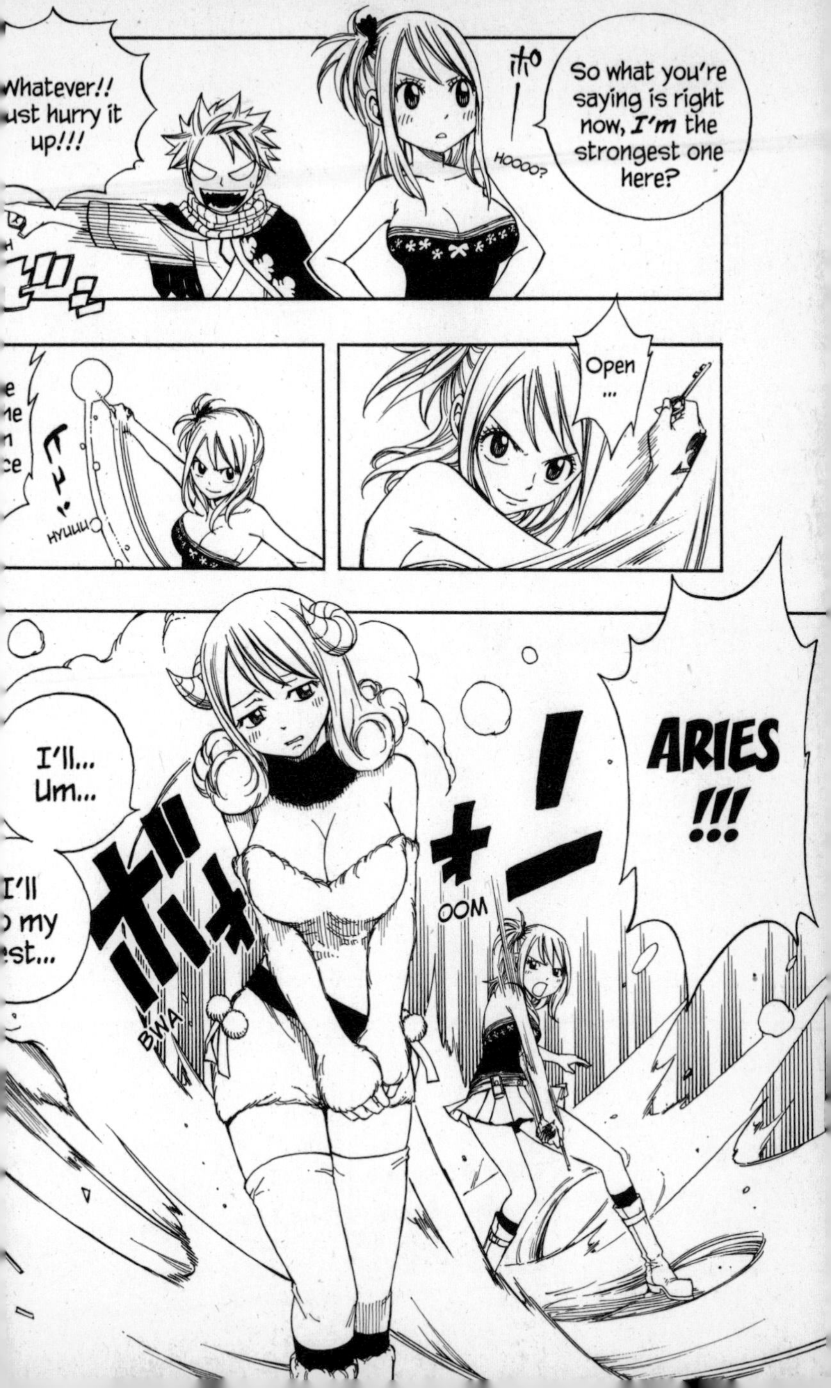
HOOOO?
So what you're saying is right now, I'm the strongest one here?
Whatever!! ust hurry it up!!!
Open ...
HYUUU
ARIES !!!
OOM
BWA
I'll... Um...
I'll o my est...

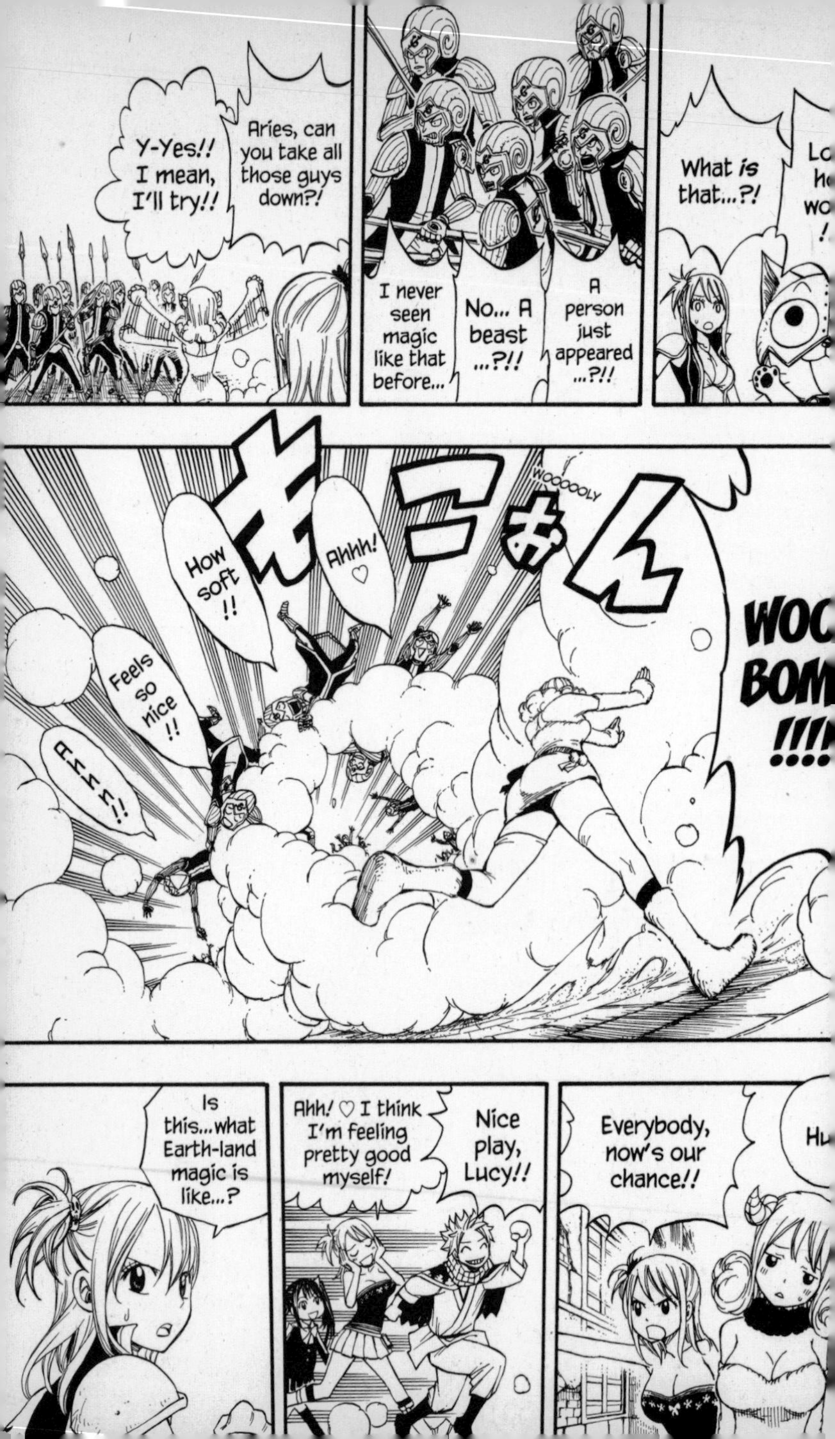
What is that...?!
A person just appeared ...?!!
No... A beast ...?!!
I never seen magic like that before...
Aries, can you take all those guys down?!
Y-Yes!! I mean, I'll try!!
もこぉん
WOOOOOOLY
Ahhh! ♡
How soft !!
Feels so nice !!
Ahhhh!!
Everybody, now's our chance!!
Nice play, Lucy!!
Ahh! ♡ I think I'm feeling pretty good myself!
Is this...what Earth-land magic is like...?

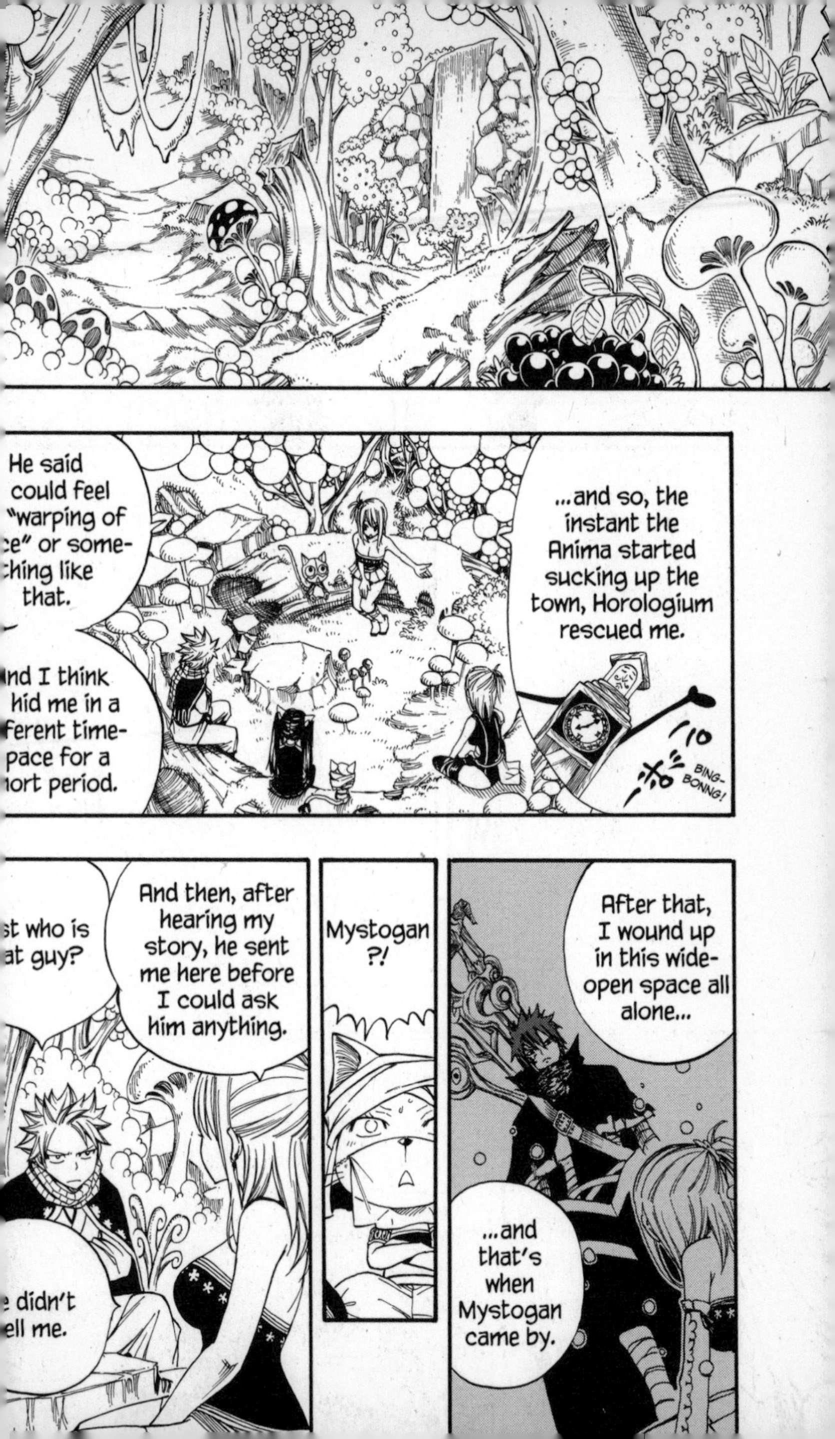
...and so, the instant the Anima started sucking up the town, Horologium rescued me.
BING-BONNG!
He said could feel "warping of ce" or some-thing like that.
nd I think hid me in a ferent time-pace for a ort period.
After that, I wound up in this wide-open space all alone...
...and that's when Mystogan came by.
Mystogan?!
And then, after hearing my story, he sent me here before I could ask him anything.
st who is at guy?
e didn't ell me.

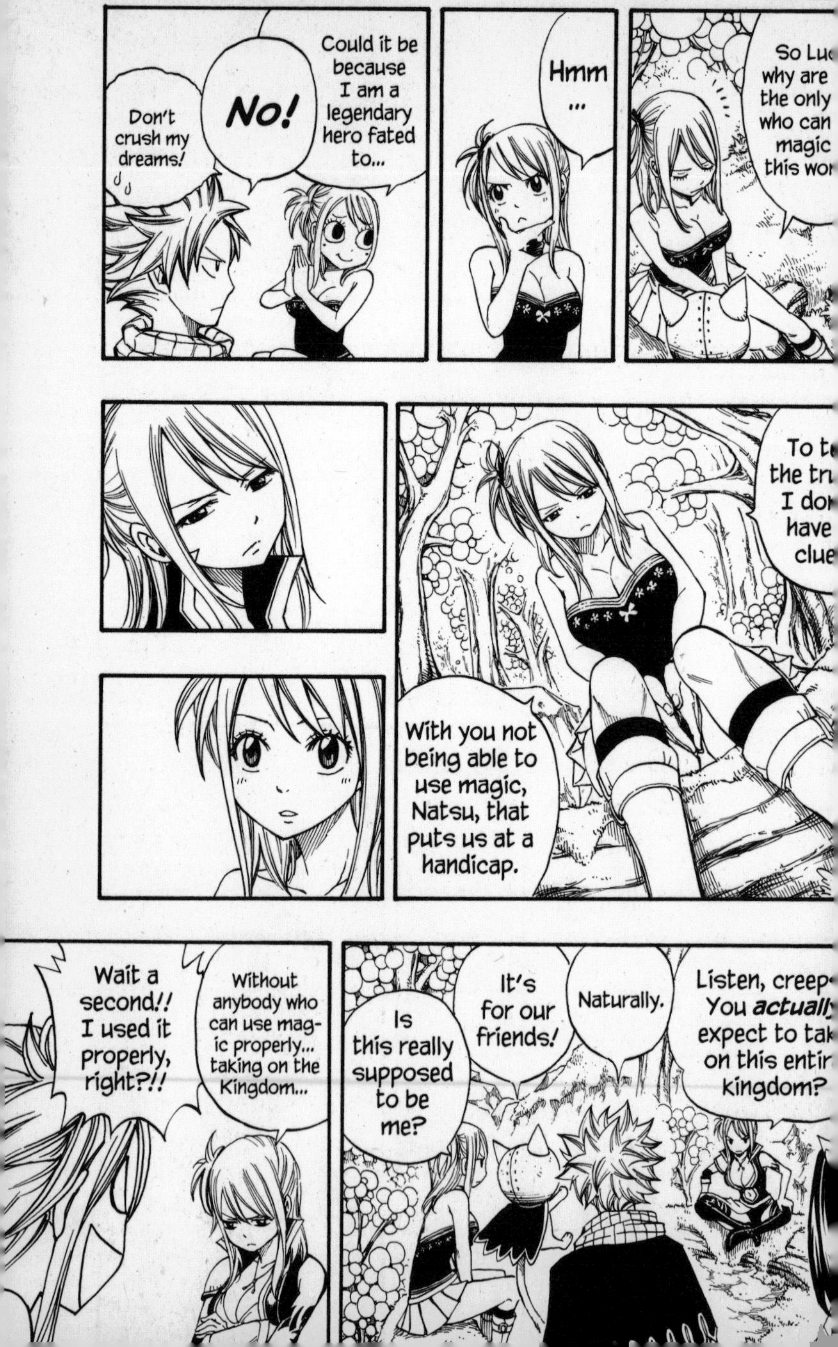
So Lu why are the only who can magic this wor
Hmm ...
Could it be because I am a legendary hero fated to...
No!
Don't crush my dreams!
To t the tr I do have clue
With you not being able to use magic, Natsu, that puts us at a handicap.
Listen, creep You *actuall* expect to tak on this entir kingdom?
Naturally.
It's for our friends!
Is this really supposed to be me?
Without anybody who can use magic properly... taking on the Kingdom...
Wait a second!! I used it properly, right?!!

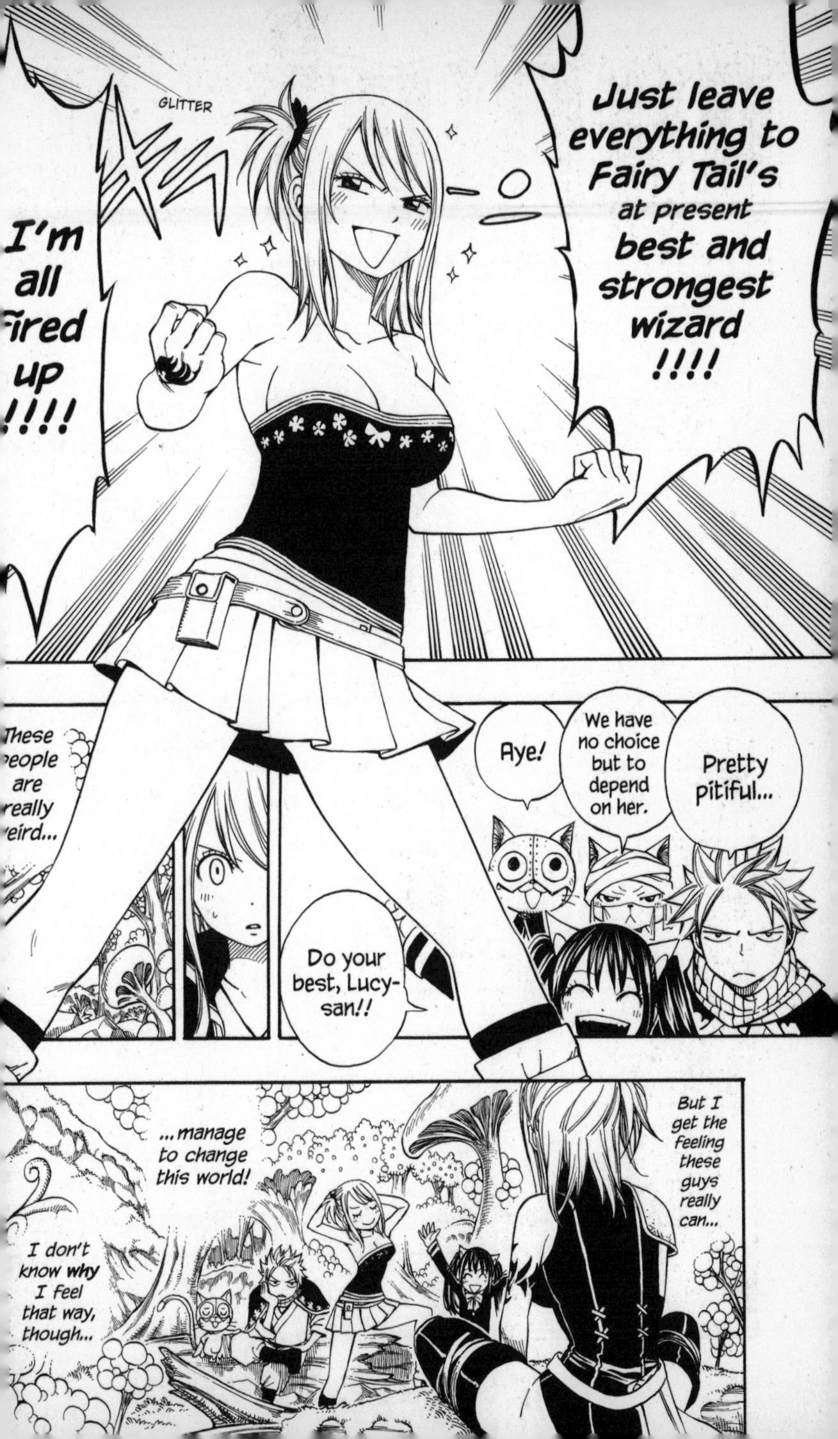

Just leave everything to Fairy Tail's at present best and strongest wizard !!!!
GLITTER
I'm all fired up !!!!
Pretty pitiful...
We have no choice but to depend on her.
Aye!
Do your best, Lucy-san!!
These eople are really eird...
But I get the feeling these guys really can...
...manage to change this world!
I don't know why I feel that way, though...

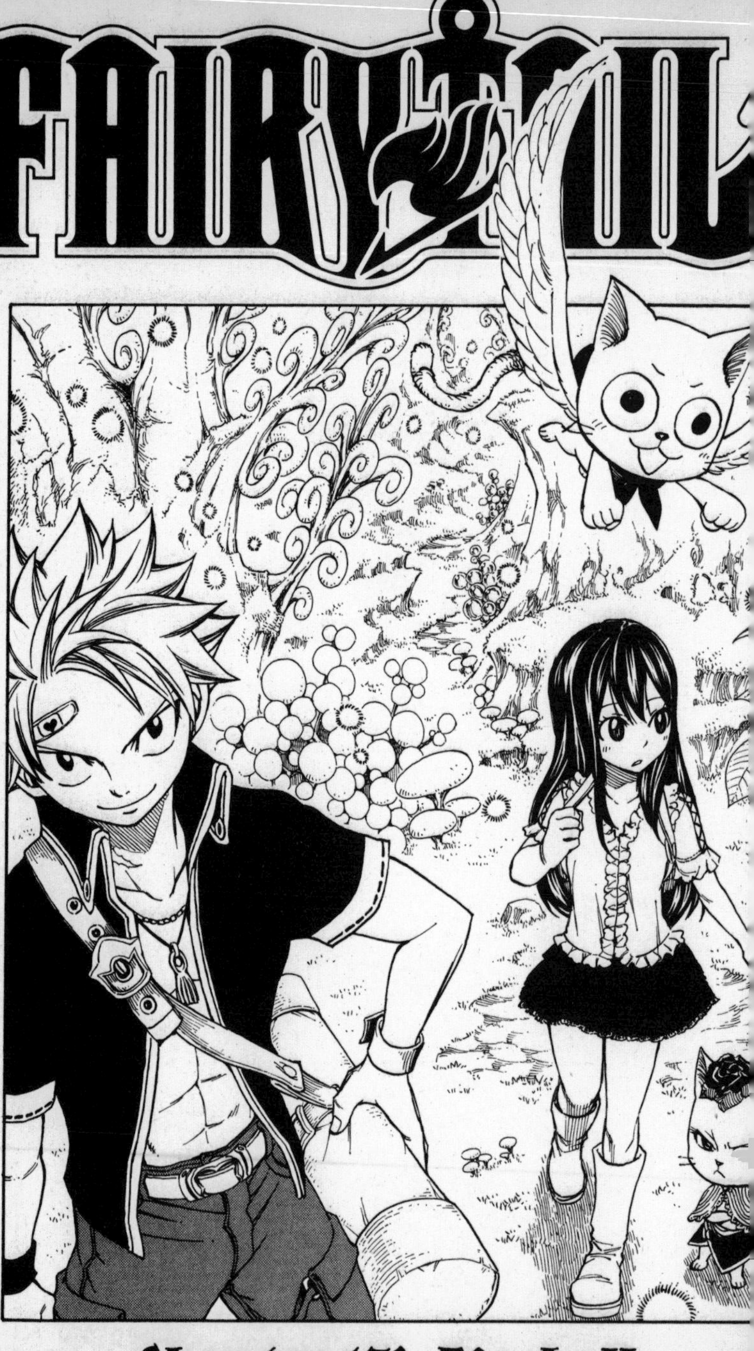

Chapter 173, Fireball

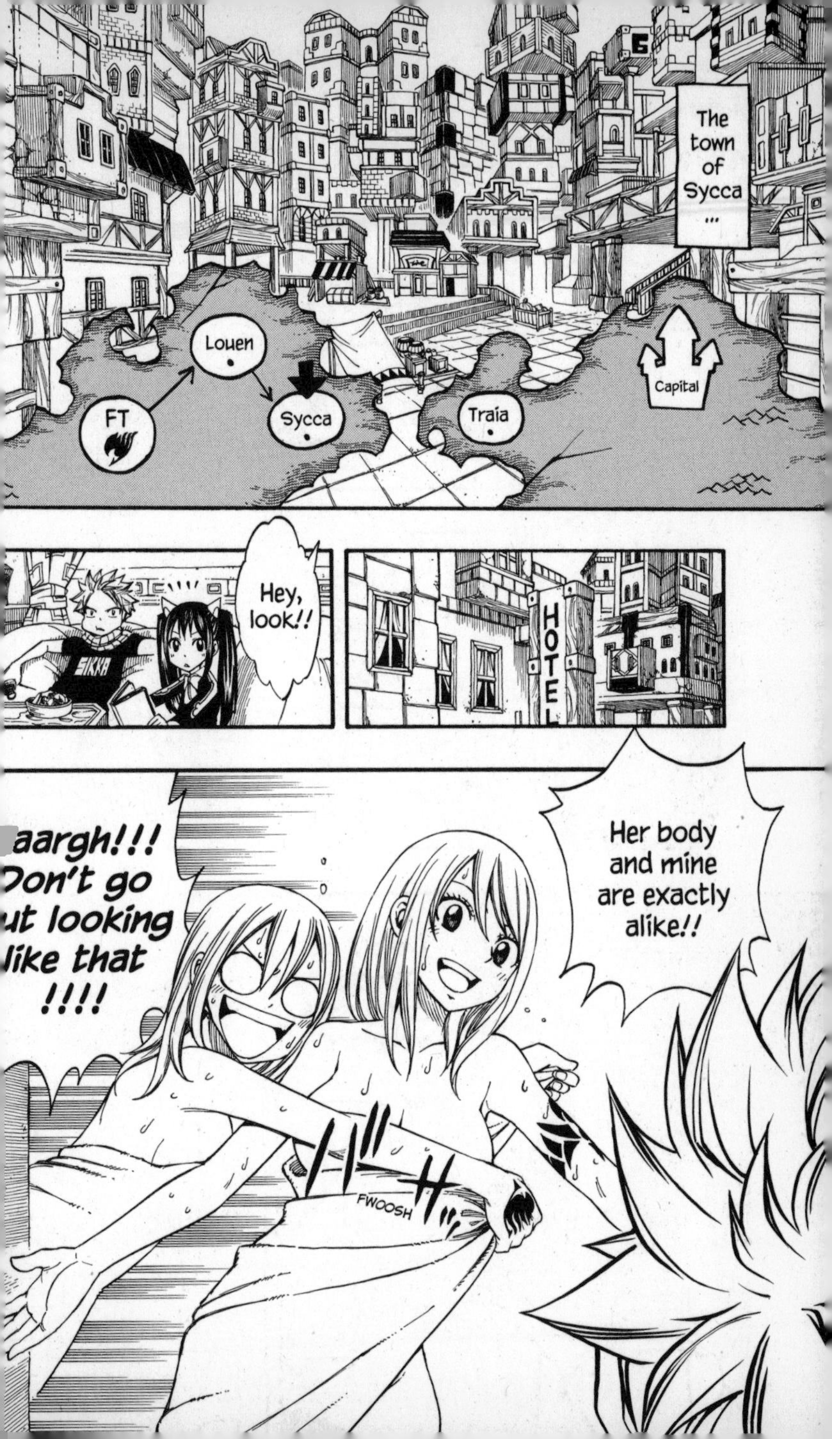
The town of Sycca ...
FT
Louen
Sycca
Traia
Capital
HOTEL
Hey, look!!
Her body and mine are exactly alike!!
aargh!!! Don't go ut looking like that !!!!
FWOOSH

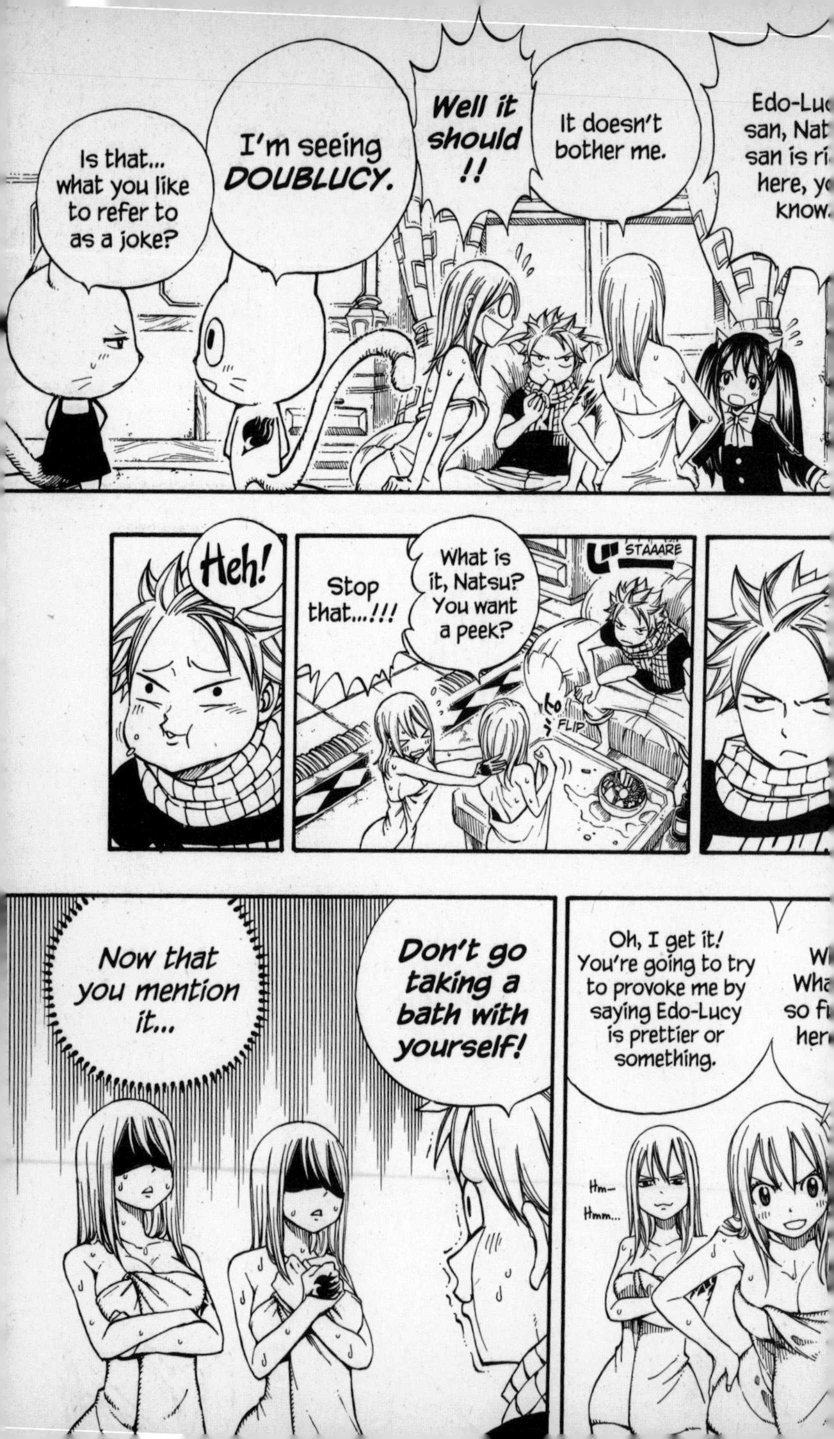
Edo-Luc san, Nat san is ri here, yo know.
It doesn't bother me.
Well it should !!
I'm seeing DOUBLUCY.
Is that... what you like to refer to as a joke?
STAAARE
What is it, Natsu? You want a peek?
Stop that...!!!
FLIP
Heh!
Wh Wha so f her
Oh, I get it! You're going to try to provoke me by saying Edo-Lucy is prettier or something.
Hm- Hmm...
Don't go taking a bath with yourself!
Now that you mention it...

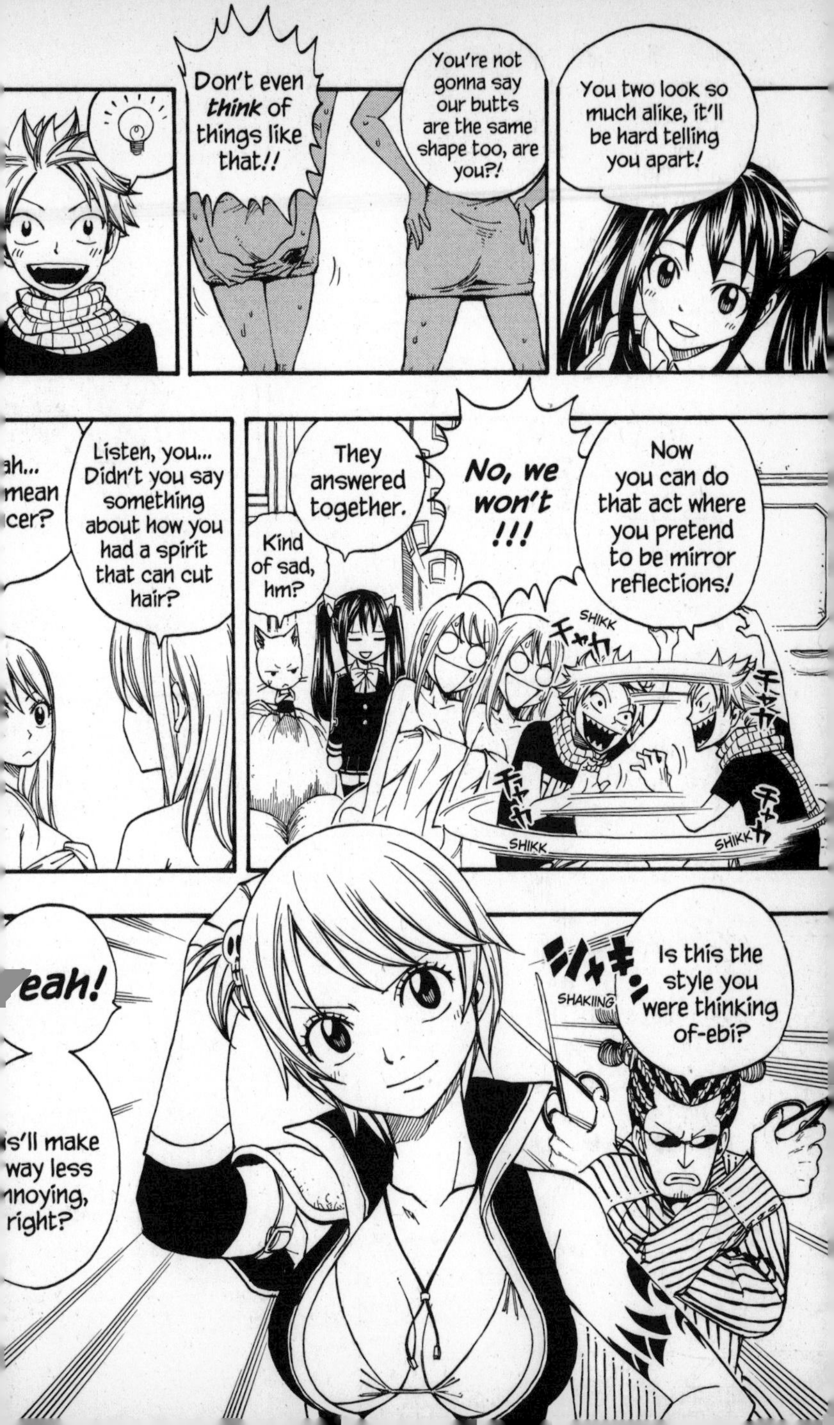

You two look so much alike, it'll be hard telling you apart!
You're not gonna say our butts are the same shape too, are you?!
Don't even *think* of things like that!!
Now you can do that act where you pretend to be mirror reflections!
No, we won't!!!
They answered together.
Kind of sad, hm?
SHIKK
SHIKK
SHIKK
Listen, you... Didn't you say something about how you had a spirit that can cut hair?
ah... mean cer?
SHAKIING
Is this the style you were thinking of-ebi?
eah!
s'll make way less nnoying, right?

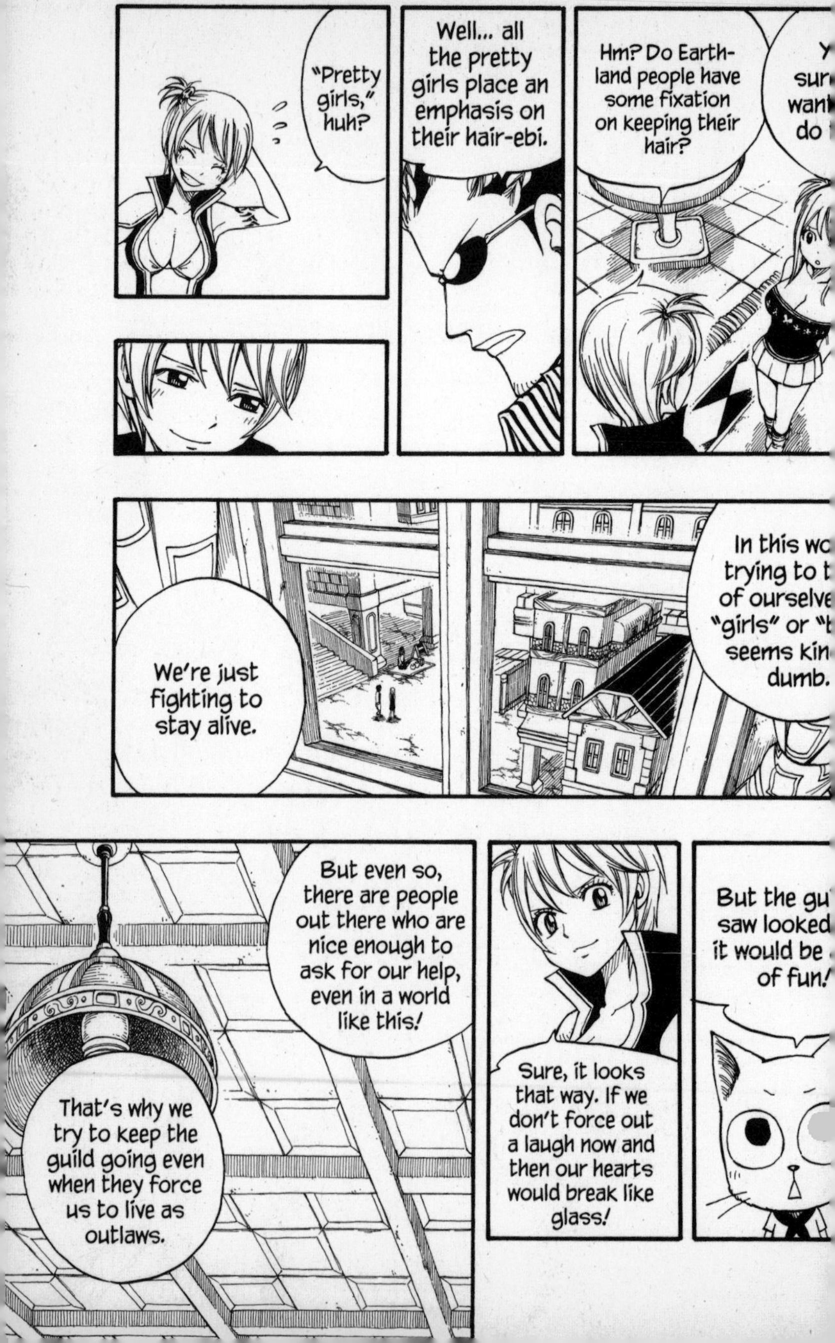
Y sur want do
Hm? Do Earth-land people have some fixation on keeping their hair?
Well... all the pretty girls place an emphasis on their hair-ebi.
"Pretty girls," huh?
In this wo trying to t of ourselve "girls" or "b seems kin dumb.
We're just fighting to stay alive.
But the gu saw looked it would be of fun!
Sure, it looks that way. If we don't force out a laugh now and then our hearts would break like glass!
But even so, there are people out there who are nice enough to ask for our help, even in a world like this!
That's why we try to keep the guild going even when they force us to live as outlaws.

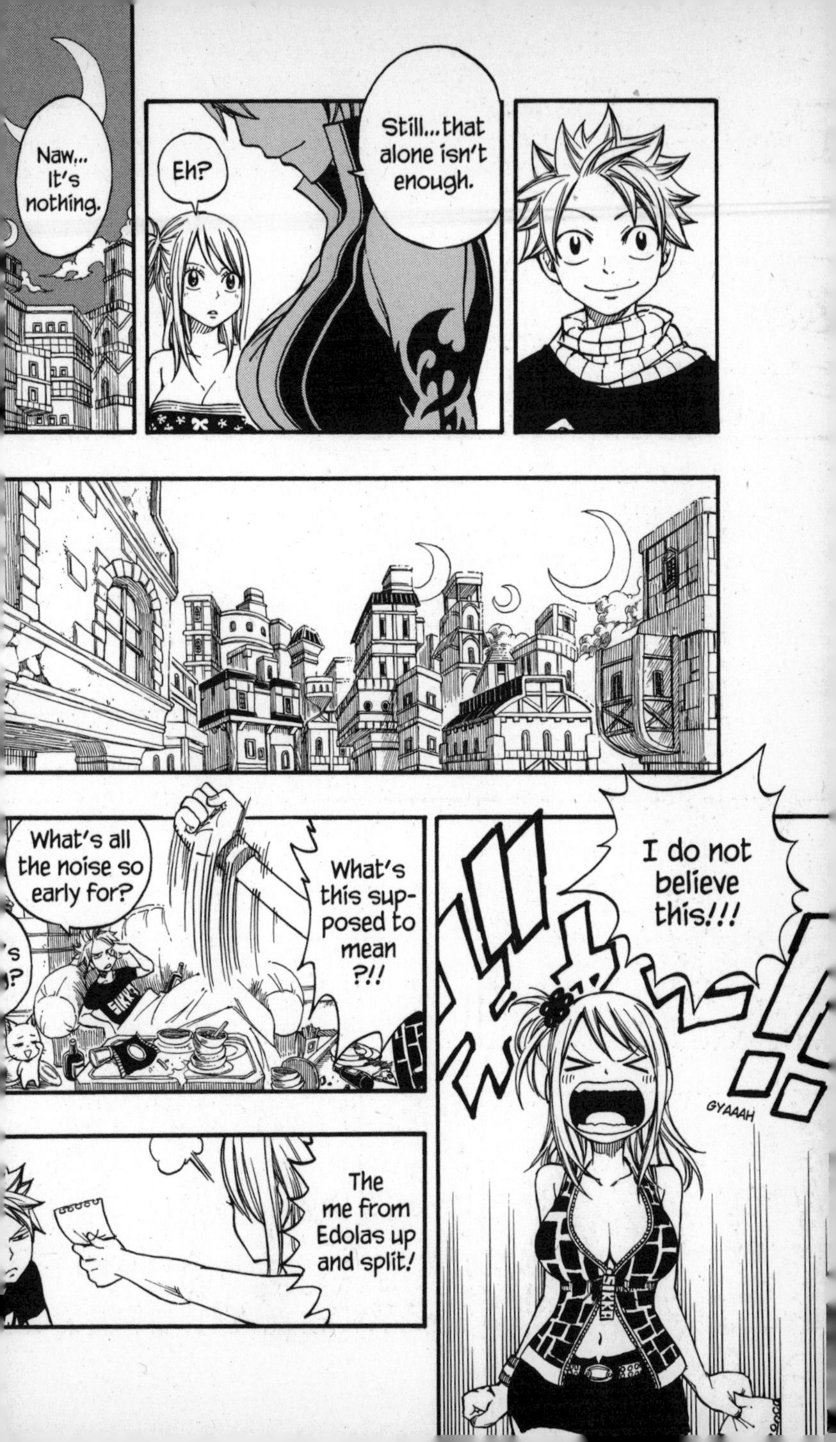
Still...that alone isn't enough.
Eh?
Naw... It's nothing.
I do not believe this!!!
GYAAAH
What's this sup-posed to mean?!!
What's all the noise so early for?
The me from Edolas up and split!

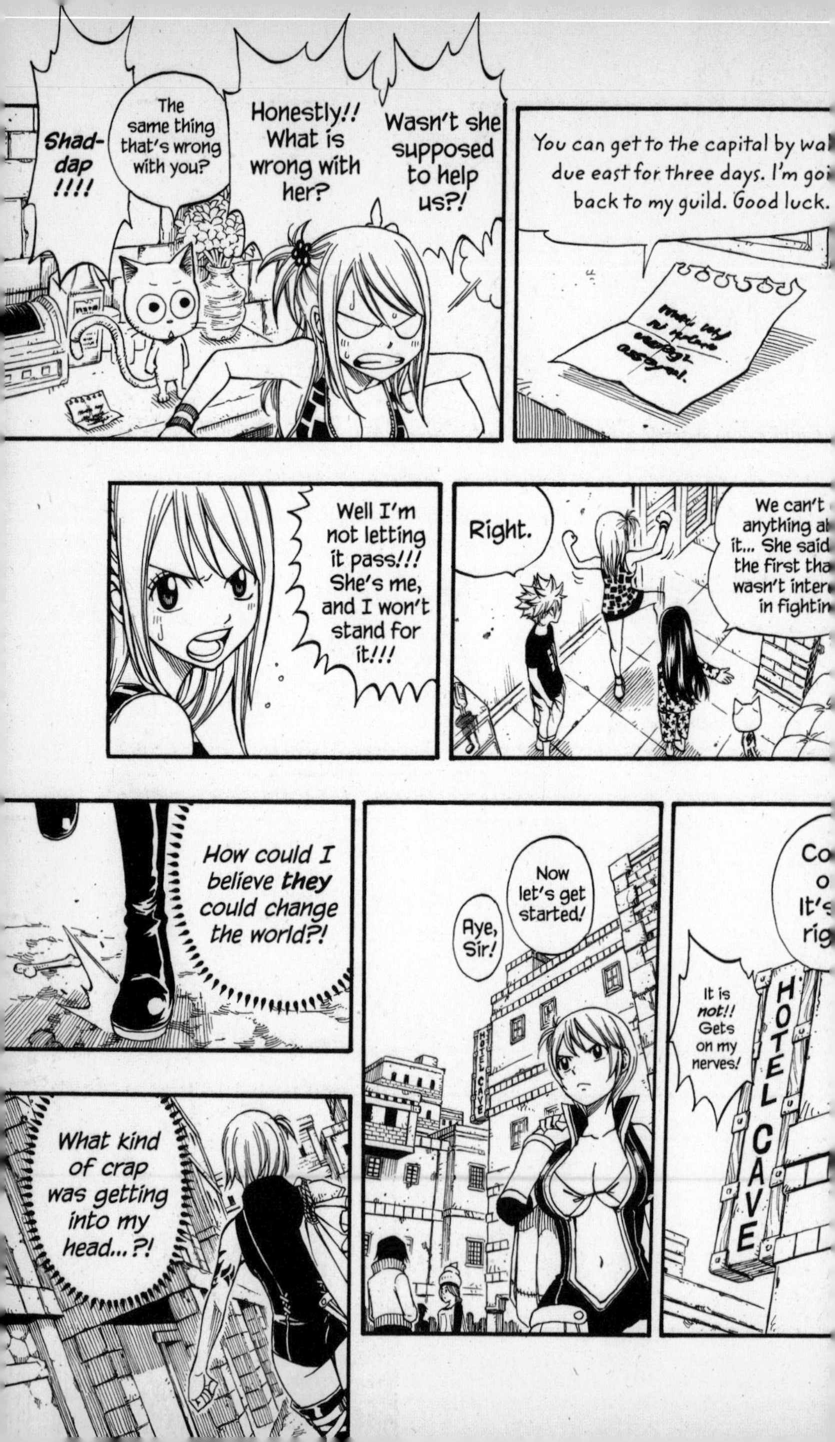
You can get to the capital by wa due east for three days. I'm goi back to my guild. Good luck.
Wasn't she supposed to help us?!
Honestly!! What is wrong with her?
The same thing that's wrong with you?
Shad-dap!!!!
We can't anything a it... She said the first tha wasn't inter in fightin
Right.
Well I'm not letting it pass!!! She's me, and I won't stand for it!!!
Co o It's rig
HOTEL CAVE
It is not!! Gets on my nerves!
Now let's get started!
Aye, Sir!
HOTEL CAVE
How could I believe they could change the world?!
What kind of crap was getting into my head...?!

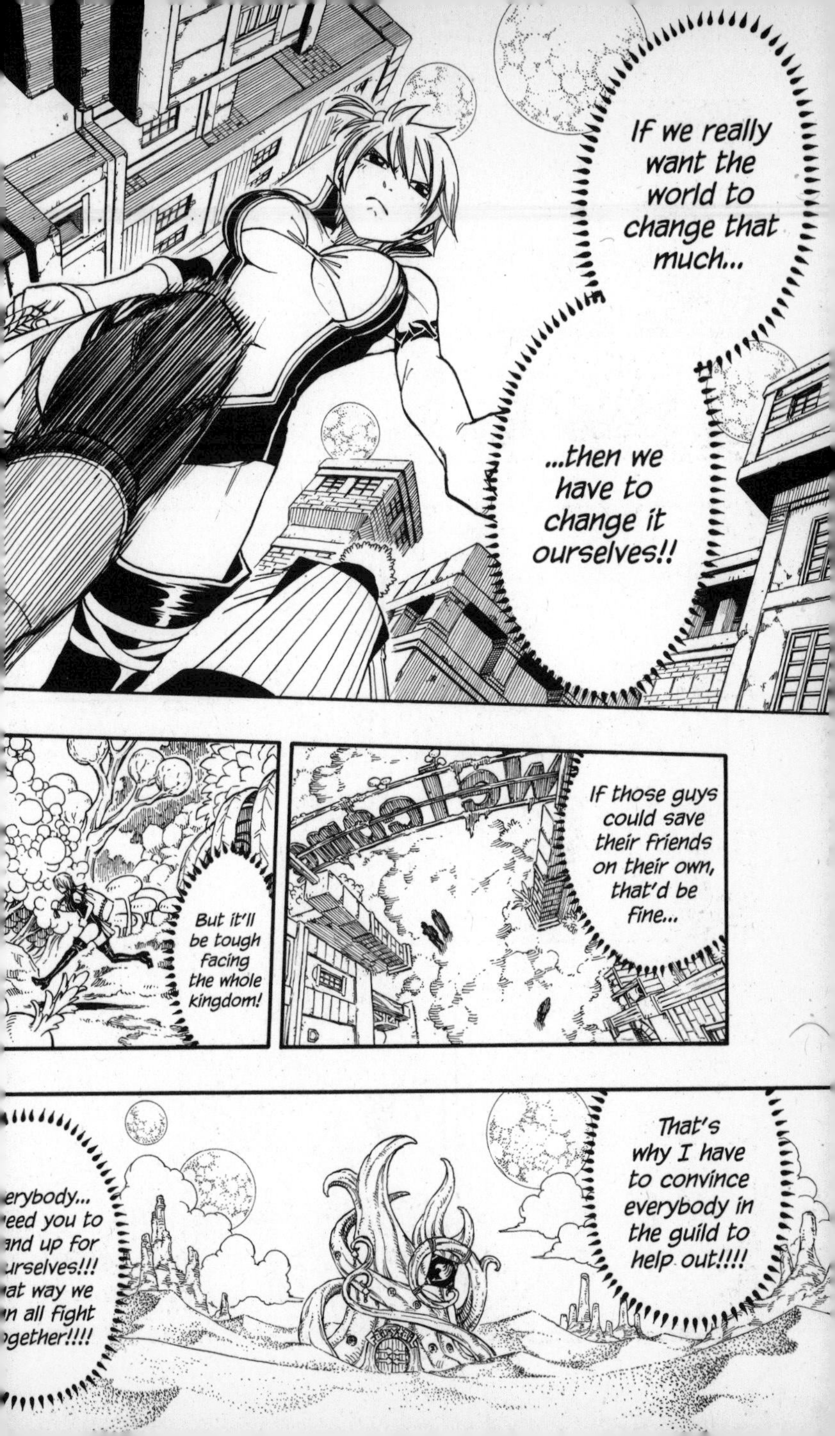
If we really want the world to change that much...
...then we have to change it ourselves!!
If those guys could save their friends on their own, that'd be fine...
But it'll be tough facing the whole kingdom!
That's why I have to convince everybody in the guild to help out!!!!
erybody... eed you to and up for urselves!!! at way we n all fight gether!!!!

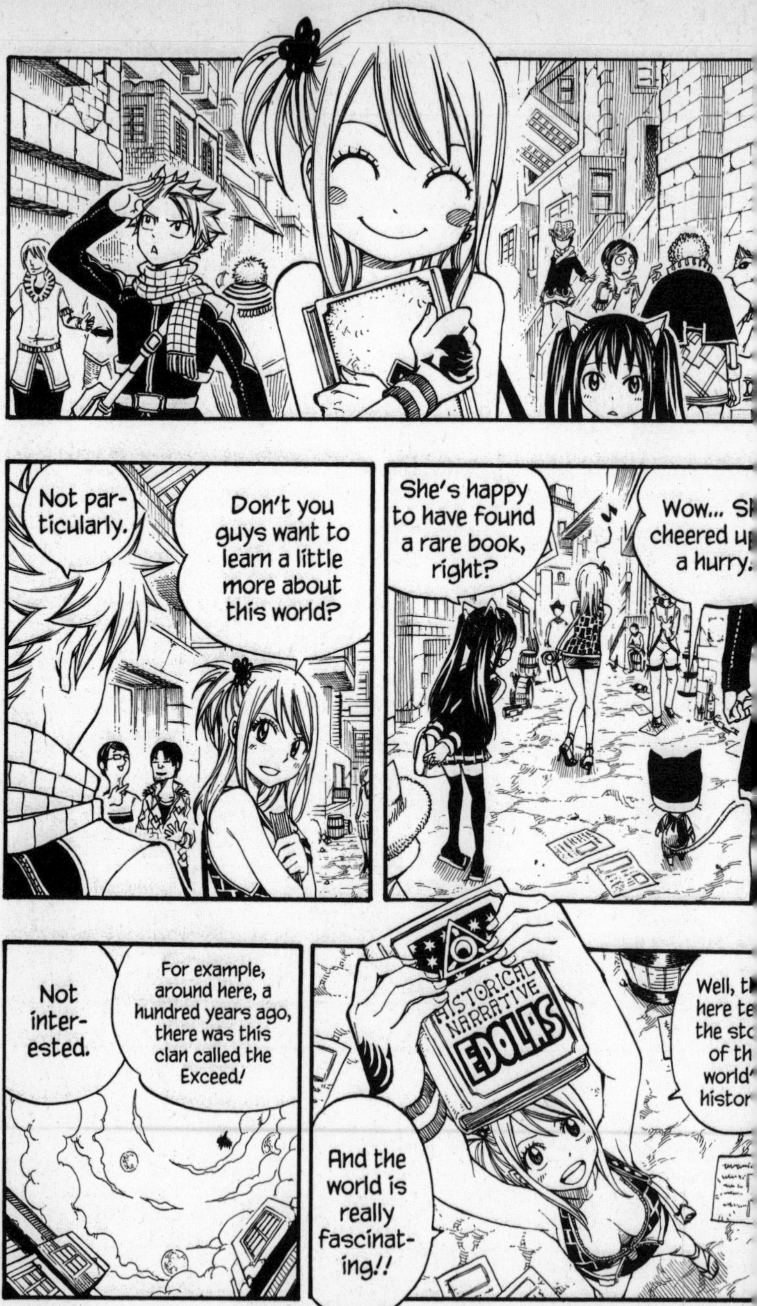
Wow... S cheered u a hurry.
She's happy to have found a rare book, right?
Don't you guys want to learn a little more about this world?
Not particularly.
Well, t here te the sto of th world' histor
HISTORICAL NARRATIVE EDOLAS
And the world is really fascinating!!
For example, around here, a hundred years ago, there was this clan called the Exceed!
Not interested.

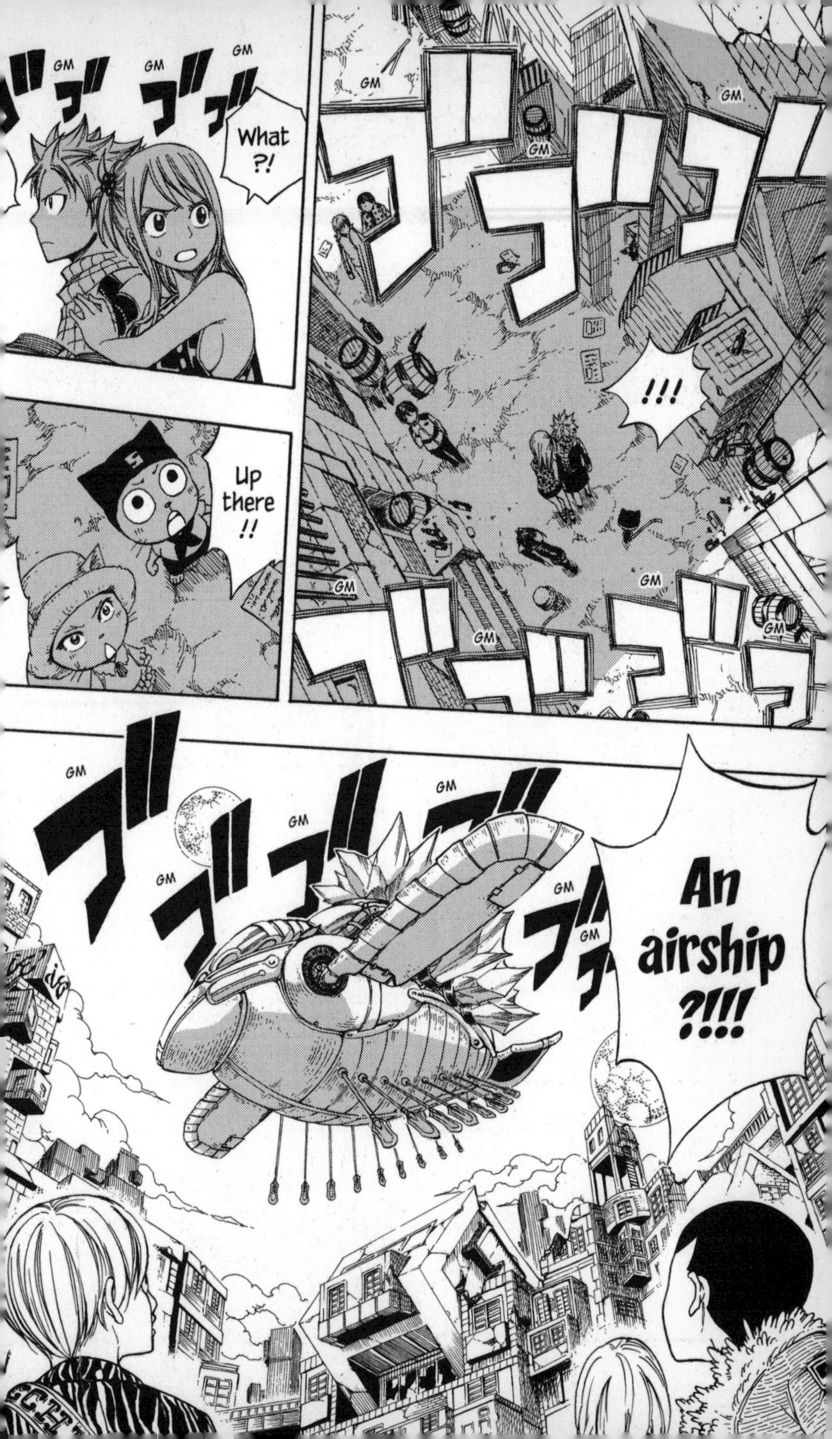

GM
GM
GM
!!!
GM
GM
GM
GM
GM
GM
GM
What ?!
Up there !!
GM
GM
GM
GM
GM
GM
An airship ?!!!

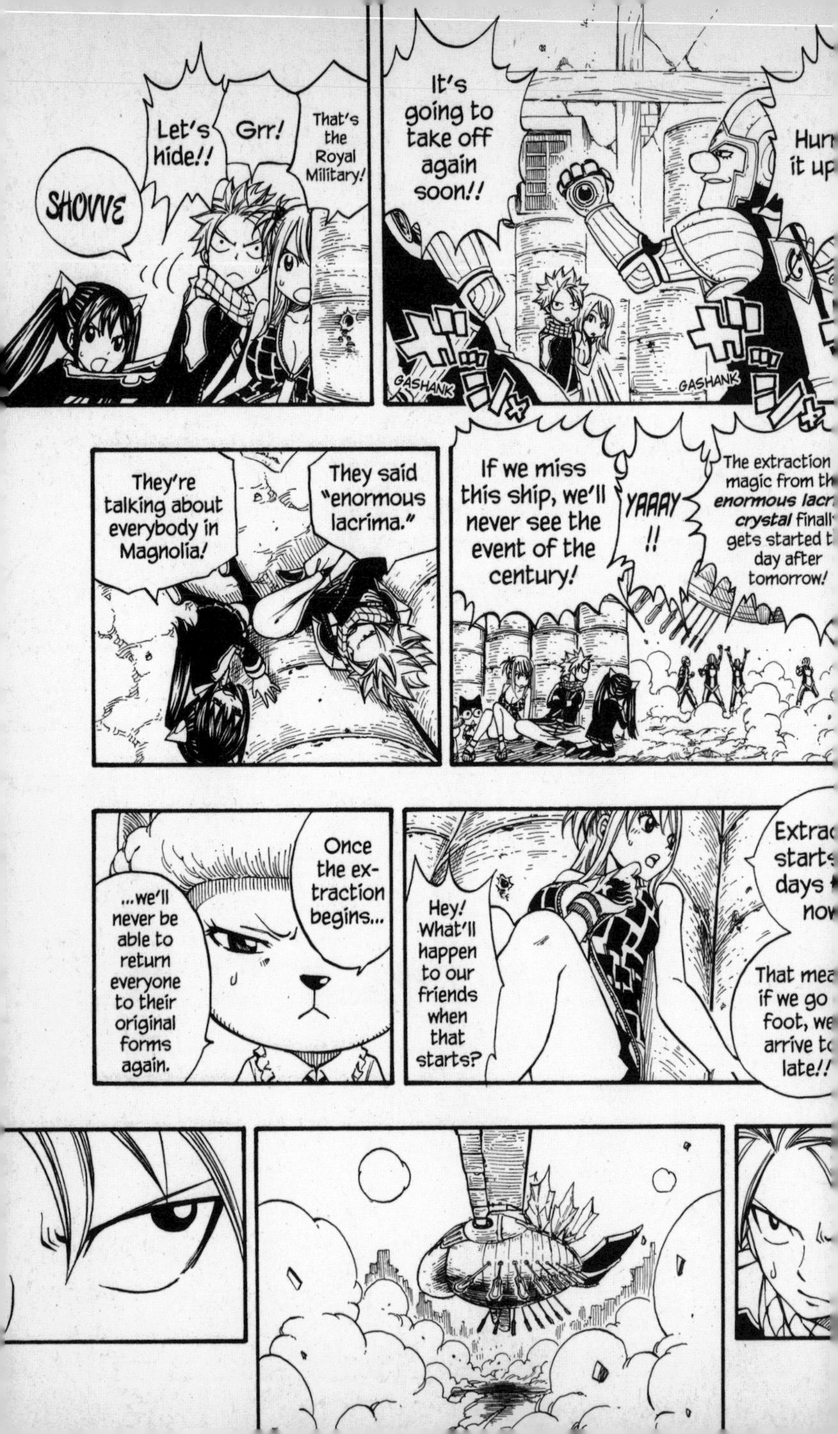

Hurr it up
It's going to take off again soon!!
GASHANK
GASHANK
That's the Royal Military!
Grr!
Let's hide!!
SHOVVE
The extraction magic from th enormous lacr crystal finall gets started t day after tomorrow!
YAAAY!!
If we miss this ship, we'll never see the event of the century!
They said "enormous lacrima."
They're talking about everybody in Magnolia!
Extrac starts days now
That mea if we go foot, we arrive to late!!
Hey! What'll happen to our friends when that starts?
Once the extraction begins...
...we'll never be able to return everyone to their original forms again.

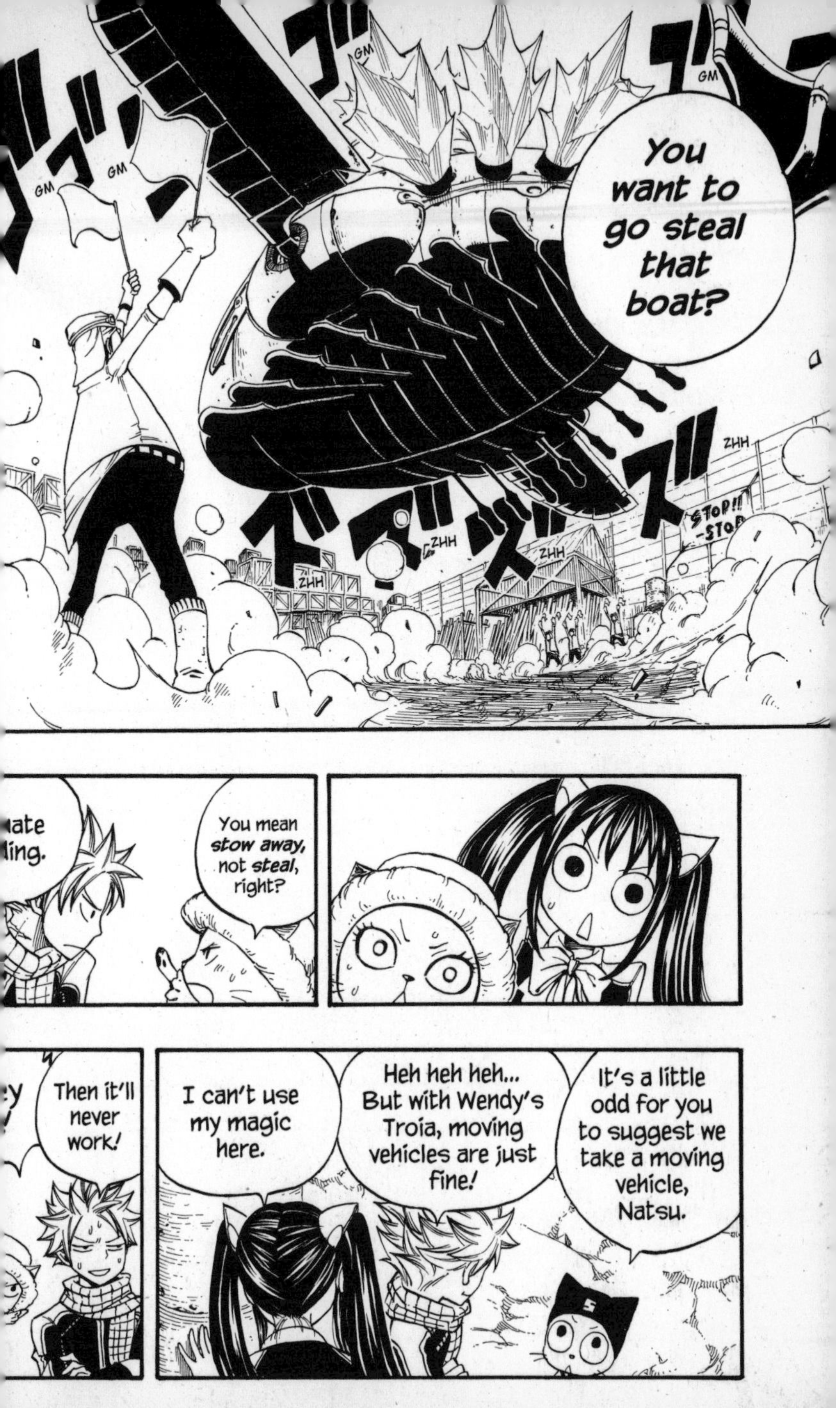
GM
GM
GM
GM
You want to go steal that boat?
ZHH
ZHH
ZHH
ZHH
STOP!! -STOP
You mean *stow away*, not *steal*, right?
It's a little odd for you to suggest we take a moving vehicle, Natsu.
Heh heh heh... But with Wendy's Troia, moving vehicles are just fine!
I can't use my magic here.
Then it'll never work!

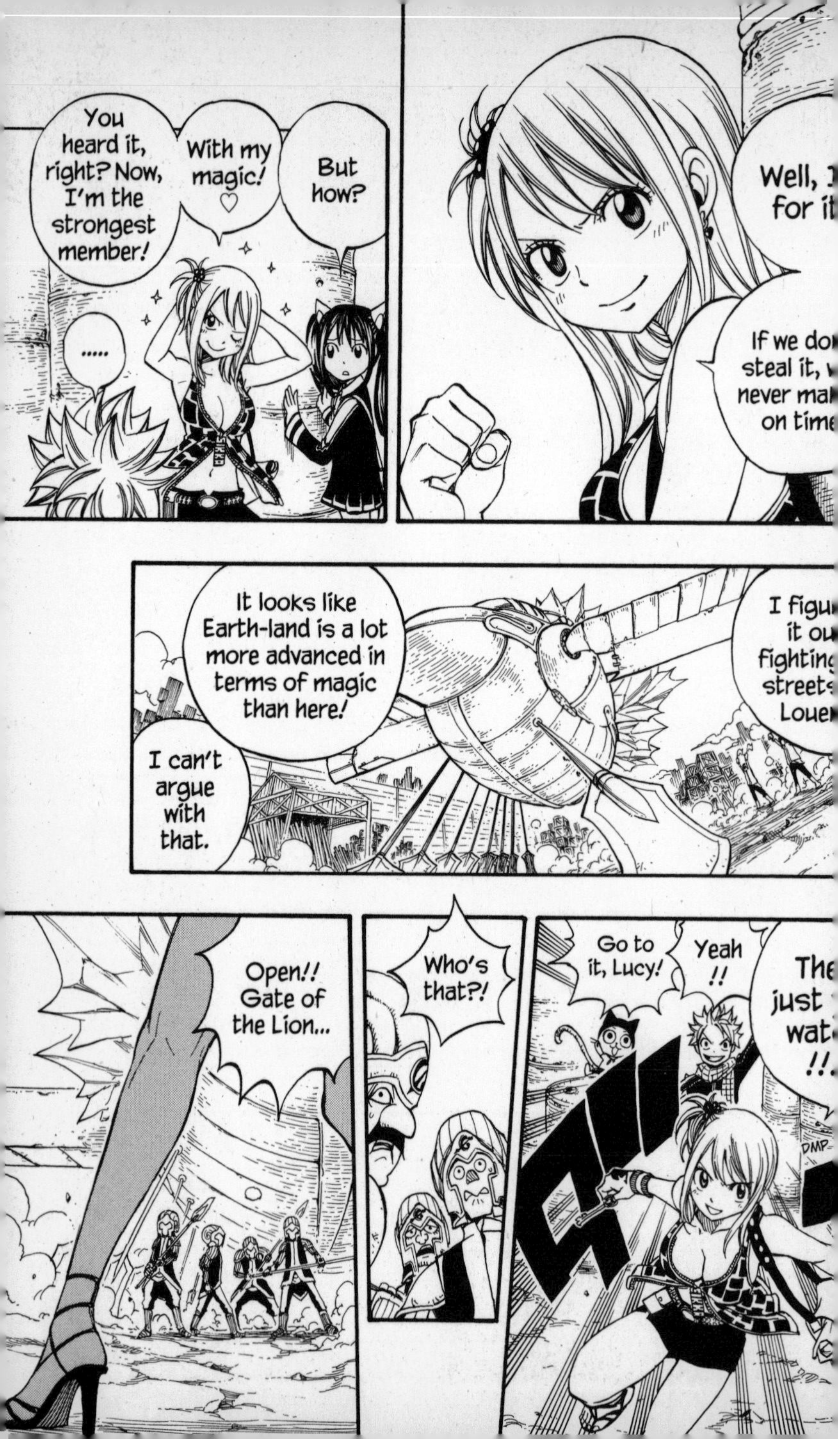
Well, I
for it
If we do
steal it,
never ma
on time
But how?
With my magic! ♡
You heard it, right? Now, I'm the strongest member!
.....
I figu
it ou
fighting
streets
Louen
It looks like Earth-land is a lot more advanced in terms of magic than here!
I can't argue with that.
The
just
wat
!!
Yeah !!
Go to it, Lucy!
DMP
Who's that?!
Open!! Gate of the Lion...

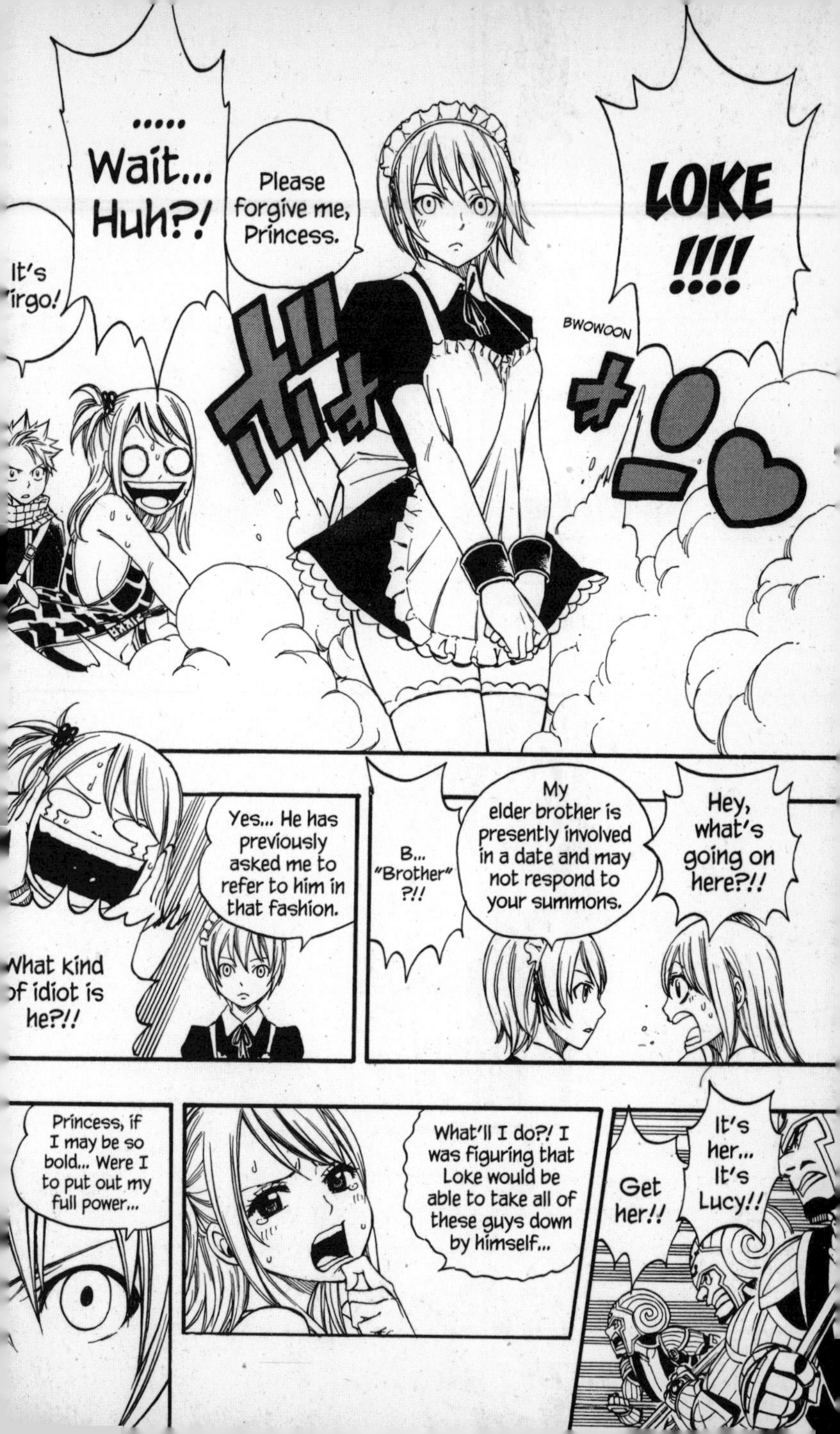
LOKE !!!!
BWOWOON
Please forgive me, Princess.
..... Wait... Huh?!
It's irgo!
Hey, what's going on here?!!
My elder brother is presently involved in a date and may not respond to your summons.
B... "Brother" ?!!
Yes... He has previously asked me to refer to him in that fashion.
What kind of idiot is he?!!
It's her... It's Lucy!!
Get her!!
What'll I do?! I was figuring that Loke would be able to take all of these guys down by himself...
Princess, if I may be so bold... Were I to put out my full power...

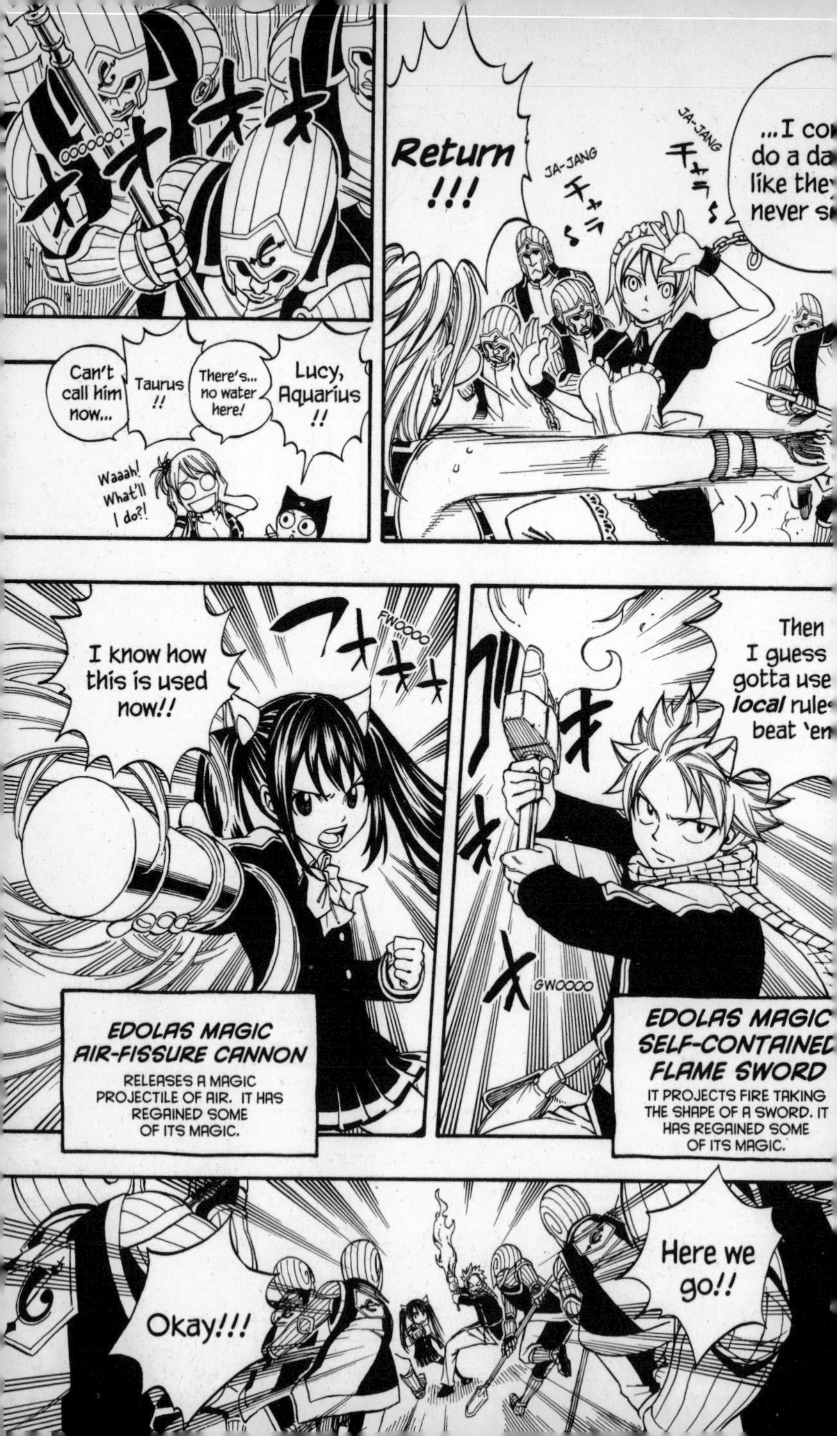
Return!!!
JA-JANG
JA-JANG
...I co
do a da
like they
never s
Lucy, Aquarius!!
There's... no water here!
Taurus!!
Can't call him now...
Waaah! What'll I do?!
Then I guess gotta use *local* rule beat 'en
GWOOOO
EDOLAS MAGIC SELF-CONTAINED FLAME SWORD
IT PROJECTS FIRE TAKING THE SHAPE OF A SWORD. IT HAS REGAINED SOME OF ITS MAGIC.
FWOOOO
I know how this is used now!!
EDOLAS MAGIC AIR-FISSURE CANNON
RELEASES A MAGIC PROJECTILE OF AIR. IT HAS REGAINED SOME OF ITS MAGIC.
Here we go!!
Okay!!!

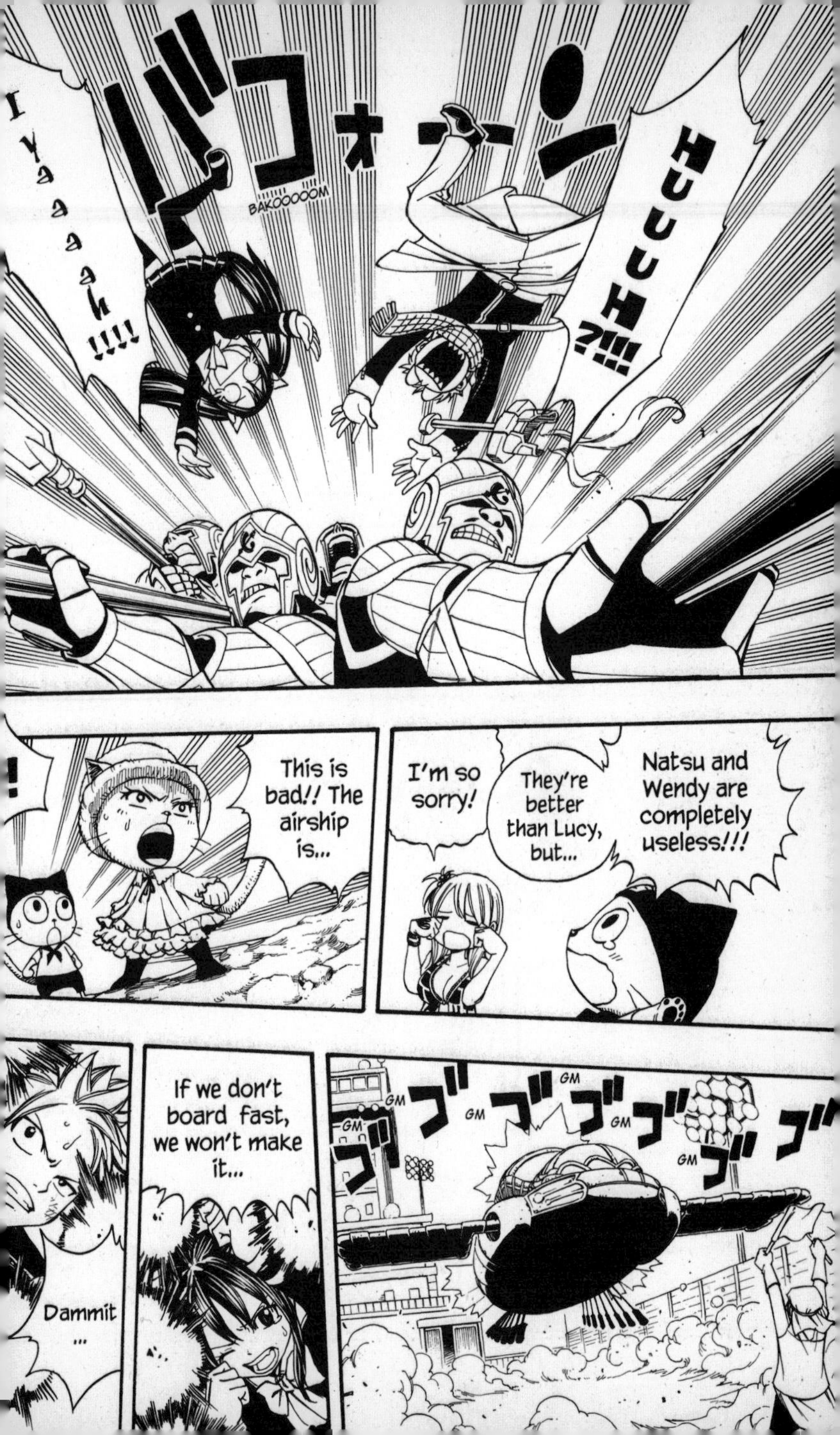
HUUUUH?!!!
バコォーン
BAKOOOOOM
Iyaaaaah!!!!
Natsu and Wendy are completely useless!!!
They're better than Lucy, but...
I'm so sorry!
This is bad!! The airship is...
!
ゴ GM ゴ GM ゴ GM ゴ GM ゴ GM ゴ GM ゴ
If we don't board fast, we won't make it...
Dammit ...

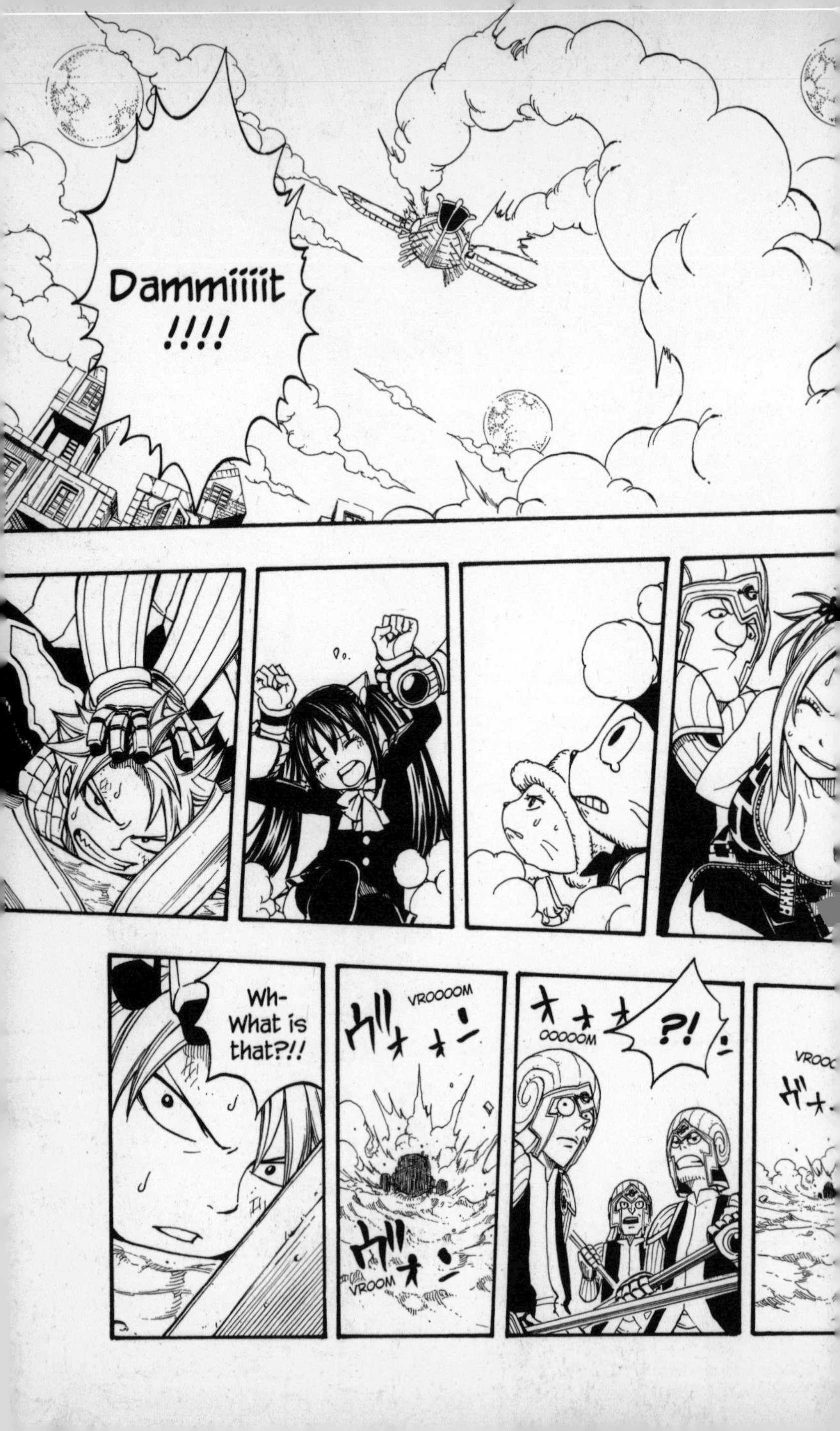
Dammiiiit !!!!
VROOO
OOOOOM
?!
VROOOOM
VROOM
Wh- What is that?!!

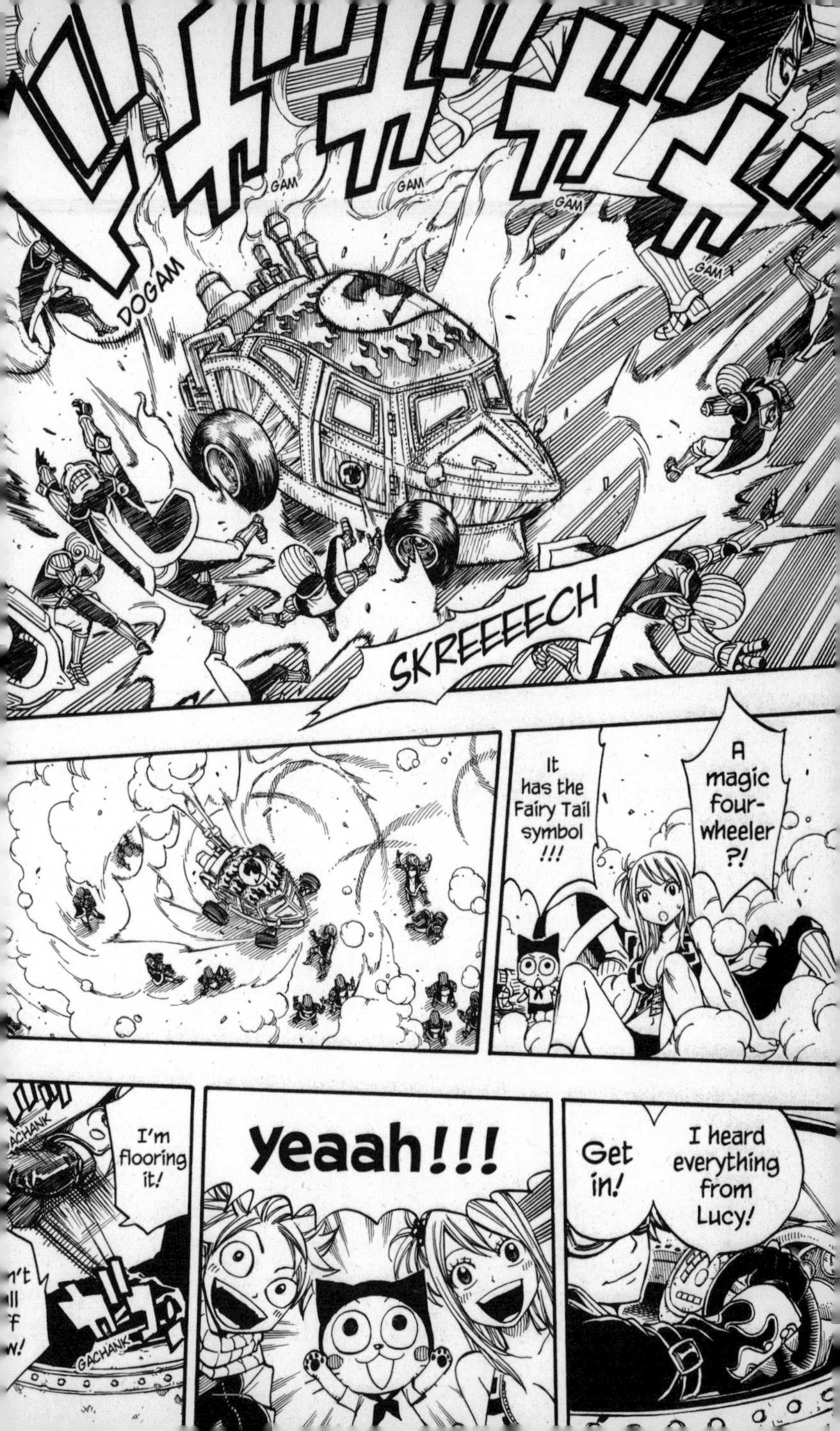
GAM
GAM
GAM
GAM
DOGAM
SKREEEECH
A magic four-wheeler ?!
It has the Fairy Tail symbol !!!
I heard everything from Lucy!
Get in!
yeaah!!!
I'm flooring it!
GACHANK
GACHANK

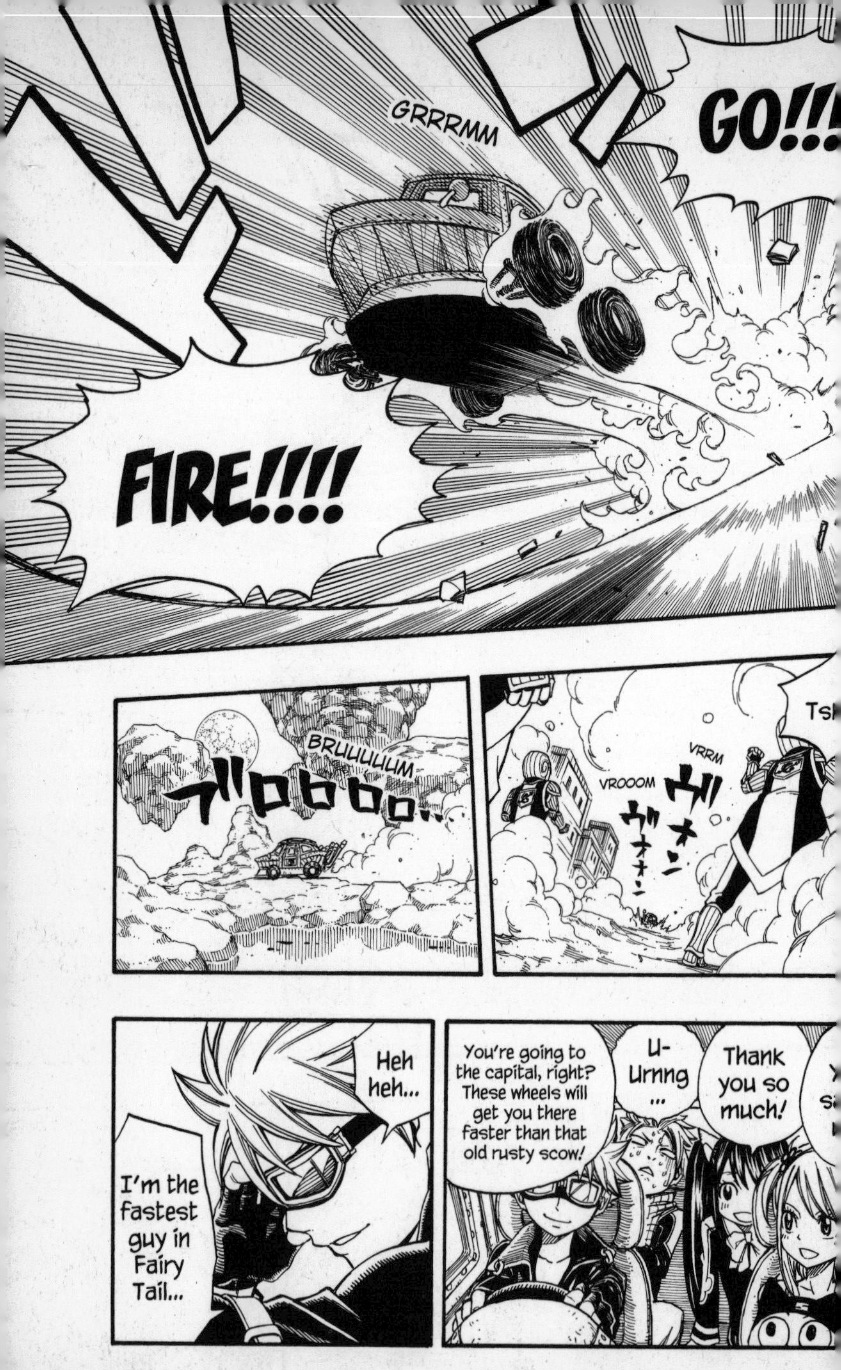
GO!!!
GRRRMM
FIRE!!!!
VRRM
VROOM
BRUUUUUM
Thank you so much!
U-Urnng...
You're going to the capital, right? These wheels will get you there faster than that old rusty scow!
Heh heh...
I'm the fastest guy in Fairy Tail...

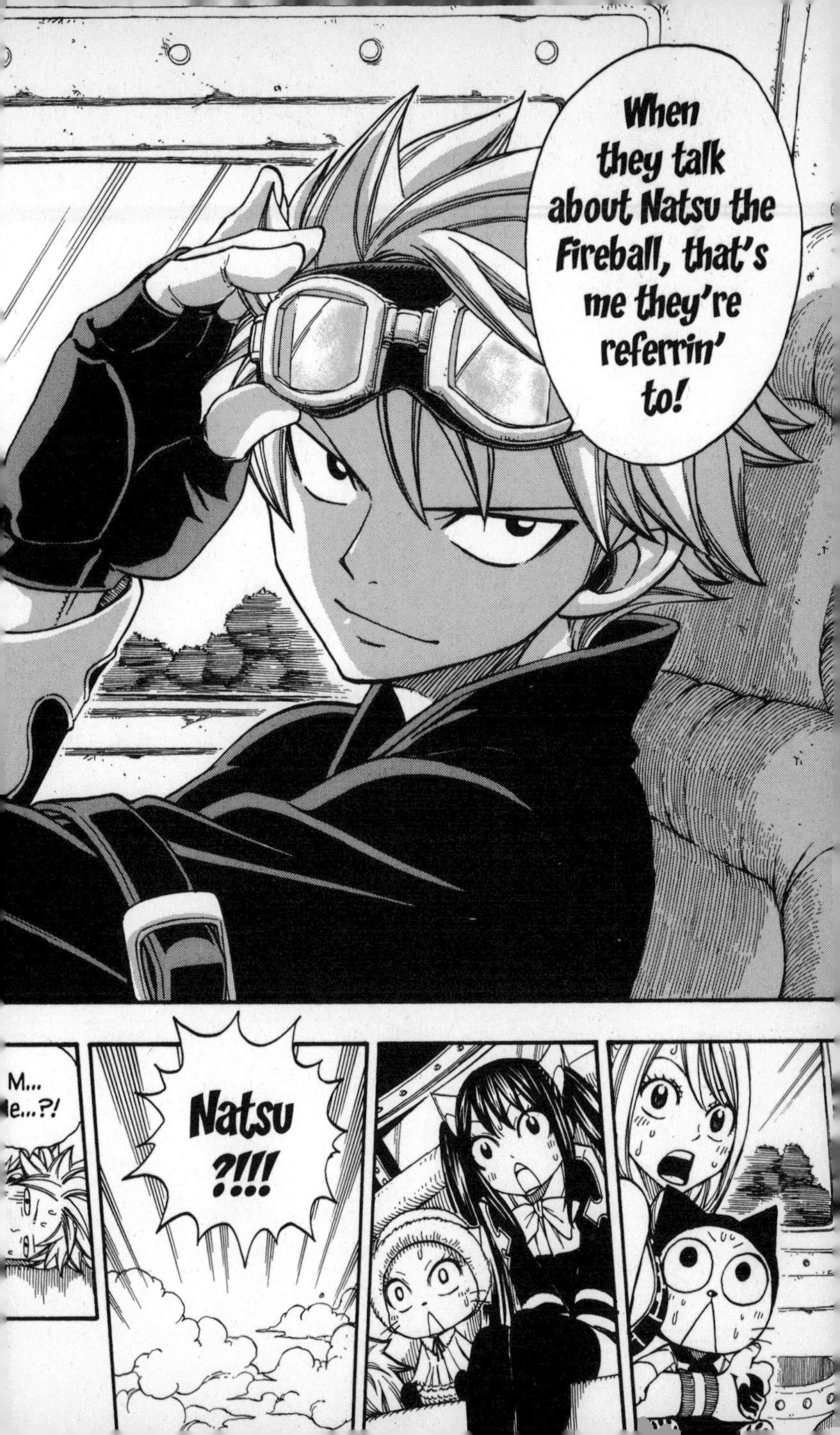

When they talk about Natsu the Fireball, that's me they're referrin' to!
Natsu ?!!!
M... e...?!

FAIRY TAIL
フェアリーテイル

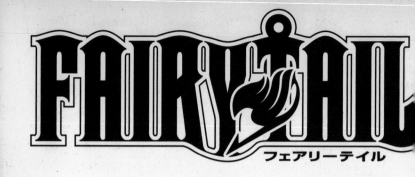

Chapter 174, Revelation

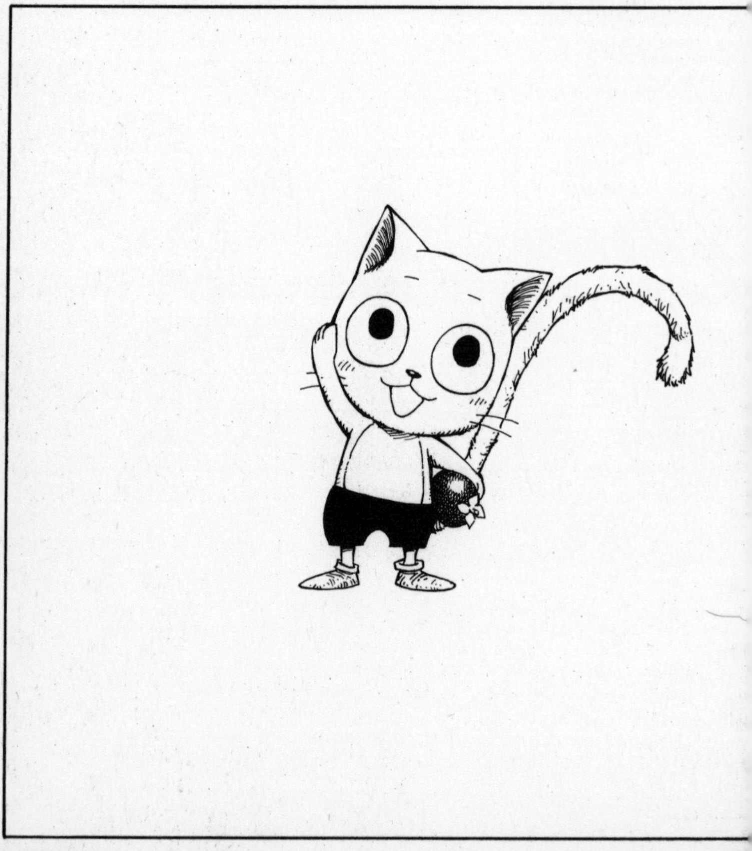

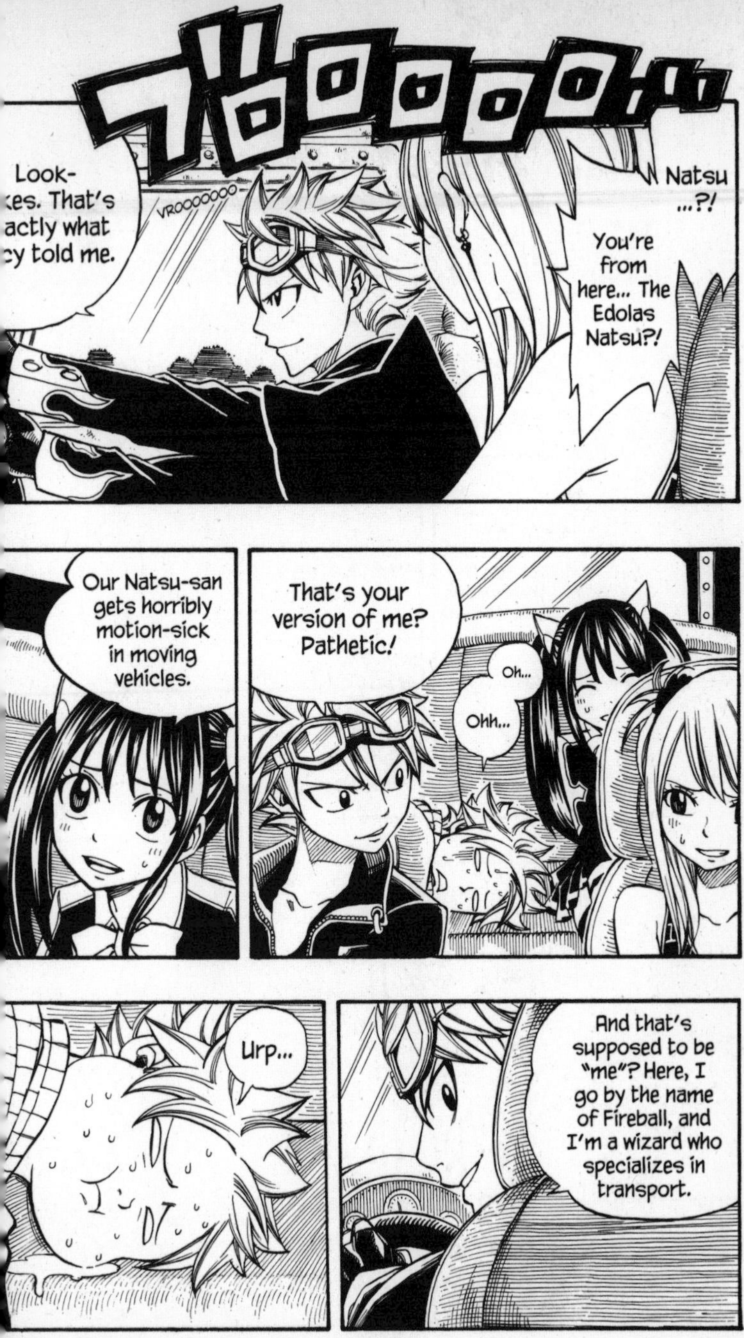
Natsu ...?!
You're from here... The Edolas Natsu?!
VROOOOOOO
Look- es. That's actly what cy told me.
Oh...
Ohh...
That's your version of me? Pathetic!
Our Natsu-san gets horribly motion-sick in moving vehicles.
And that's supposed to be "me"? Here, I go by the name of Fireball, and I'm a wizard who specializes in transport.
Urp...

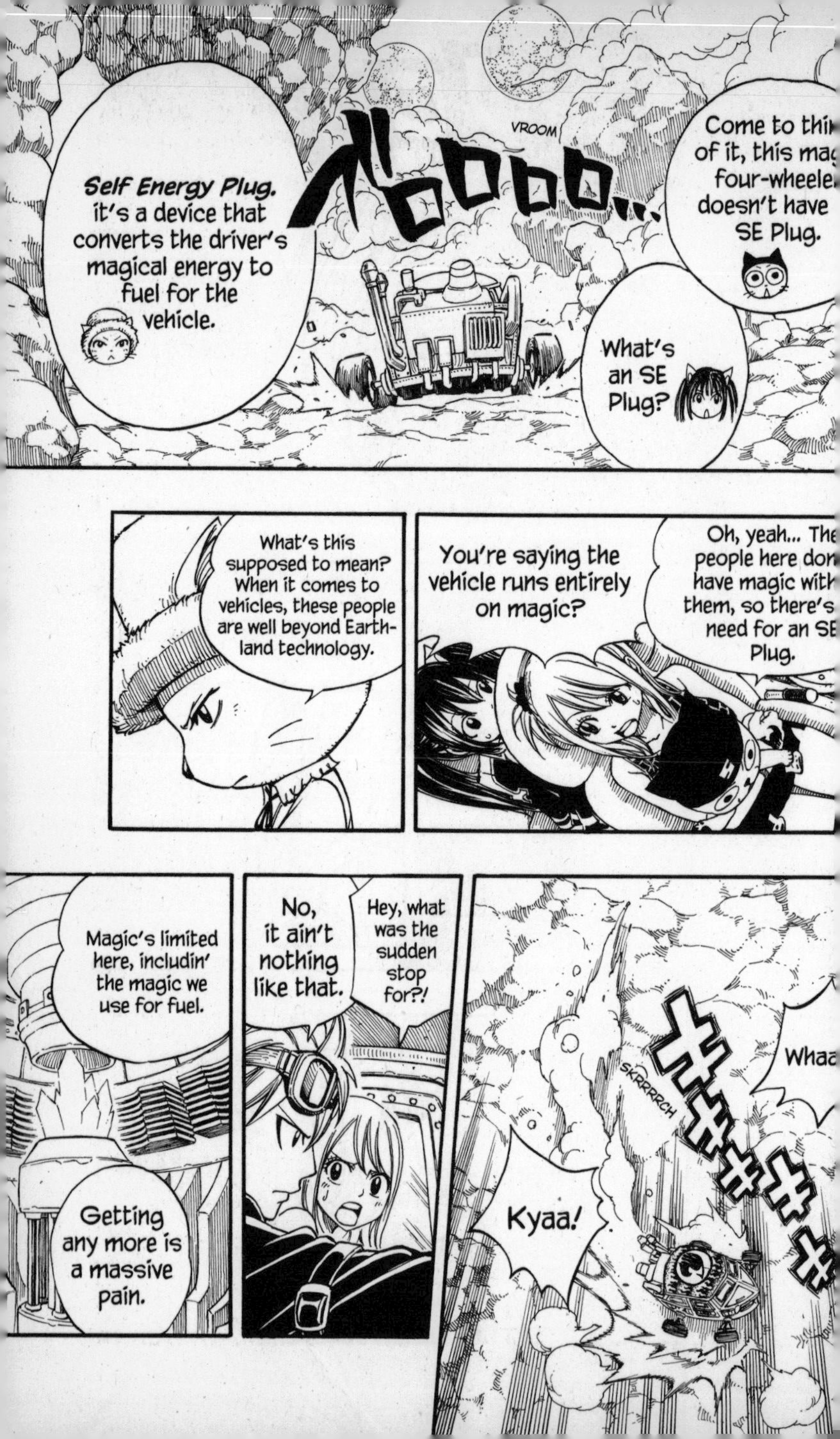

Come to thi
of it, this ma
four-wheele
doesn't have
SE Plug.
What's an SE Plug?
VROOM
Self Energy Plug. it's a device that converts the driver's magical energy to fuel for the vehicle.
Oh, yeah... The
people here do
have magic wit
them, so there's
need for an SE
Plug.
You're saying the vehicle runs entirely on magic?
What's this supposed to mean? When it comes to vehicles, these people are well beyond Earth-land technology.
Whaa
SKRRRRCH
Kyaa!
Hey, what was the sudden stop for?!
No, it ain't nothing like that.
Magic's limited here, includin' the magic we use for fuel.
Getting any more is a massive pain.

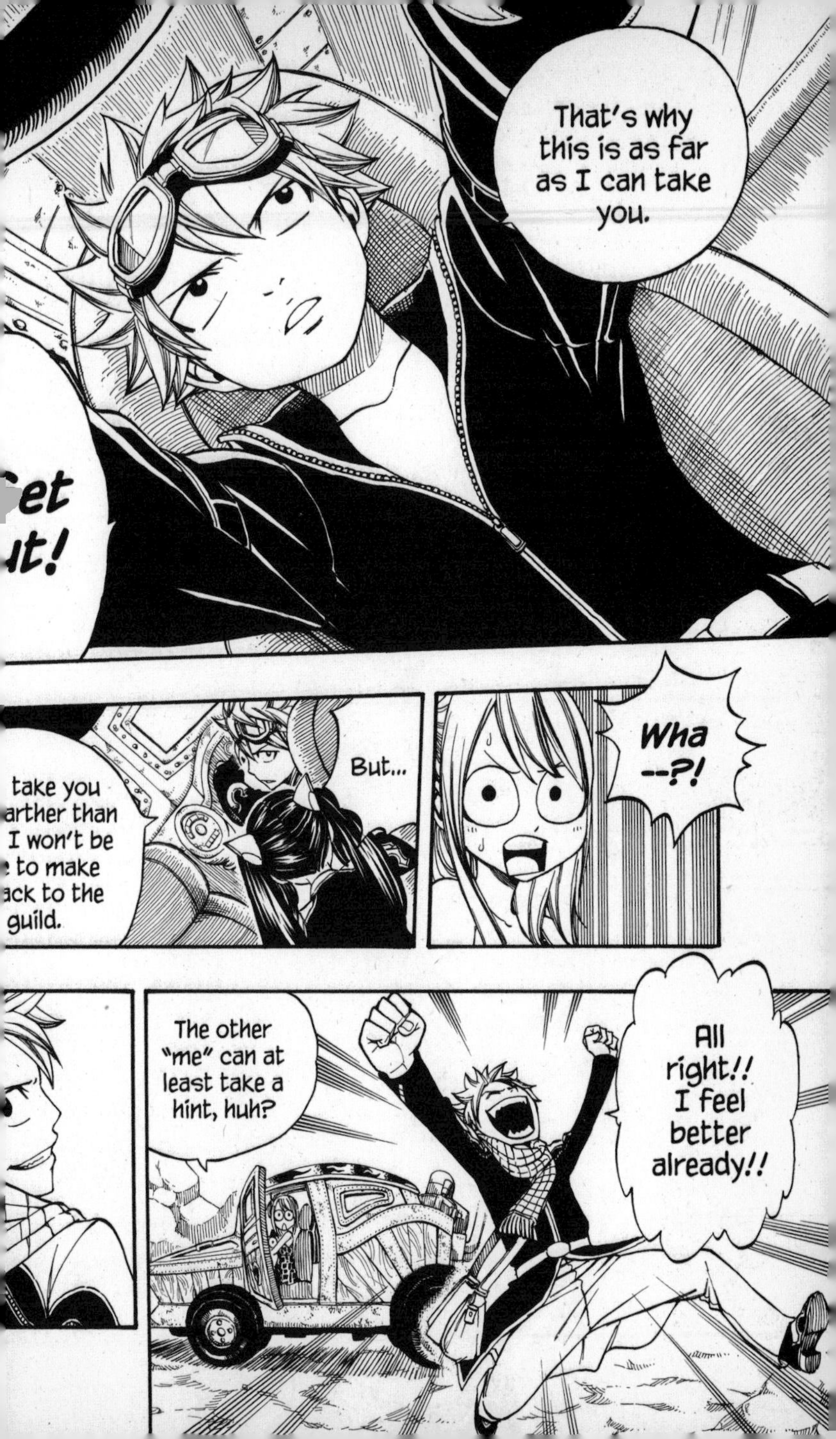
That's why this is as far as I can take you.
Wha --?!
But...
take you arther than I won't be to make ack to the guild.
All right!! I feel better already!!
The other "me" can at least take a hint, huh?

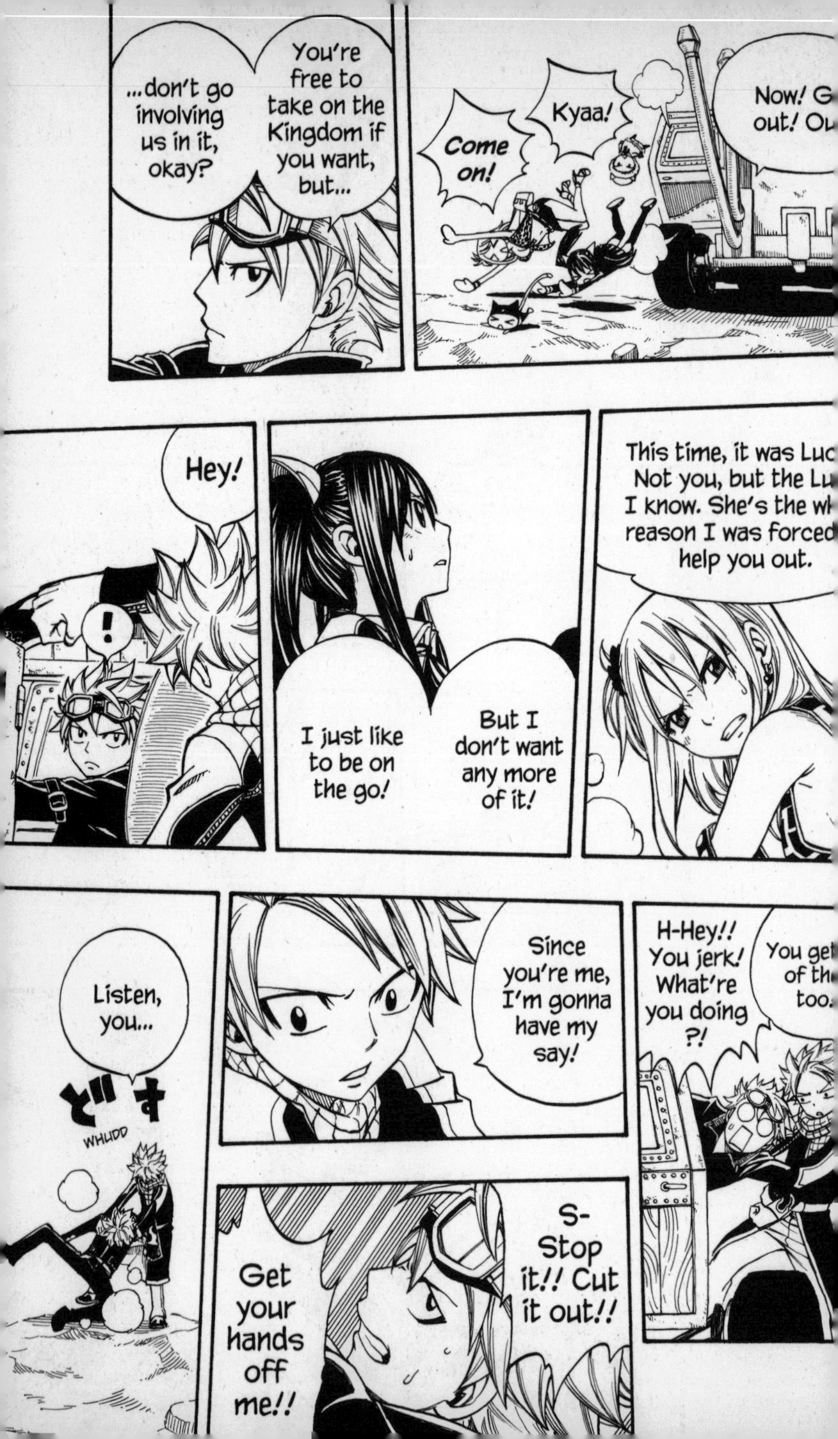

Now! G
out! Ou
Kyaa!
Come on!
You're free to take on the Kingdom if you want, but...
...don't go involving us in it, okay?
This time, it was Luc
Not you, but the Lu
I know. She's the wh
reason I was forced
help you out.
But I don't want any more of it!
I just like to be on the go!
Hey!
!
You get
of th
too.
H-Hey!! You jerk! What're you doing ?!
Since you're me, I'm gonna have my say!
S-Stop it!! Cut it out!!
Get your hands off me!!
Listen, you...
どす
WHUDD

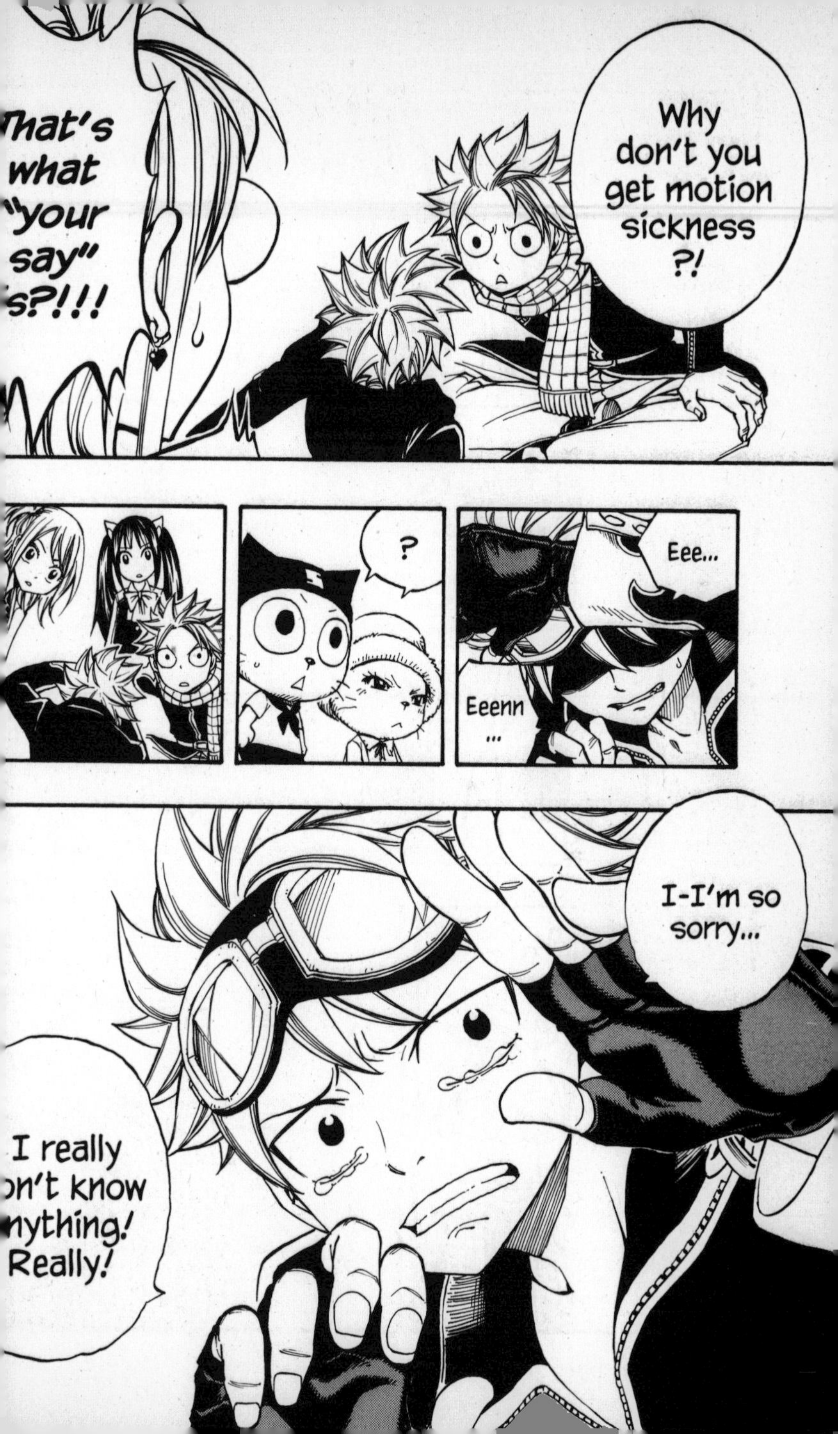
Why don't you get motion sickness ?!
hat's what "your say" s?!!!
Eee...
Eeenn ...
?
I-I'm so sorry...
I really on't know nything! Really!

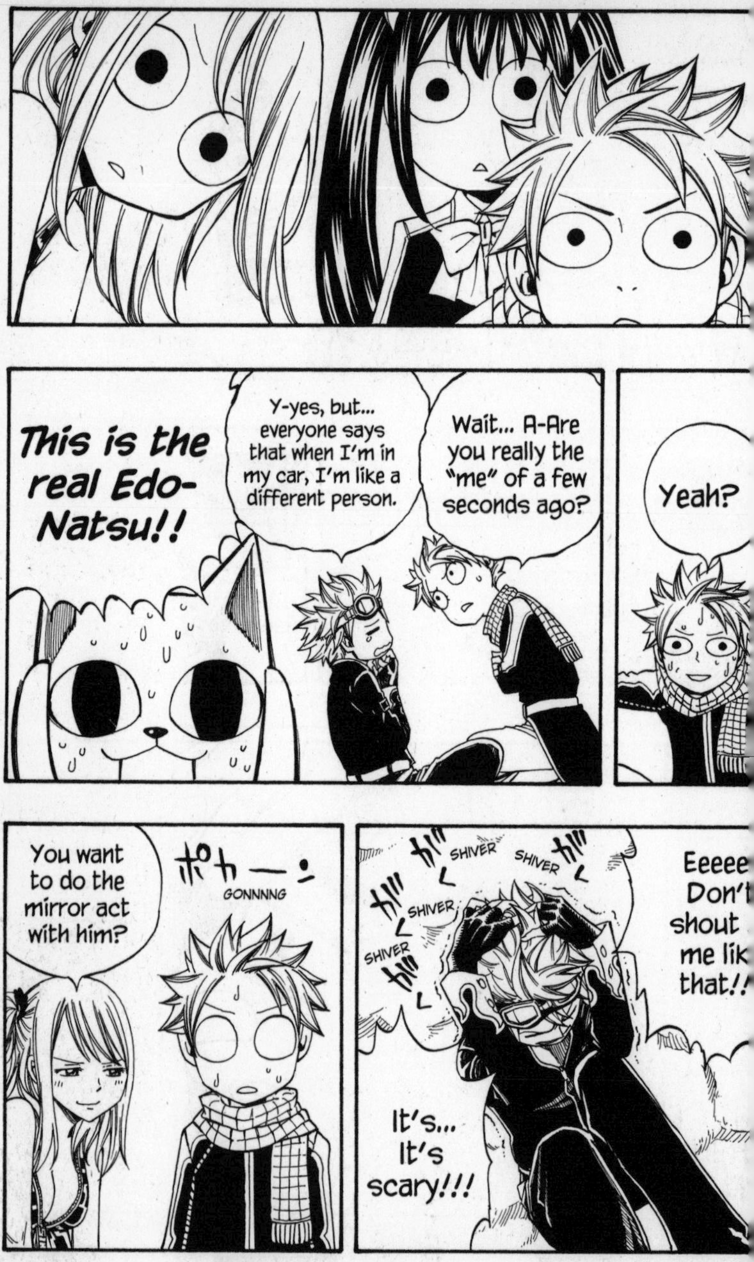
Yeah?
Wait... A-Are you really the "me" of a few seconds ago?
Y-yes, but... everyone says that when I'm in my car, I'm like a different person.
This is the real Edo-Natsu!!
Eeeee Don't shout me lik that!!
ガ SHIVER
ガ SHIVER
ガ SHIVER
ガ SHIVER
It's... It's scary!!!
ポカーン
GONNNNG
You want to do the mirror act with him?

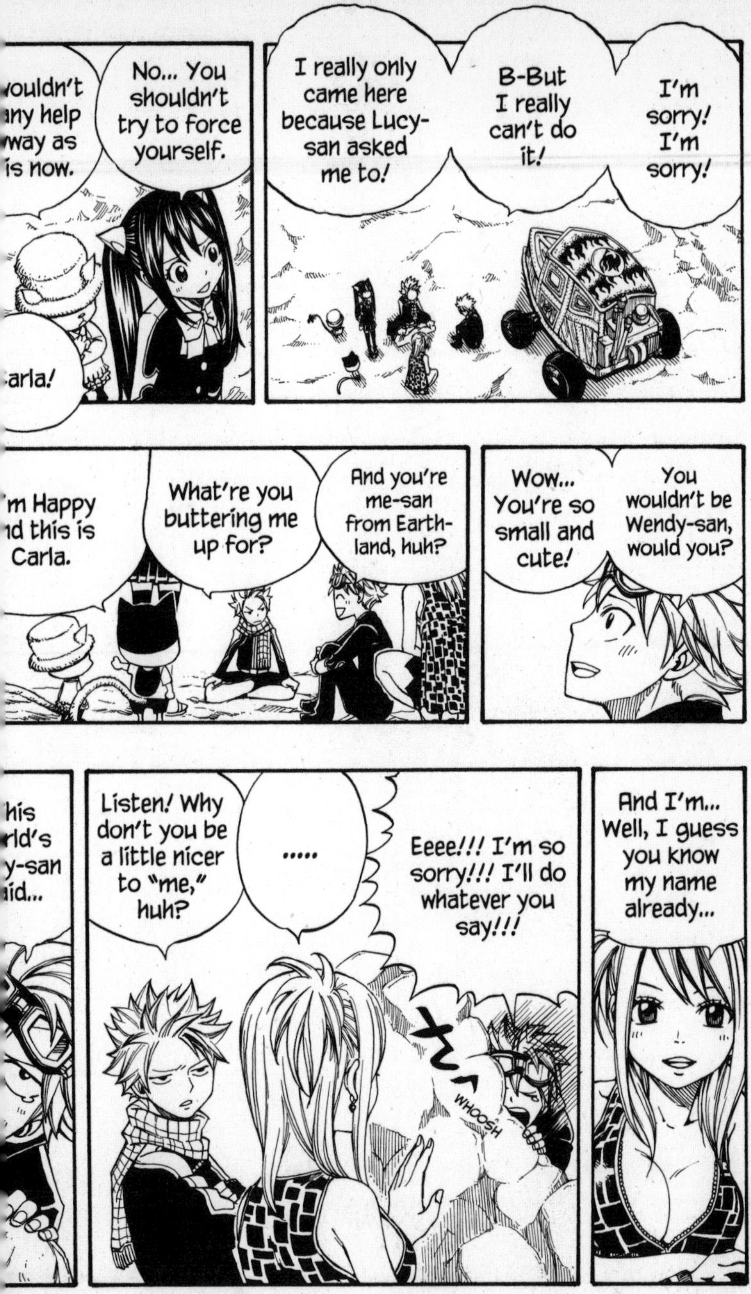

I'm sorry! I'm sorry!
B-But I really can't do it!
I really only came here because Lucy-san asked me to!
No... You shouldn't try to force yourself.
ouldn't any help way as is now.
arla!
You wouldn't be Wendy-san, would you?
Wow... You're so small and cute!
And you're me-san from Earth-land, huh?
What're you buttering me up for?
'm Happy d this is Carla.
And I'm... Well, I guess you know my name already...
Eeee!!! I'm so sorry!!! I'll do whatever you say!!!
WHOOSH
.....
Listen! Why don't you be a little nicer to "me," huh?
his rld's y-san id...

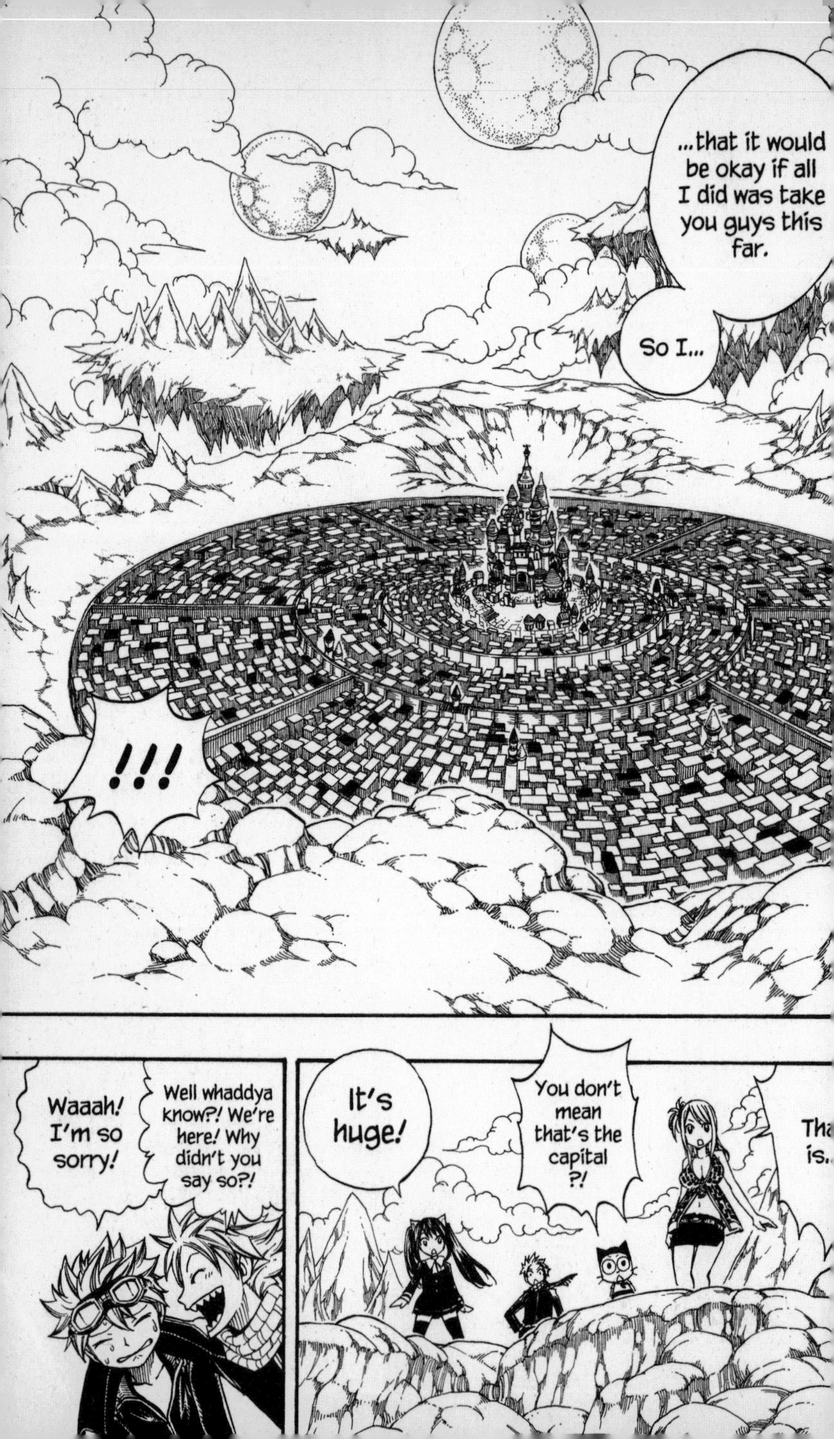
...that it would be okay if all I did was take you guys this far.
So I...
!!!
Tha is...
You don't mean that's the capital ?!
It's huge!
Well whaddya know?! We're here! Why didn't you say so?!
Waaah! I'm so sorry!

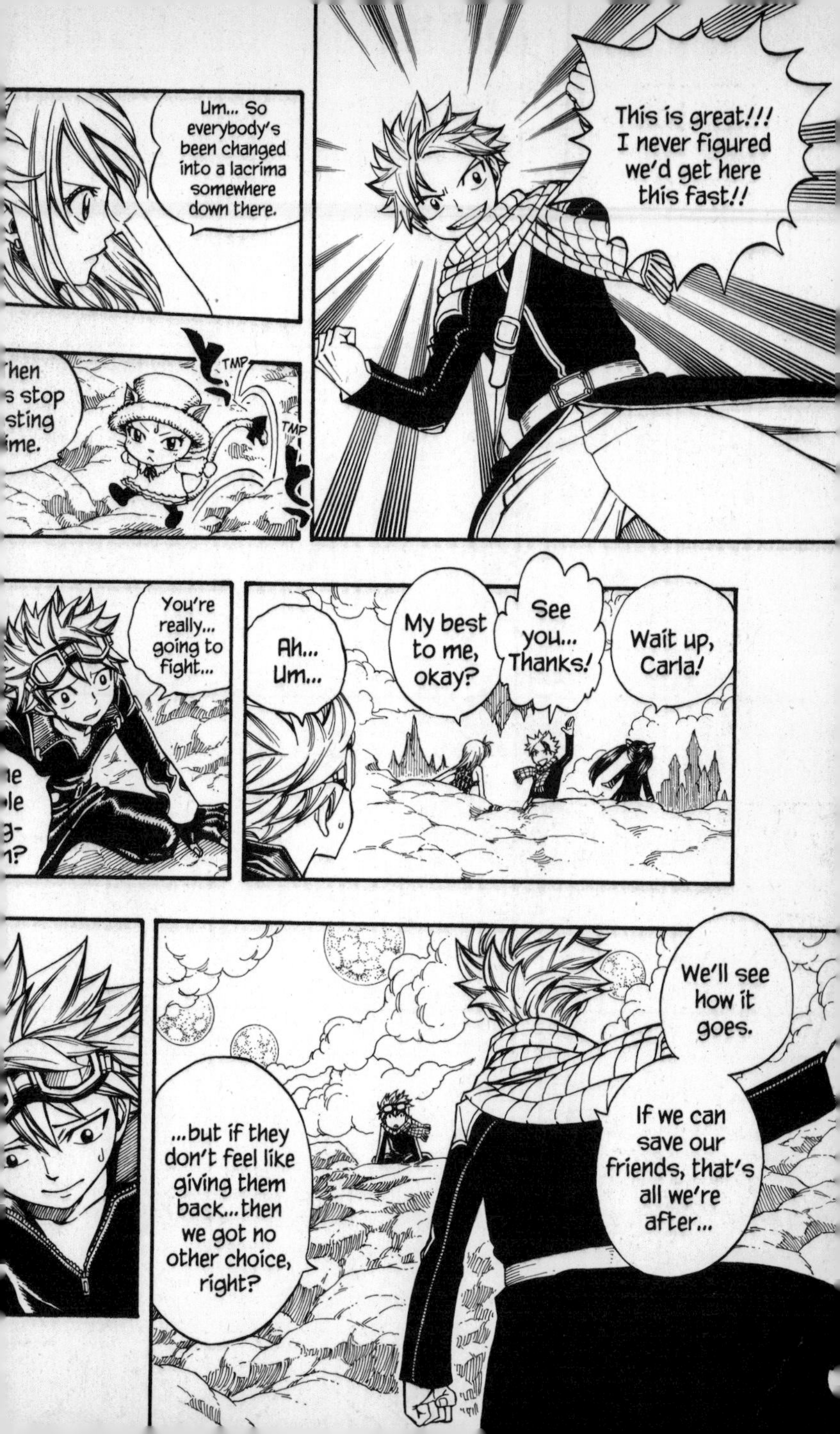

This is great!!! I never figured we'd get here this fast!!
Um... So everybody's been changed into a lacrima somewhere down there.
TMP
TMP
Wait up, Carla!
See you... Thanks!
My best to me, okay?
Ah... Um...
You're really... going to fight...
We'll see how it goes.
If we can save our friends, that's all we're after...
...but if they don't feel like giving them back...then we got no other choice, right?

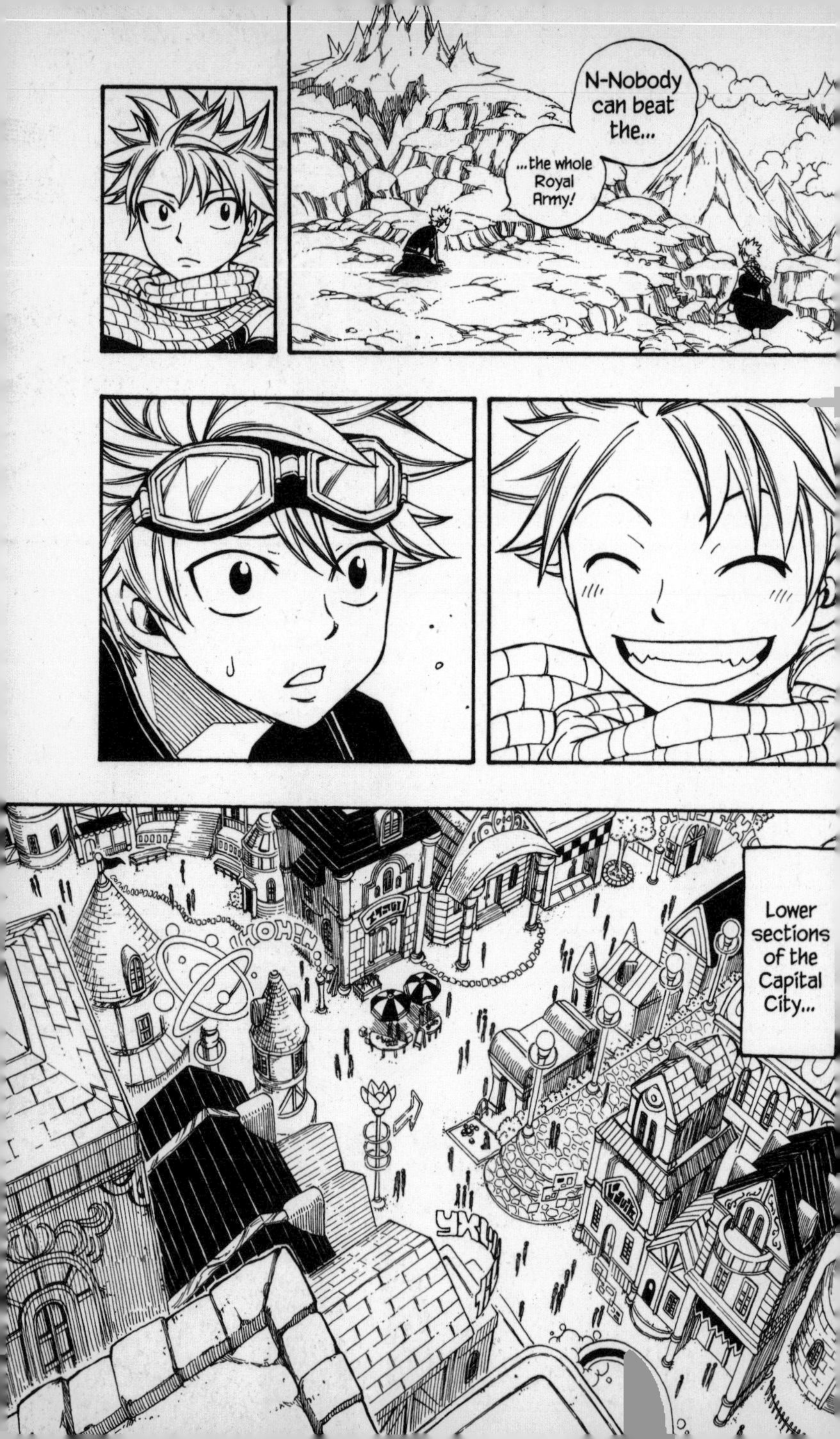
N-Nobody can beat the...
...the whole Royal Army!
Lower sections of the Capital City...

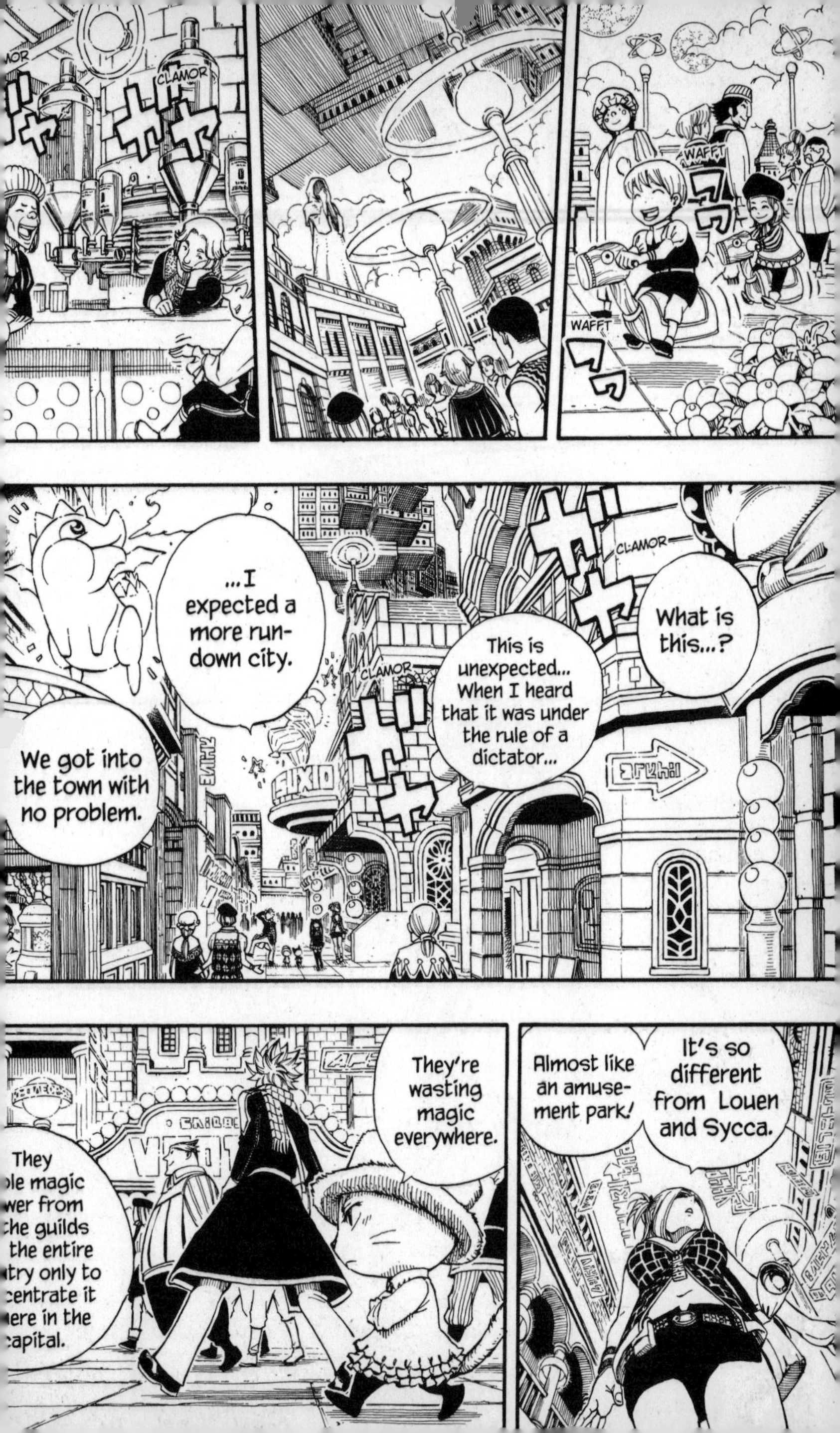
WAFFT
WAFFT
CLAMOR
MOR
What is this...?
This is unexpected... When I heard that it was under the rule of a dictator...
CLAMOR
CLAMOR
...I expected a more run-down city.
We got into the town with no problem.
It's so different from Louen and Sycca.
Almost like an amusement park!
They're wasting magic everywhere.
They ole magic wer from che guilds the entire try only to centrate it ere in the capital.

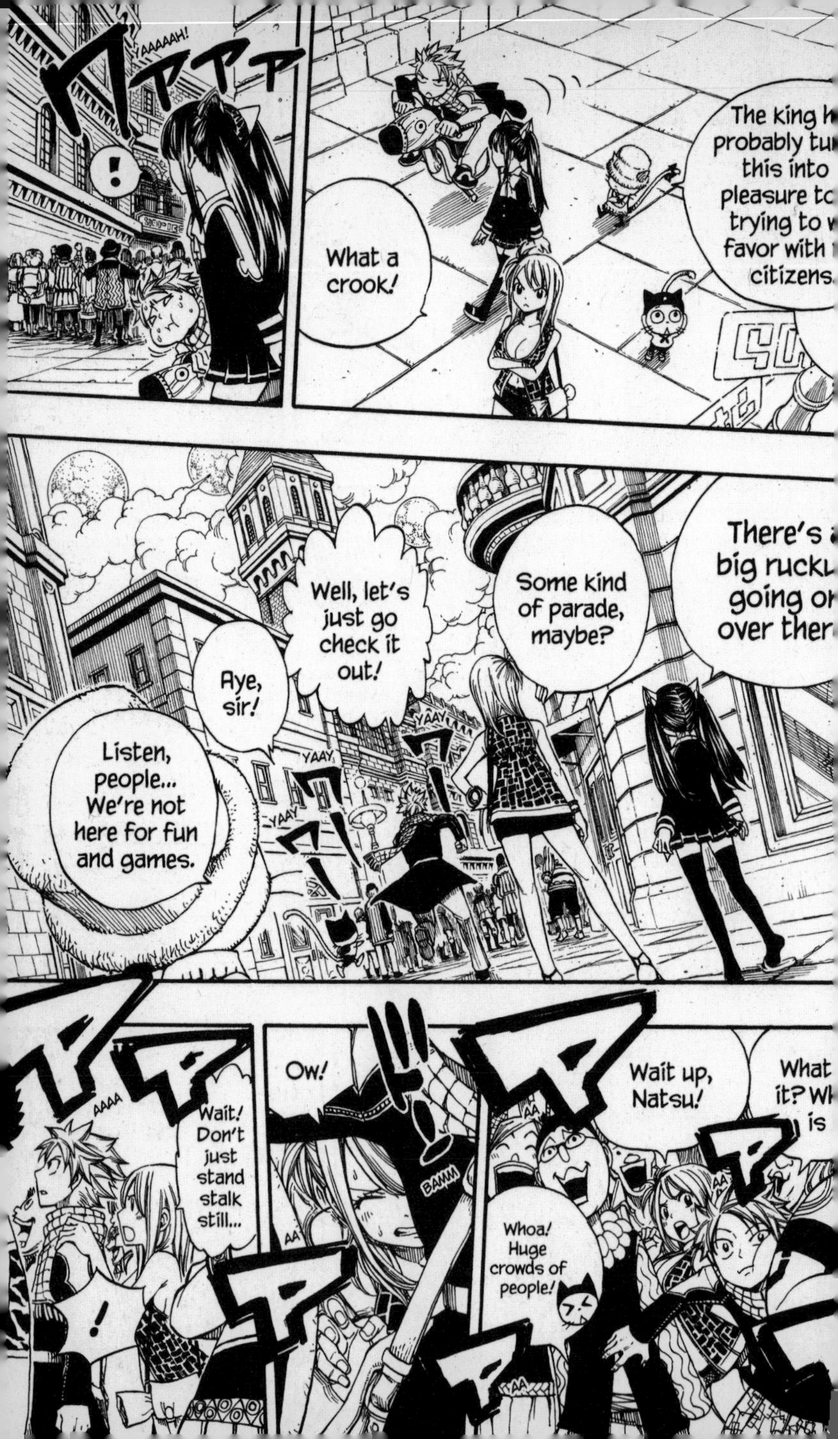
The king h
probably tu
this into
pleasure to
trying to w
favor with
citizens.
What a crook!
YAAAAH!
!
There's a
big ruck
going o
over ther
Some kind of parade, maybe?
Well, let's just go check it out!
YAAY
YAAY
YAAY
Aye, sir!
Listen, people... We're not here for fun and games.
What
it? Wh
is
Wait up, Natsu!
AA
AA
Whoa! Huge crowds of people!
AA
Ow!
BAMM
AA
AAAA
Wait! Don't just stand stalk still...
!

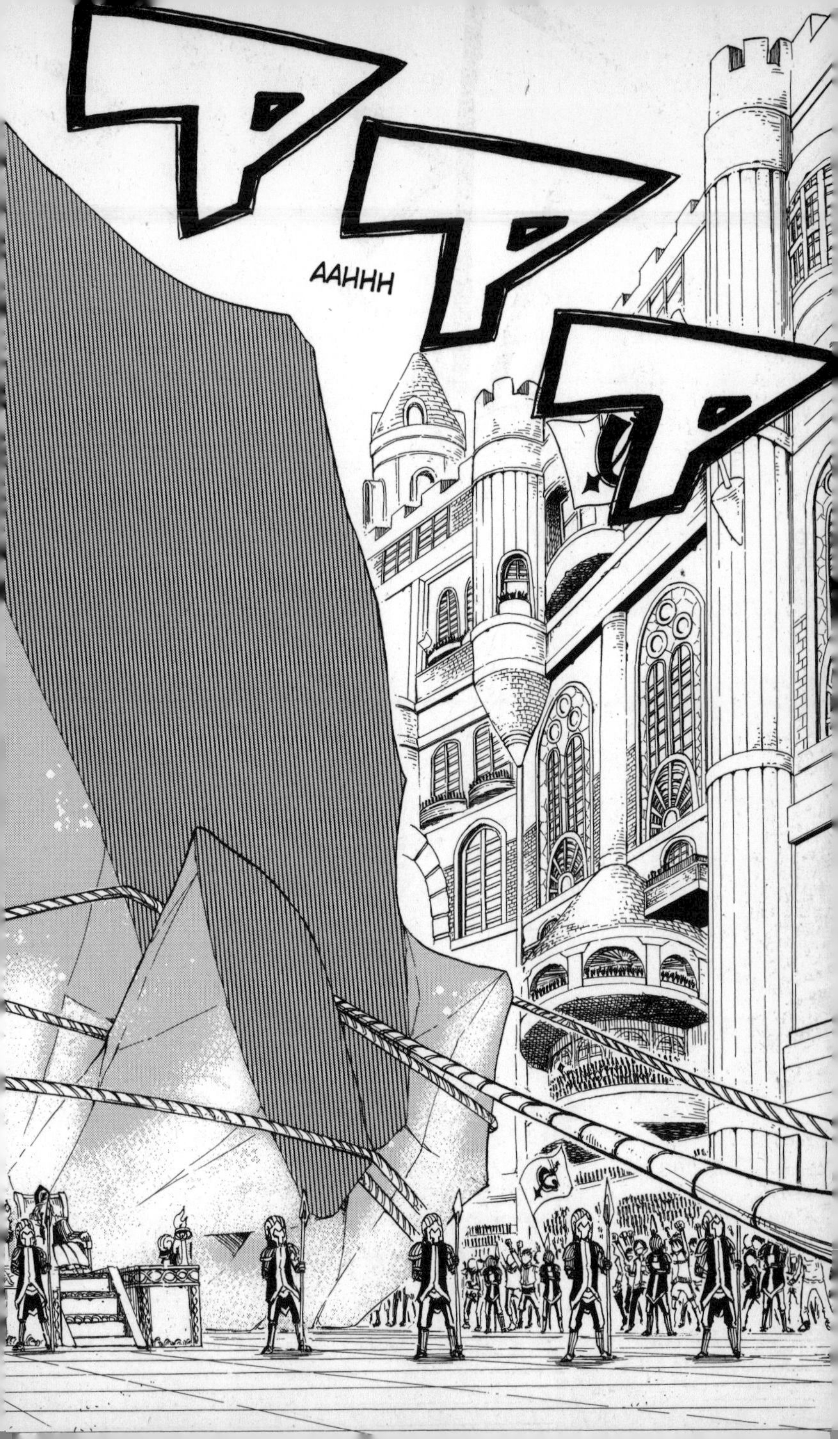
AAHHH

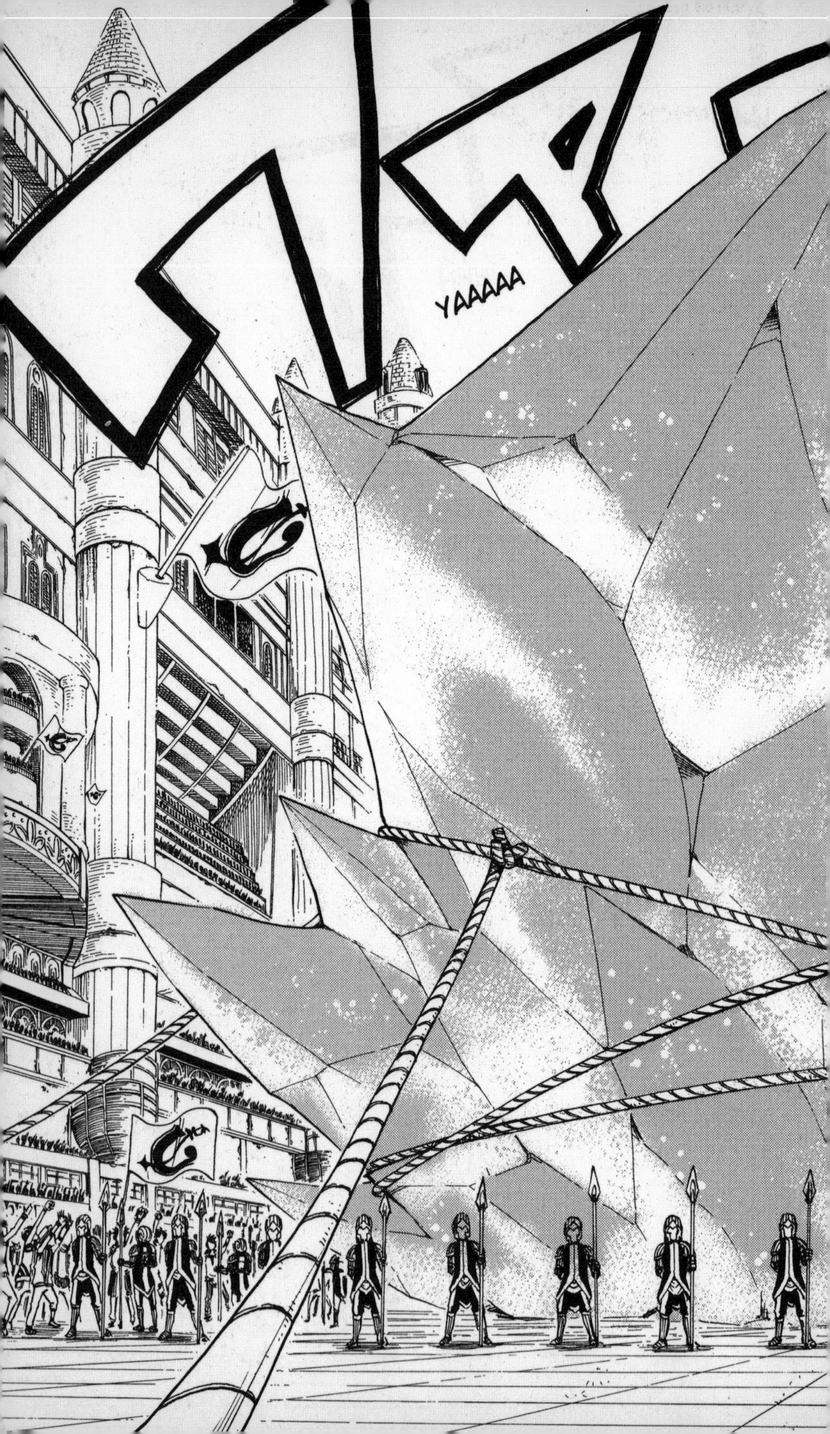
YAAAAA

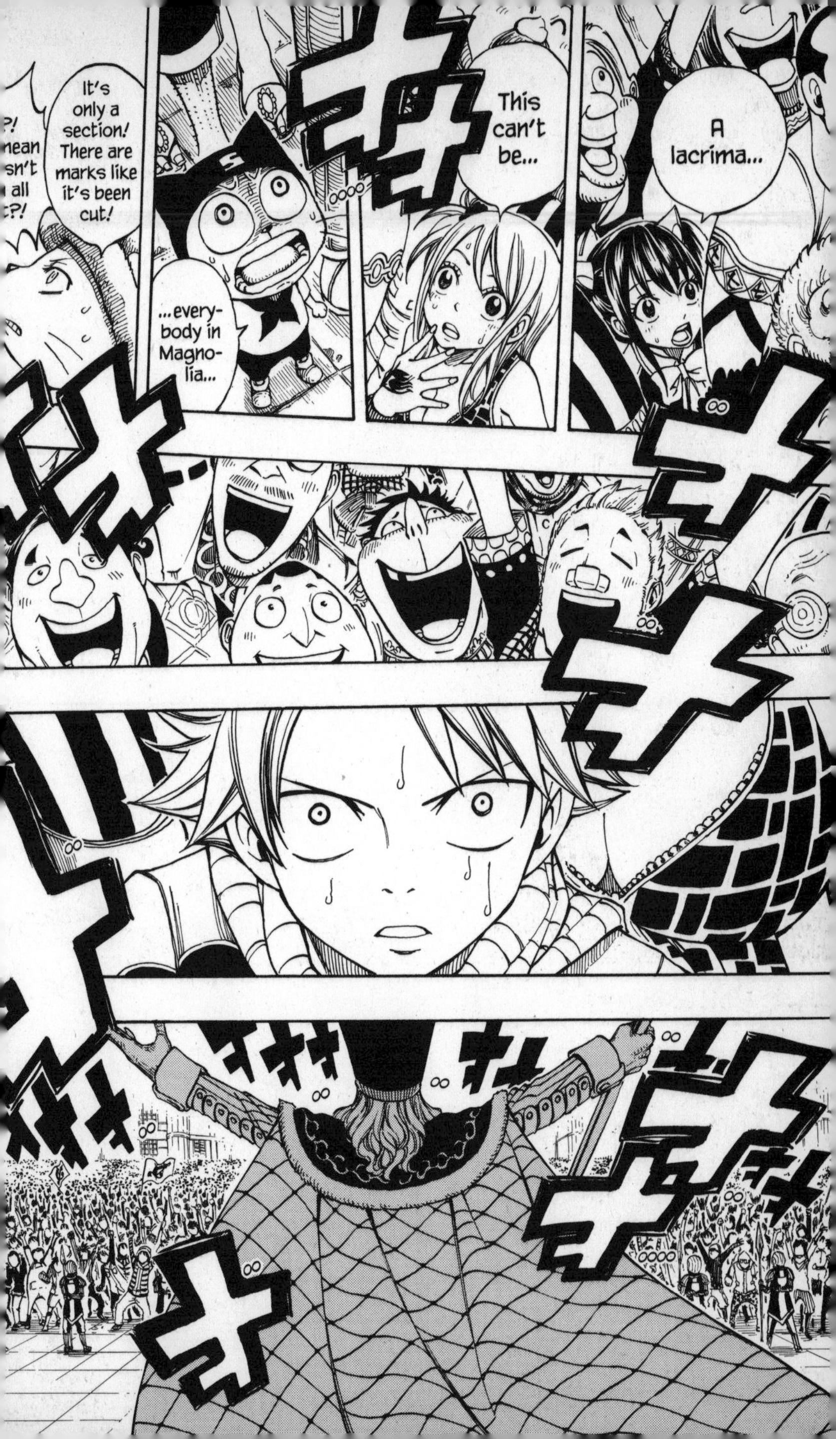
A lacrima...
This can't be...
It's only a section! There are marks like it's been cut!
...everybody in Magnolia...

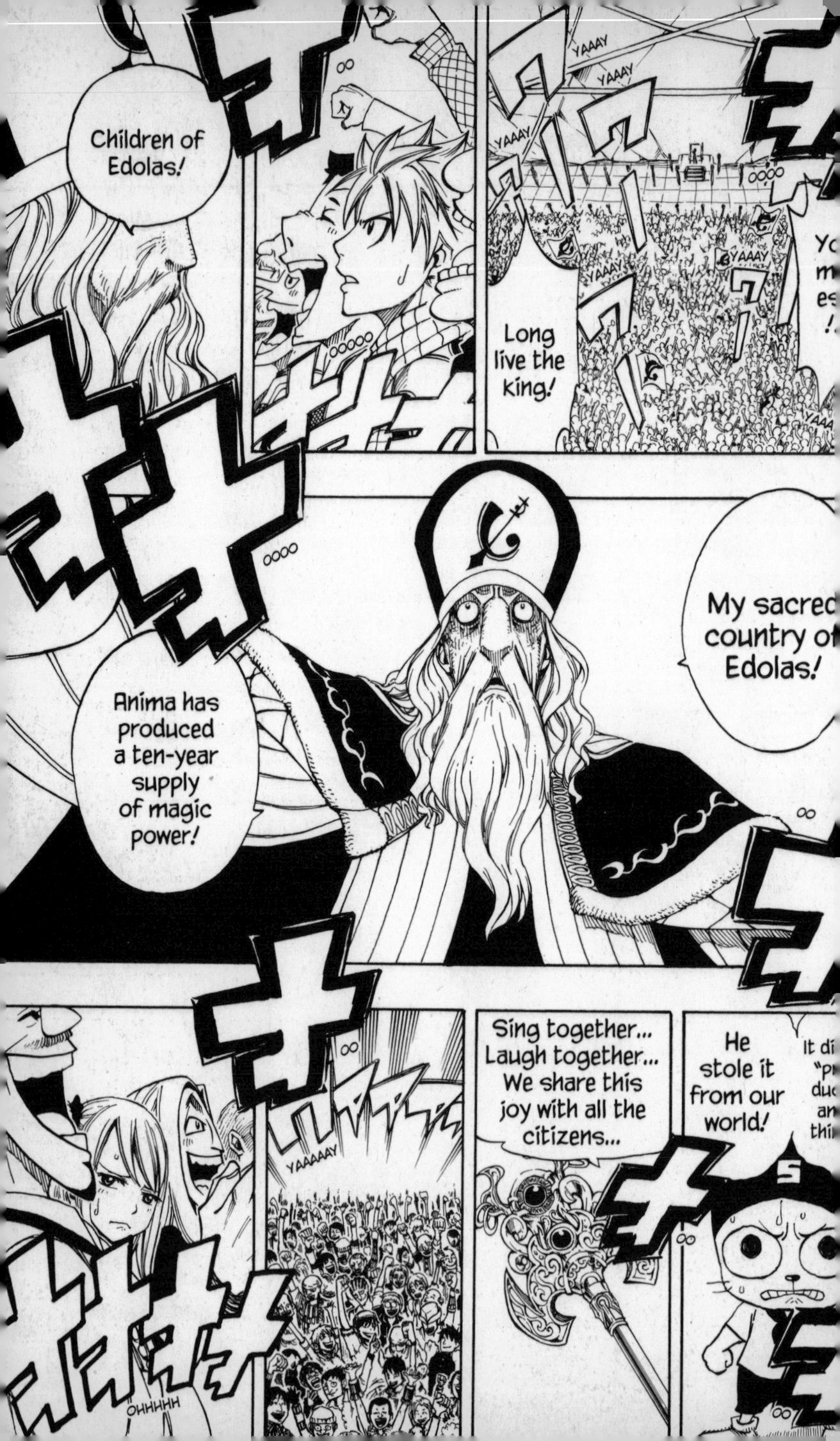
YAAAY
YAAAY
YAAAY
YAAAY
YAAAY
Long live the king!
Children of Edolas!
My sacred country of Edolas!
Anima has produced a ten-year supply of magic power!
He stole it from our world!
Sing together... Laugh together... We share this joy with all the citizens...
YAAAAAY
OHHHHH

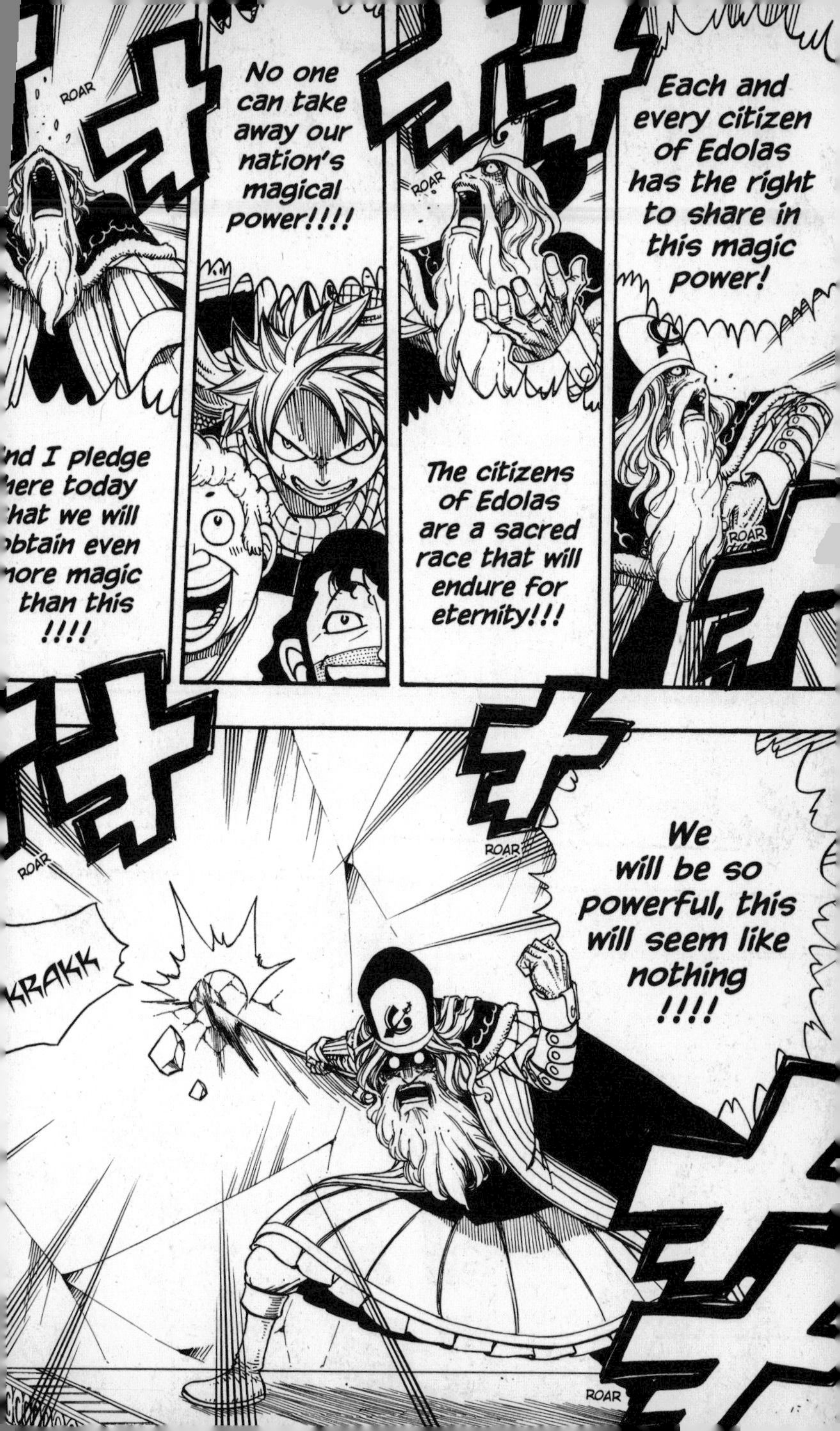
Each and every citizen of Edolas has the right to share in this magic power!
ROAR
ROAR
The citizens of Edolas are a sacred race that will endure for eternity!!!
No one can take away our nation's magical power!!!!
ROAR
nd I pledge here today that we will btain even nore magic than this !!!!
We will be so powerful, this will seem like nothing !!!!
ROAR
ROAR
KRAKK
ROAR

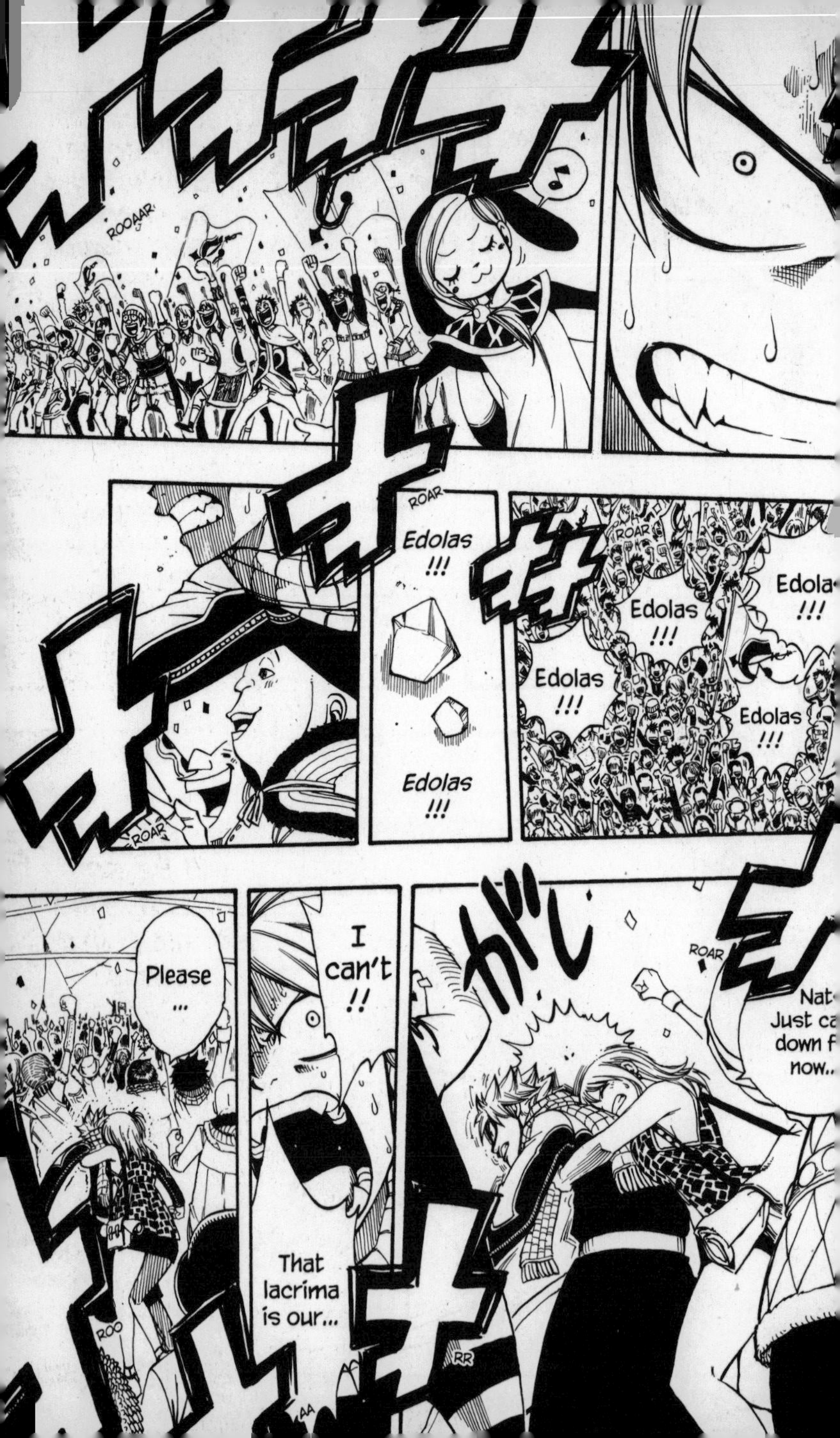
ROOAAR
Edola !!!
Edolas !!!
Edolas !!!
Edolas !!!
ROAR
ROAR
Edolas !!!
Edolas !!!
ROAR
ROAR
Nat Just ca down f now..
RR
I can't !!
That lacrima is our...
AA
Please ...
ROO

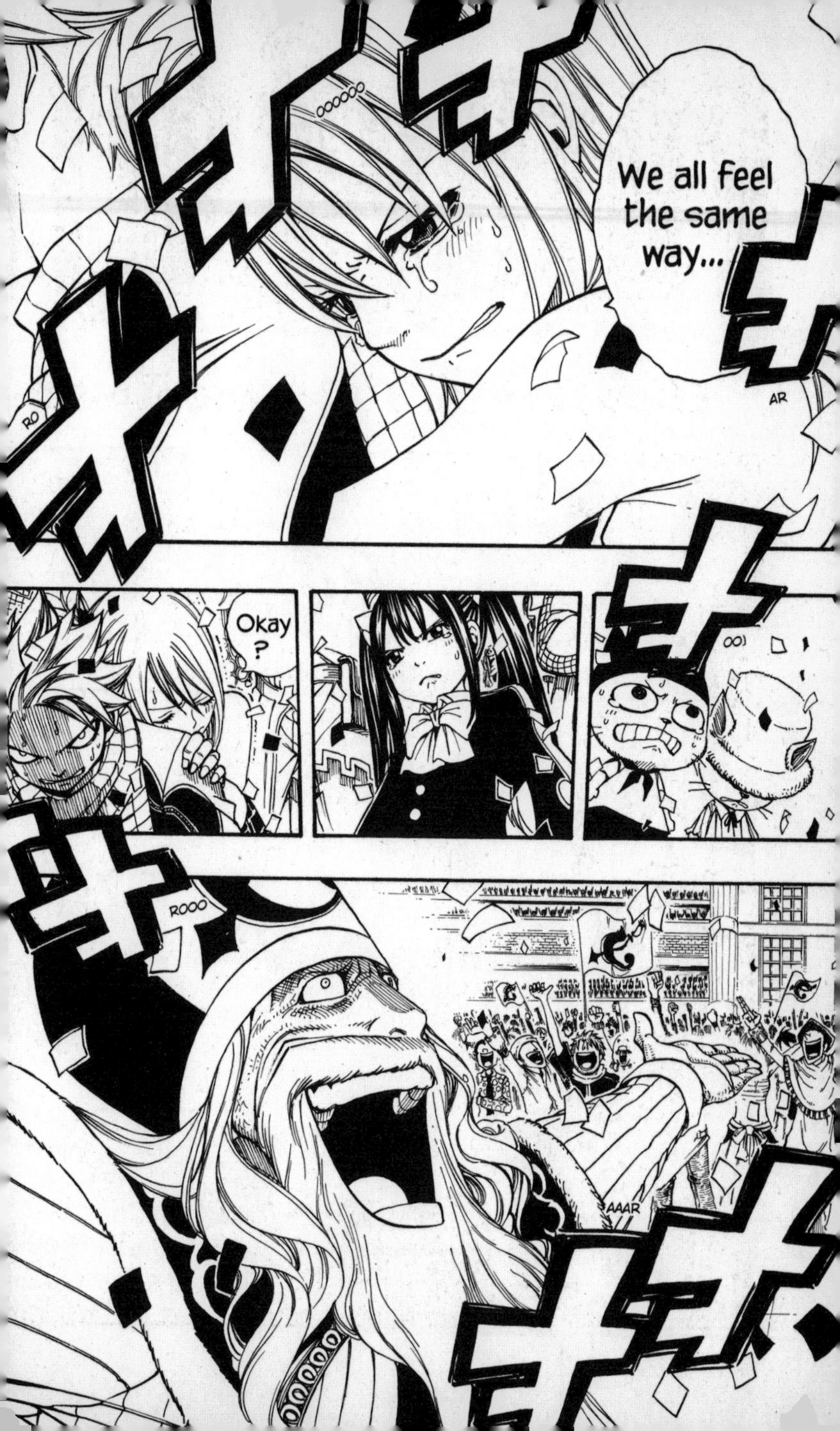
We all feel the same way...
AR
RO
OO
Okay ?
ROOO
AAAR

FAIRY TAIL

フェアリーテイル

Chapter 175, Welcome Home

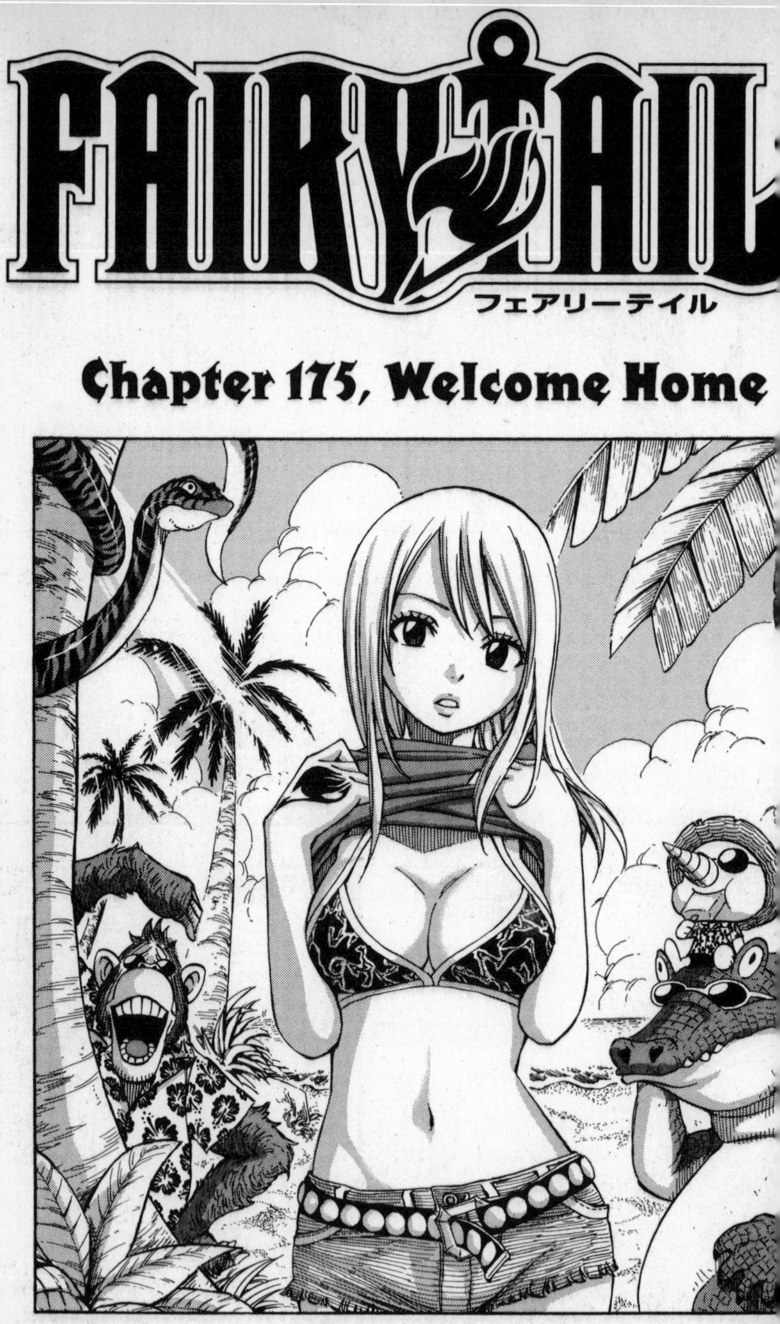

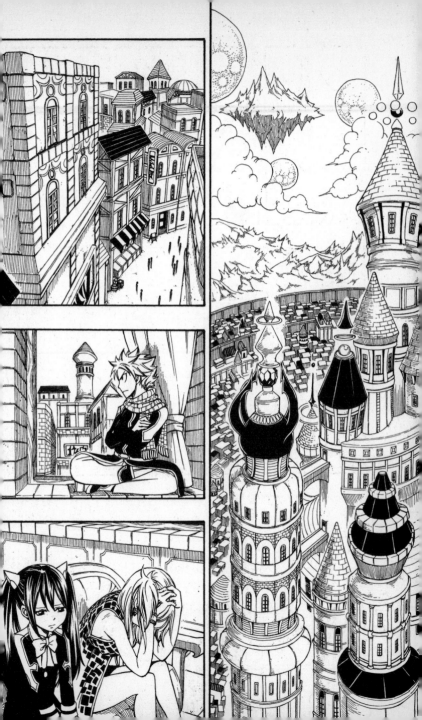

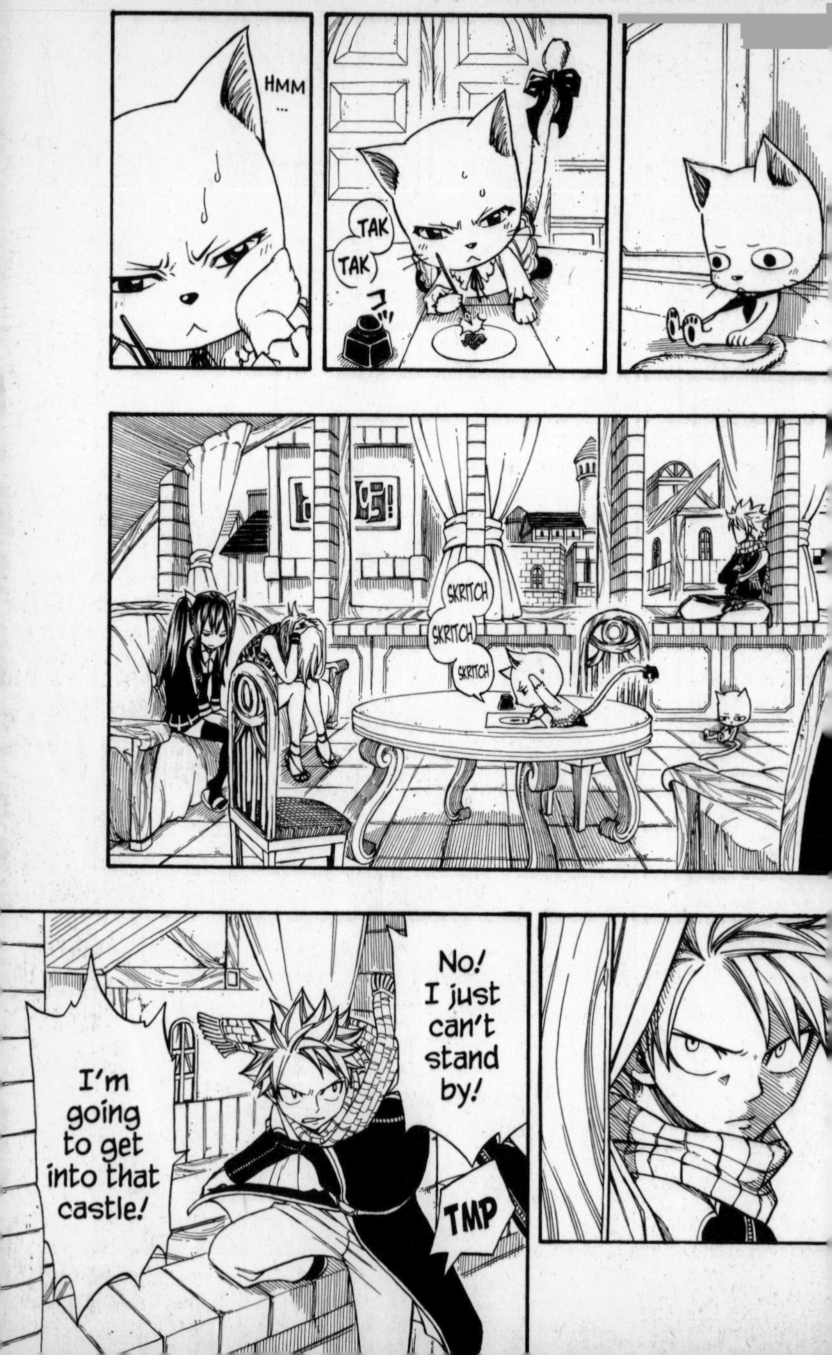
TAK
TAK
HMM...
SKRITCH
SKRITCH
SKRITCH
No! I just can't stand by!
I'm going to get into that castle!
TMP

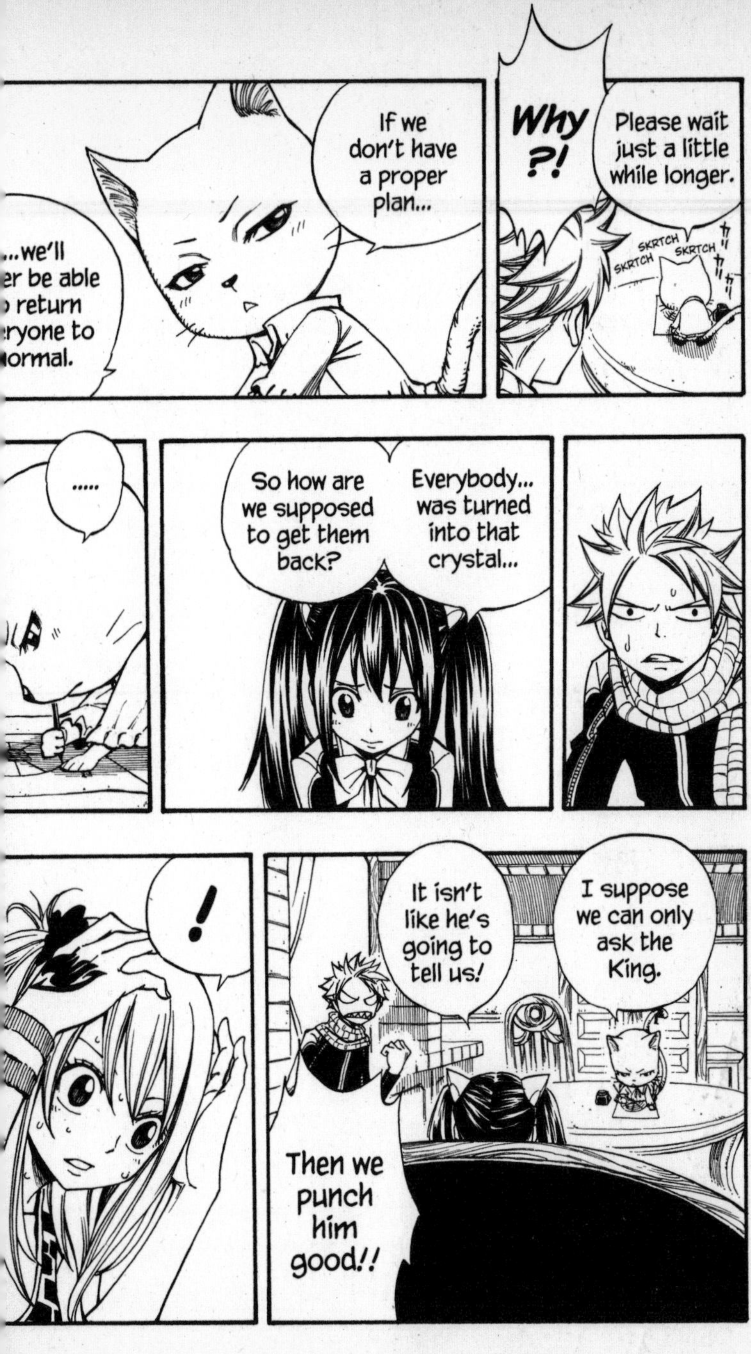
Please wait just a little while longer.
SKRTCH SKRTCH SKRTCH
Why?!
If we don't have a proper plan...
...we'll
er be able
return
ryone to
ormal.
Everybody... was turned into that crystal...
So how are we supposed to get them back?
.....
I suppose we can only ask the King.
It isn't like he's going to tell us!
Then we punch him good!!
!

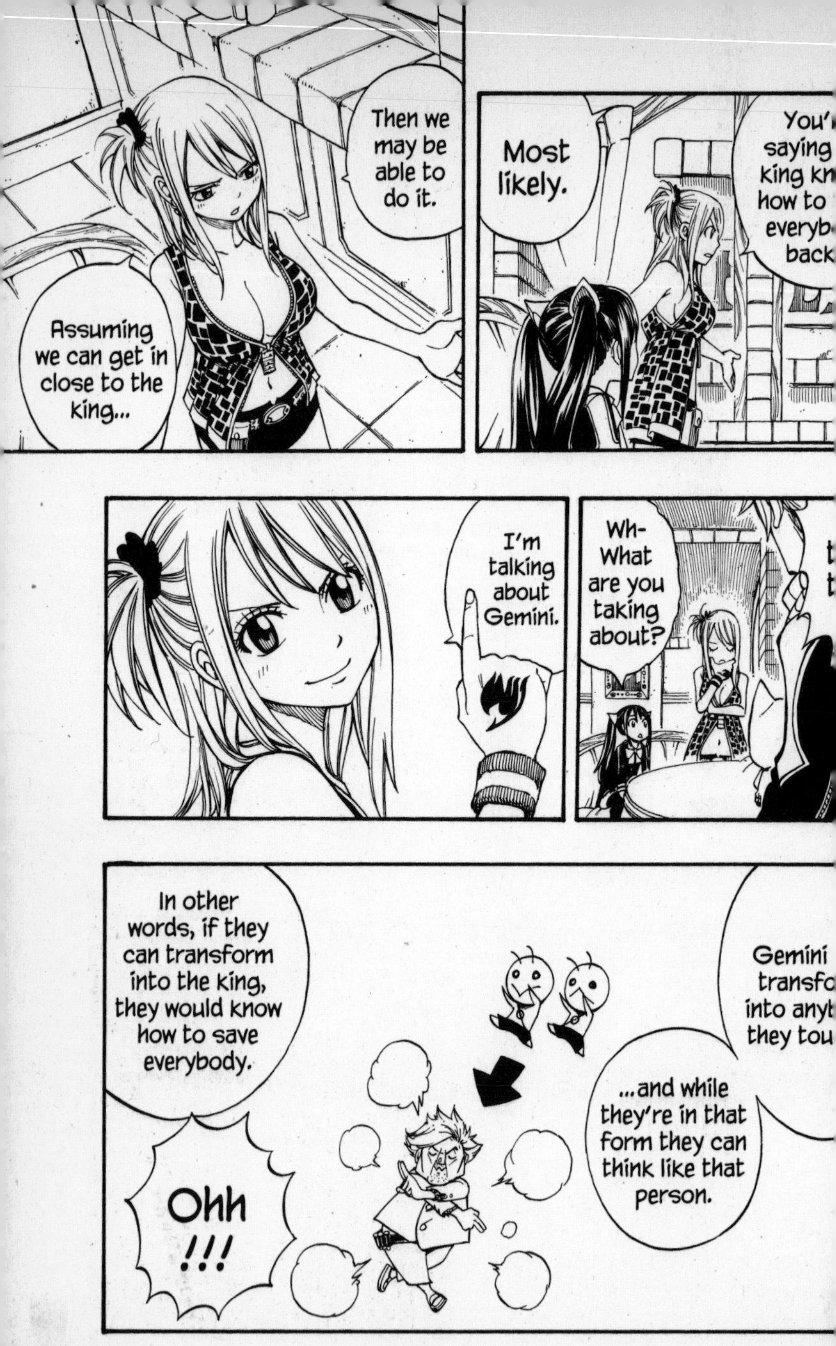
You'
saying
king kn
how to
everyb
back
Most likely.
Then we may be able to do it.
Assuming we can get in close to the king...
Wh- What are you taking about?
I'm talking about Gemini.
Gemini
transfo
into anyb
they tou
...and while they're in that form they can think like that person.
In other words, if they can transform into the king, they would know how to save everybody.
Ohh !!!

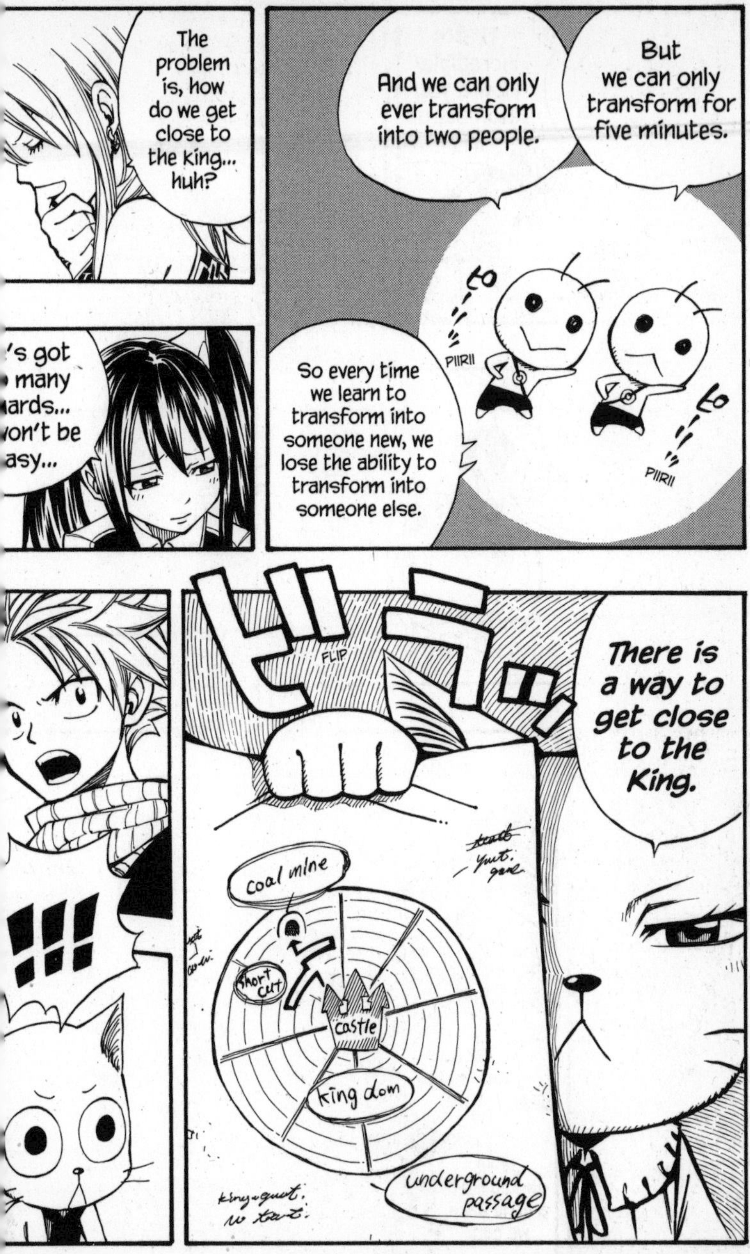
But we can only transform for five minutes.
And we can only ever transform into two people.
to
PIIRII
to
PIIRII
So every time we learn to transform into someone new, we lose the ability to transform into someone else.
The problem is, how do we get close to the king... huh?
's got
many
ards...
on't be
asy...
There is a way to get close to the King.
FLIP
coal mine
short cut
castle
kingdom
underground passage
!!!

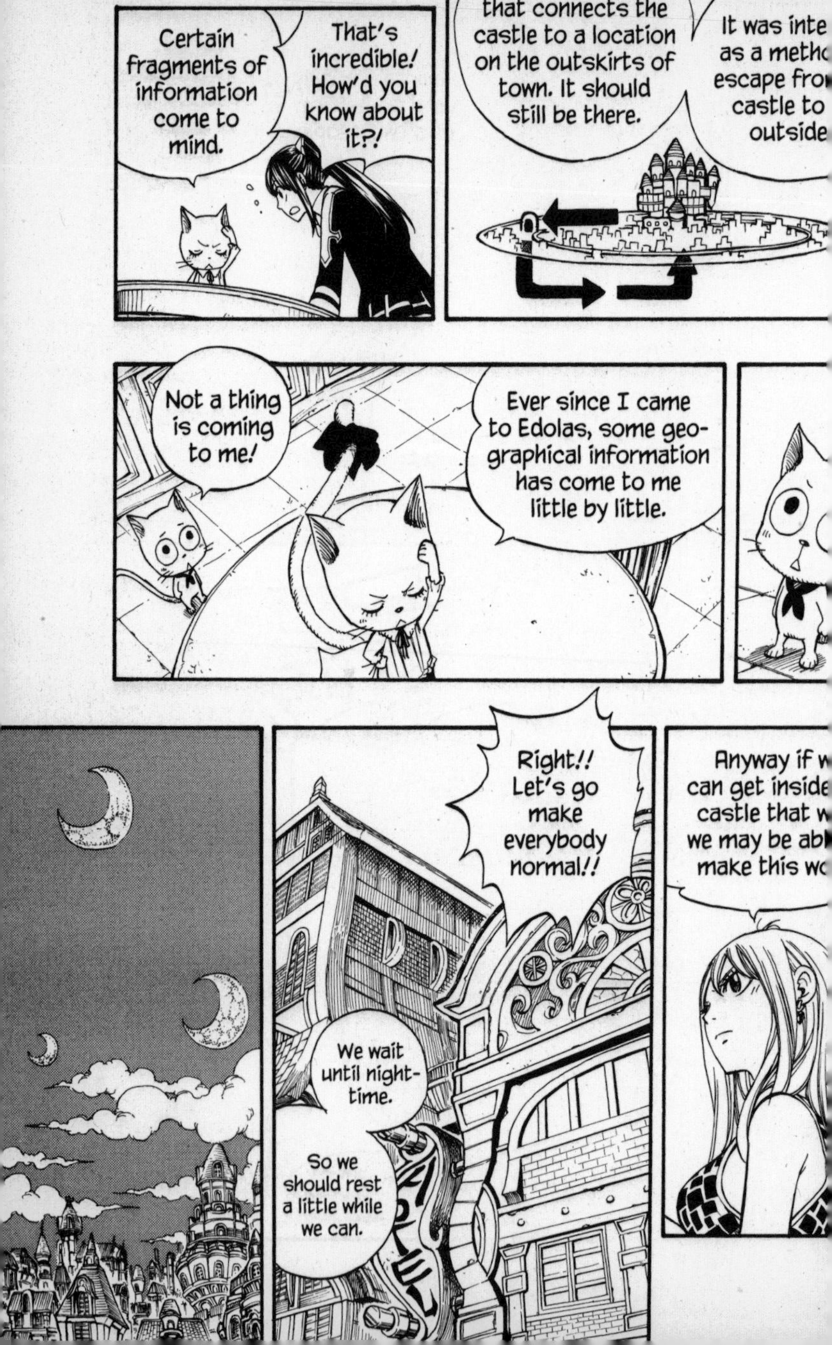
It was inte
as a metho
escape fro
castle to
outside
...but it *is* a tunnel that connects the castle to a location on the outskirts of town. It should still be there.
That's incredible! How'd you know about it?!
Certain fragments of information come to mind.
Ever since I came to Edolas, some geo-graphical information has come to me little by little.
Not a thing is coming to me!
Anyway if w
can get inside
castle that w
we may be ab
make this wo
Right!! Let's go make everybody normal!!
We wait until night-time.
So we should rest a little while we can.

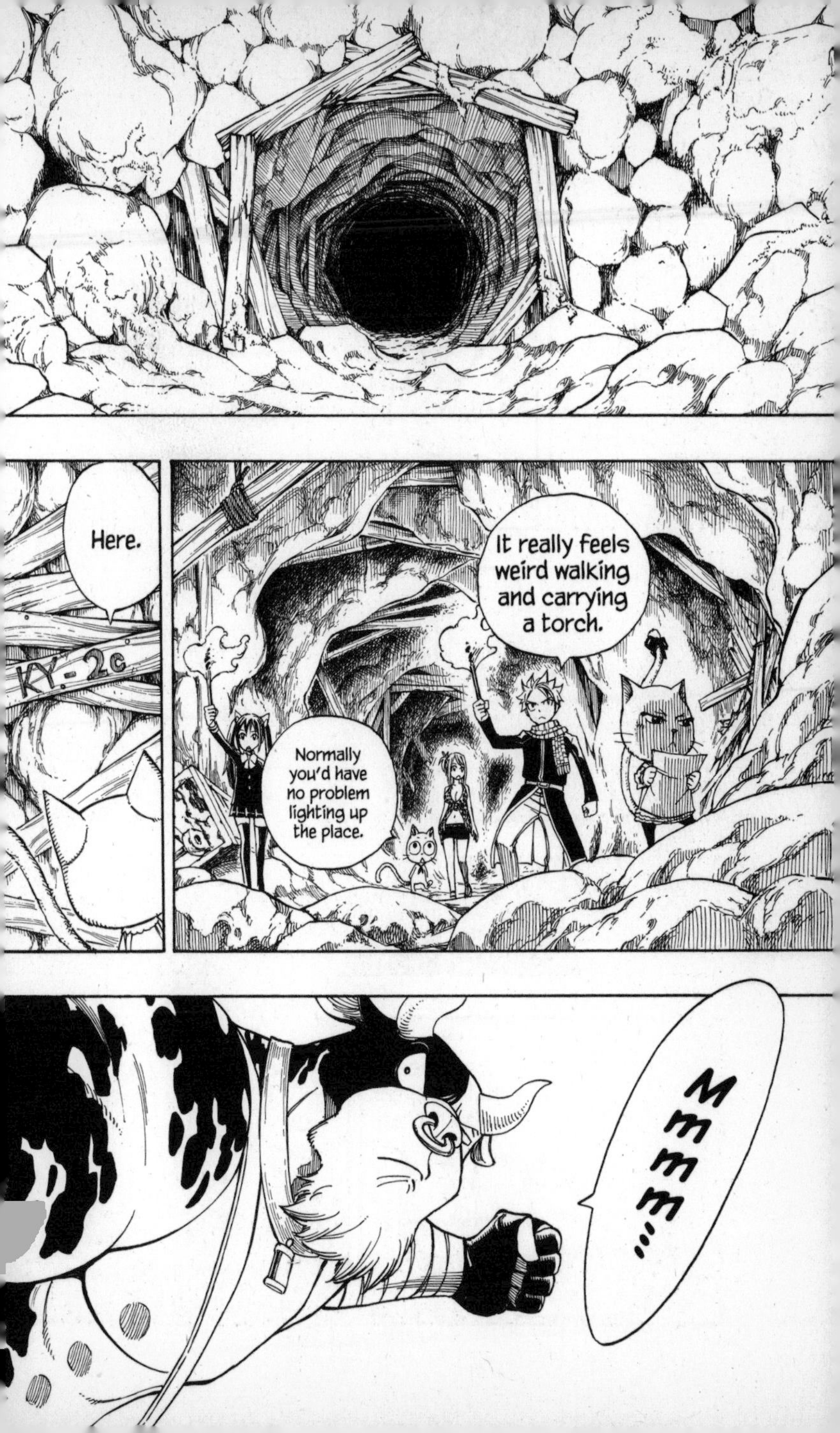
It really feels weird walking and carrying a torch.
Normally you'd have no problem lighting up the place.
Here.
KY-2c
Mmmm...

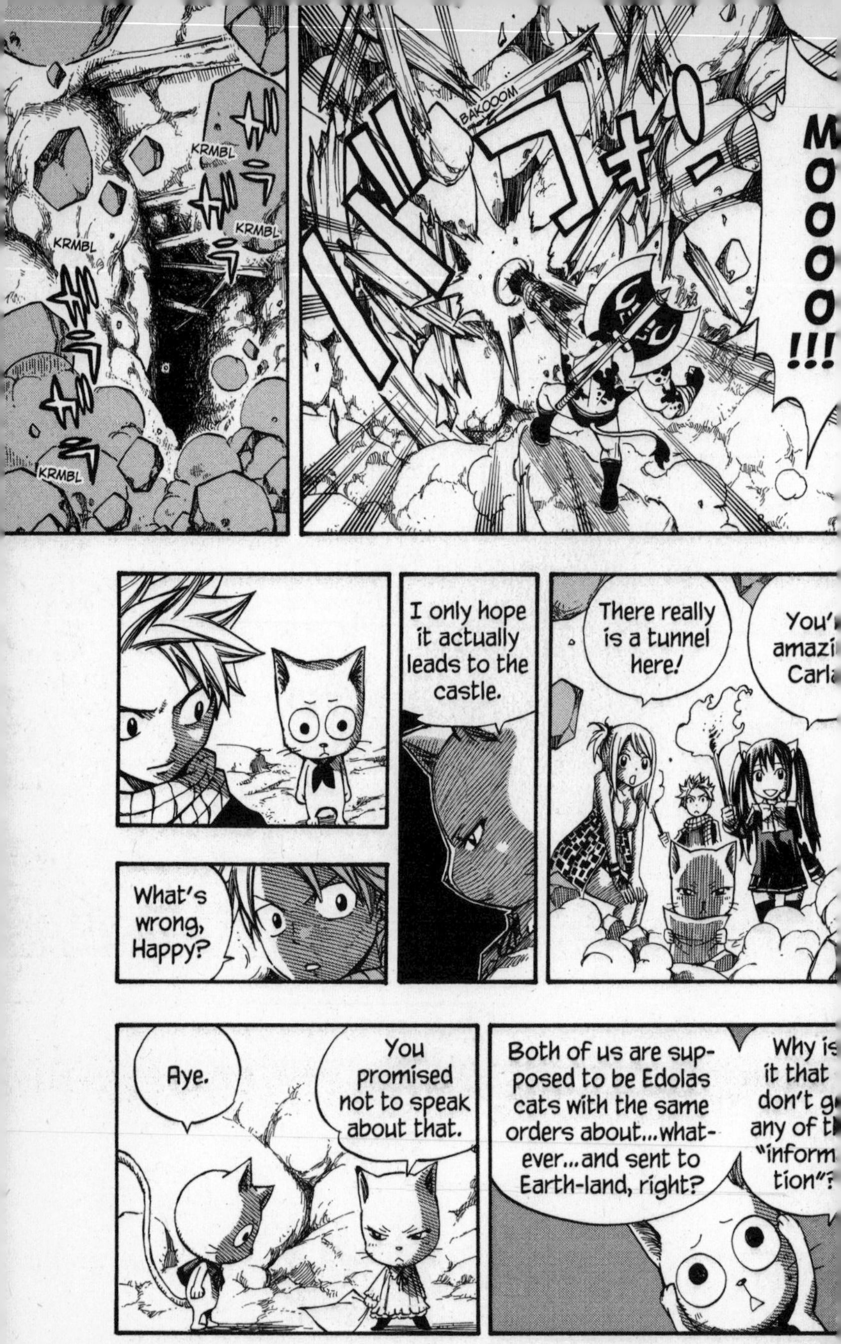
MOOOOO!!!
BAKOOOM
KRMBL
KRMBL
KRMBL
KRMBL
You' amazi Carla
There really is a tunnel here!
I only hope it actually leads to the castle.
What's wrong, Happy?
Why is it that don't g any of t "inform tion"?
Both of us are sup-posed to be Edolas cats with the same orders about...what-ever...and sent to Earth-land, right?
You promised not to speak about that.
Aye.

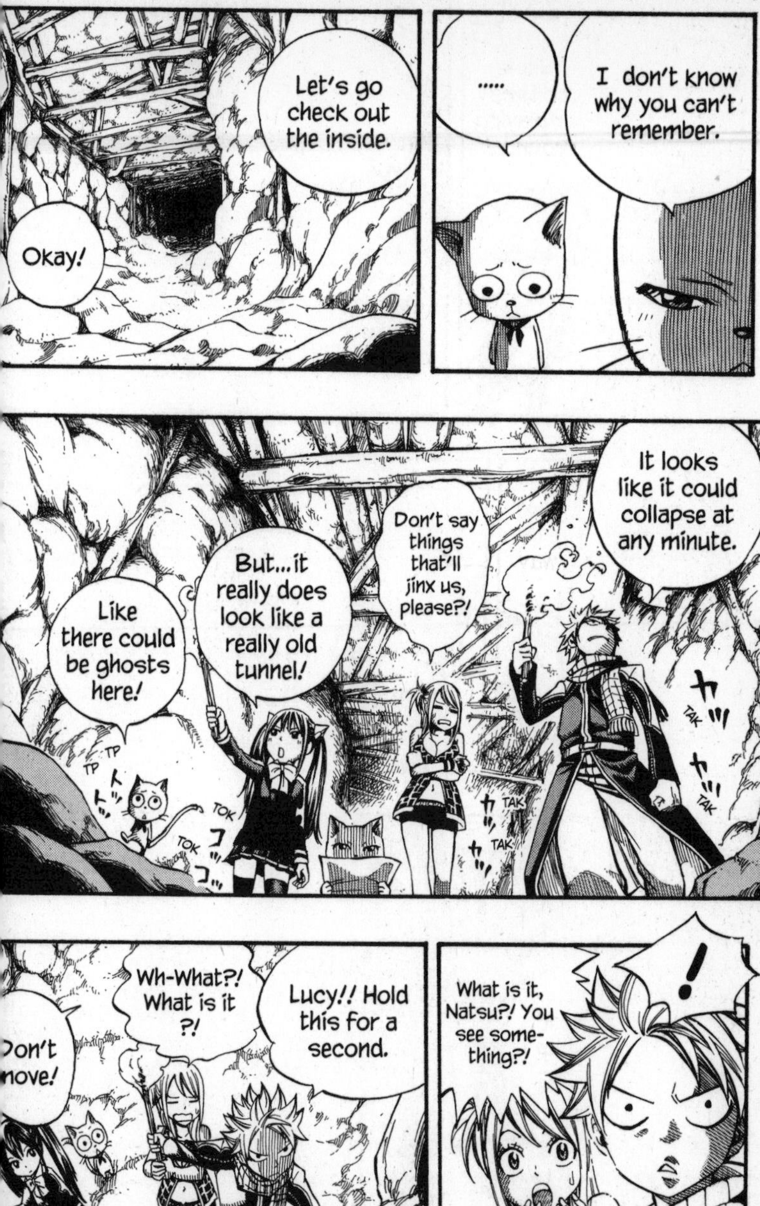
I don't know why you can't remember.
.....
Let's go check out the inside.
Okay!
It looks like it could collapse at any minute.
TAK
TAK
Don't say things that'll jinx us, please?!
TAK
TAK
But...it really does look like a really old tunnel!
Like there could be ghosts here!
TOK
TOK
TP
TP
What is it, Natsu?! You see some-thing?!
Lucy!! Hold this for a second.
Wh-What?! What is it ?!
Don't move!

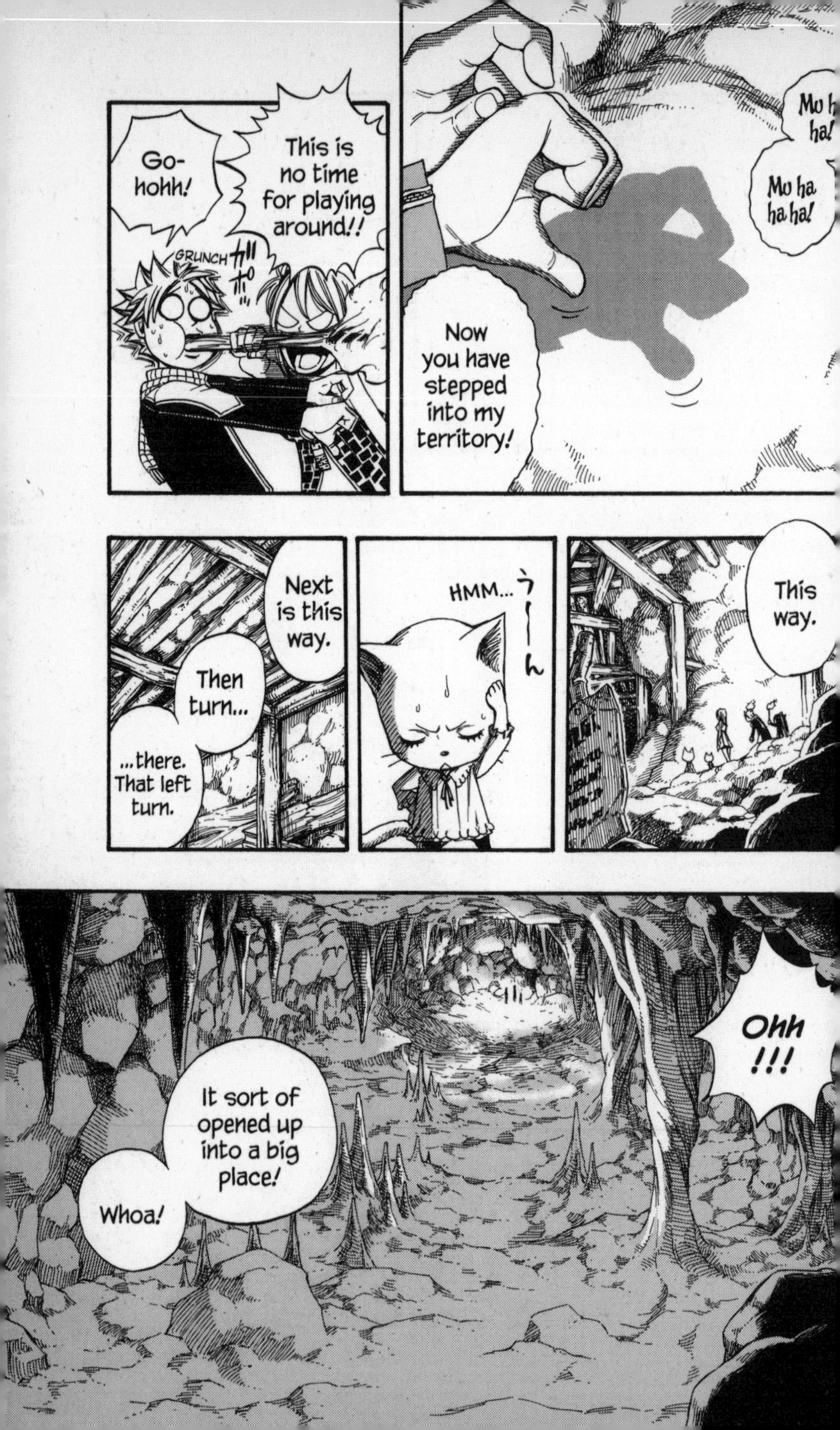
Mo h
ha!
Mo ha ha ha!
Now you have stepped into my territory!
This is no time for playing around!!
Go-hohh!
GRUNCH
This way.
HMM...
Next is this way.
Then turn...
...there. That left turn.
Ohh !!!
It sort of opened up into a big place!
Whoa!

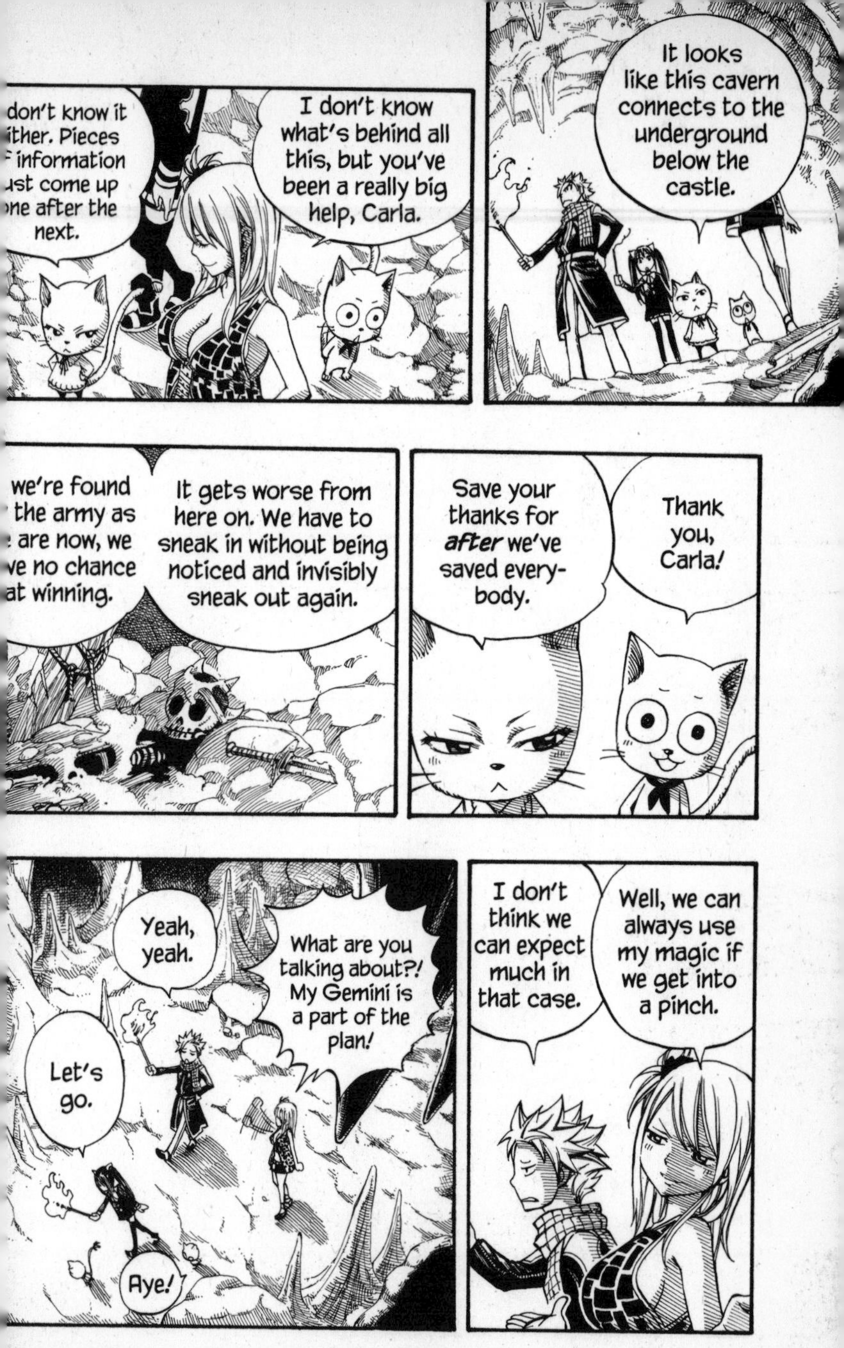
It looks like this cavern connects to the underground below the castle.
I don't know what's behind all this, but you've been a really big help, Carla.
don't know it ither. Pieces information ust come up ne after the next.
Thank you, Carla!
Save your thanks for *after* we've saved every-body.
It gets worse from here on. We have to sneak in without being noticed and invisibly sneak out again.
we're found the army as are now, we ve no chance at winning.
Well, we can always use my magic if we get into a pinch.
I don't think we can expect much in that case.
What are you talking about?! My Gemini is a part of the plan!
Yeah, yeah.
Let's go.
Aye!

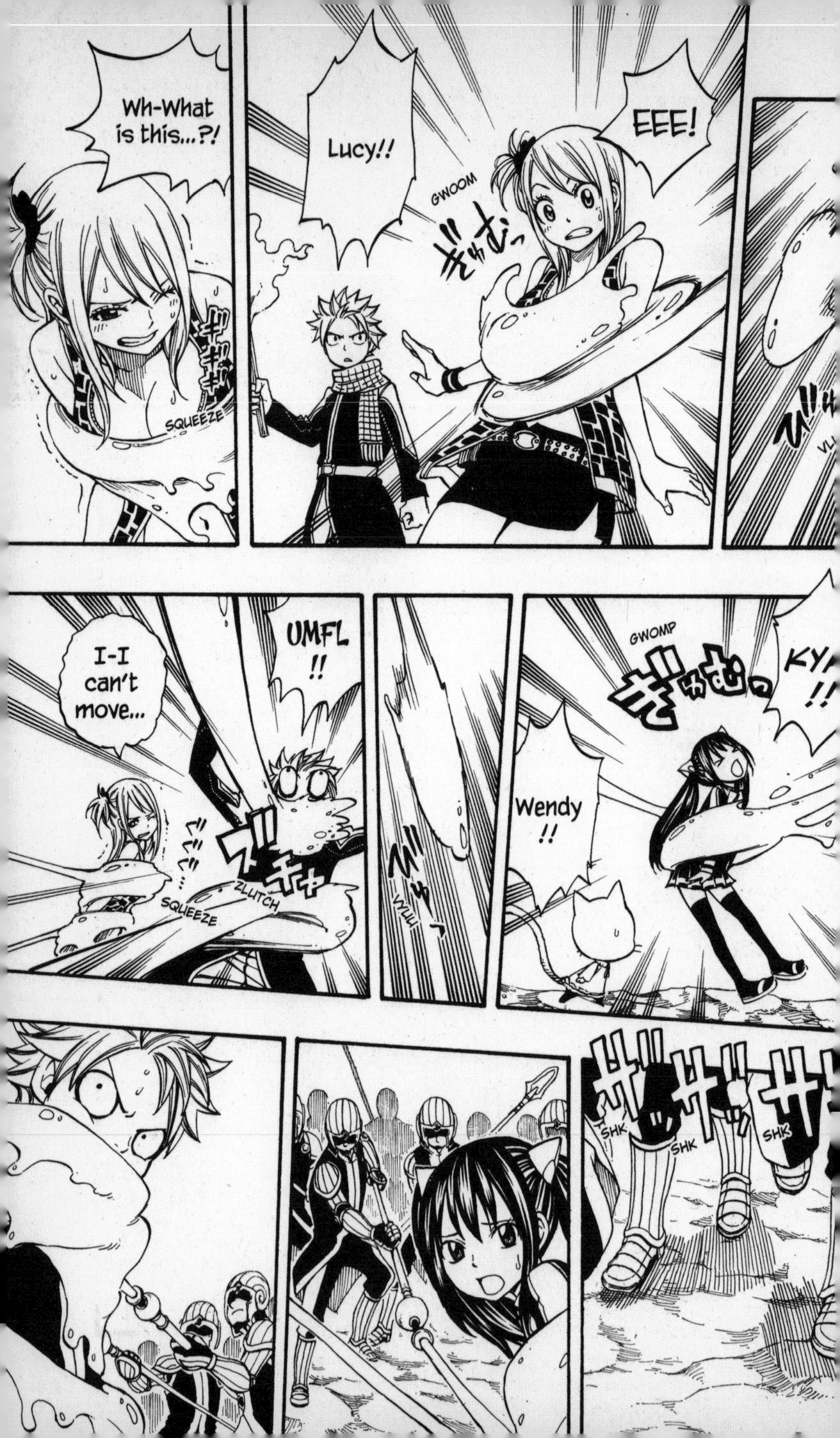

VLI
EEE!
GWOOM
ぎゅむっ
Lucy!!
Wh-What is this...?!
ギギギ
SQUEEZE
KY
!!
GWOMP
ぎゅむっ
Wendy
!!
VLLI
UMFL
!!
I-I can't move...
ブチャ
ZLUTCH
SQUEEZE
ザッザッザッ
SHK
SHK
SHK

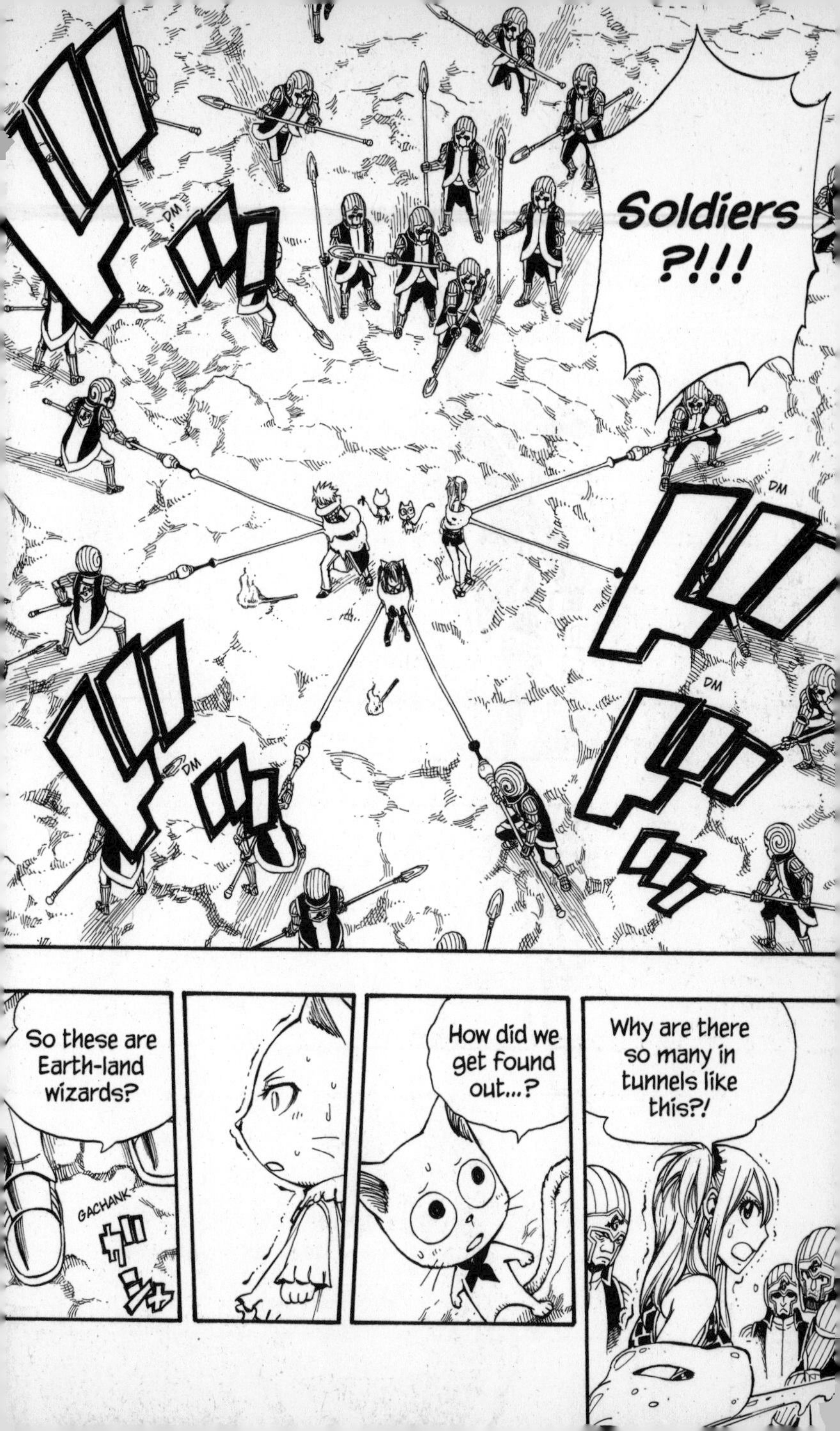
Soldiers?!!!
DM
DM
DM
DM
Why are there so many in tunnels like this?!
How did we get found out...?
So these are Earth-land wizards?
GACHANK

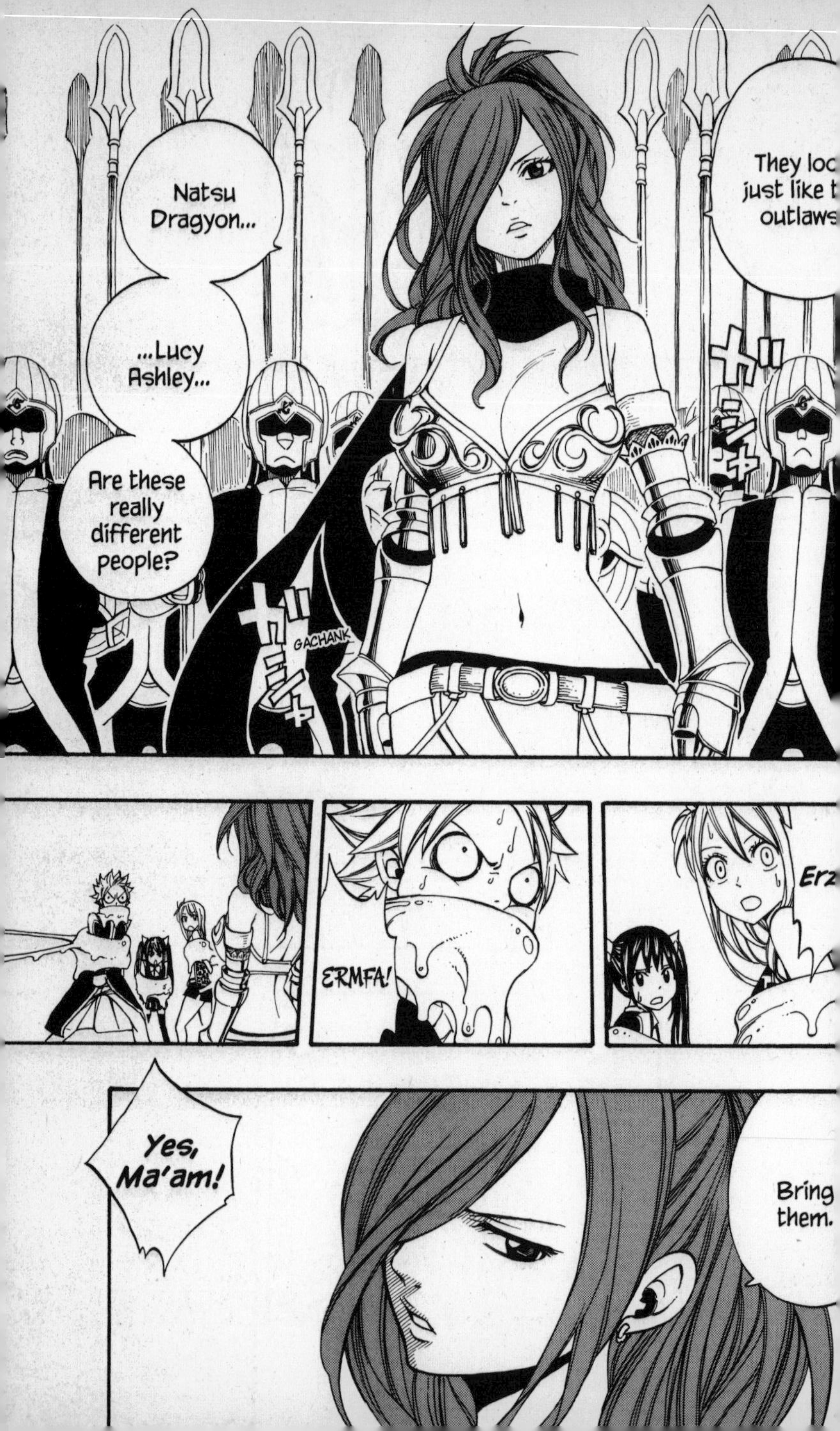
They lo just like t outlaws
Natsu Dragyon...
...Lucy Ashley...
Are these really different people?
GACHANK
Erz
ERMFA!
Bring them.
Yes, Ma'am!

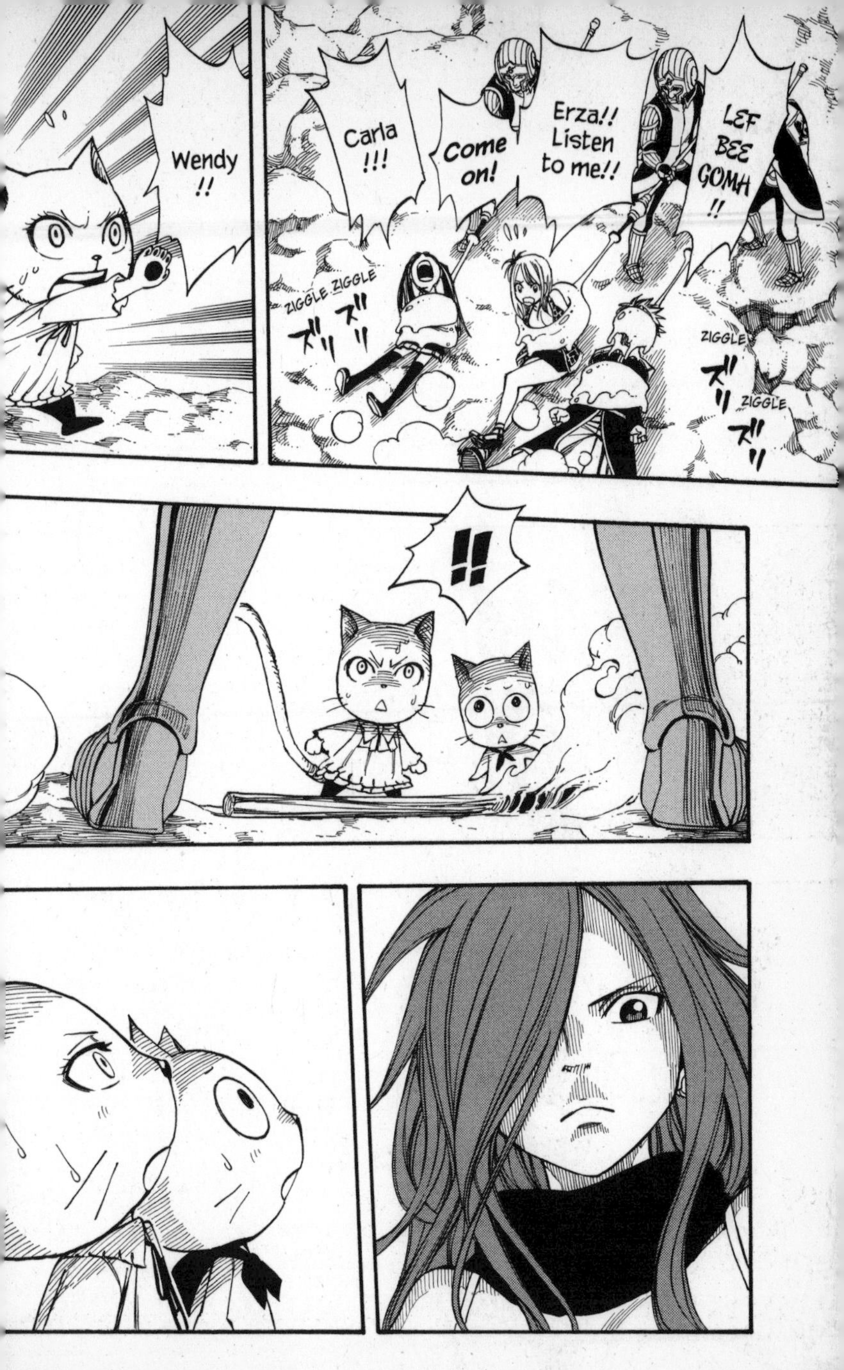
LEF BEE GOMA!!
Erza!! Listen to me!!
Come on!
Carla!!!
ZIGGLE
ZIGGLE
ZIGGLE ZIGGLE
Wendy!!
!!

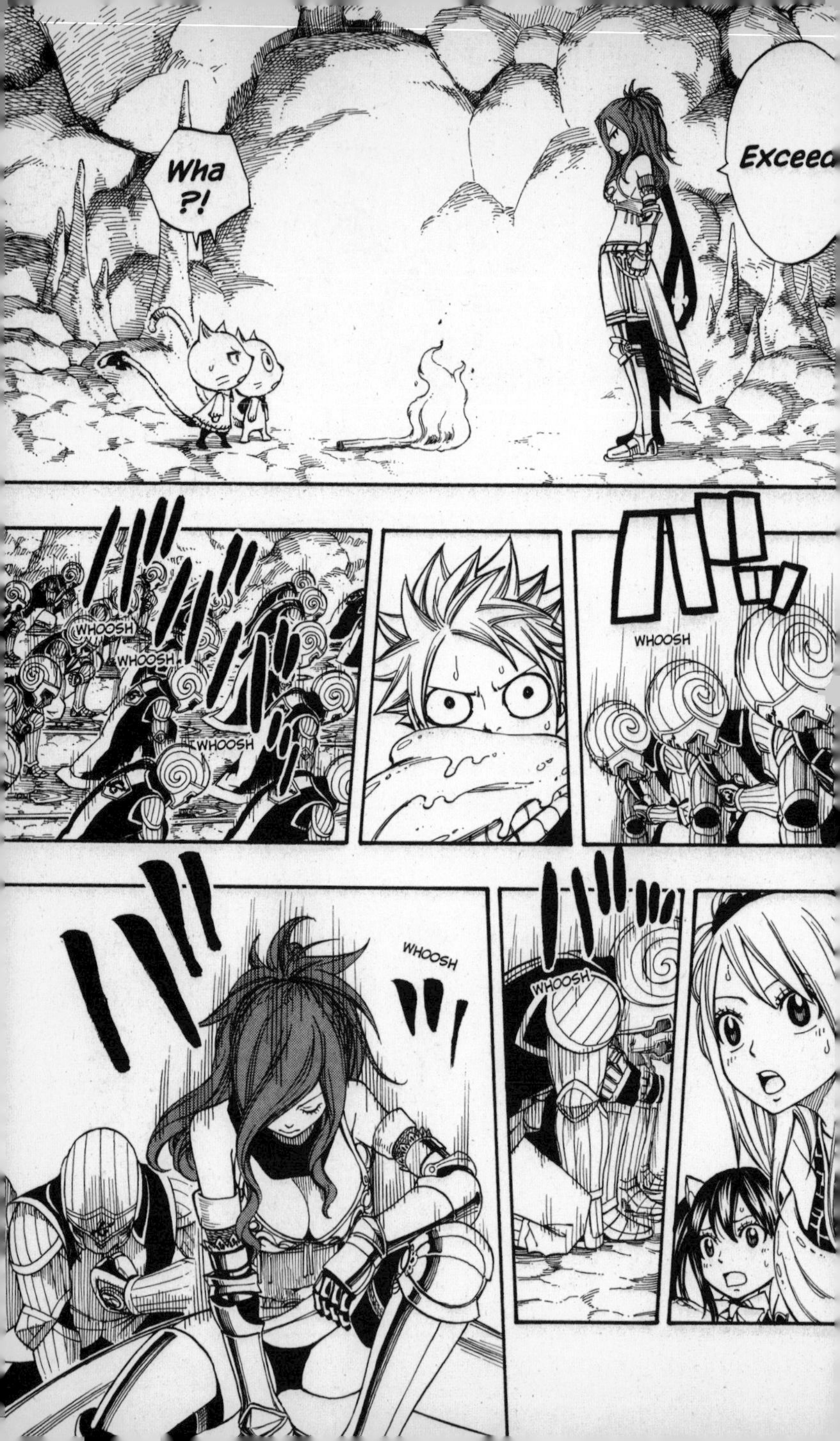
Exceed
Wha ?!
WHOOSH
WHOOSH
WHOOSH
WHOOSH
WHOOSH
WHOOSH

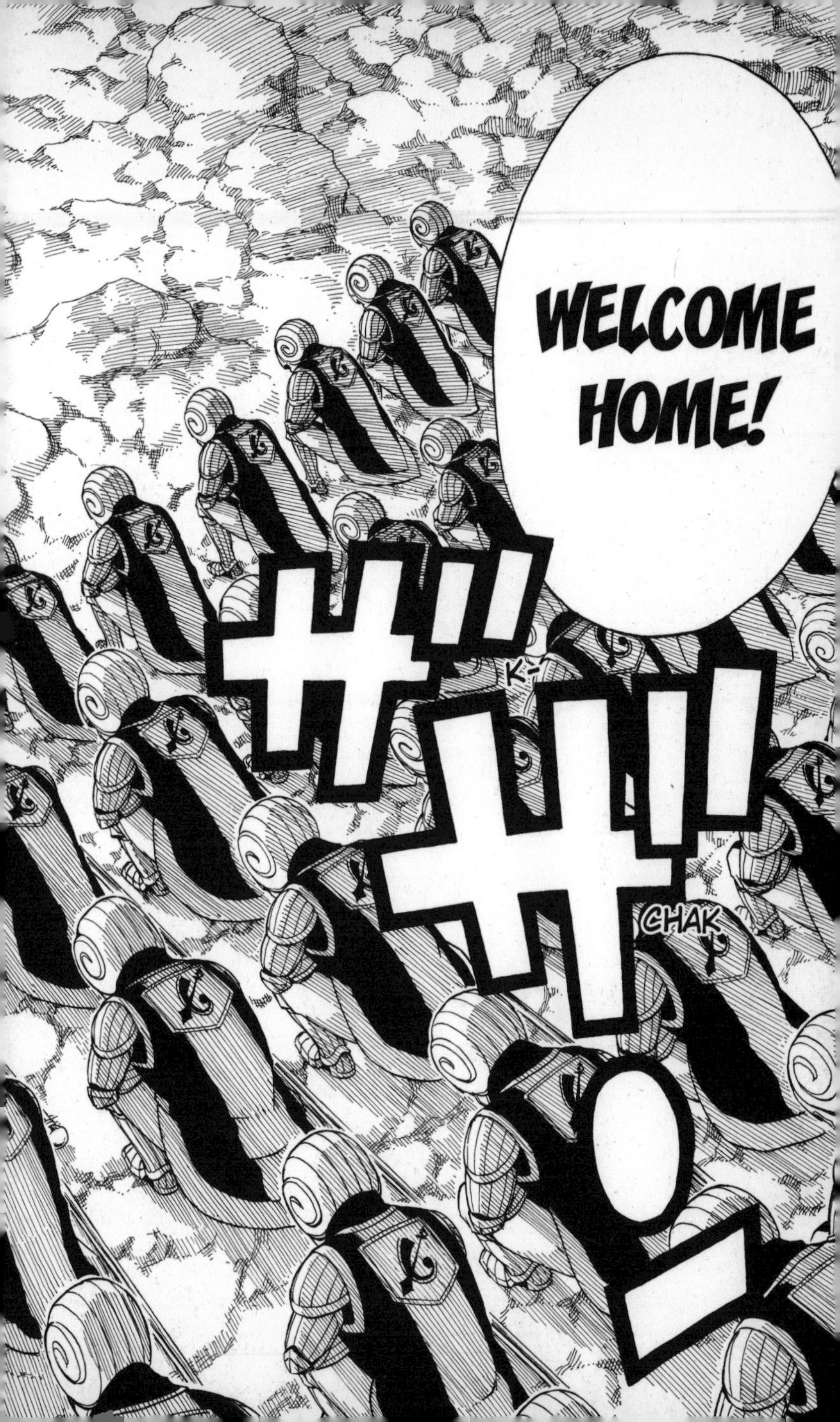
WELCOME HOME!
K-
CHAK

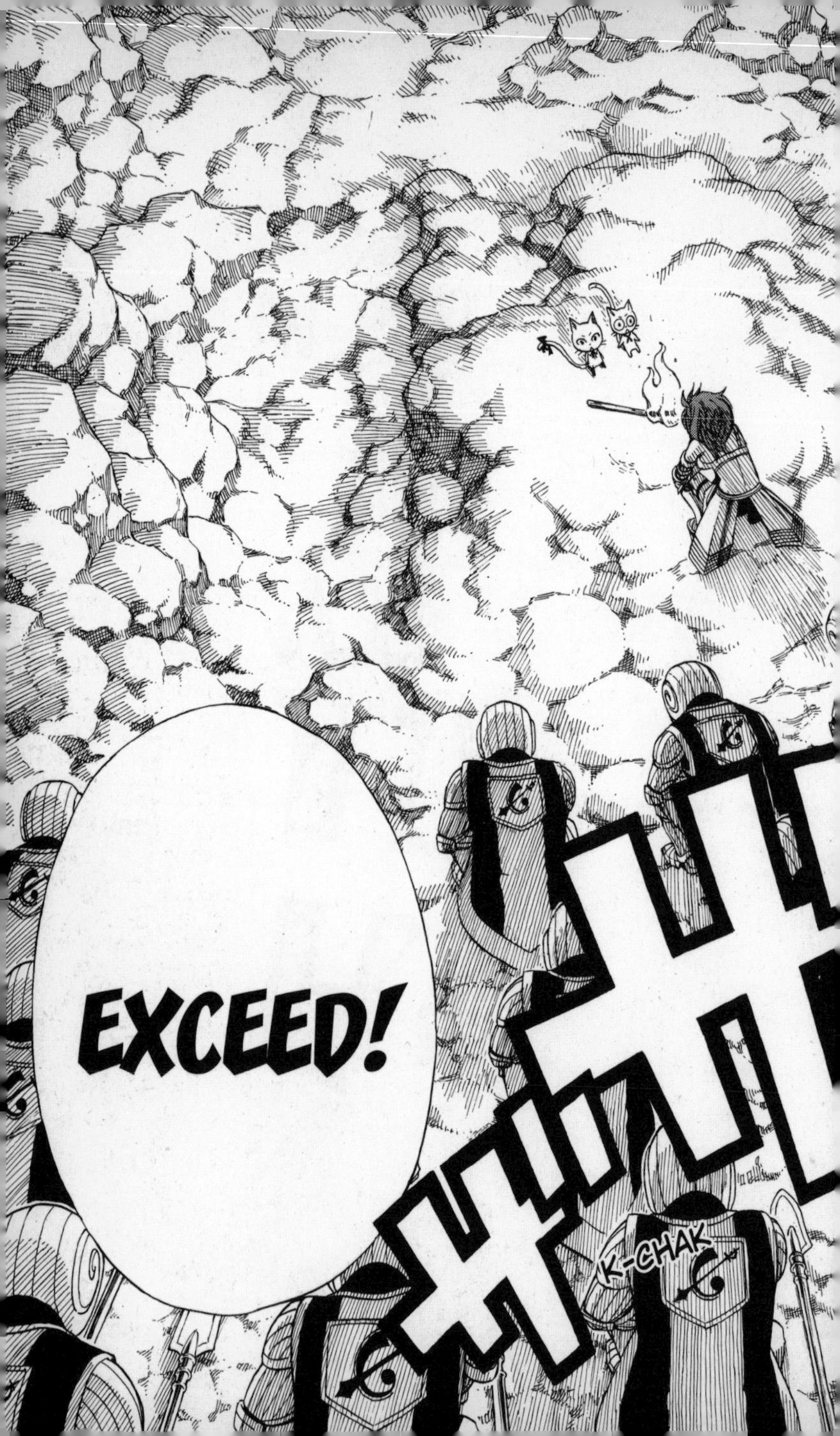
EXCEED!
K-CHAK

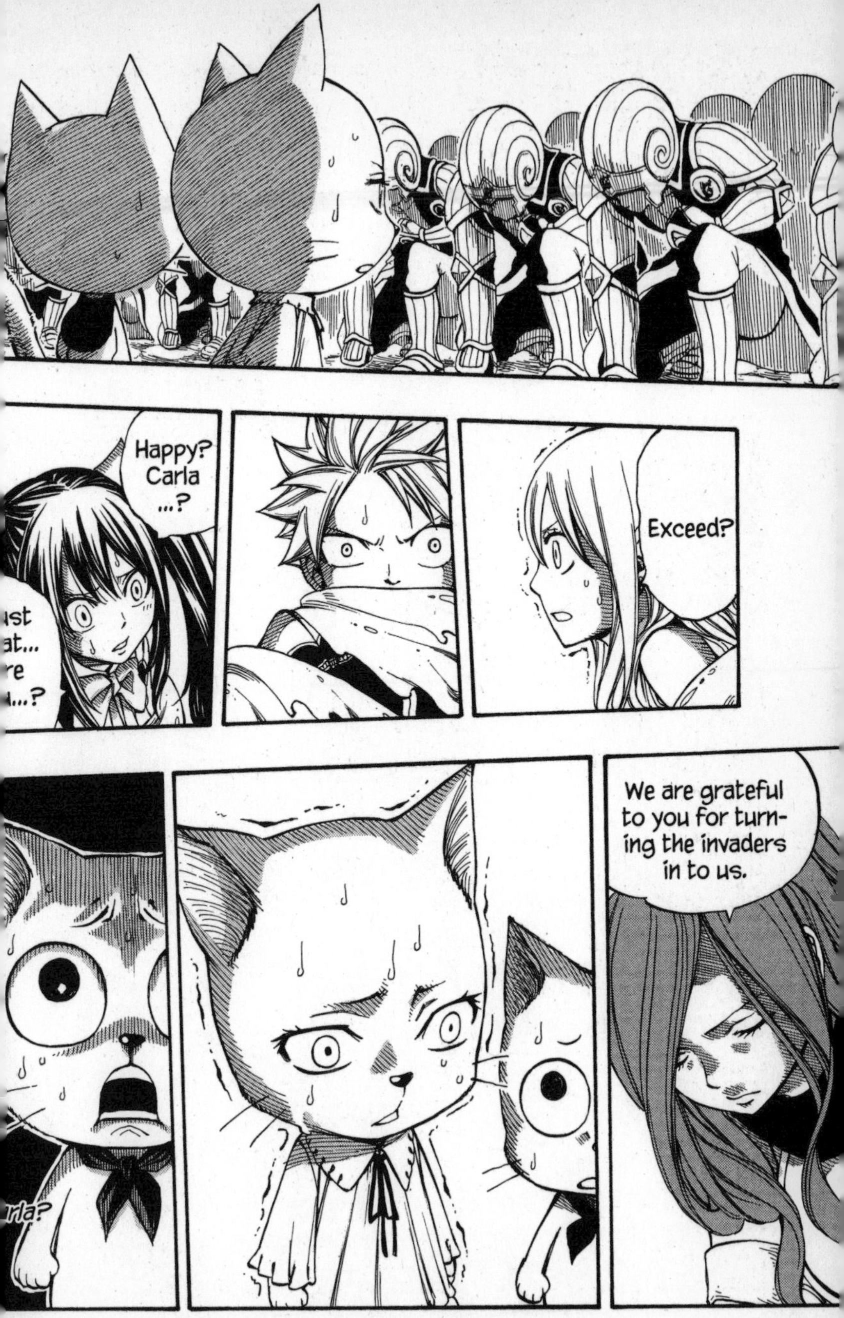
Exceed?
Happy? Carla ...?
We are grateful to you for turn-ing the invaders in to us.

Chapter 176, Extalia

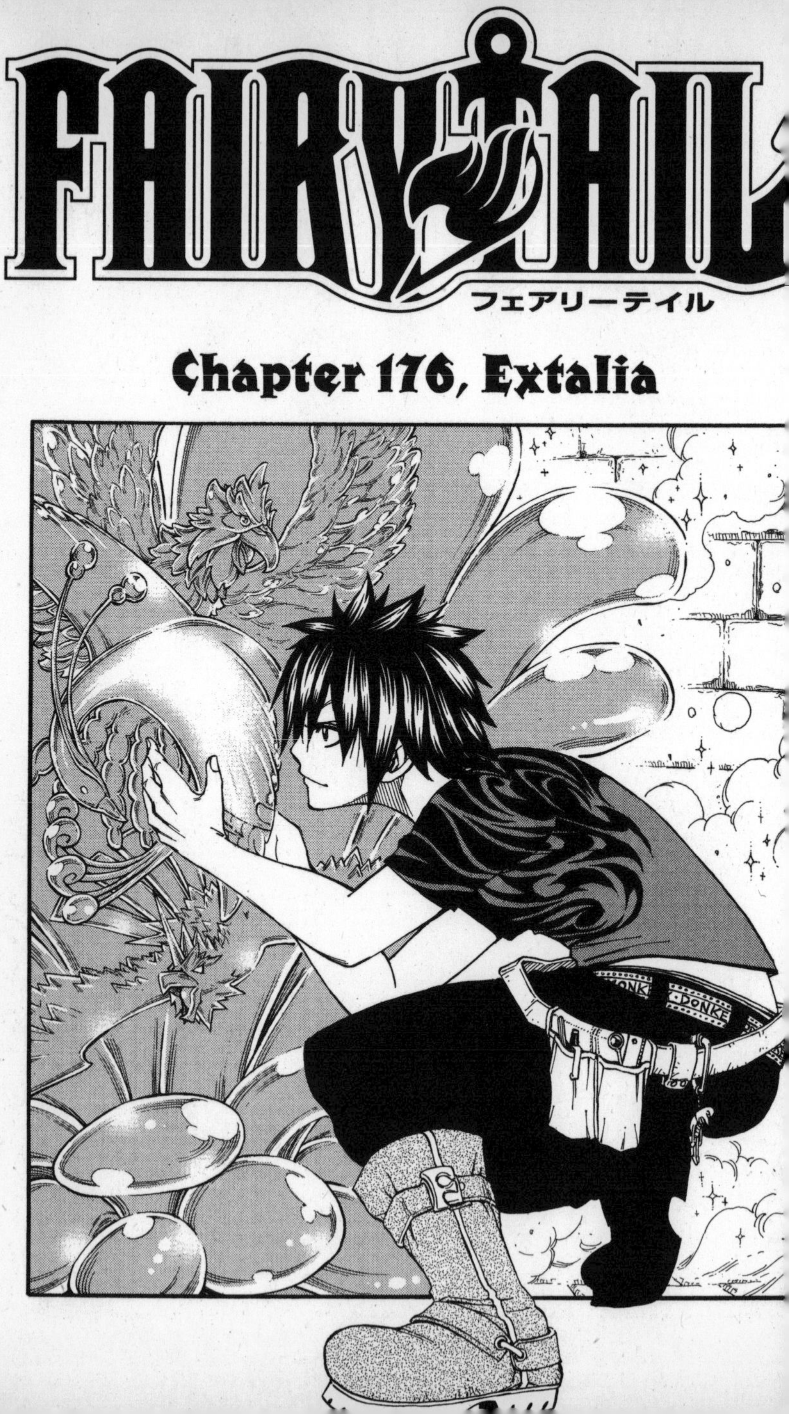

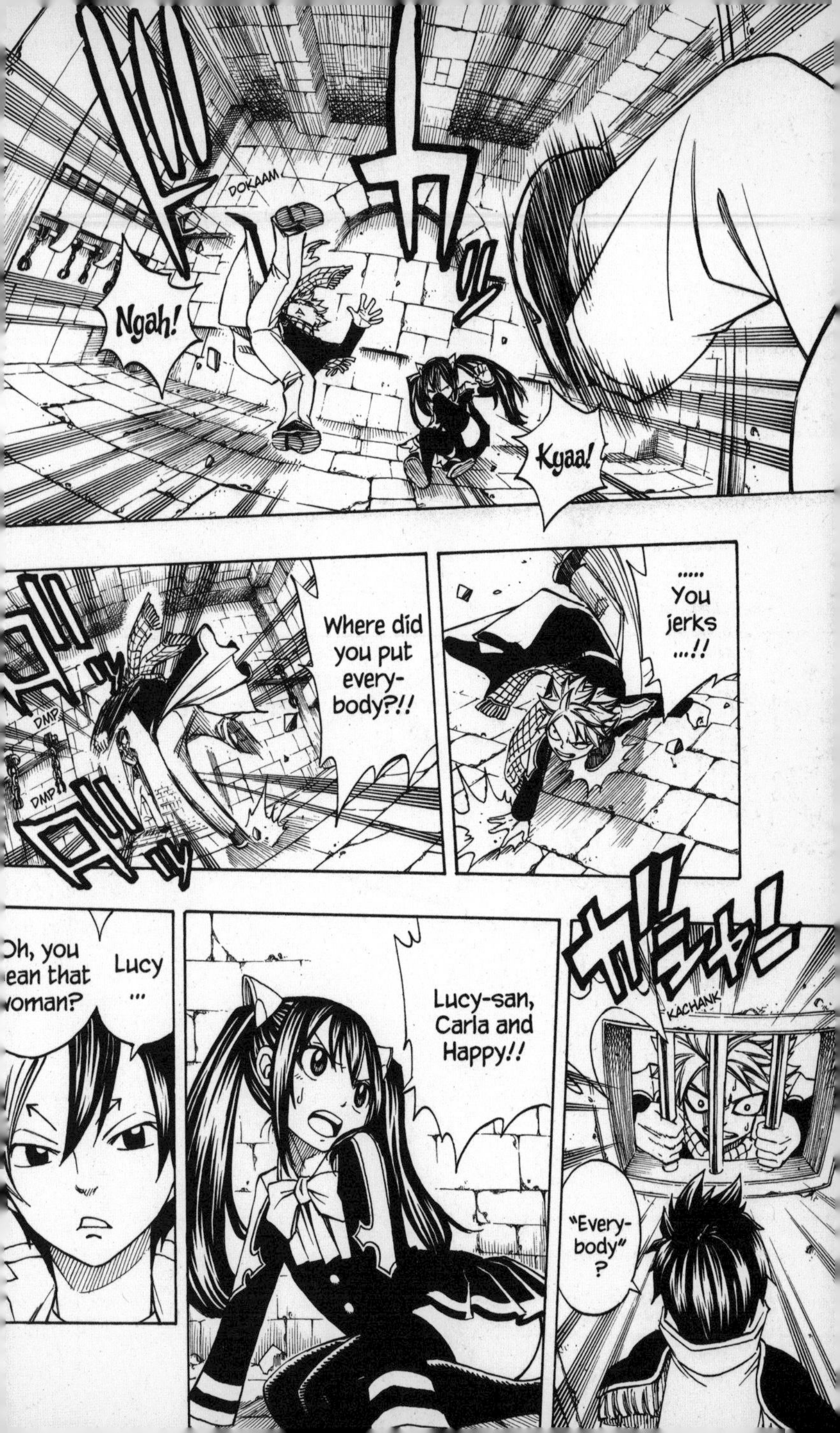
DOKAAM
Ngah!
Kyaa!
..... You jerks ...!!
Where did you put every-body?!!
DMP
DMP
KACHANK
"Every-body"?
Lucy-san, Carla and Happy!!
Lucy ...
Oh, you ean that oman?

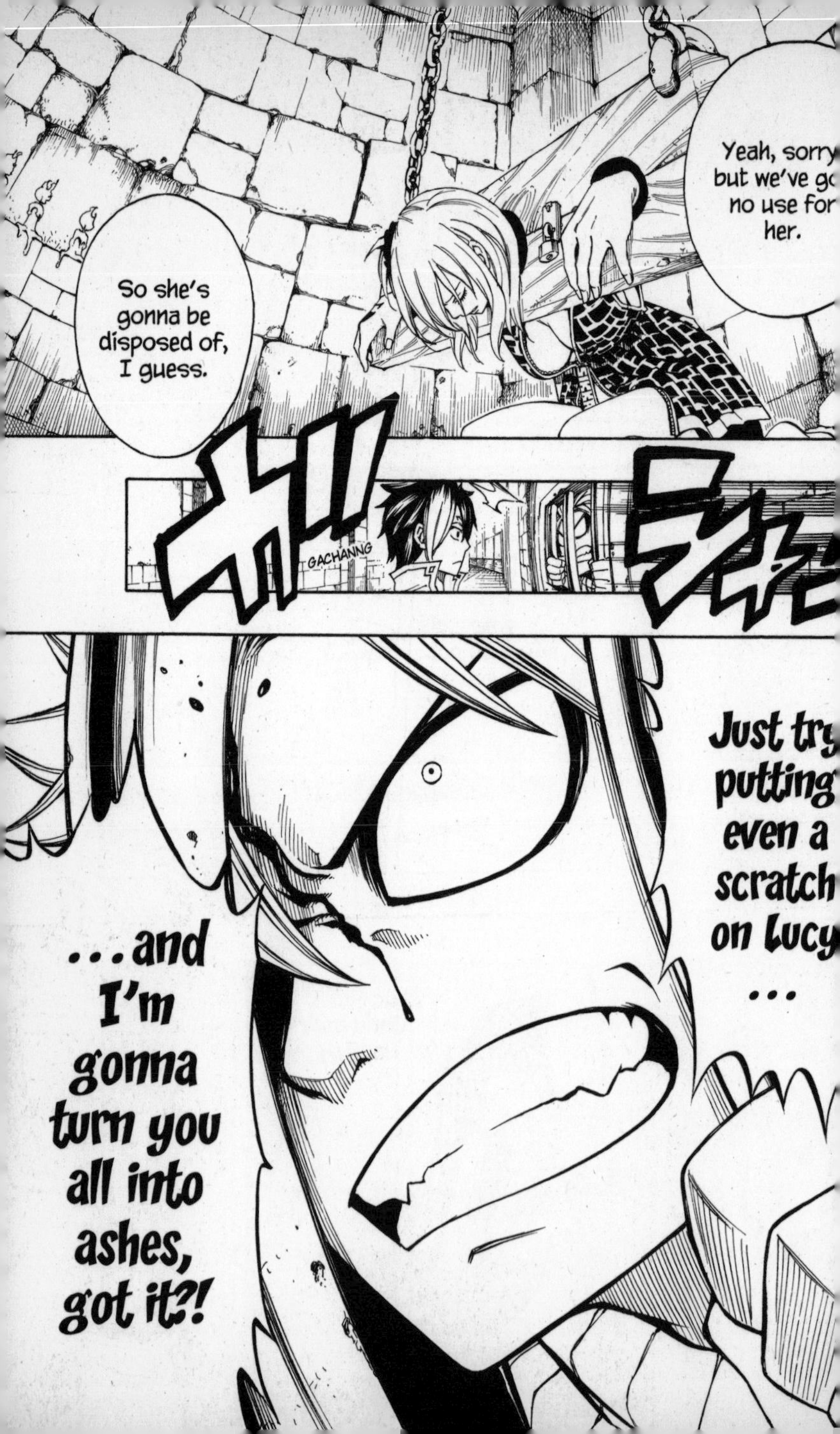
Yeah, sorry but we've go no use for her.
So she's gonna be disposed of, I guess.
GACHANNG
Just try putting even a scratch on Lucy ...
...and I'm gonna turn you all into ashes, got it?!

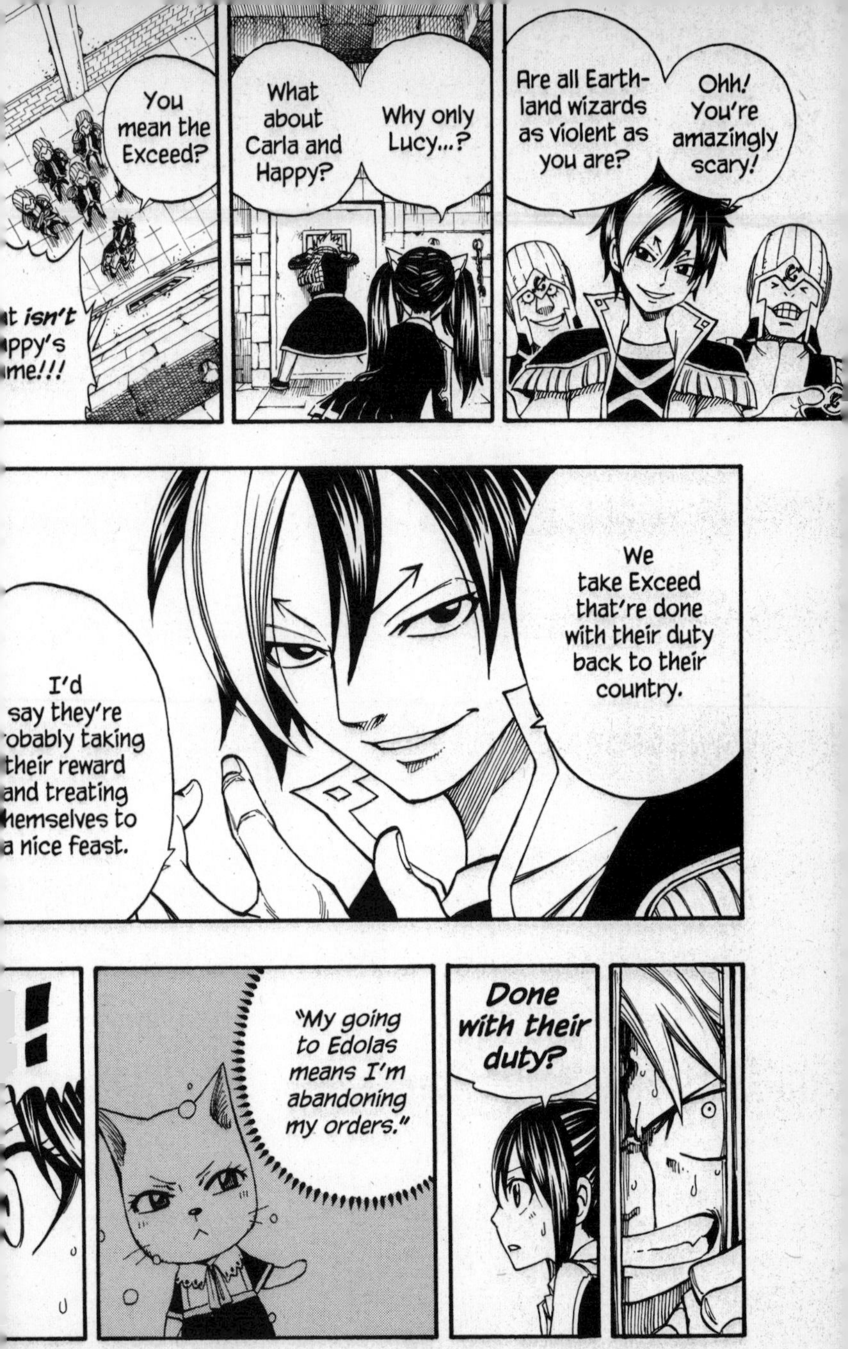
Ohh! You're amazingly scary!
Are all Earth-land wizards as violent as you are?
Why only Lucy...?
What about Carla and Happy?
You mean the Exceed?
t isn't ppy's me!!!
We take Exceed that're done with their duty back to their country.
I'd say they're robably taking their reward and treating hemselves to a nice feast.
Done with their duty?
"My going to Edolas means I'm abandoning my orders."
!!

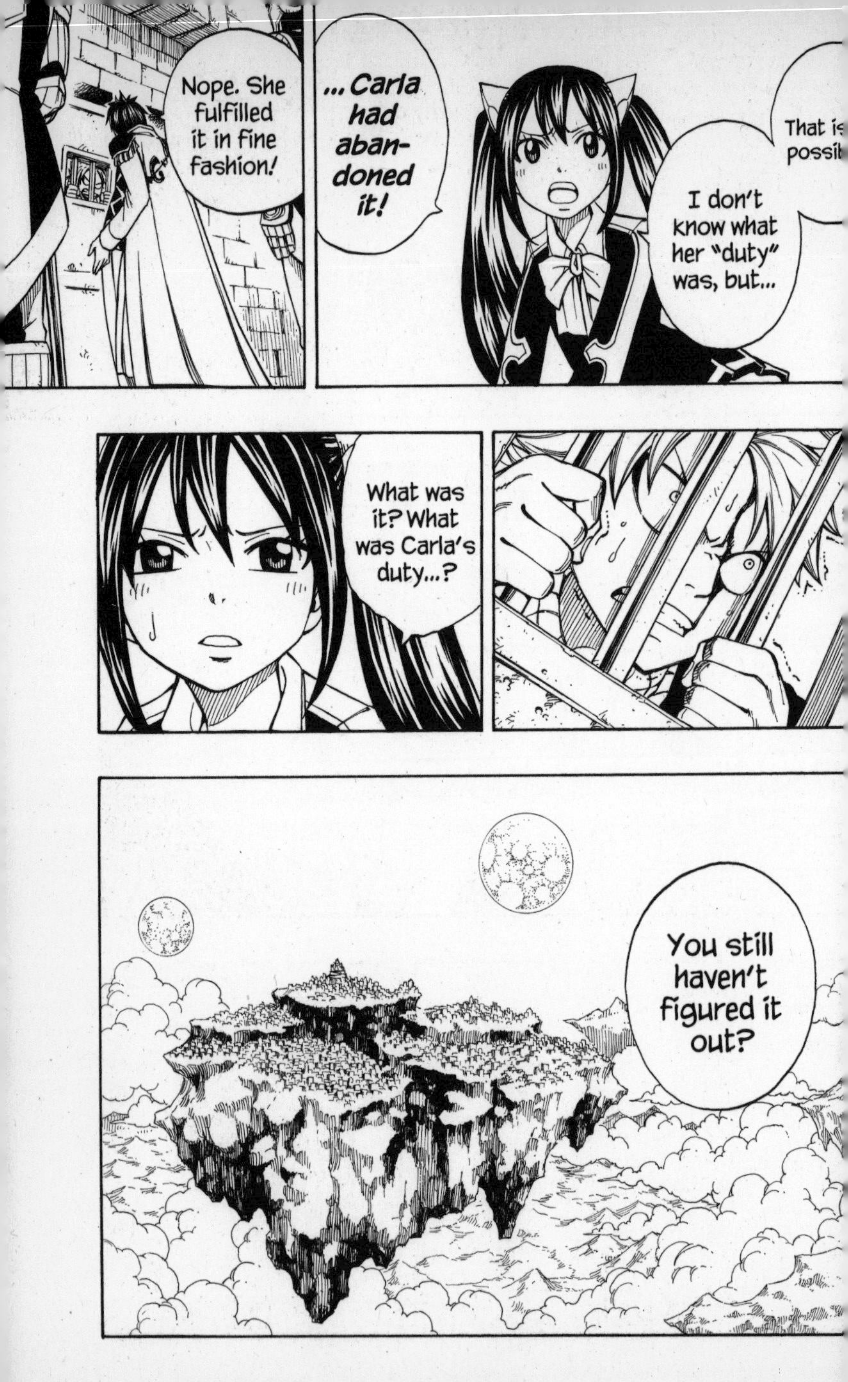
That is
I don't know what her "duty" was, but...
...Carla had aban-doned it!
Nope. She fulfilled it in fine fashion!
What was it? What was Carla's duty...?
You still haven't figured it out?

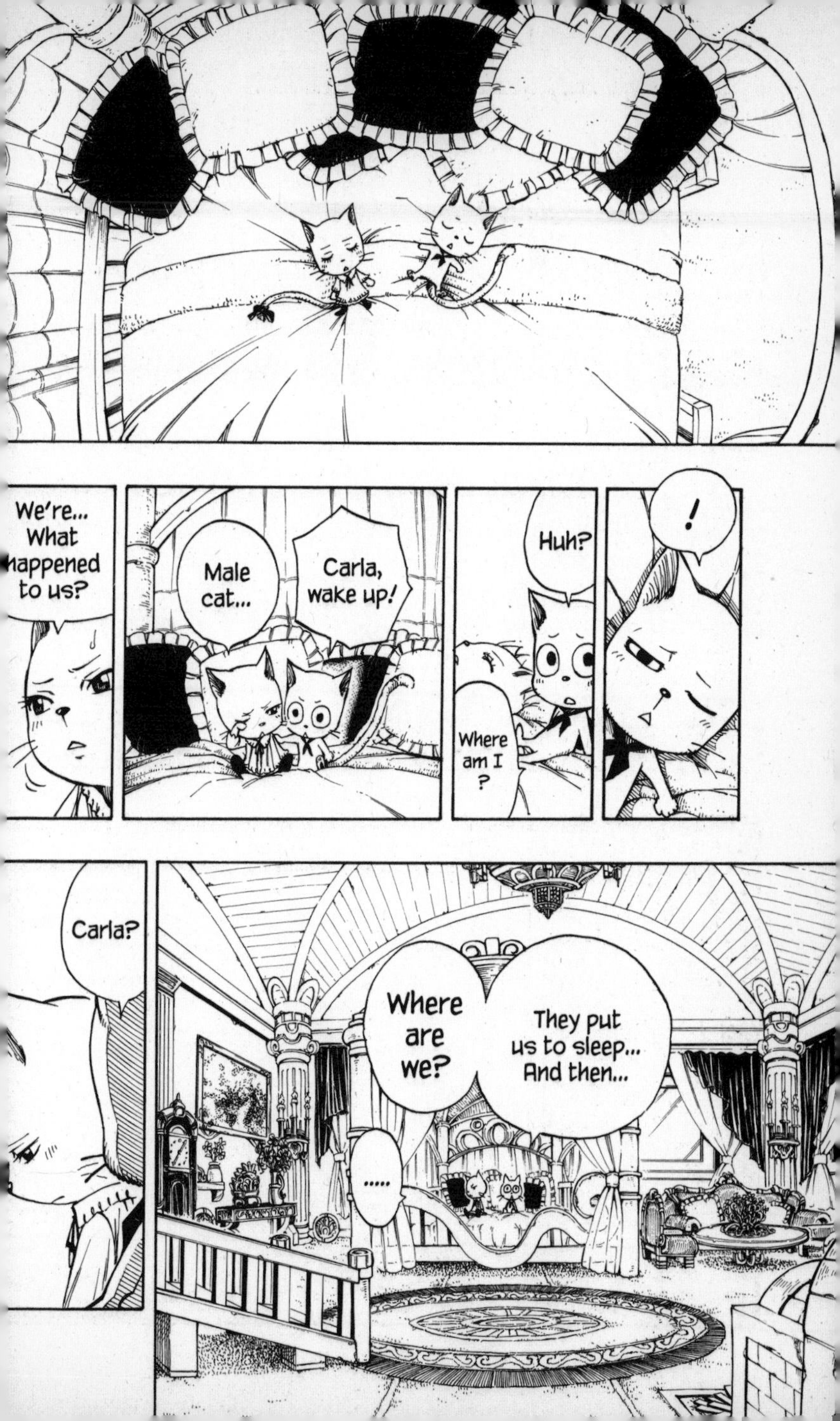
!
Huh?
Where am I ?
Carla, wake up!
Male cat...
We're... What happened to us?
They put us to sleep... And then...
Where are we?
.....
Carla?

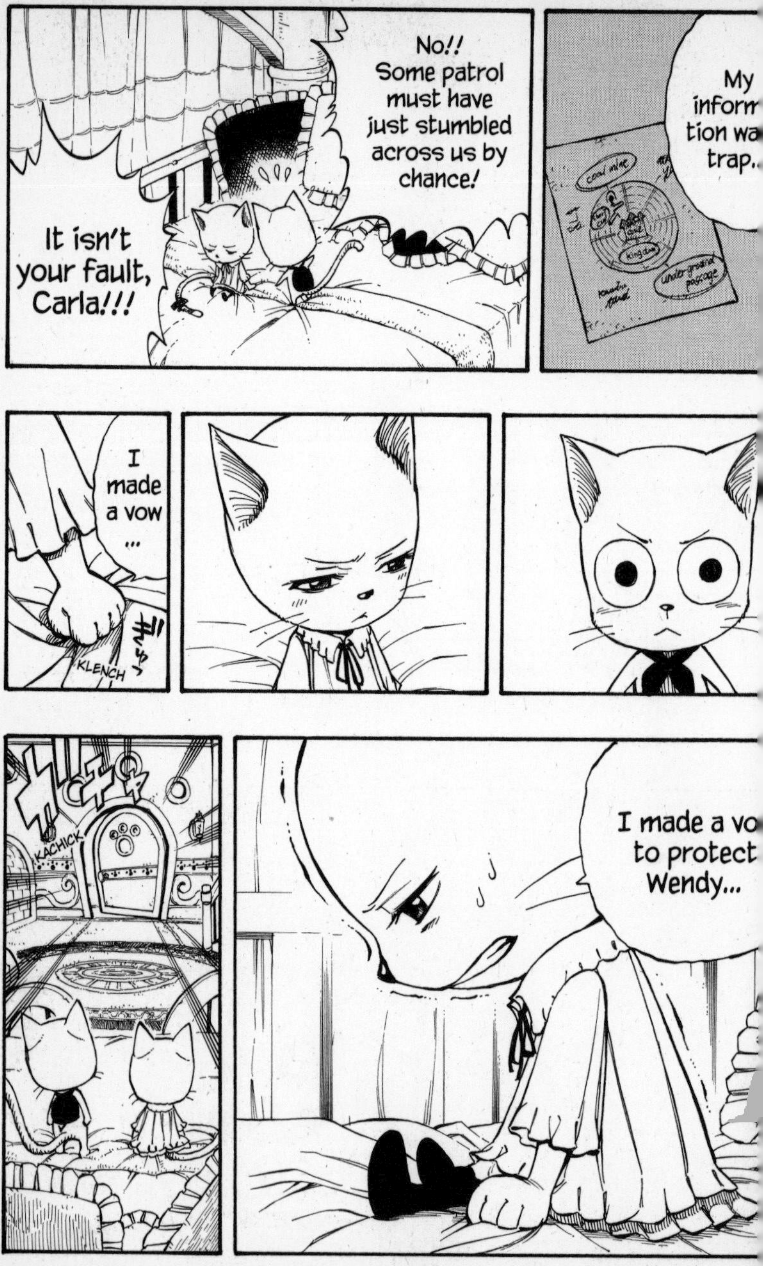
My inform tion wa trap..
coal mine
kingdom
underground passage
No!! Some patrol must have just stumbled across us by chance!
It isn't your fault, Carla!!!
I made a vow ...
KLENCH
I made a vo to protect Wendy...
KACHICK

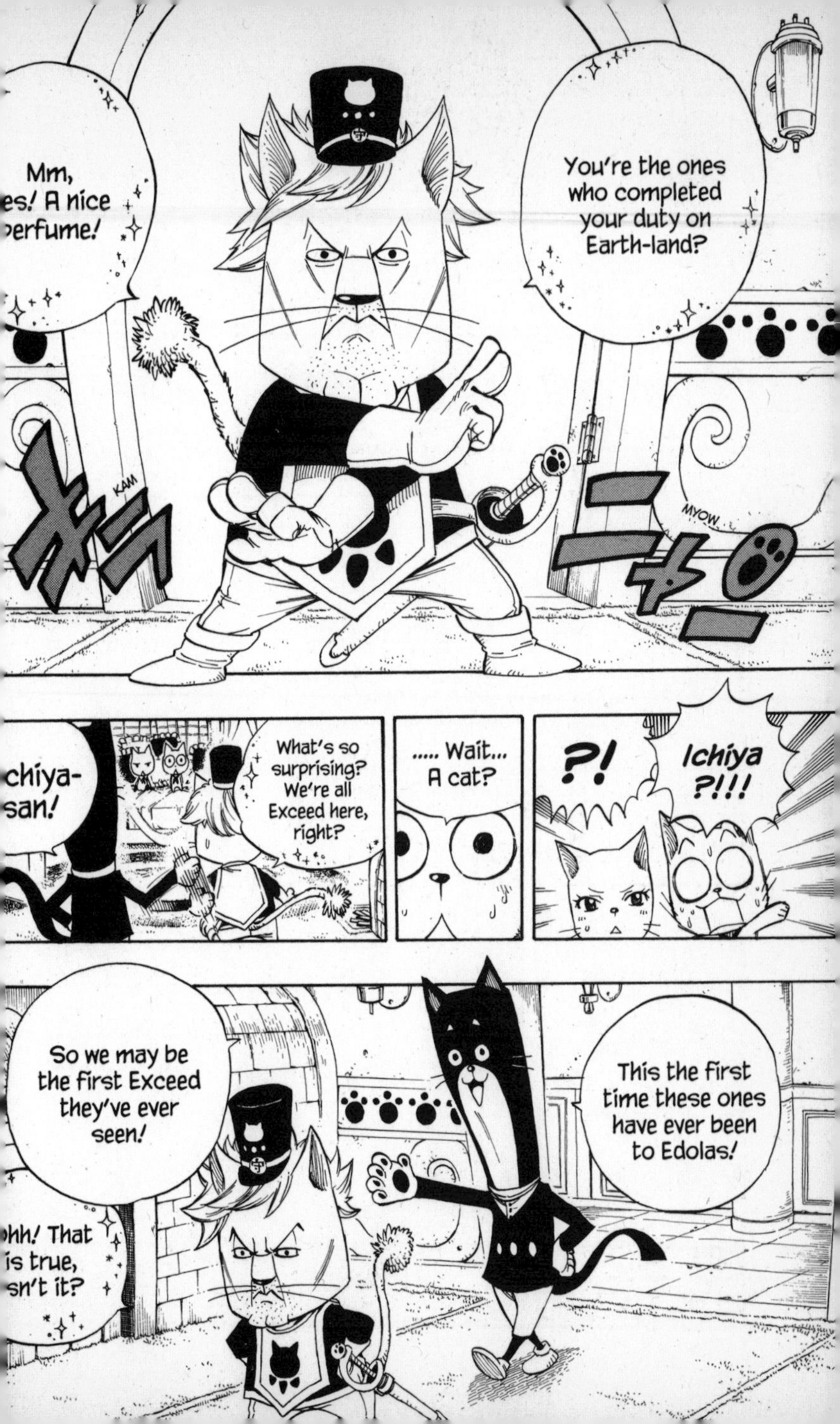
You're the ones who completed your duty on Earth-land?
MYOW
Mm, es! A nice erfume!
KAM
?!
Ichiya ?!!!
..... Wait... A cat?
What's so surprising? We're all Exceed here, right?
chiya- san!
This the first time these ones have ever been to Edolas!
So we may be the first Exceed they've ever seen!
hh! That is true, sn't it?

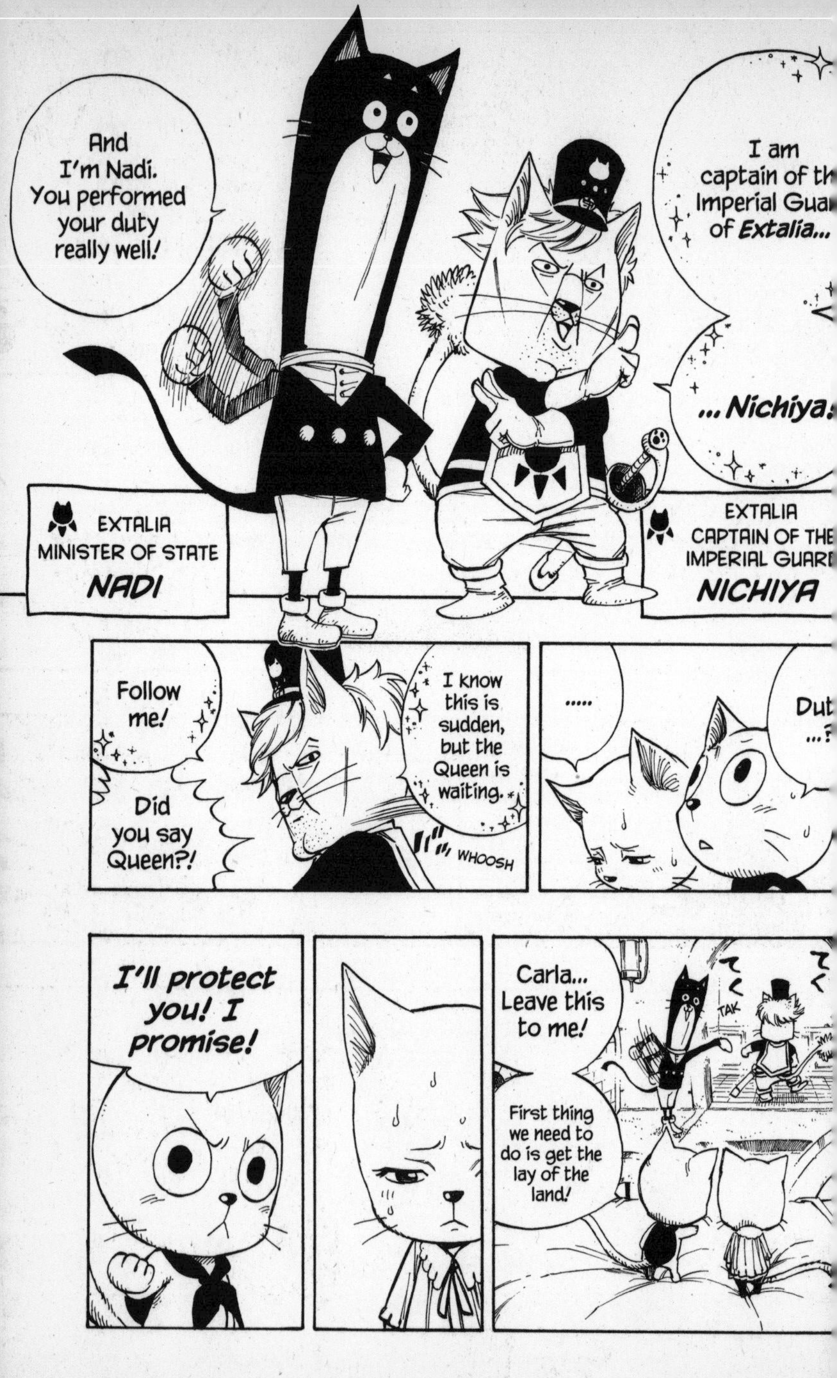

I am captain of th Imperial Gua of Extalia...
... Nichiya
EXTALIA CAPTAIN OF THE IMPERIAL GUAR NICHIYA
And I'm Nadi. You performed your duty really well!
EXTALIA MINISTER OF STATE NADI
Dut ...?
.....
I know this is sudden, but the Queen is waiting.
WHOOSH
Follow me!
Did you say Queen?!
Carla... Leave this to me!
First thing we need to do is get the lay of the land!
TAK
I'll protect you! I promise!

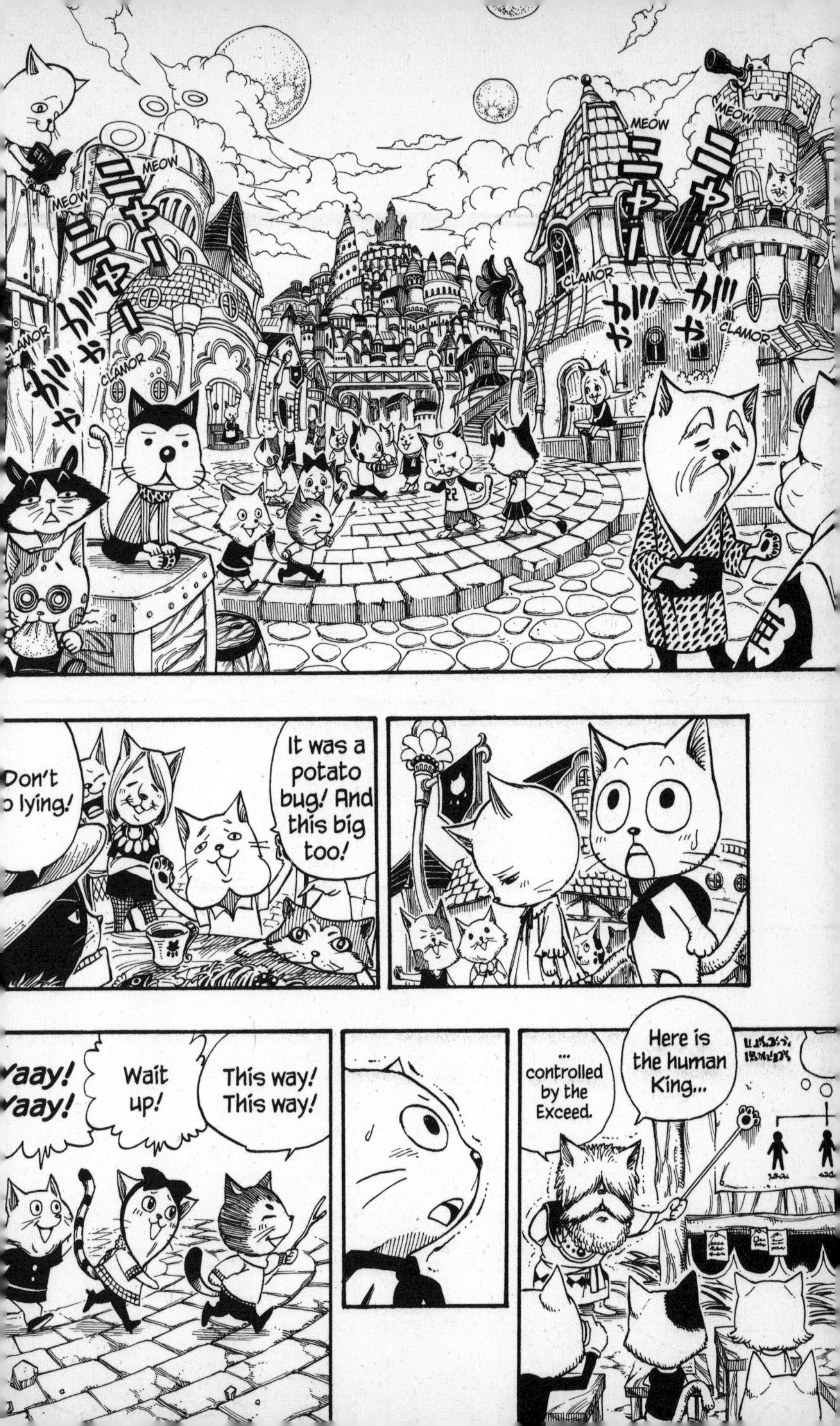
MEOW
MEOW
CLAMOR
CLAMOR
MEOW
MEOW
CLAMOR
CLAMOR
It was a potato bug! And this big too!
Don't o lying!
Here is the human King...
... controlled by the Exceed.
This way! This way!
Wait up!
vaay! vaay!

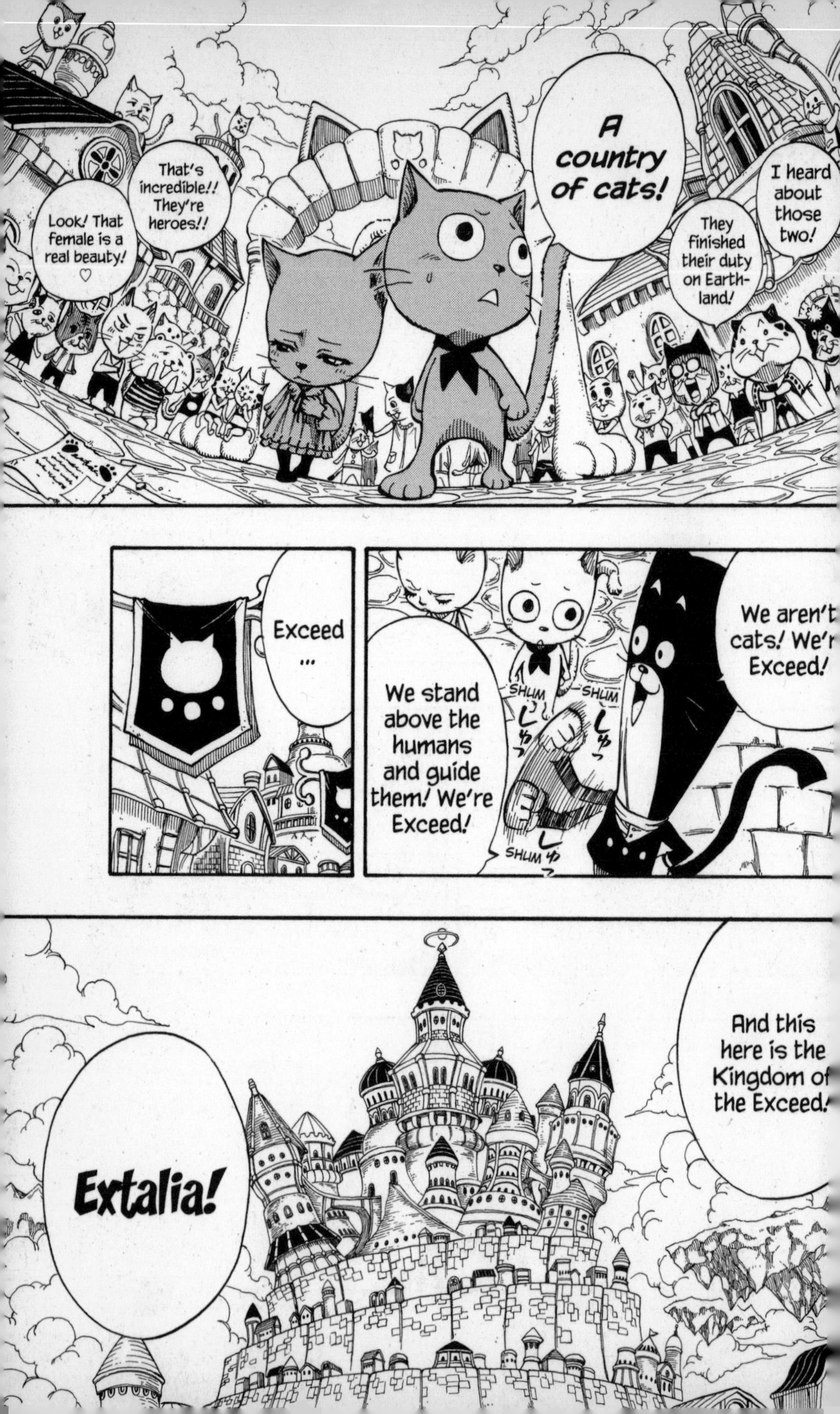
I heard about those two!
A country of cats!
They finished their duty on Earth-land!
That's incredible!! They're heroes!!
Look! That female is a real beauty! ♡
We aren't cats! We'r Exceed!
SHUM
SHUM
We stand above the humans and guide them! We're Exceed!
SHUM
Exceed ...
And this here is the Kingdom of the Exceed!
Extalia!

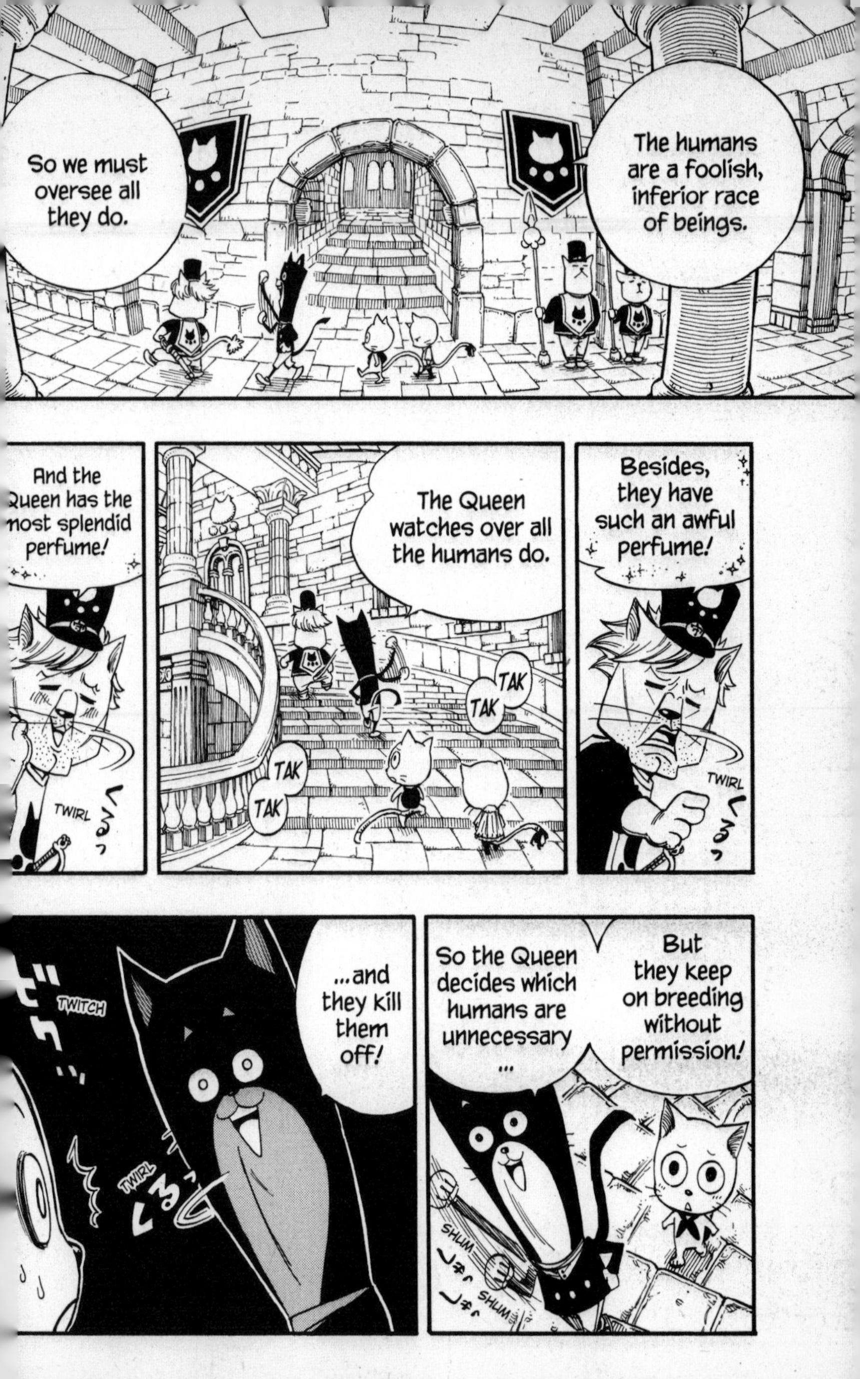
The humans are a foolish, inferior race of beings.
So we must oversee all they do.
Besides, they have such an awful perfume!
TWIRL
The Queen watches over all the humans do.
TAK
TAK
TAK
TAK
And the Queen has the most splendid perfume!
TWIRL
But they keep on breeding without permission!
So the Queen decides which humans are unnecessary ...
SHUM
SHUM
...and they kill them off!
TWITCH
TWIRL

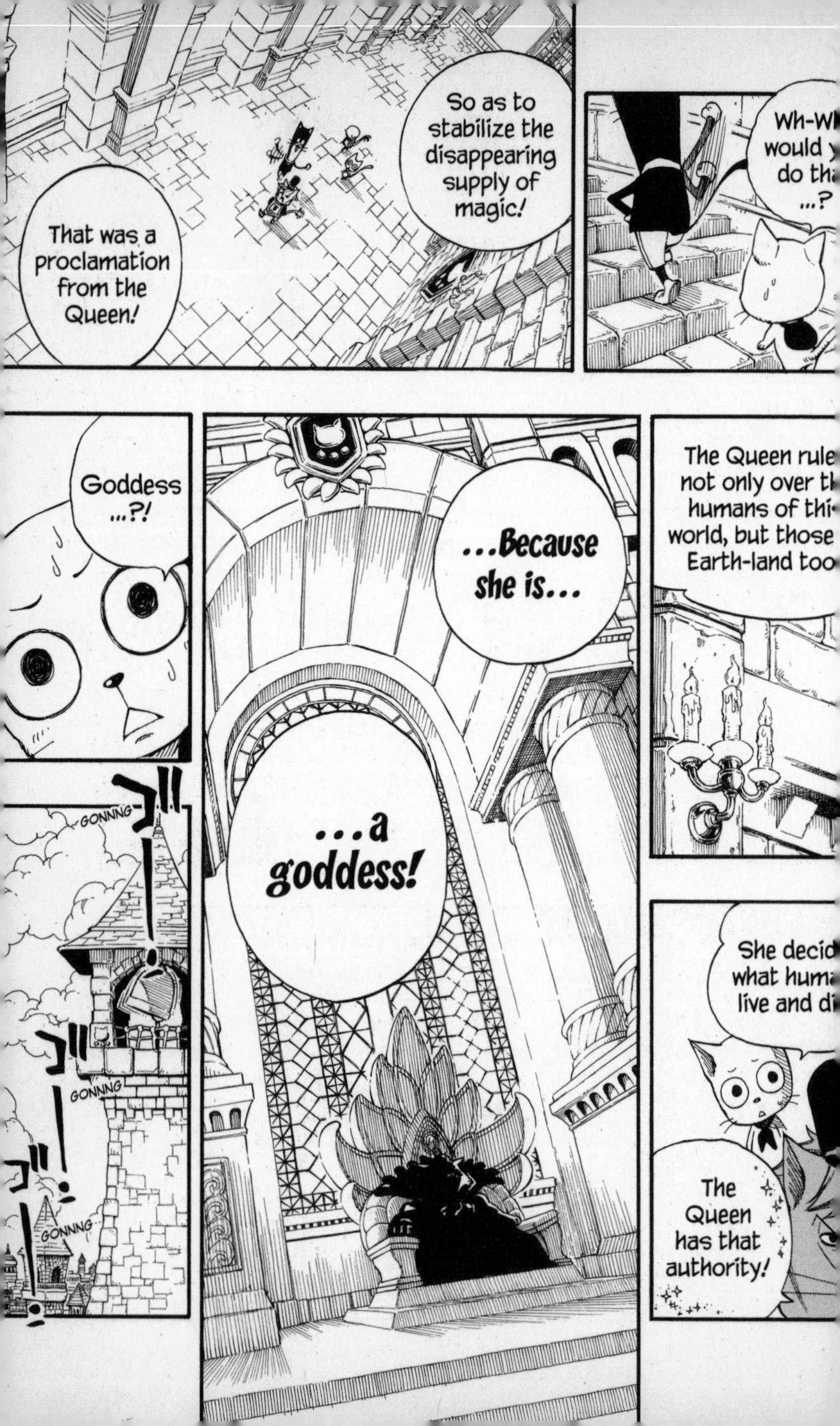

Wh-W would y do th ...?
So as to stabilize the disappearing supply of magic!
That was a proclamation from the Queen!
The Queen rule not only over th humans of thi world, but those Earth-land too
She decid what huma live and di
The Queen has that authority!
...Because she is...
...a goddess!
Goddess ...?!
GONNNG
GONNNG
GONNNG

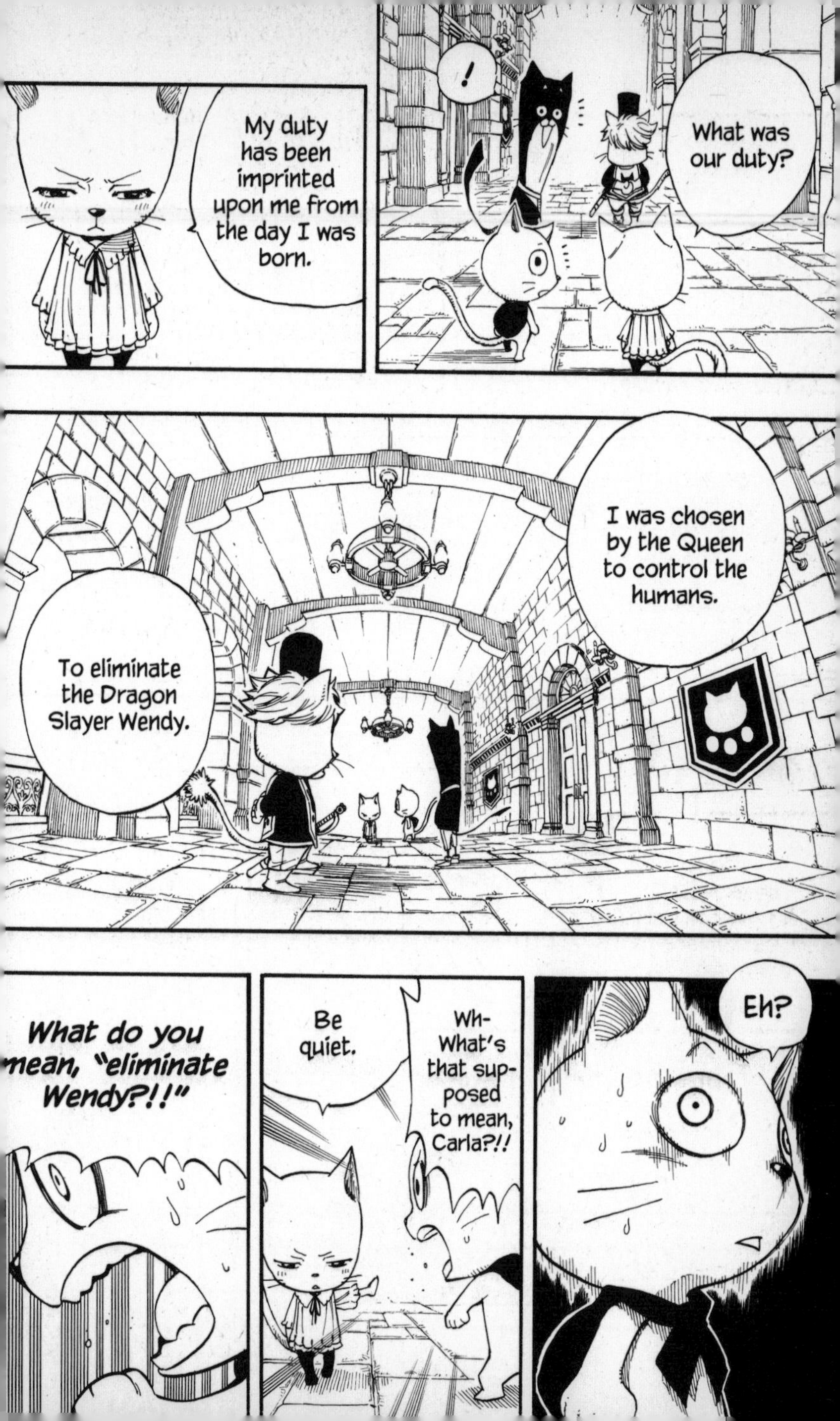
What was our duty?
!
My duty has been imprinted upon me from the day I was born.
I was chosen by the Queen to control the humans.
To eliminate the Dragon Slayer Wendy.
Eh?
Wh- What's that sup-posed to mean, Carla?!!
Be quiet.
What do you mean, "eliminate Wendy?!!"

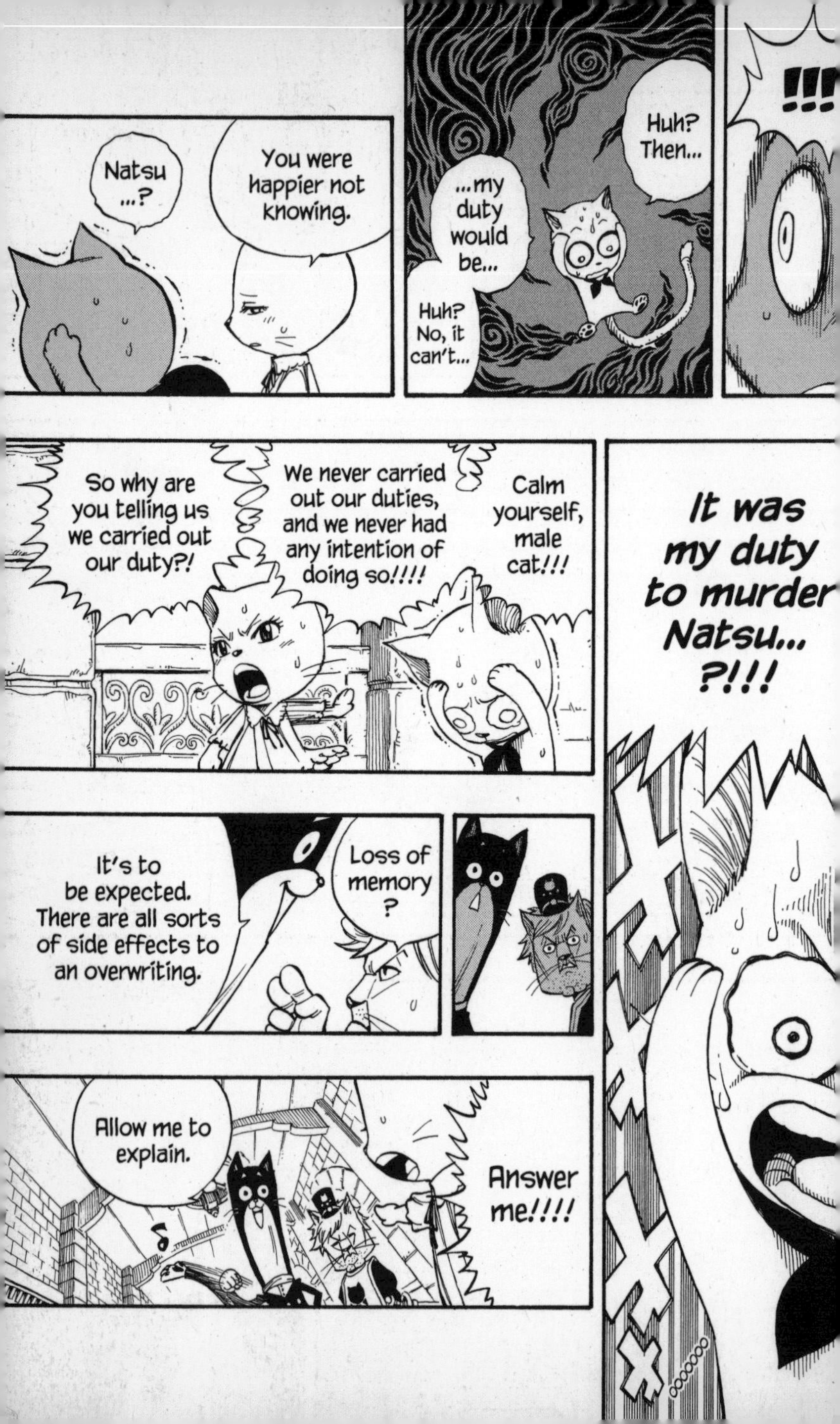
!!!
Huh? Then...
...my duty would be...
Huh? No, it can't...
You were happier not knowing.
Natsu ...?
It was my duty to murder Natsu... ?!!!
Calm yourself, male cat!!!
We never carried out our duties, and we never had any intention of doing so!!!!
So why are you telling us we carried out our duty?!
Loss of memory ?
It's to be expected. There are all sorts of side effects to an overwriting.
Answer me!!!!
Allow me to explain.

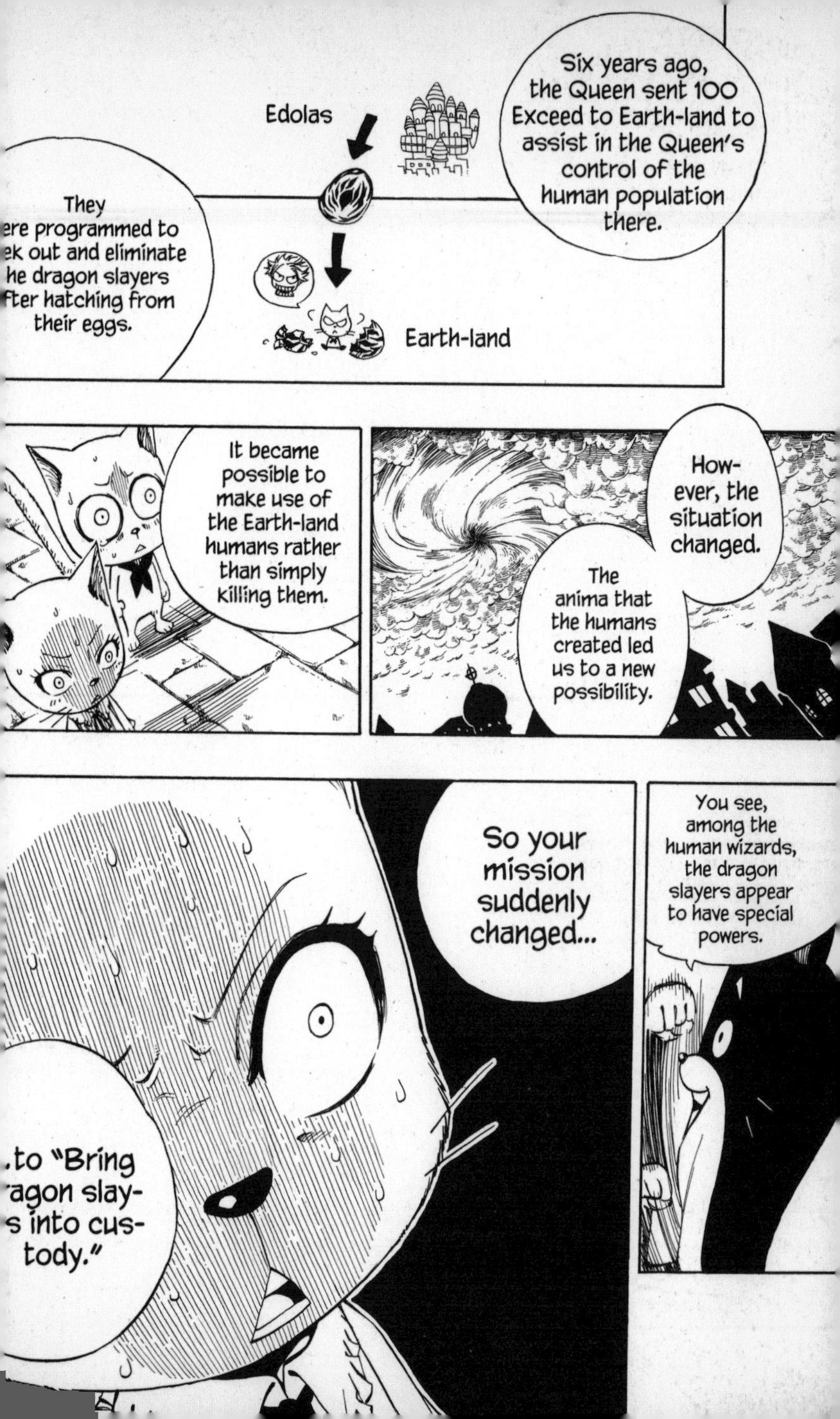

Six years ago, the Queen sent 100 Exceed to Earth-land to assist in the Queen's control of the human population there.
Edolas
Earth-land
They ere programmed to ek out and eliminate he dragon slayers fter hatching from their eggs.
How-ever, the situation changed.
The anima that the humans created led us to a new possibility.
It became possible to make use of the Earth-land humans rather than simply killing them.
You see, among the human wizards, the dragon slayers appear to have special powers.
So your mission suddenly changed...
.to "Bring ragon slay-s into cus-tody."

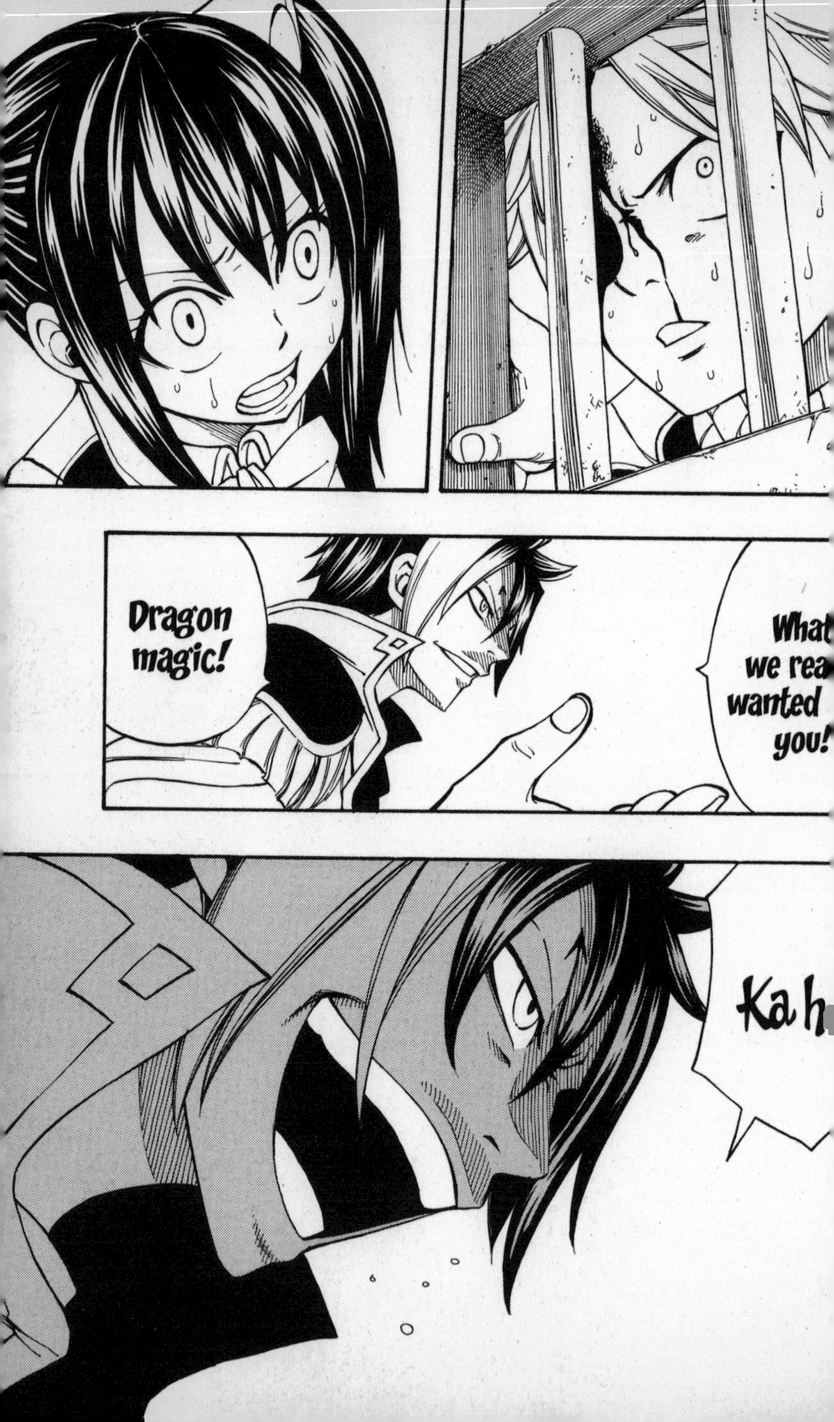
What we rea wanted you!
Dragon magic!
Ka h

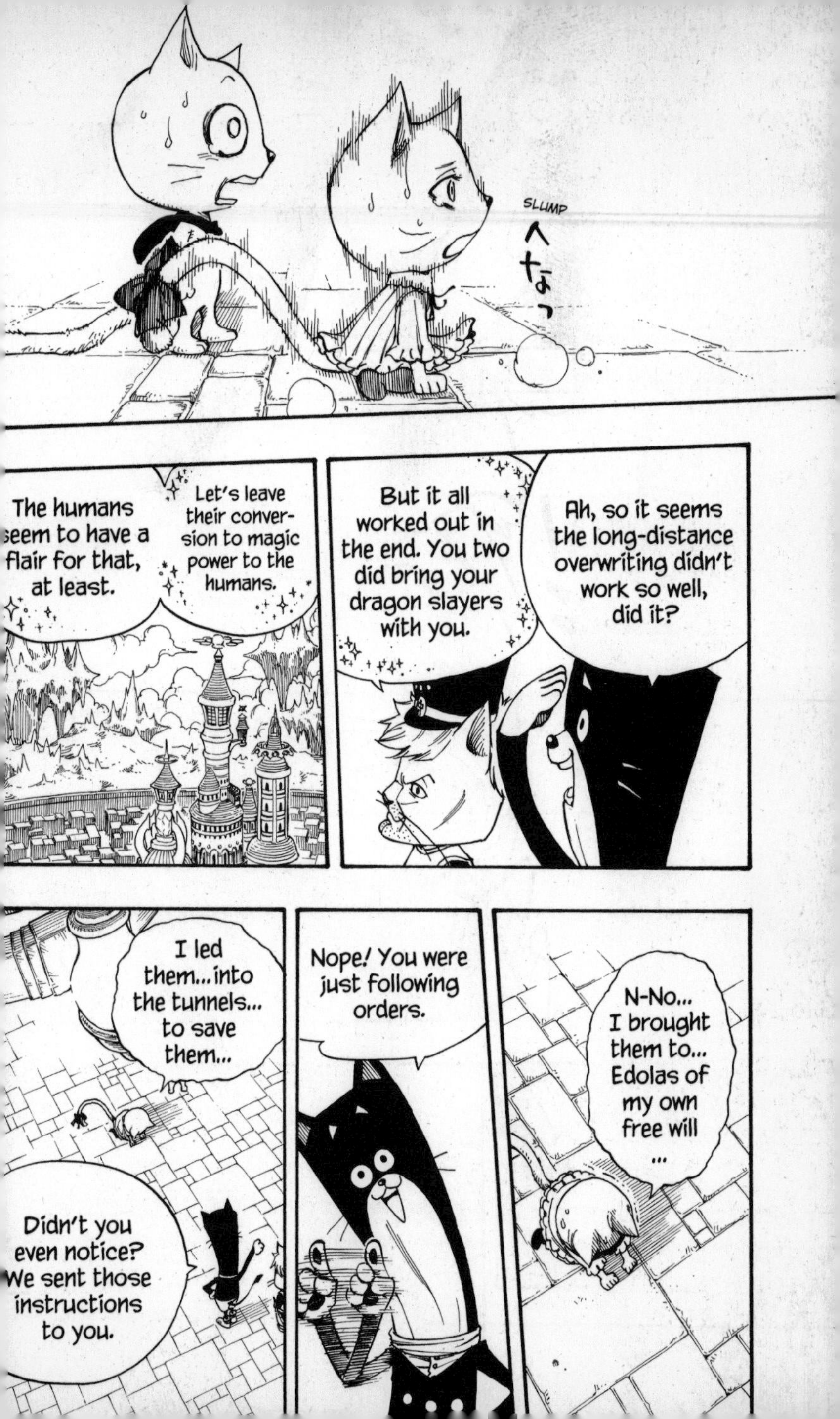
SLUMP
へなっ
Ah, so it seems the long-distance overwriting didn't work so well, did it?
But it all worked out in the end. You two did bring your dragon slayers with you.
Let's leave their conversion to magic power to the humans.
The humans seem to have a flair for that, at least.
N-No... I brought them to... Edolas of my own free will ...
Nope! You were just following orders.
I led them...into the tunnels... to save them...
Didn't you even notice? We sent those instructions to you.

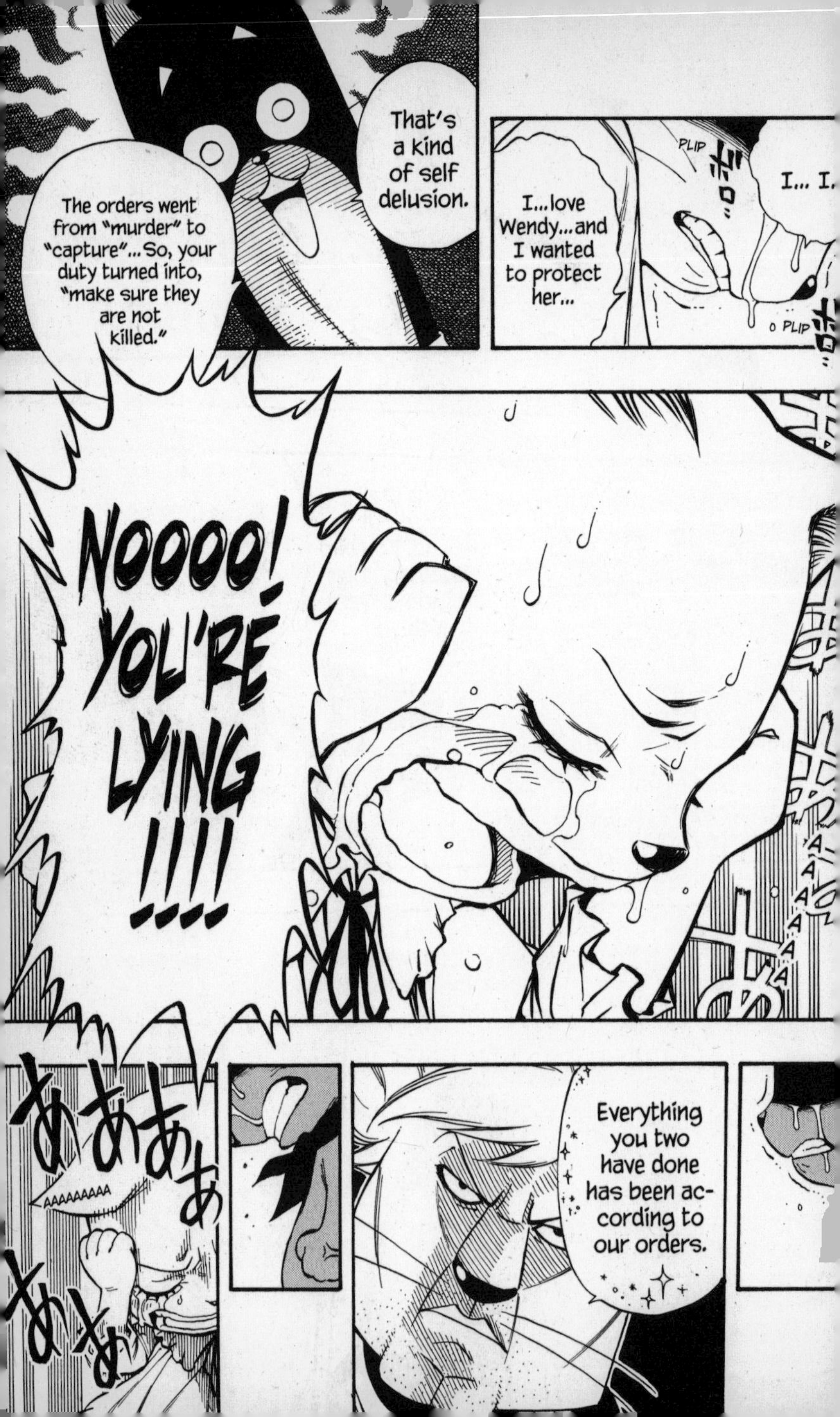

PLIP
I... I.
I...love Wendy...and I wanted to protect her...
PLIP
That's a kind of self delusion.
The orders went from "murder" to "capture"... So, your duty turned into, "make sure they are not killed."
A-AAAAAAA
NOOOO! YOU'RE LYING!!!!
Everything you two have done has been according to our orders.
AAAAAAAAA

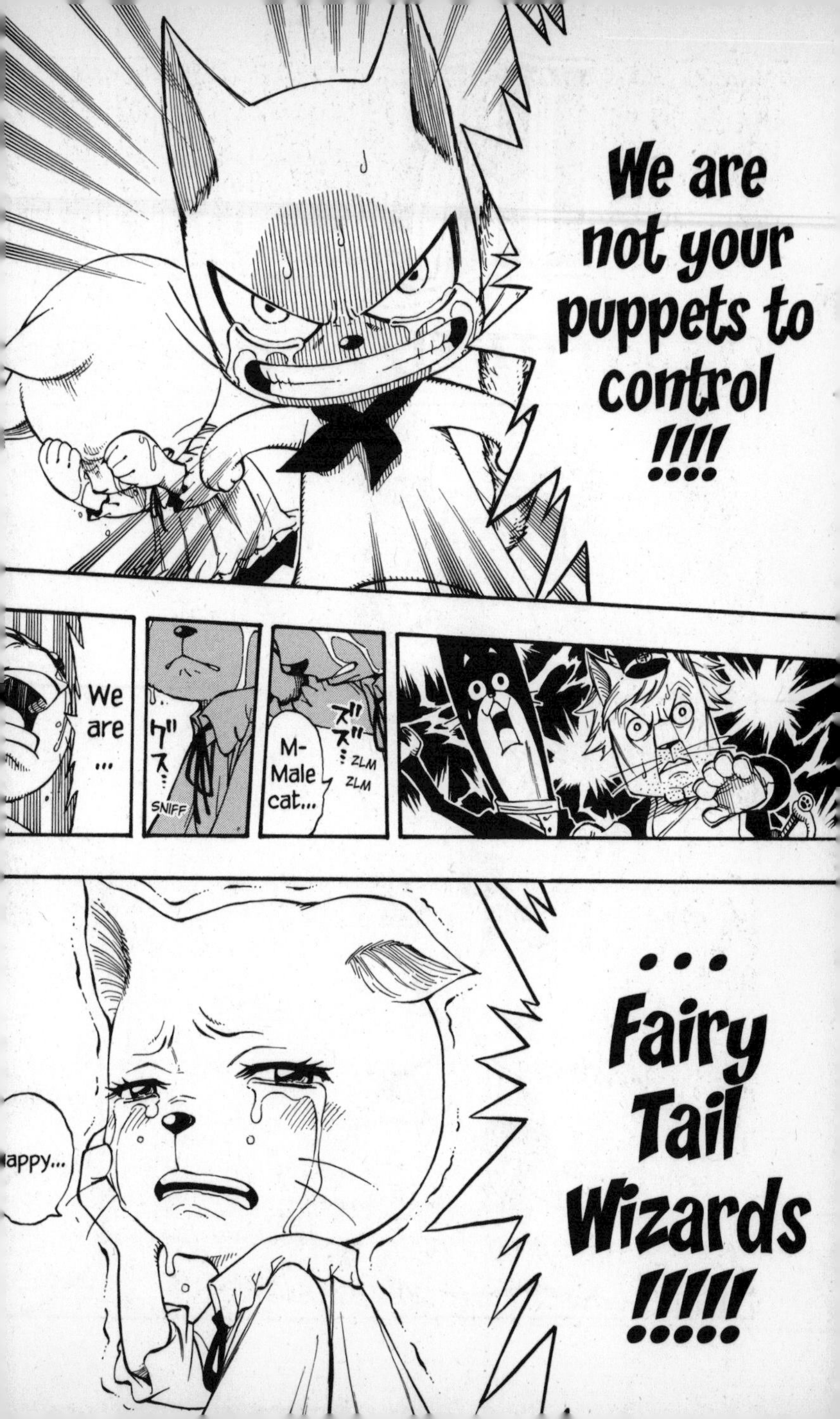
We are not your puppets to control !!!!
M-Male cat...
ズズ ZLM ZLM
グス SNIFF
We are ...
... Fairy Tail Wizards !!!!!
appy...

FAIRY TAIL

フェアリーテイル

Chapter 177, Fly to Your Friend

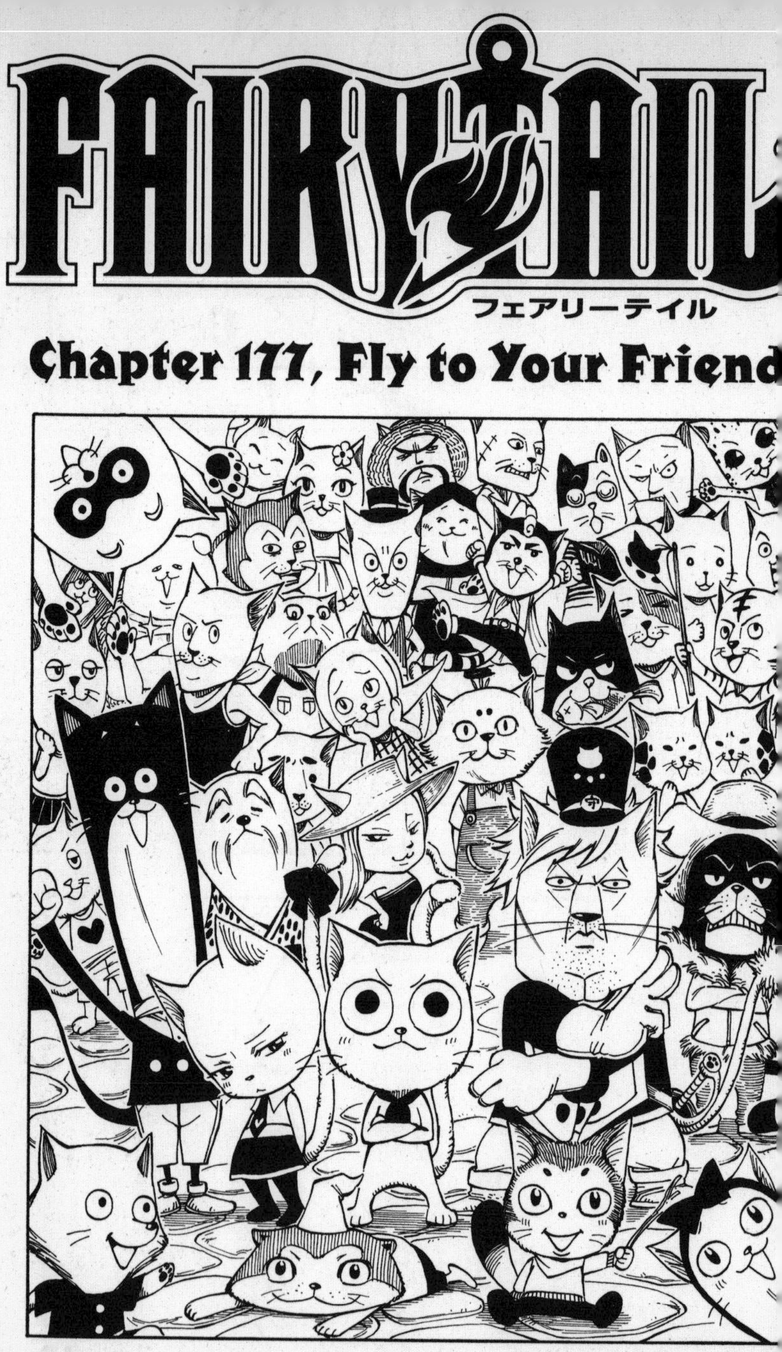

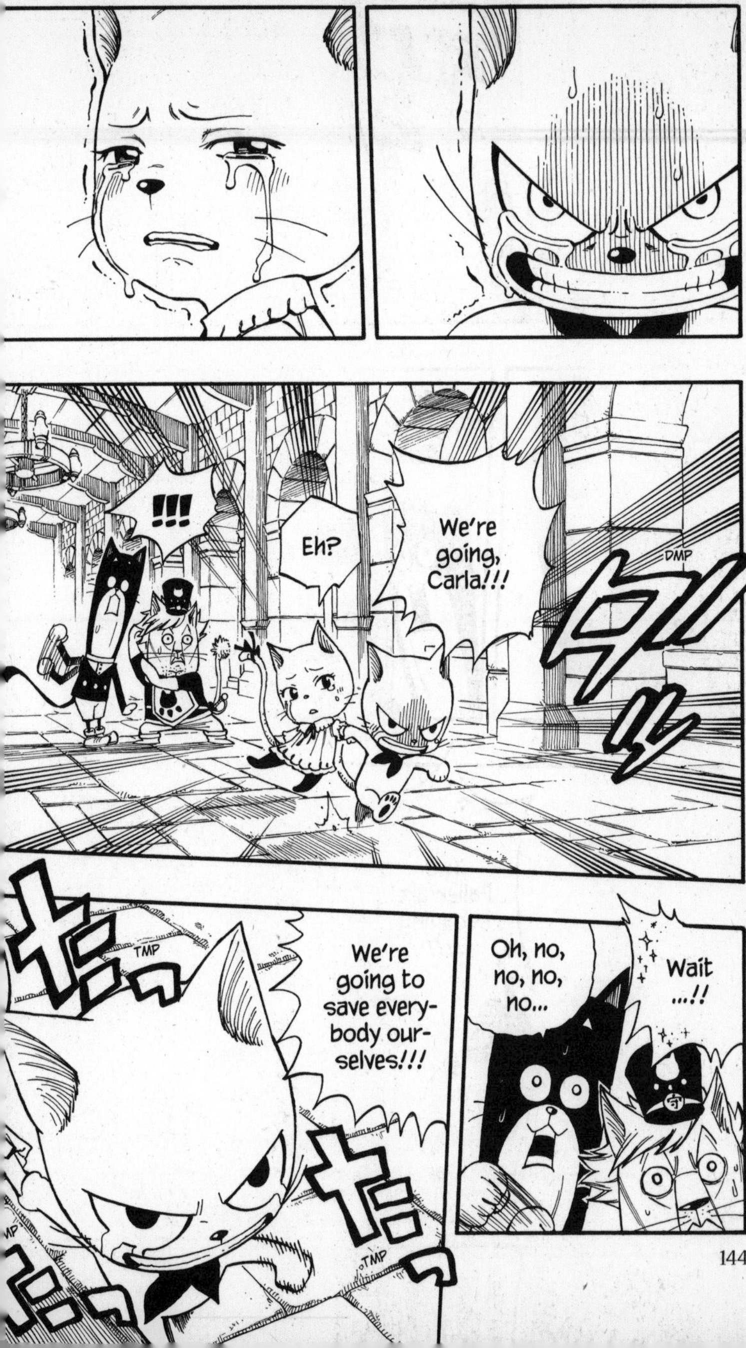
DMP
We're going, Carla!!!
Eh?
!!!
Wait ...!!
Oh, no, no, no, no...
We're going to save every-body our-selves!!!
TMP
TMP

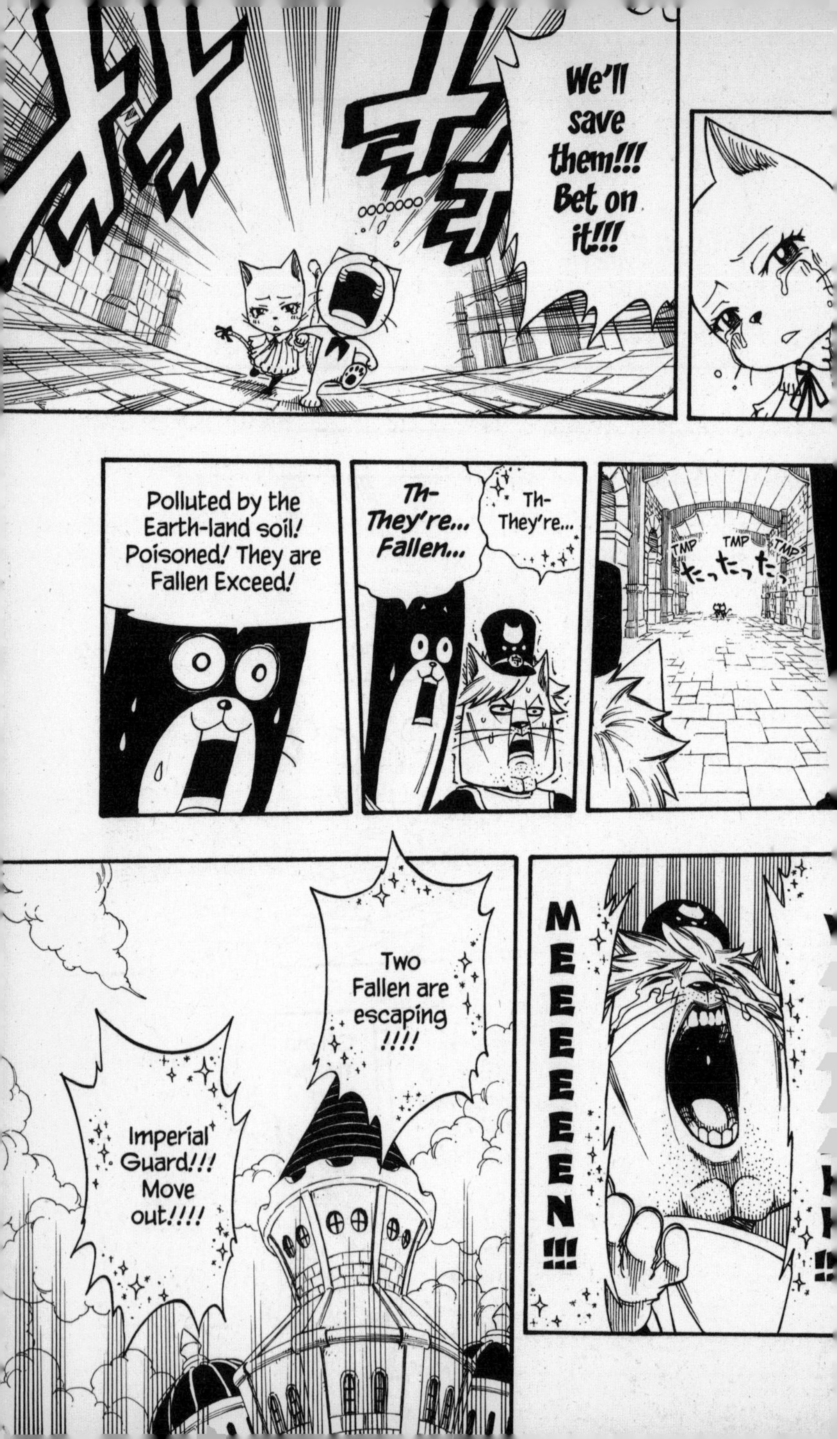
We'll save them!!! Bet on it!!!
oooooooo
TMP TMP TMP
たったった
Th- They're...
Th- They're... Fallen...
Polluted by the Earth-land soil! Poisoned! They are Fallen Exceed!
MEEEEEEN!!!
Two Fallen are escaping!!!!
Imperial Guard!!! Move out!!!!

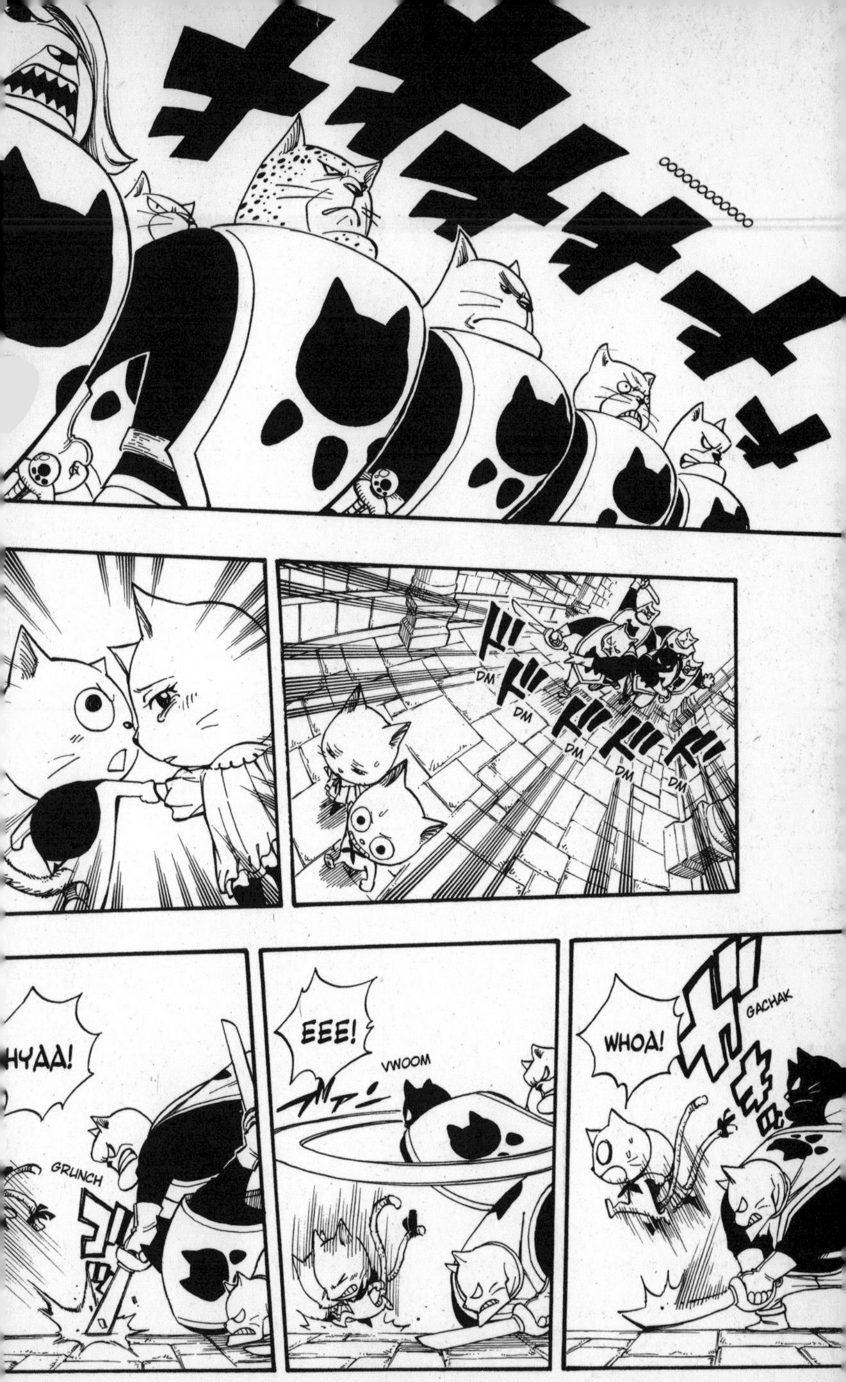
oooooooooooo
DM
DM
DM
DM
DM
WHOA!
GACHAK
EEE!
VWOOM
HYAA!
GRUNCH

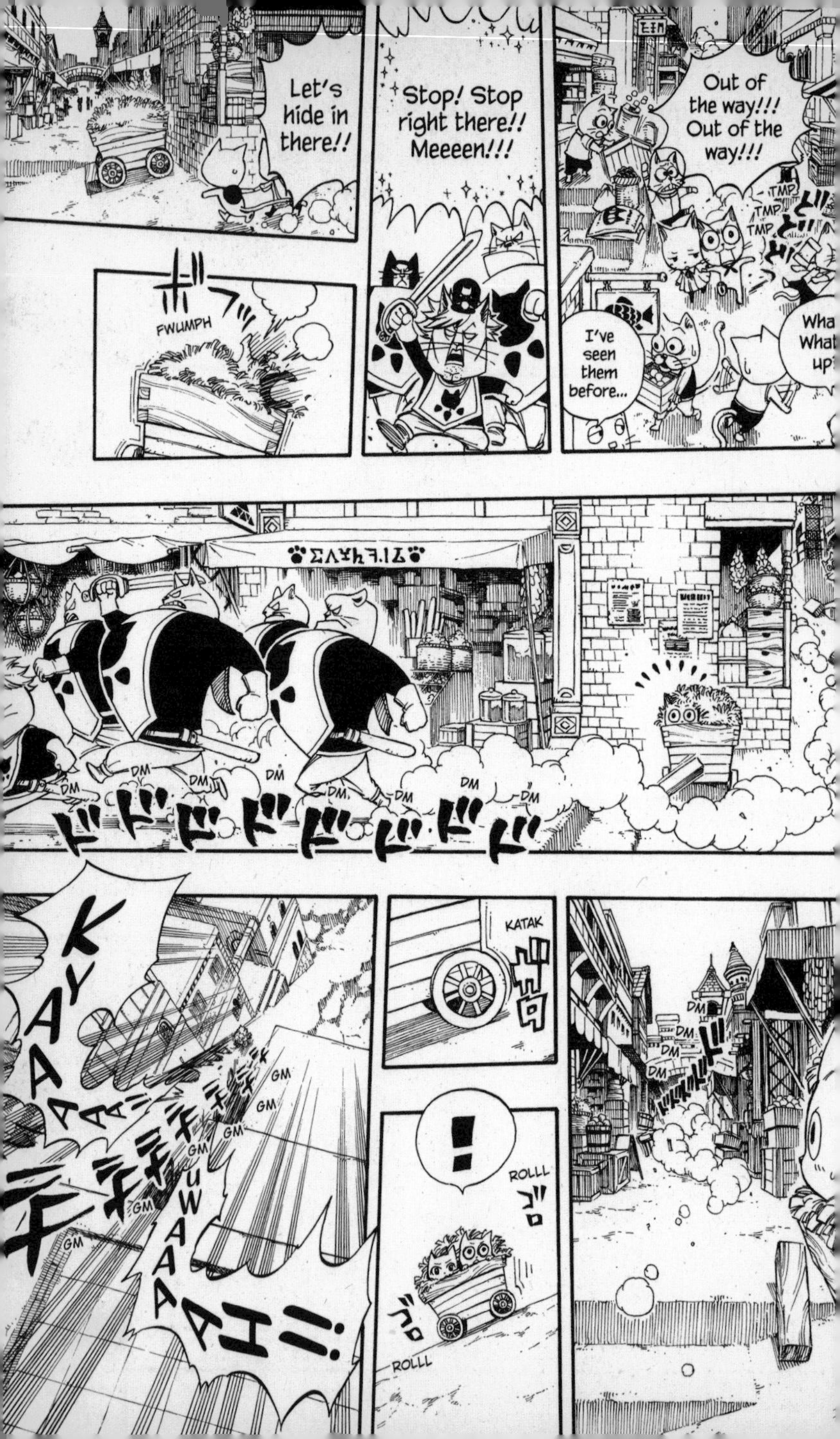
Out of the way!!! Out of the way!!!
TMP TMP TMP
I've seen them before...
Stop! Stop right there!! Meeeen!!!
Let's hide in there!!
FWUMPH
DM DM DM DM DM DM DM DM
DM DM DM DM
KATAK
!
ROLLL
ROLLL
KYAAAA!!
GM GM GM GM GM GM
UWAAAAH!!

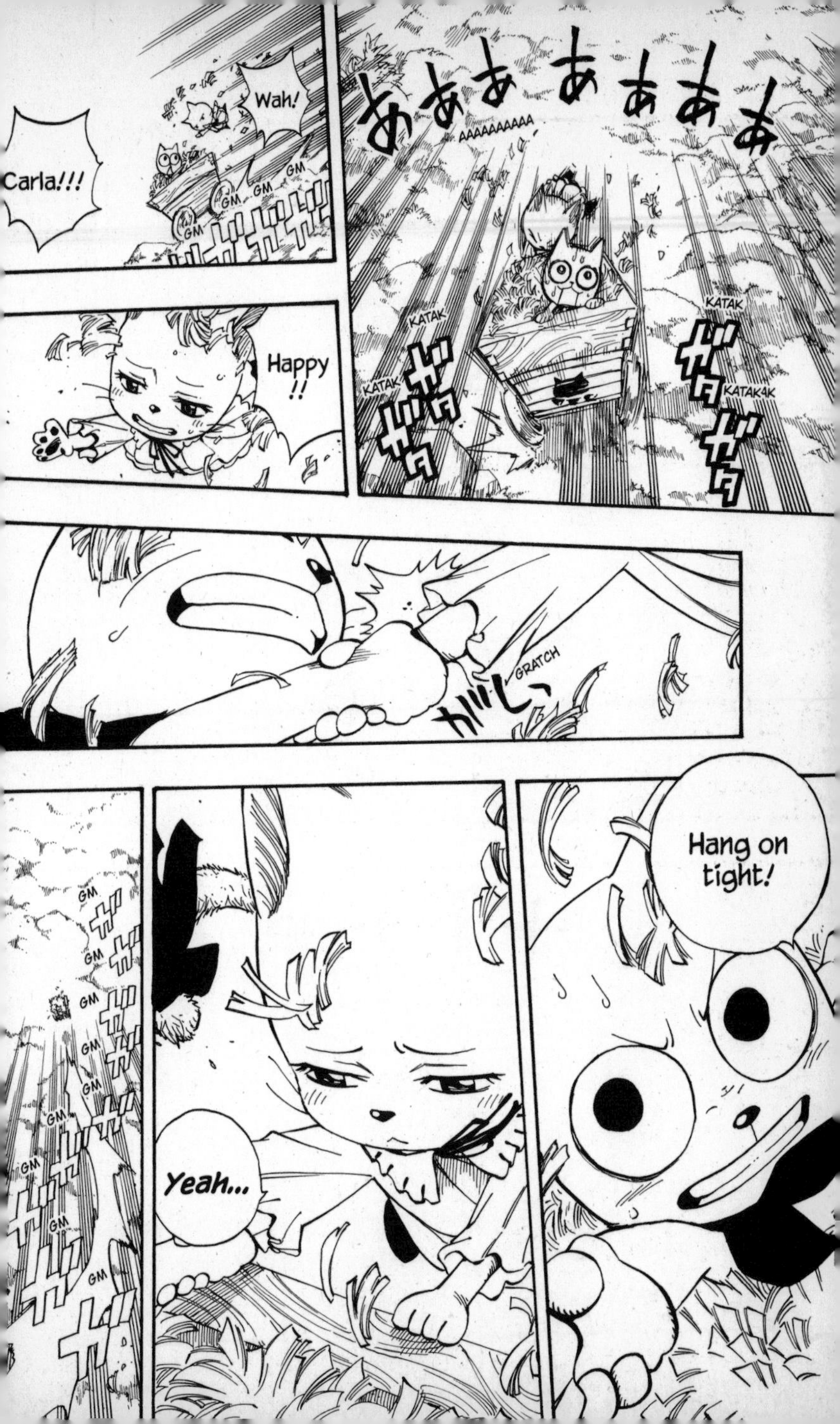

AAAAAAAAAA
KATAK
KATAK
KATAKAK
Wah!
GM
GM
GM
GM
Carla!!!
Happy!!
GRATCH
Hang on tight!
Yeah...
GM
GM
GM
GM
GM
GM
GM
GM
GM

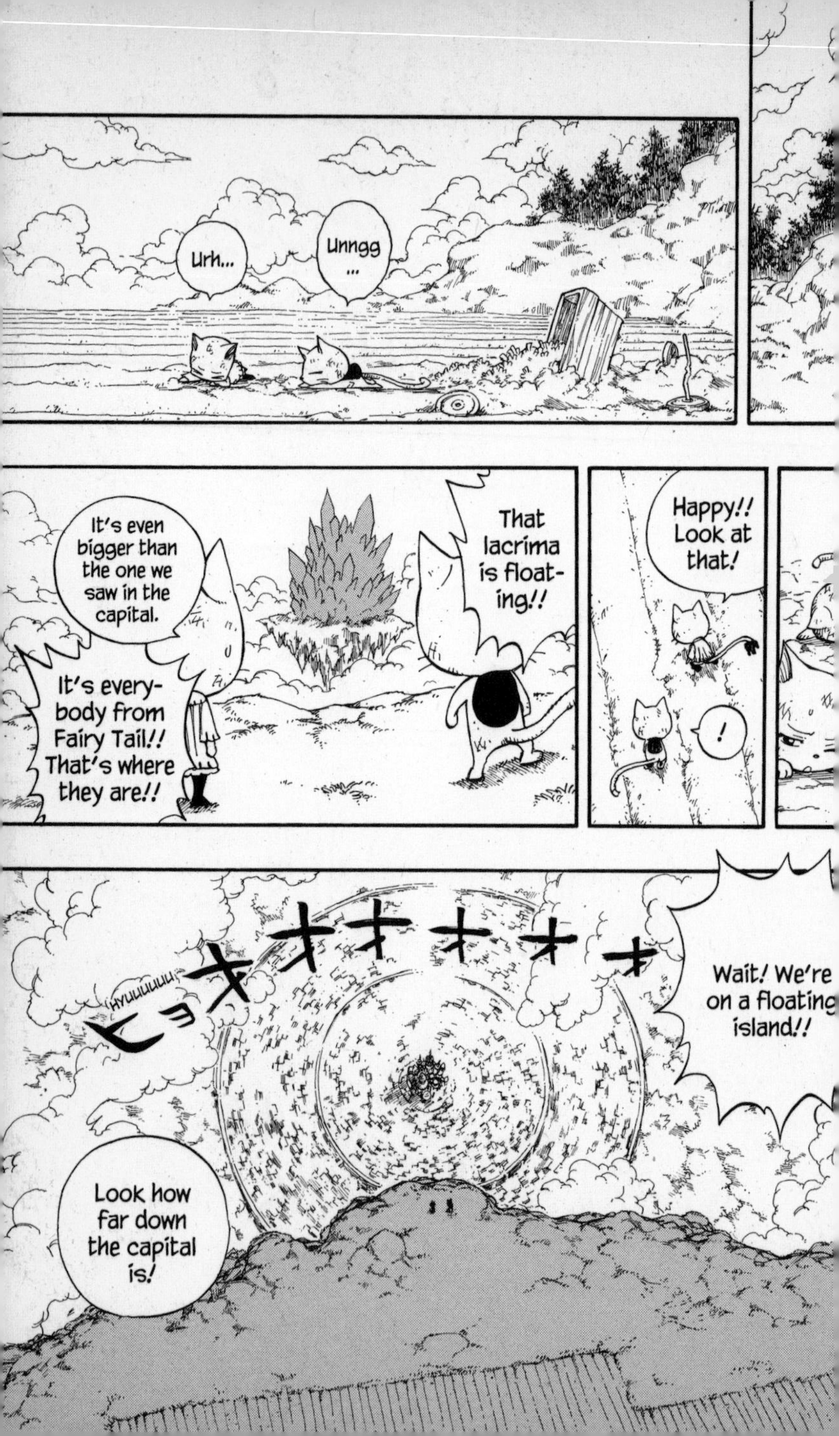
Unngg ...
Urh...
Happy!! Look at that!
!
That lacrima is floating!!
It's even bigger than the one we saw in the capital.
It's everybody from Fairy Tail!! That's where they are!!
Wait! We're on a floating island!!
ヒョオオオオオ
HYUUUUUU
Look how far down the capital is!

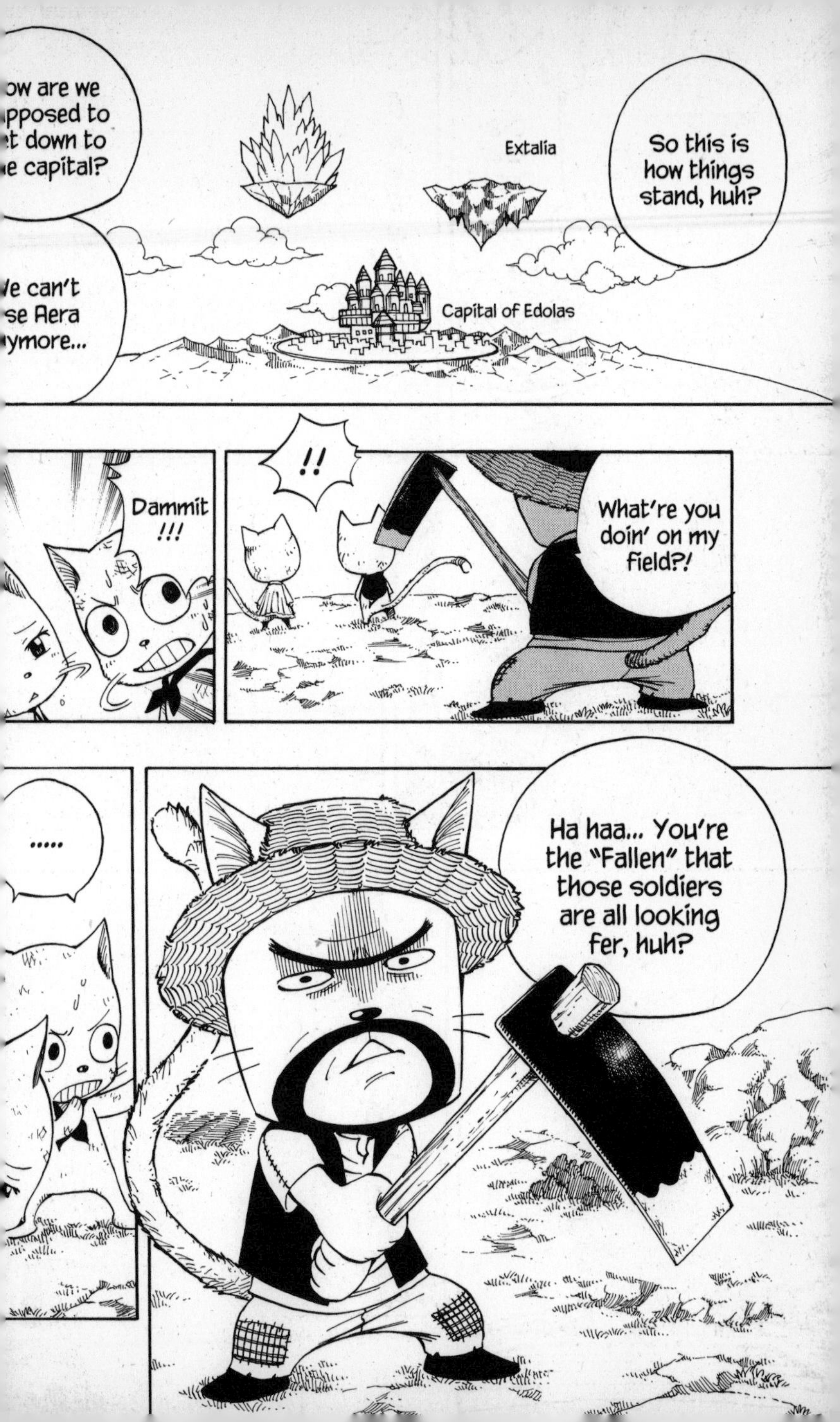
So this is how things stand, huh?
Extalia
Capital of Edolas
ow are we pposed to t down to e capital?
e can't se Aera ymore...
!!
What're you doin' on my field?!
Dammit !!!
Ha haa... You're the "Fallen" that those soldiers are all looking fer, huh?
.....

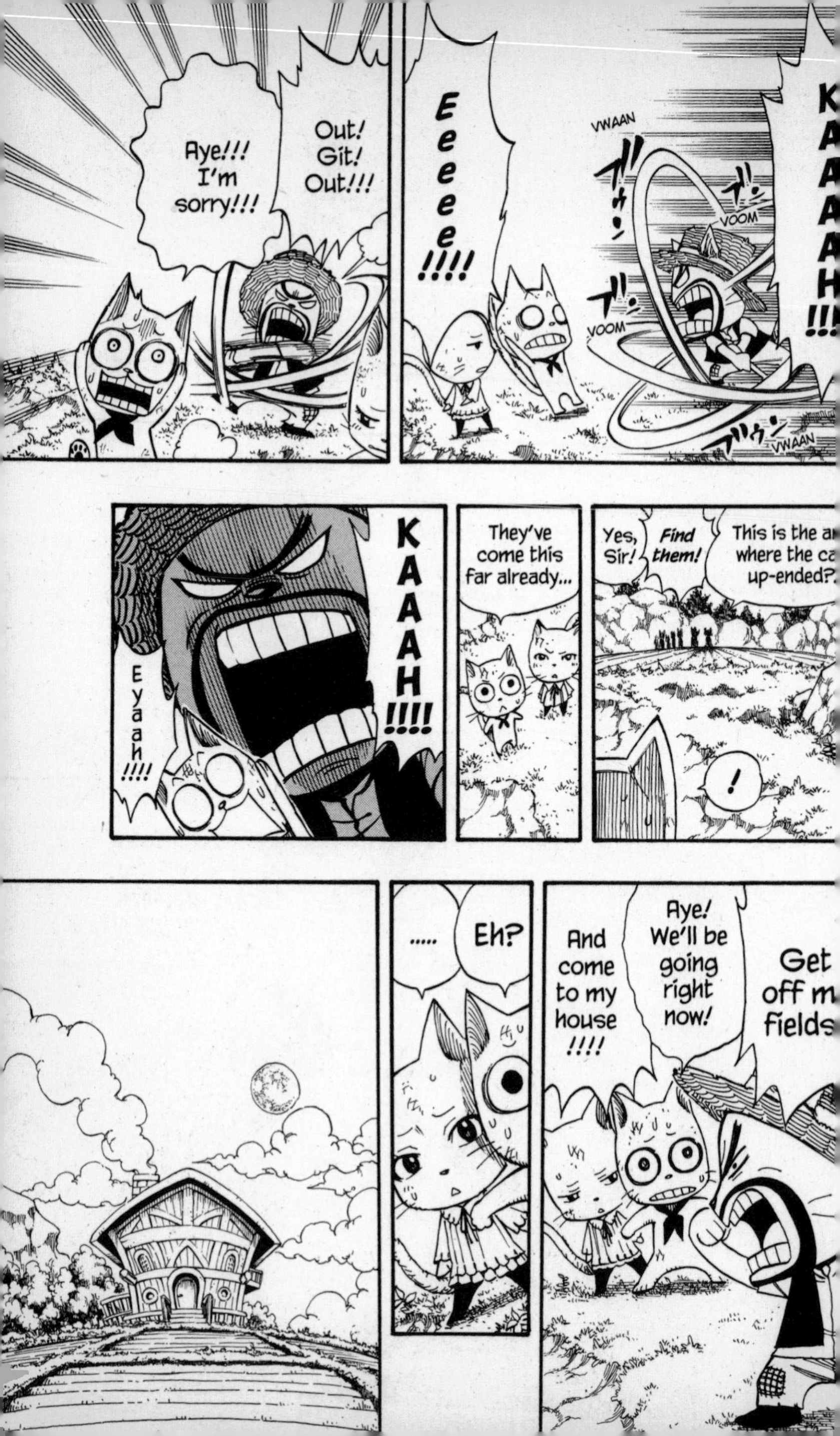
KAAAAAH!!!
VWAAN
VOOM
VOOM
VWAAN
Eeeee!!!!
Out! Git! Out!!!
Aye!!! I'm sorry!!!
This is the a where the ca up-ended?
Find them!
Yes, Sir!
!
They've come this far already...
KAAAAH!!!!
Eyaah!!!!
Get off m fields
Aye! We'll be going right now!
And come to my house!!!!
Eh?
.....

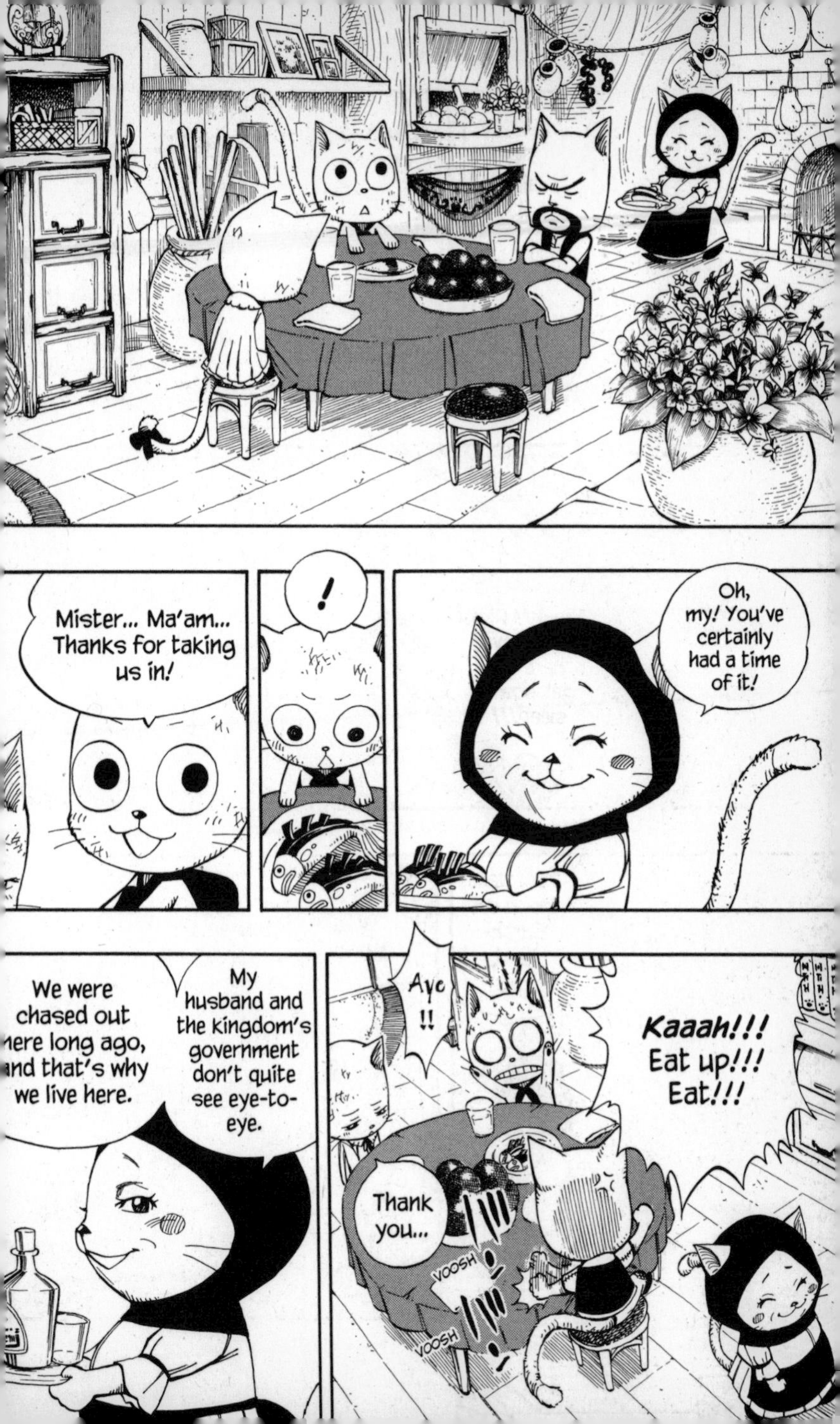
Oh, my! You've certainly had a time of it!
!
Mister... Ma'am... Thanks for taking us in!
Kaaah!!! Eat up!!! Eat!!!
Aye !!
Thank you...
VOOSH
VOOSH
My husband and the kingdom's government don't quite see eye-to-eye.
We were chased out ere long ago, nd that's why we live here.

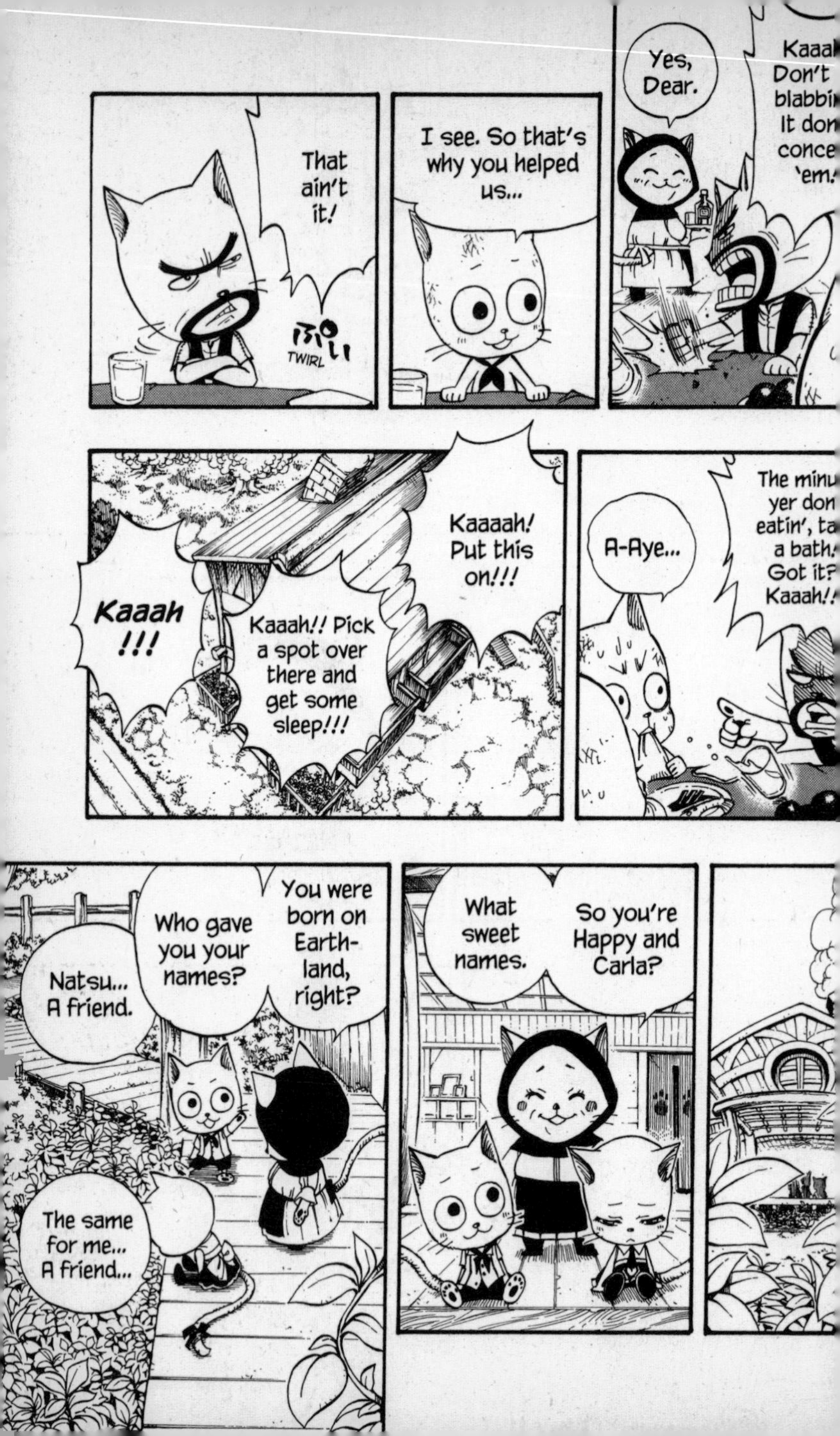
Kaaa Don't blabbi It don conce 'em!
Yes, Dear.
I see. So that's why you helped us...
That ain't it!
TWIRL
The minu yer don eatin', ta a bath. Got it? Kaaah!!
A-Aye...
Kaaaah! Put this on!!!
Kaaah!! Pick a spot over there and get some sleep!!!
Kaaah !!!
So you're Happy and Carla?
What sweet names.
You were born on Earth-land, right?
Who gave you your names?
Natsu... A friend.
The same for me... A friend...

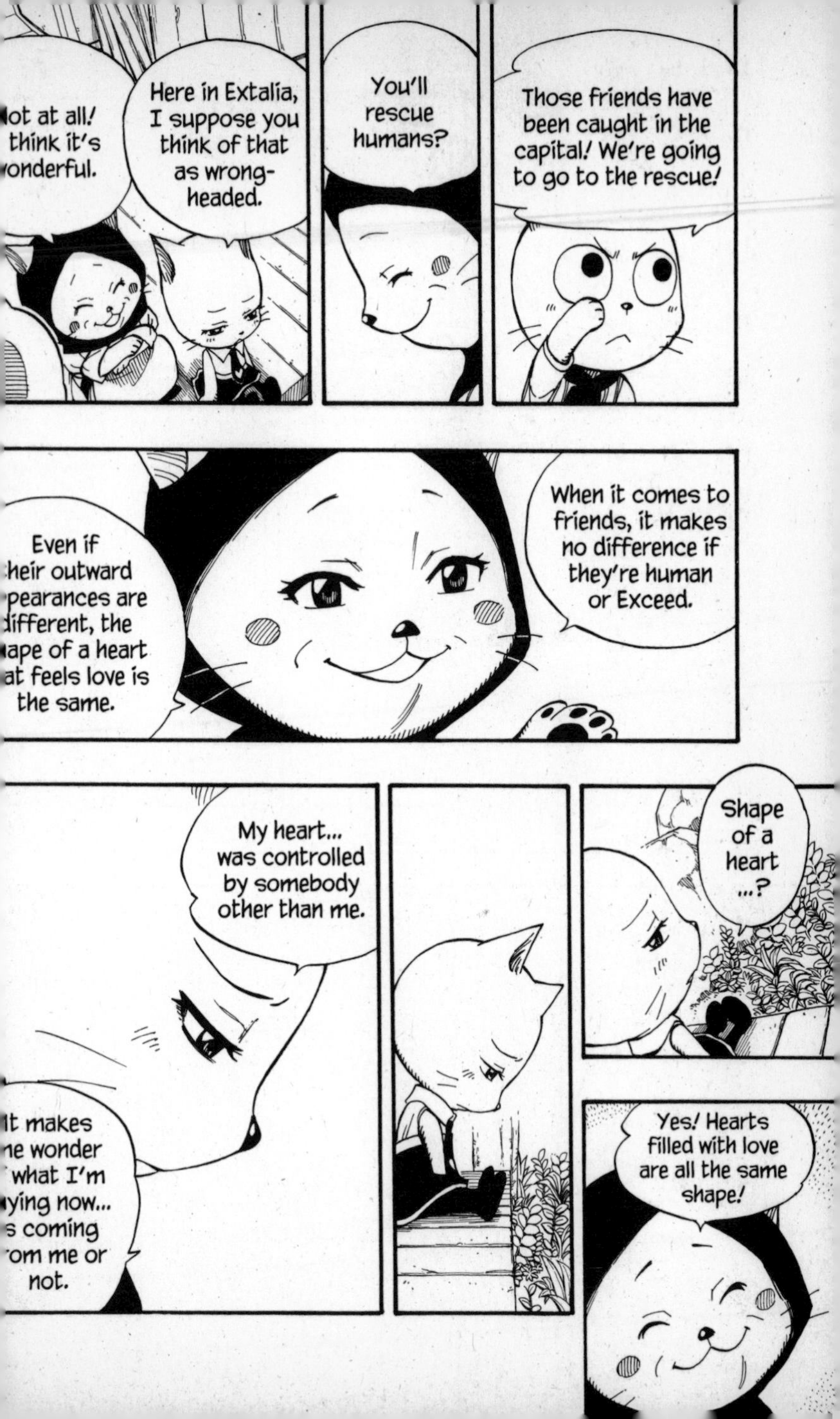
Those friends have been caught in the capital! We're going to go to the rescue!
You'll rescue humans?
Here in Extalia, I suppose you think of that as wrong-headed.
ot at all! think it's onderful.
When it comes to friends, it makes no difference if they're human or Exceed.
Even if heir outward pearances are ifferent, the ape of a heart at feels love is the same.
Shape of a heart ...?
Yes! Hearts filled with love are all the same shape!
My heart... was controlled by somebody other than me.
It makes e wonder what I'm ying now... s coming om me or not.

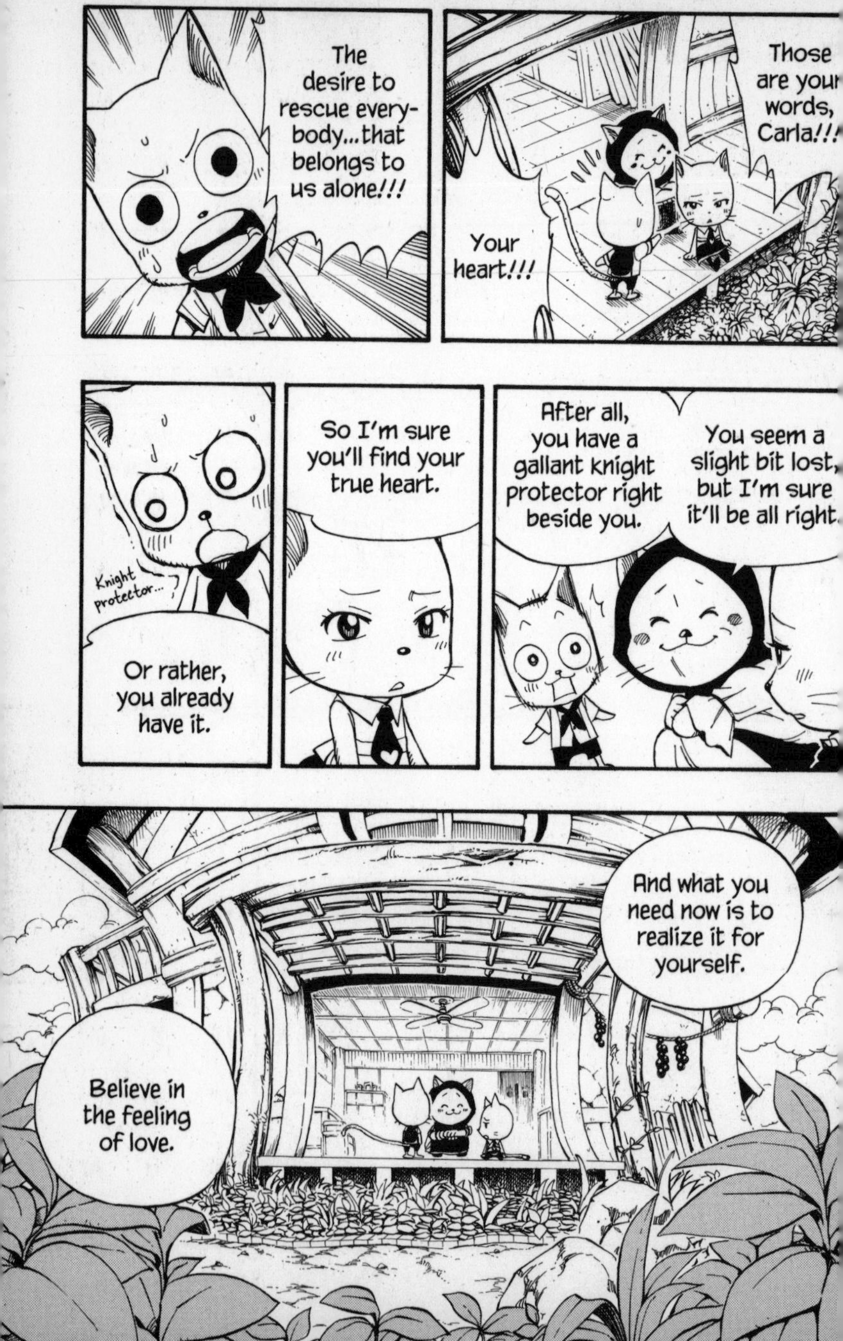
Those are your words, Carla!!!
Your heart!!!
The desire to rescue every-body...that belongs to us alone!!!
You seem a slight bit lost, but I'm sure it'll be all right.
After all, you have a gallant knight protector right beside you.
So I'm sure you'll find your true heart.
Knight protector...
Or rather, you already have it.
And what you need now is to realize it for yourself.
Believe in the feeling of love.

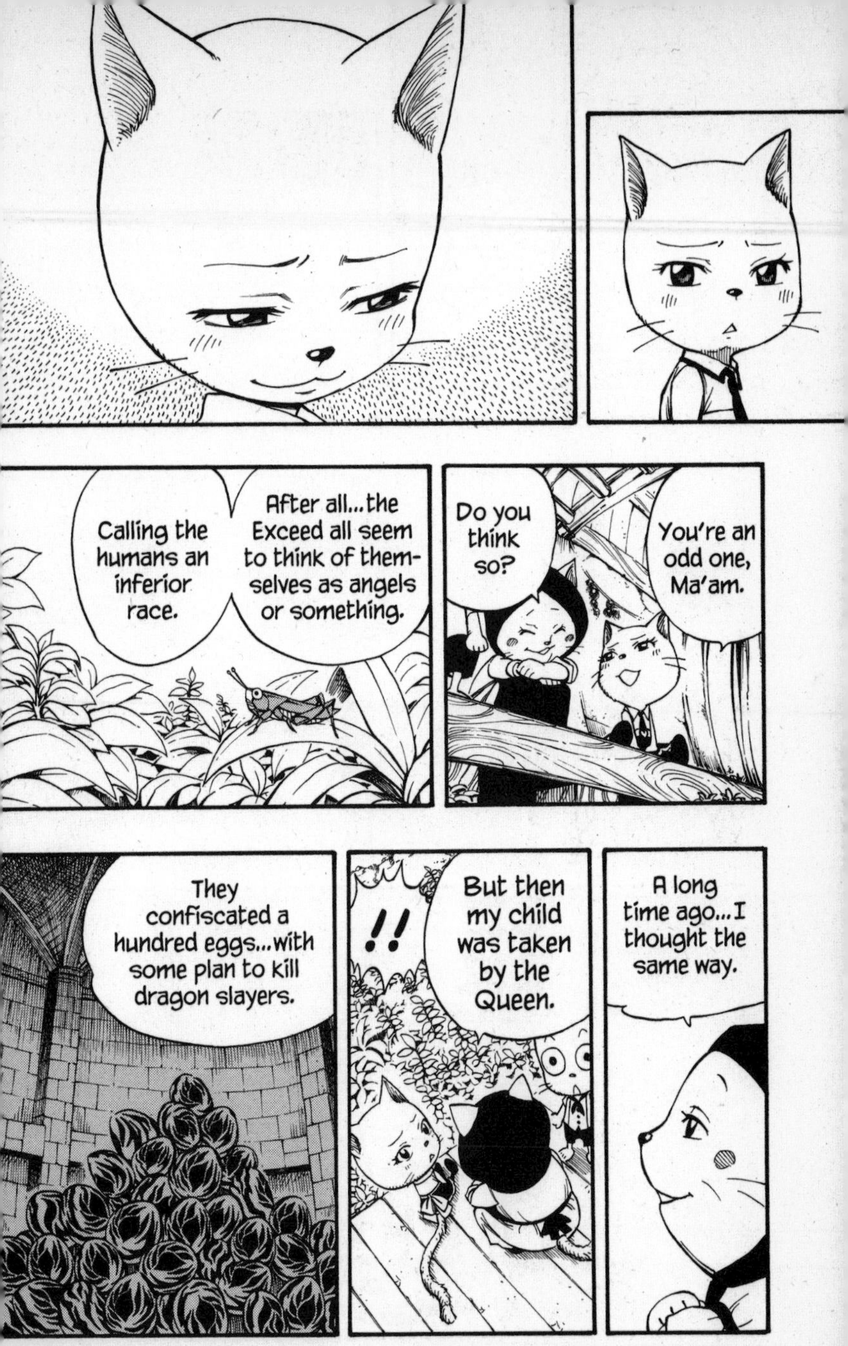
You're an odd one, Ma'am.
Do you think so?
After all...the Exceed all seem to think of them-selves as angels or something.
Calling the humans an inferior race.
A long time ago...I thought the same way.
But then my child was taken by the Queen.
!!
They confiscated a hundred eggs...with some plan to kill dragon slayers.

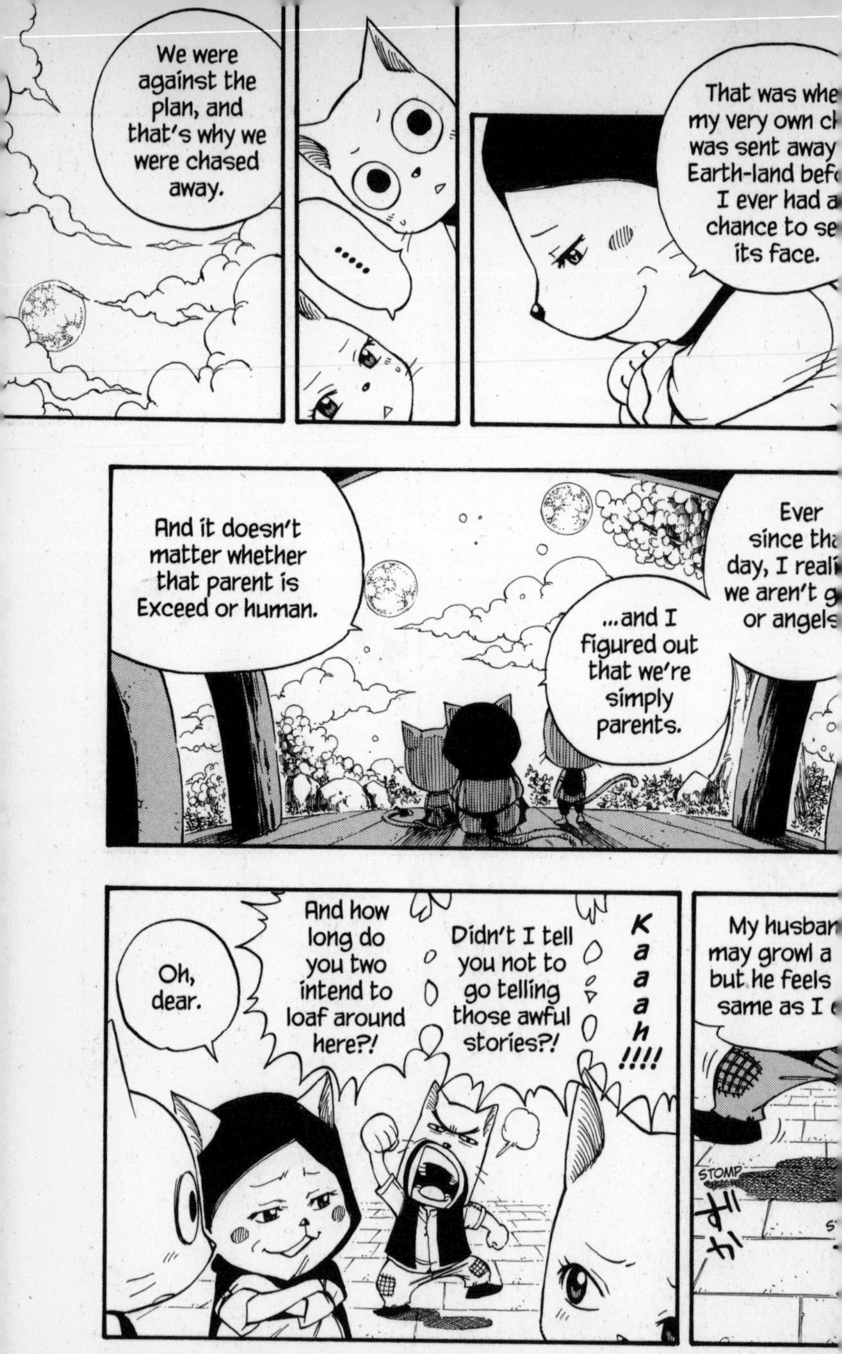
That was whe
my very own c
was sent away
Earth-land bef
I ever had a
chance to se
its face.
.....
We were against the plan, and that's why we were chased away.
Ever since th
day, I real
we aren't g
or angel
...and I figured out that we're simply parents.
And it doesn't matter whether that parent is Exceed or human.
My husban
may growl a
but he feels
same as I
STOMP
Kaaah!!!!
Didn't I tell you not to go telling those awful stories?!
And how long do you two intend to loaf around here?!
Oh, dear.

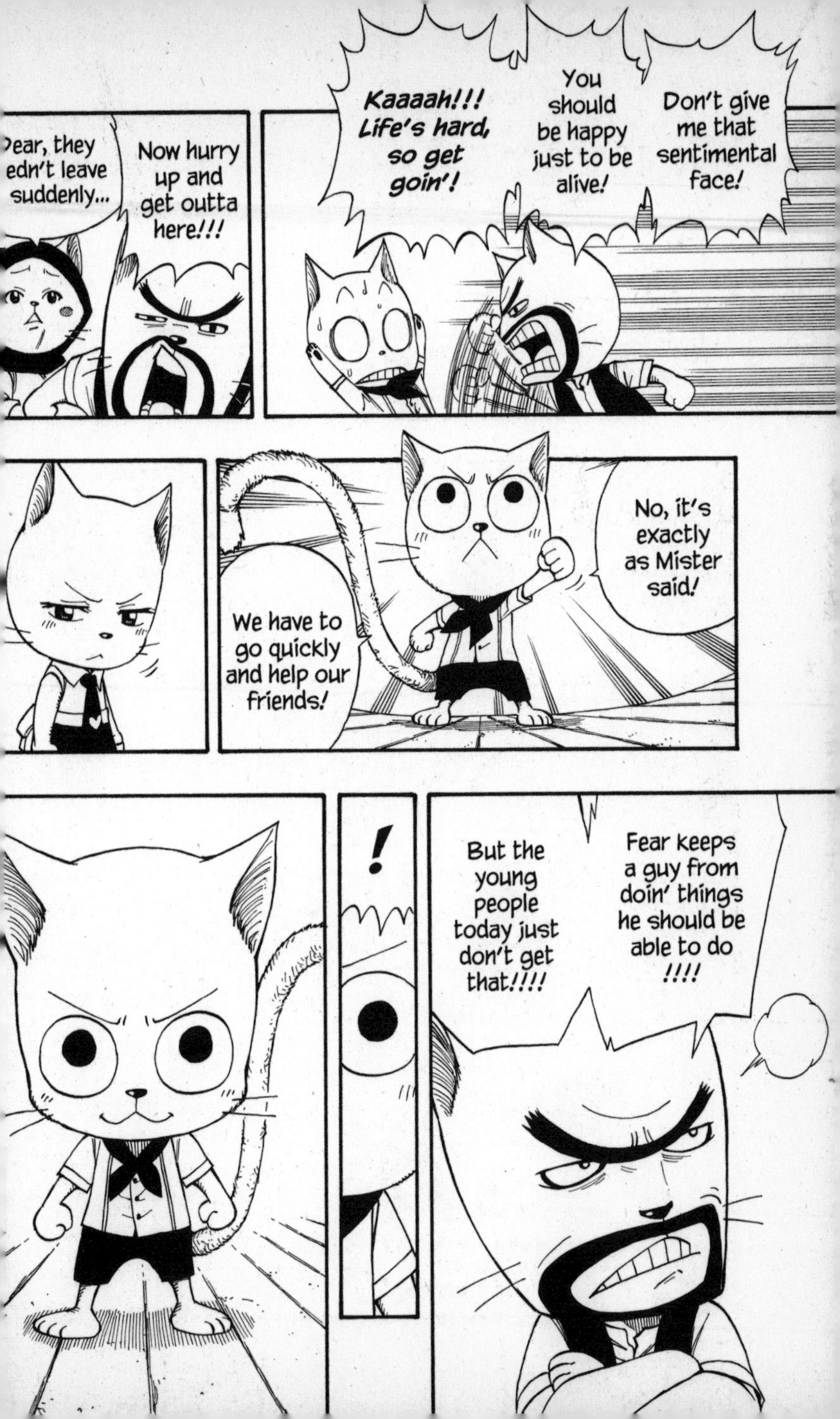

Don't give me that sentimental face!
You should be happy just to be alive!
Kaaaah!!! Life's hard, so get goin'!
Now hurry up and get outta here!!!
ear, they edn't leave suddenly...
No, it's exactly as Mister said!
We have to go quickly and help our friends!
Fear keeps a guy from doin' things he should be able to do !!!!
But the young people today just don't get that!!!!
!

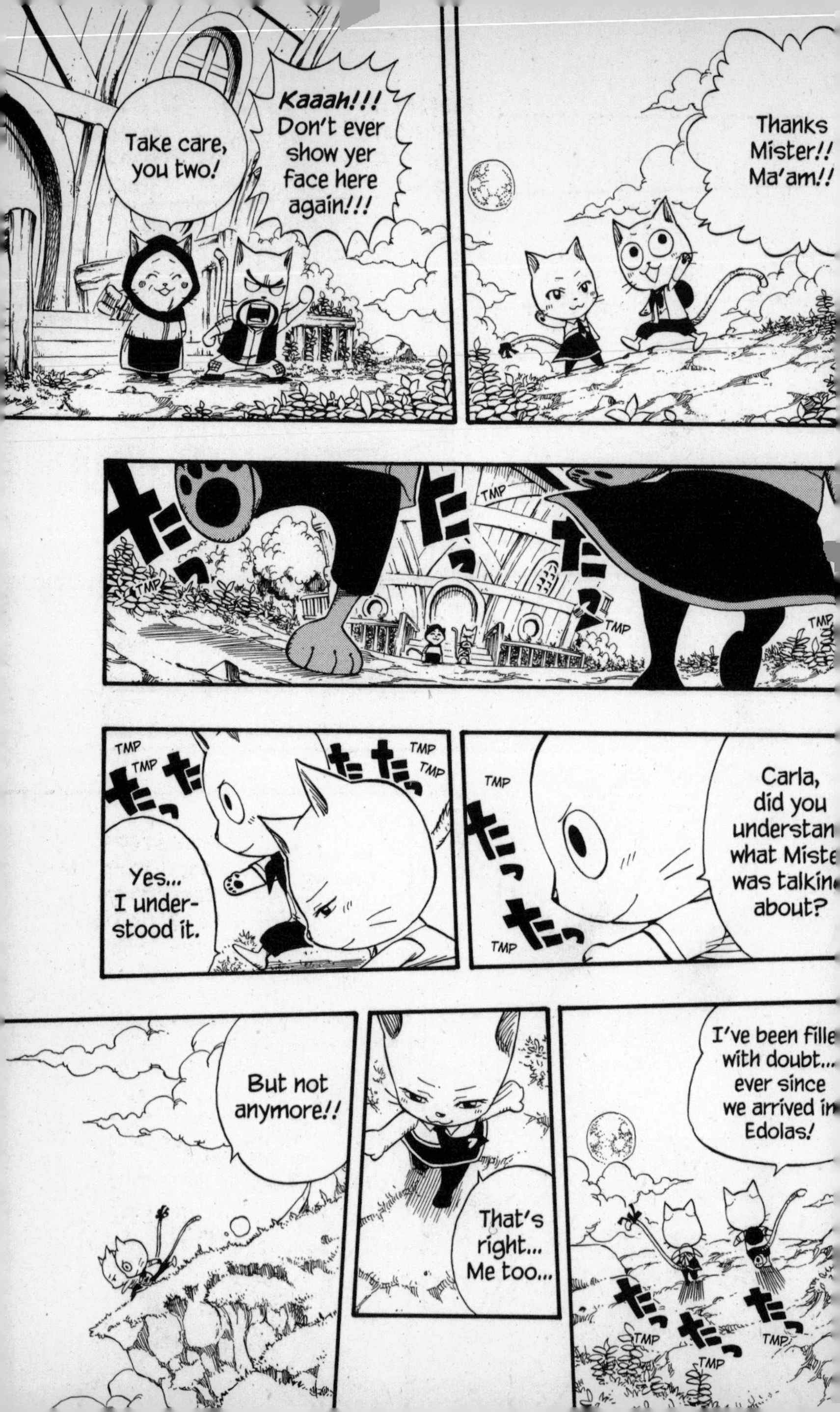
Thanks Mister!! Ma'am!!
Kaaah!!! Don't ever show yer face here again!!!
Take care, you two!
TMP
TMP
TMP
TMP
TMP
Carla, did you understan what Miste was talkin about?
TMP
TMP
TMP
TMP
TMP
TMP
Yes... I understood it.
I've been fille with doubt... ever since we arrived in Edolas!
TMP
TMP
TMP
That's right... Me too...
But not anymore!!

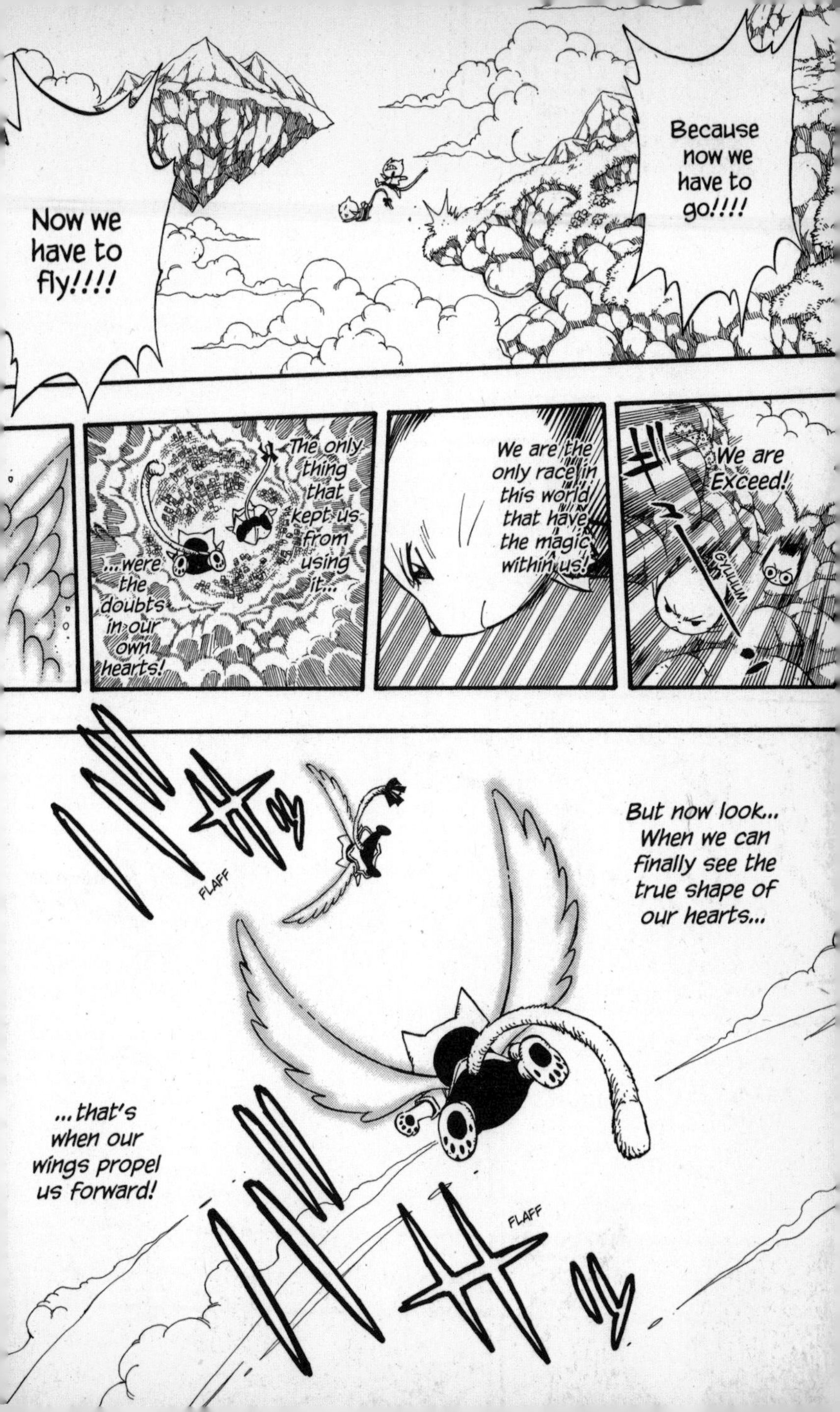
Because now we have to go!!!!
Now we have to fly!!!!
We are Exceed!
GYUUUM
We are the only race in this world that have the magic within us!
The only thing that kept us from using it...
...were the doubts in our own hearts!
But now look... When we can finally see the true shape of our hearts...
FLAFF
...that's when our wings propel us forward!
FLAFF

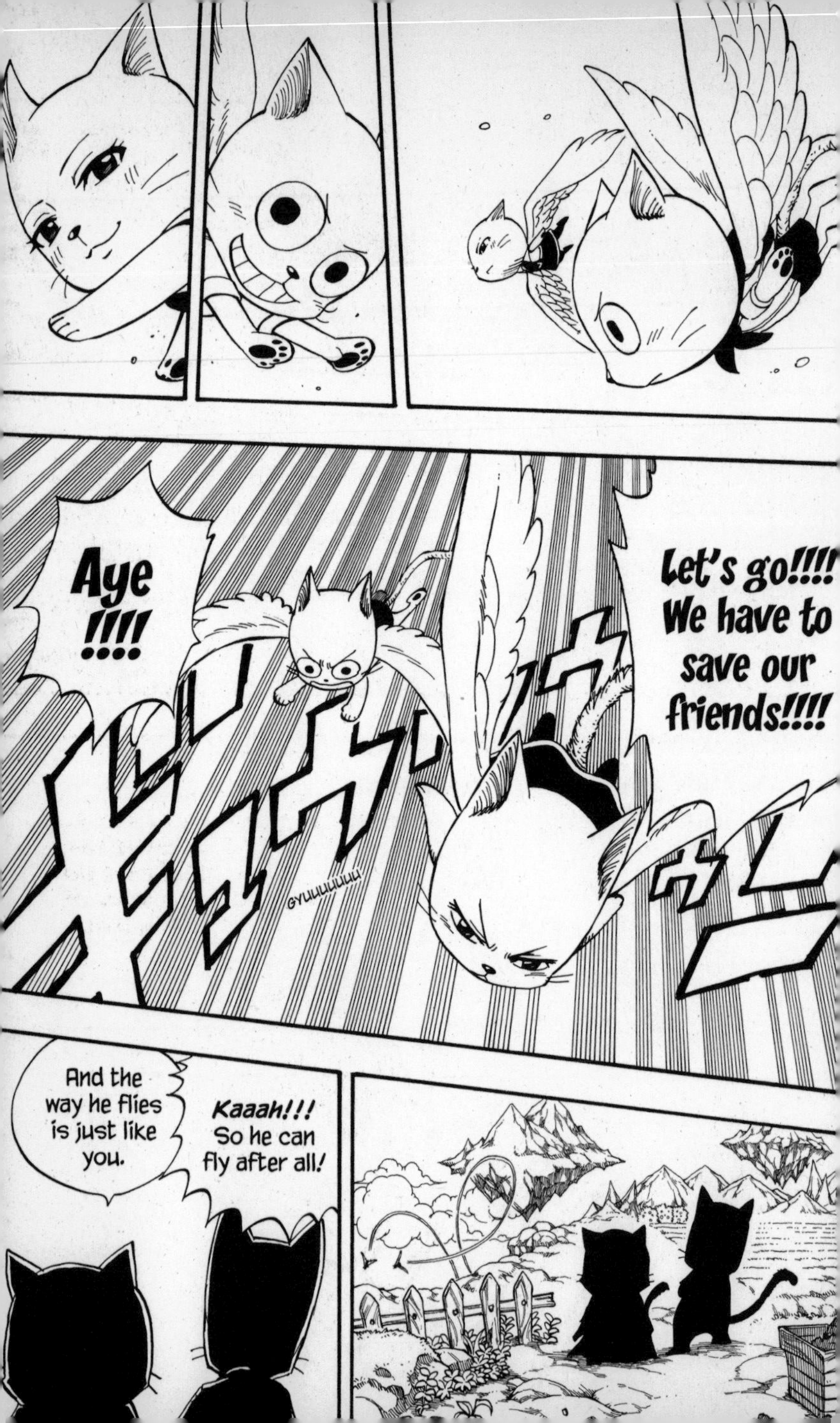
Let's go!!!! We have to save our friends!!!!
Aye !!!!
Kaaah!!! So he can fly after all!
And the way he flies is just like you.

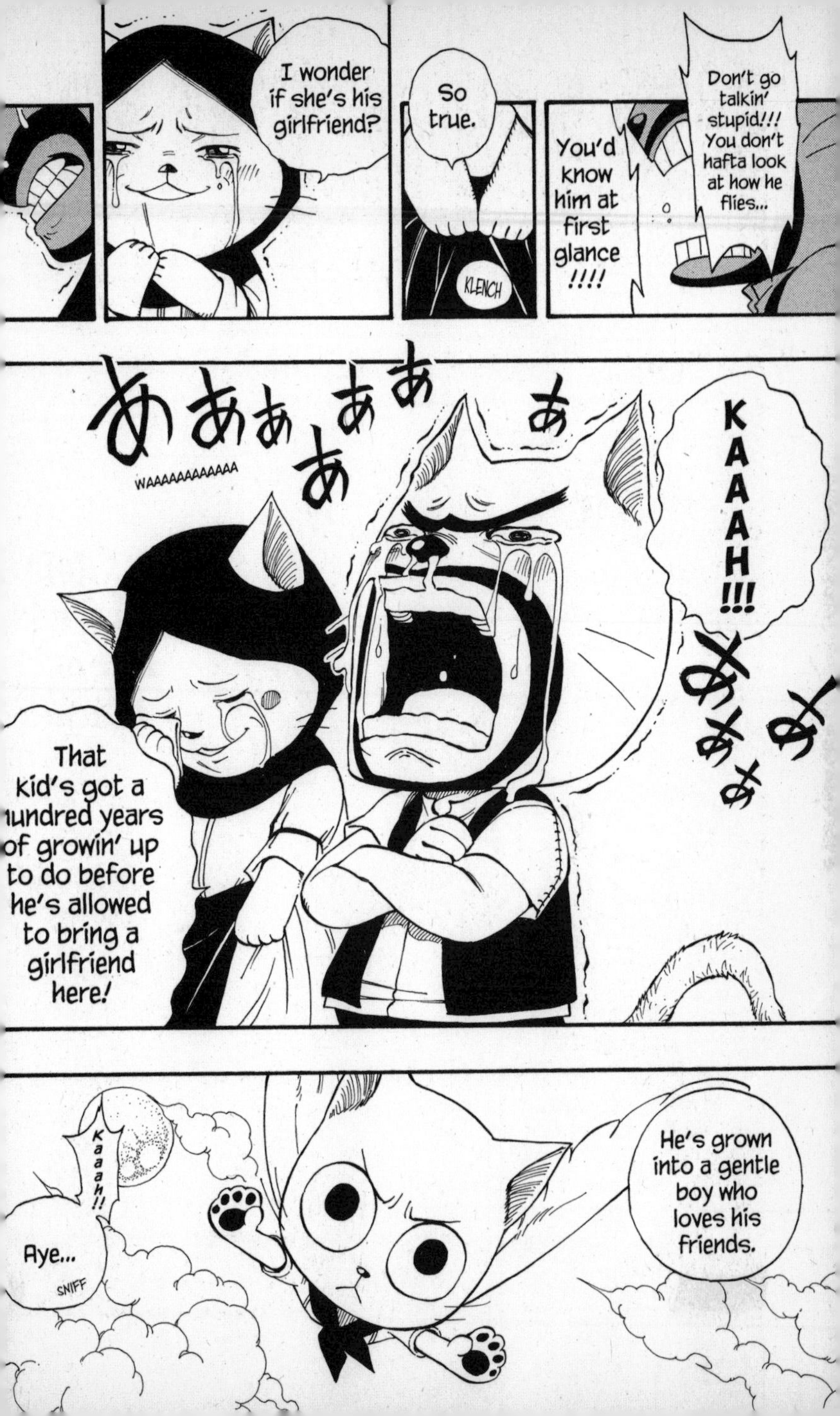
Don't go talkin' stupid!!! You don't hafta look at how he flies...
You'd know him at first glance!!!!
So true.
KLENCH
I wonder if she's his girlfriend?
KAAAH!!!
あああぁ
ああぁあああ
WAAAAAAAAAAAA
That kid's got a hundred years of growin' up to do before he's allowed to bring a girlfriend here!
He's grown into a gentle boy who loves his friends.
Kaaah!!
Aye...
SNIFF

FAIRY TAIL

フェアリーテイル

Chapter 178, Because I'm By Your Sid

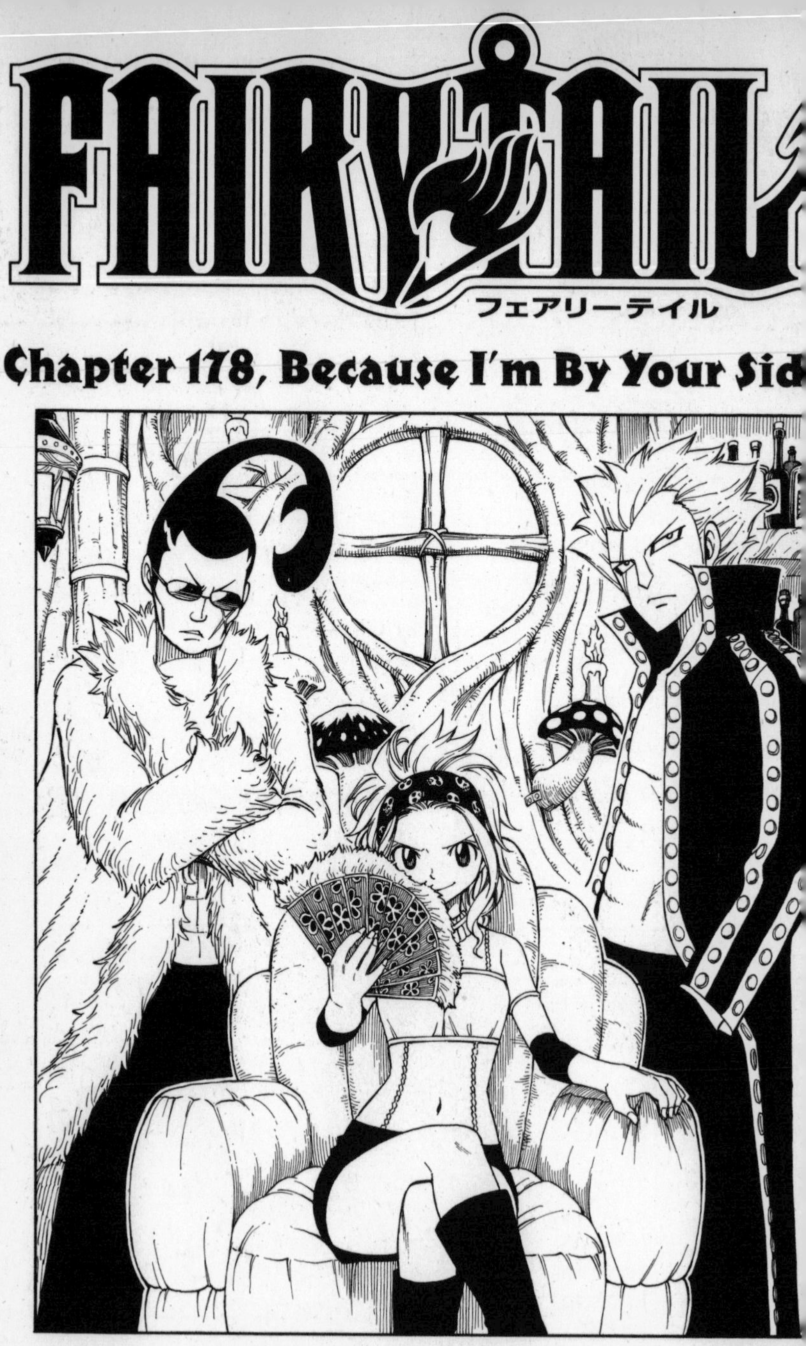

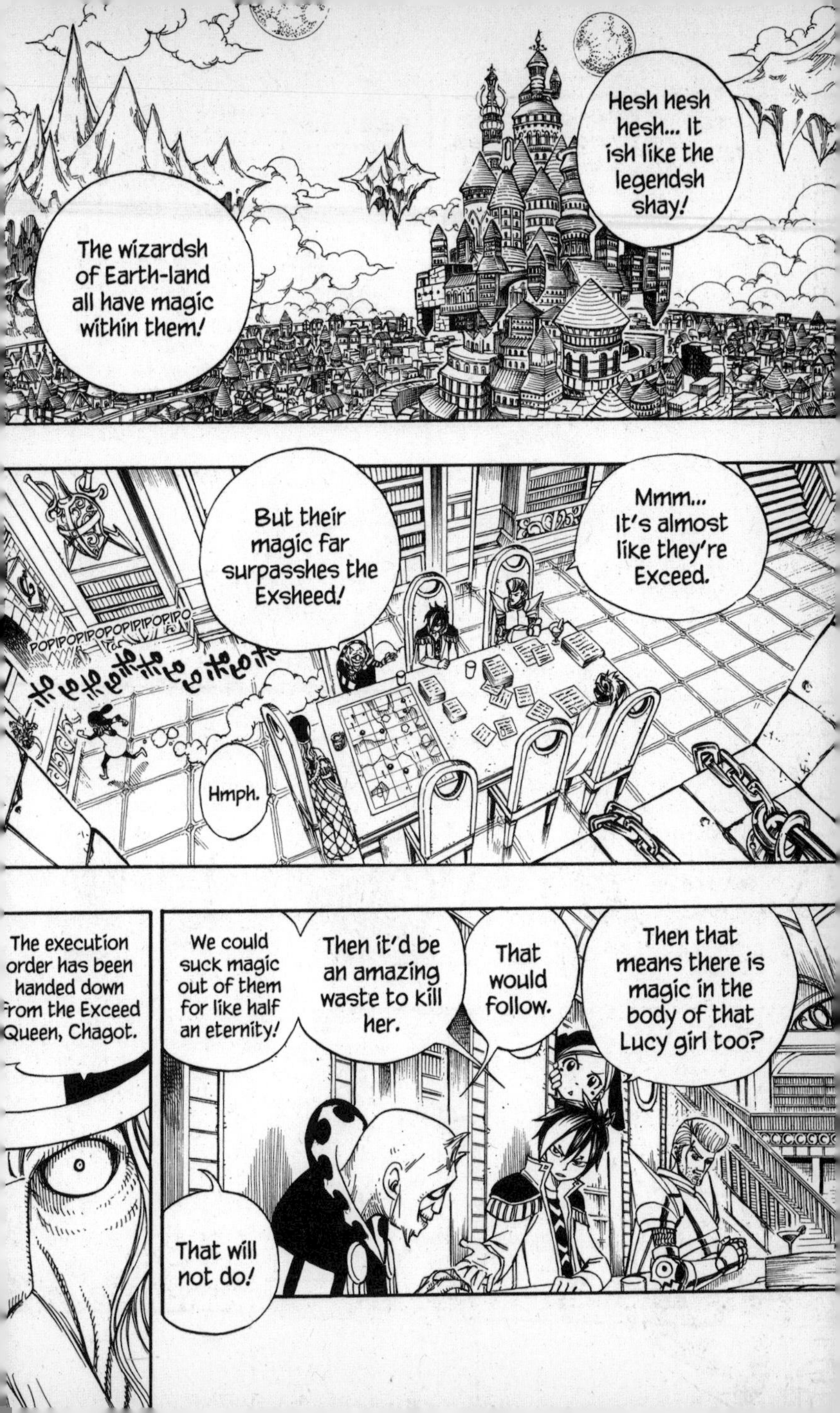

Hesh hesh hesh... It ish like the legendsh shay!
The wizardsh of Earth-land all have magic within them!
Mmm... It's almost like they're Exceed.
But their magic far surpasshes the Exsheed!
POPIPOPIPOPOPIPIPOPIPO
Hmph.
Then that means there is magic in the body of that Lucy girl too?
That would follow.
Then it'd be an amazing waste to kill her.
We could suck magic out of them for like half an eternity!
That will not do!
The execution order has been handed down from the Exceed Queen, Chagot.

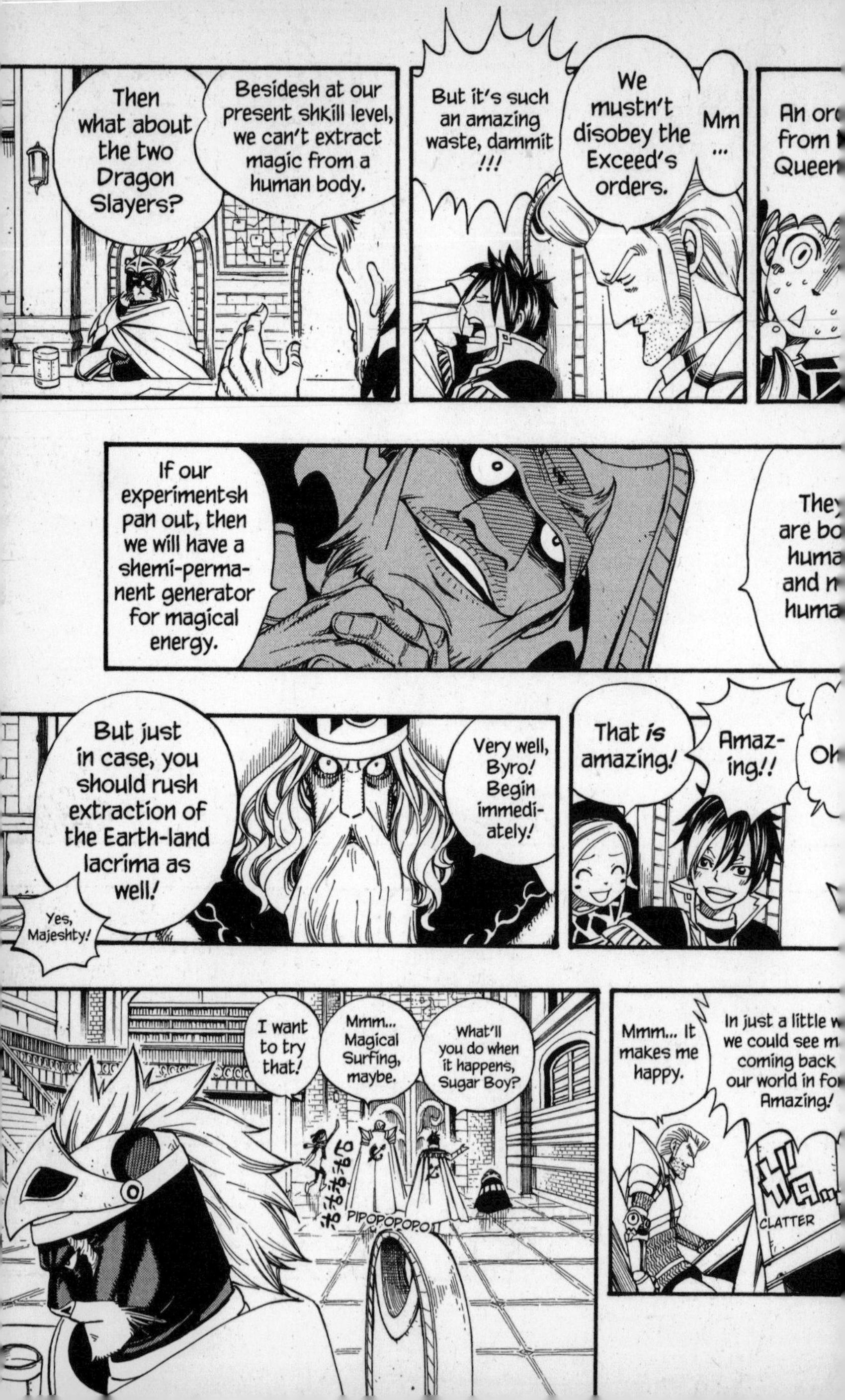

An or
from
Queen
Mm ...
We mustn't disobey the Exceed's orders.
But it's such an amazing waste, dammit!!!
Besidesh at our present shkill level, we can't extract magic from a human body.
Then what about the two Dragon Slayers?
They
are bo
huma
and n
huma
If our experimentsh pan out, then we will have a shemi-permanent generator for magical energy.
Oh
Amazing!!
That *is* amazing!
Very well, Byro! Begin immediately!
But just in case, you should rush extraction of the Earth-land lacrima as well!
Yes, Majeshty!
In just a little w
we could see m
coming back
our world in fo
Amazing!
Mmm... It makes me happy.
CLATTER
What'll you do when it happens, Sugar Boy?
Mmm... Magical Surfing, maybe.
I want to try that!
PIPOPOPOPO

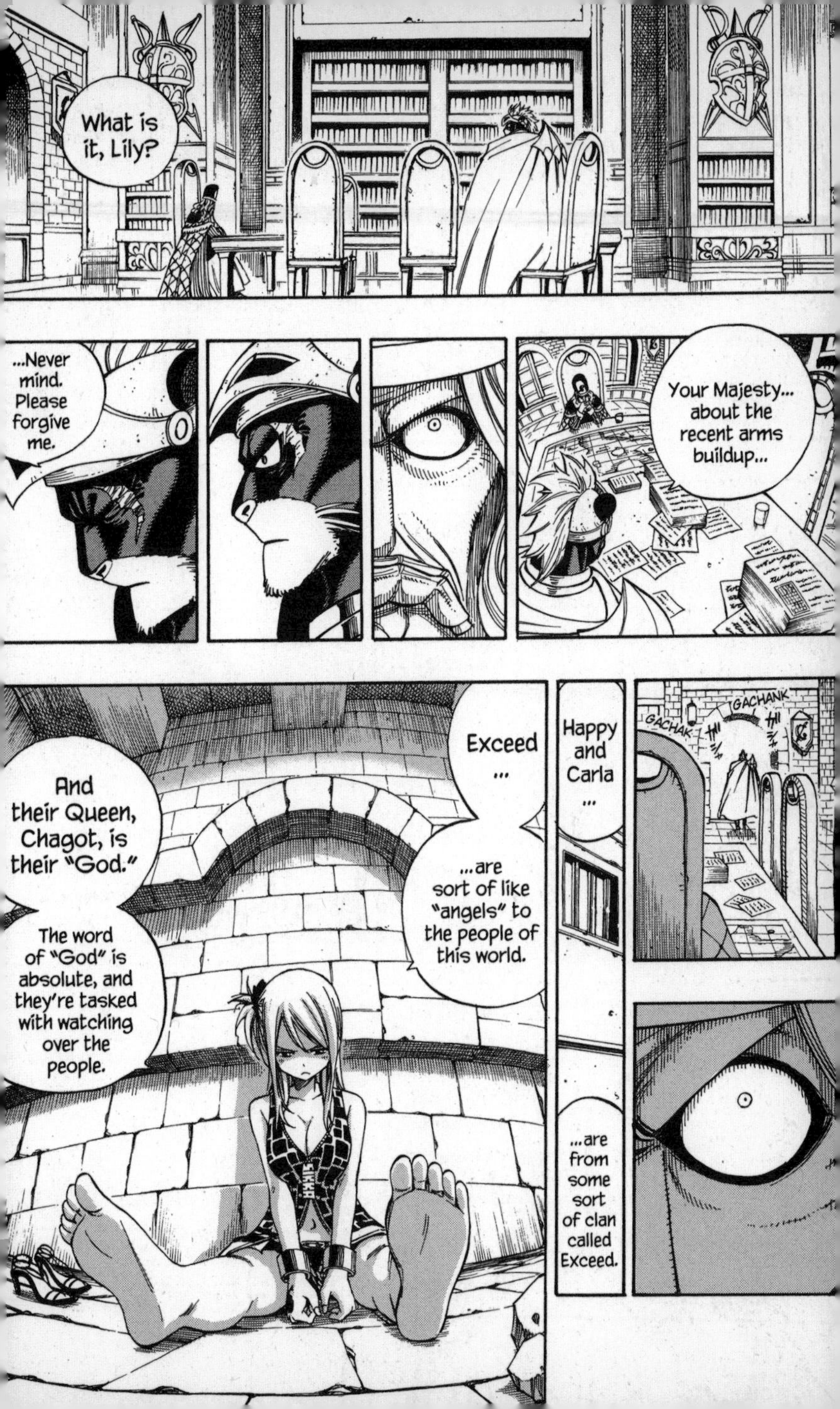
What is it, Lily?
Your Majesty... about the recent arms buildup...
...Never mind. Please forgive me.
GACHANK
GACHAK
Happy and Carla...
...are from some sort of clan called Exceed.
Exceed...
...are sort of like "angels" to the people of this world.
And their Queen, Chagot, is their "God."
The word of "God" is absolute, and they're tasked with watching over the people.

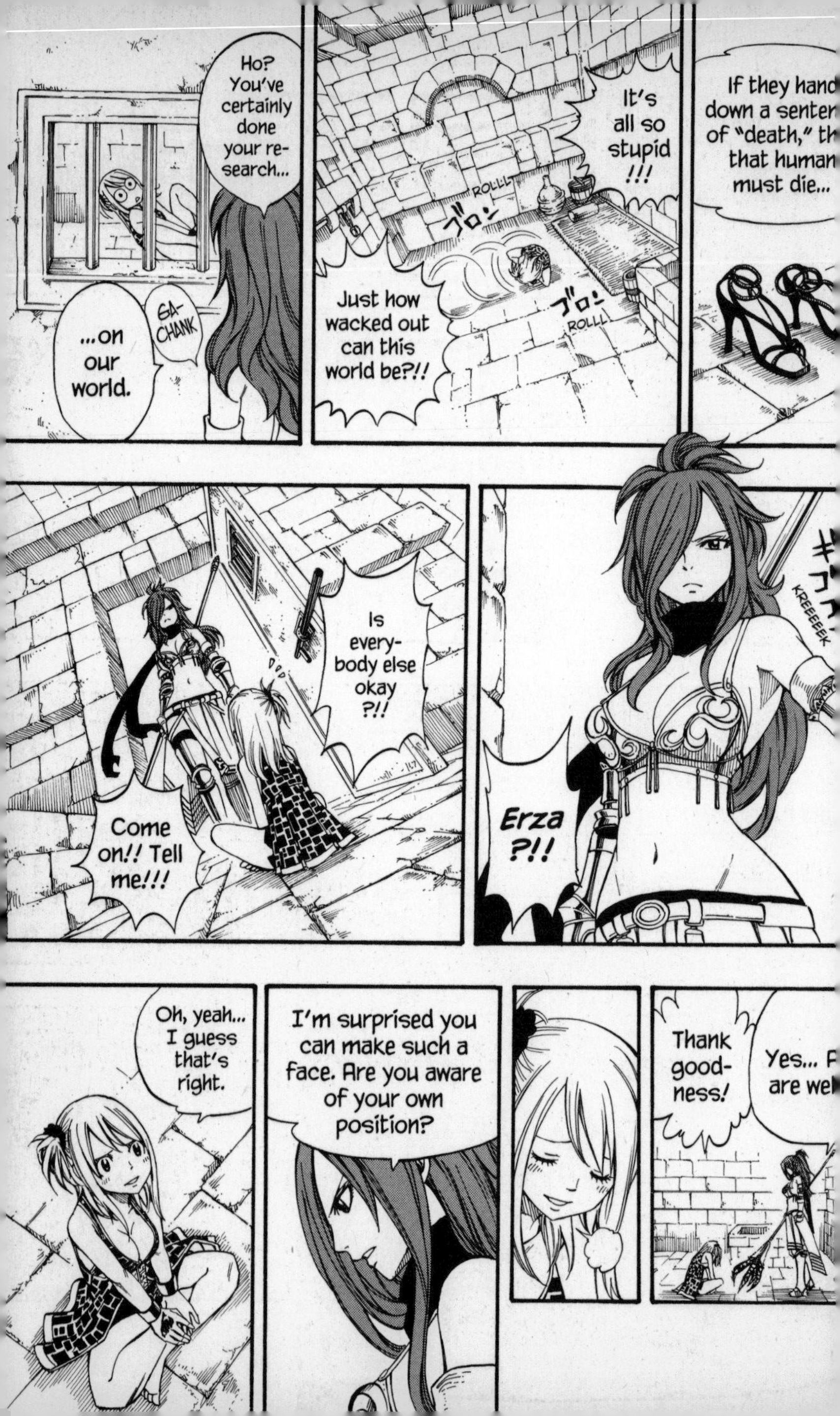

If they hand down a senter of "death," th that human must die...
It's all so stupid!!!
ROLLL
ROLLL
Just how wacked out can this world be?!!
Ho? You've certainly done your re-search...
GA-CHANK
...on our world.
KREEEEEK
Erza?!!
Is every-body else okay?!!
Come on!! Tell me!!!
Yes... are we
Thank good-ness!
I'm surprised you can make such a face. Are you aware of your own position?
Oh, yeah... I guess that's right.

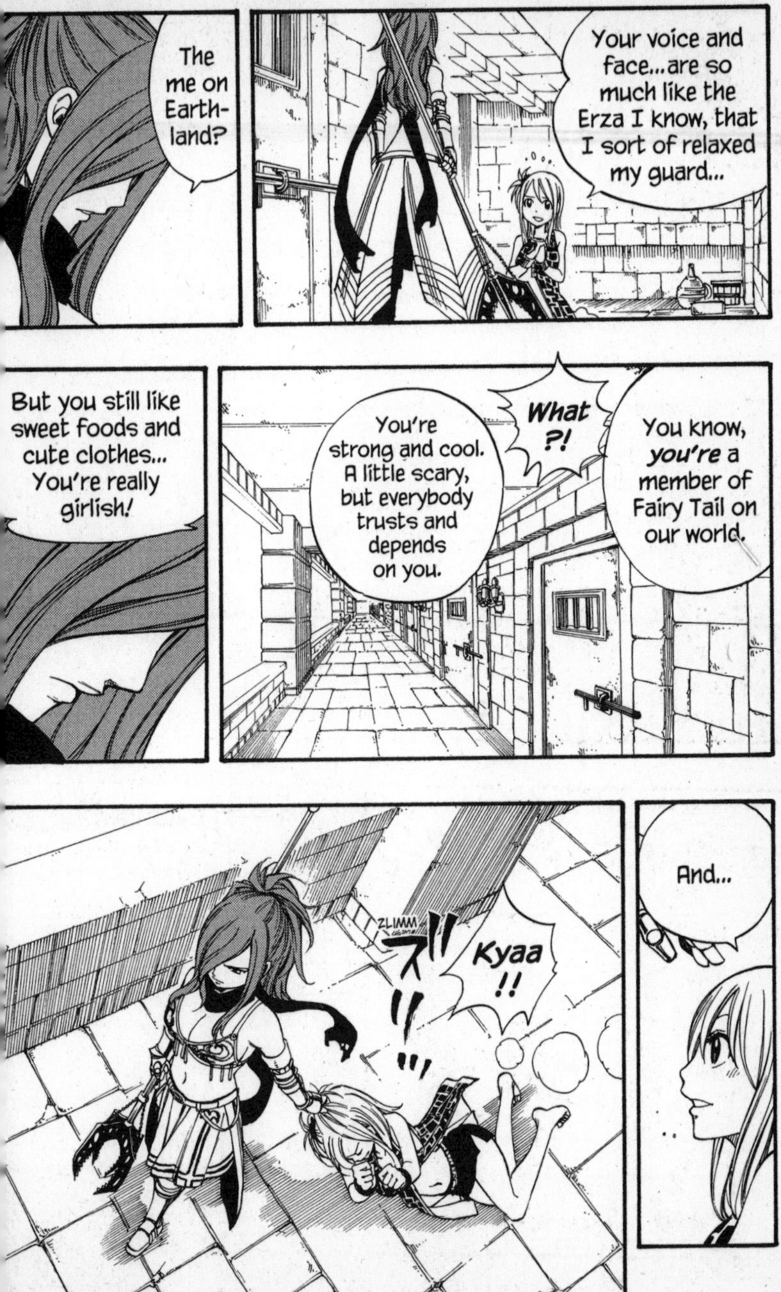
Your voice and face...are so much like the Erza I know, that I sort of relaxed my guard...
The me on Earth-land?
You know, *you're* a member of Fairy Tail on our world.
What?!
You're strong and cool. A little scary, but everybody trusts and depends on you.
But you still like sweet foods and cute clothes... You're really girlish!
And...
ZLIMM
Kyaa!!

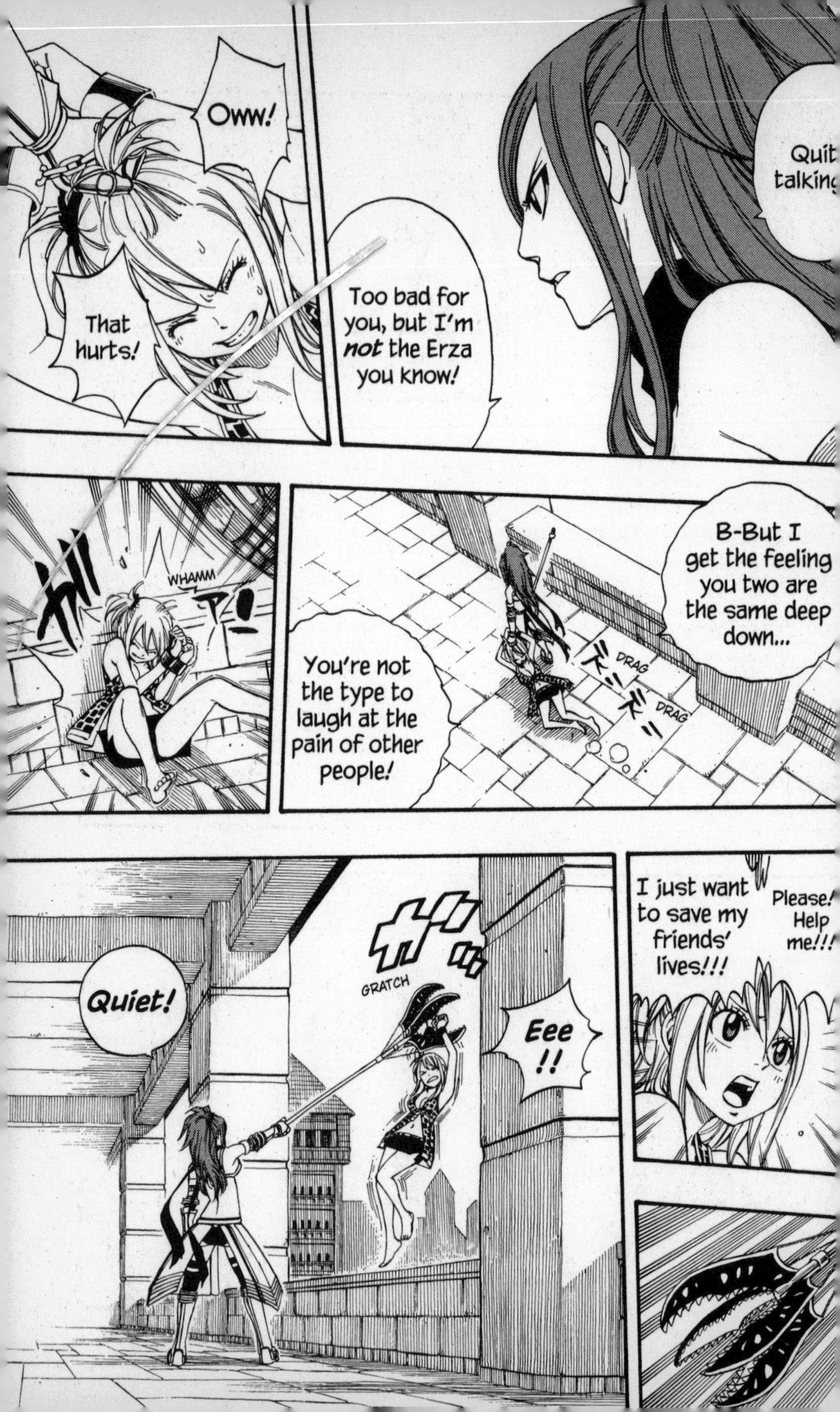
Quit talkin
Too bad for you, but I'm *not* the Erza you know!
Oww!
That hurts!
B-But I get the feeling you two are the same deep down...
DRAG
DRAG
You're not the type to laugh at the pain of other people!
WHAMM
Please! Help me!!!
I just want to save my friends' lives!!!
GRATCH
Eee !!
Quiet!

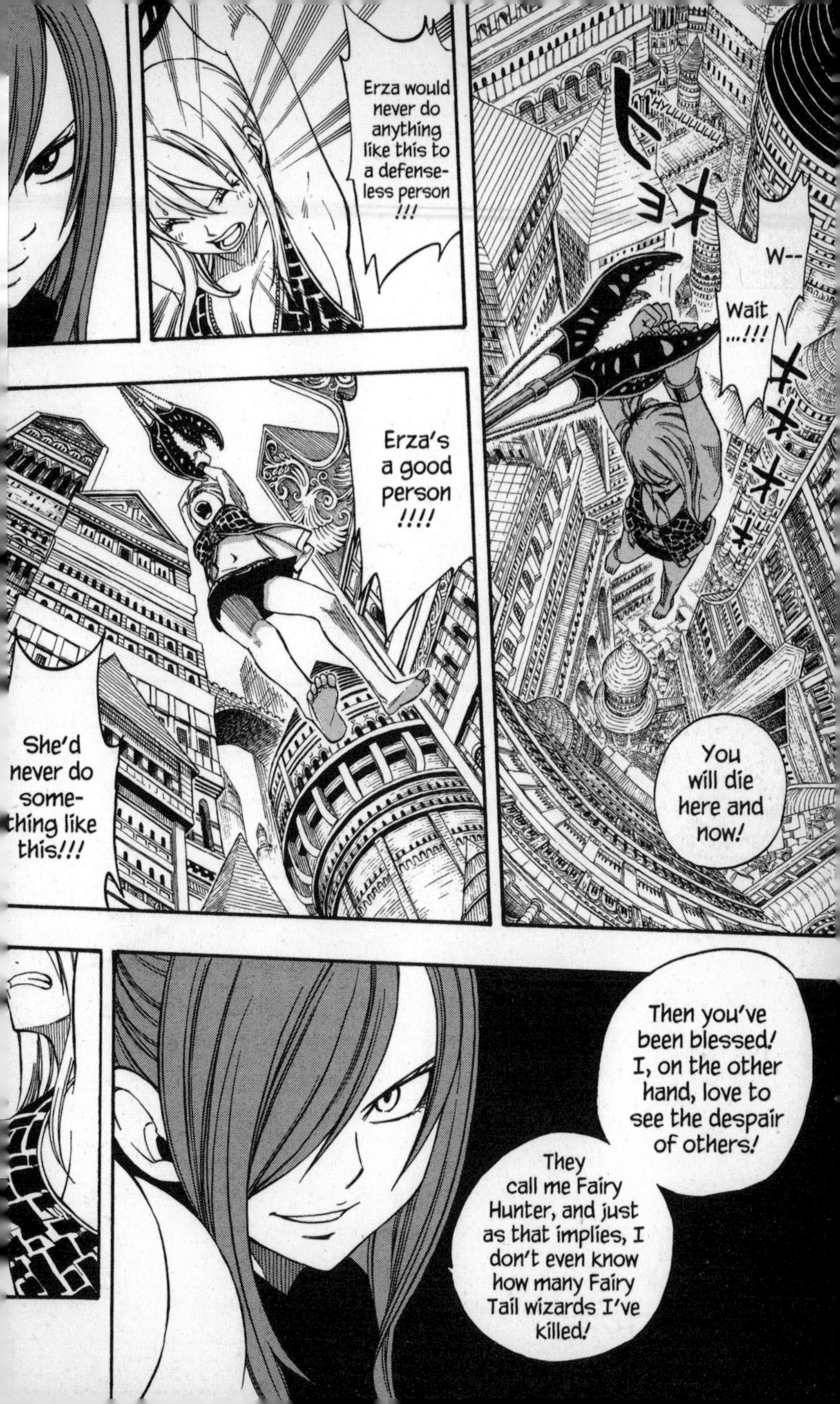

W--
Wait ...!!!
You will die here and now!
Erza would never do anything like this to a defenseless person !!!
Erza's a good person !!!!
She'd never do some-thing like this!!!
Then you've been blessed! I, on the other hand, love to see the despair of others!
They call me Fairy Hunter, and just as that implies, I don't even know how many Fairy Tail wizards I've killed!

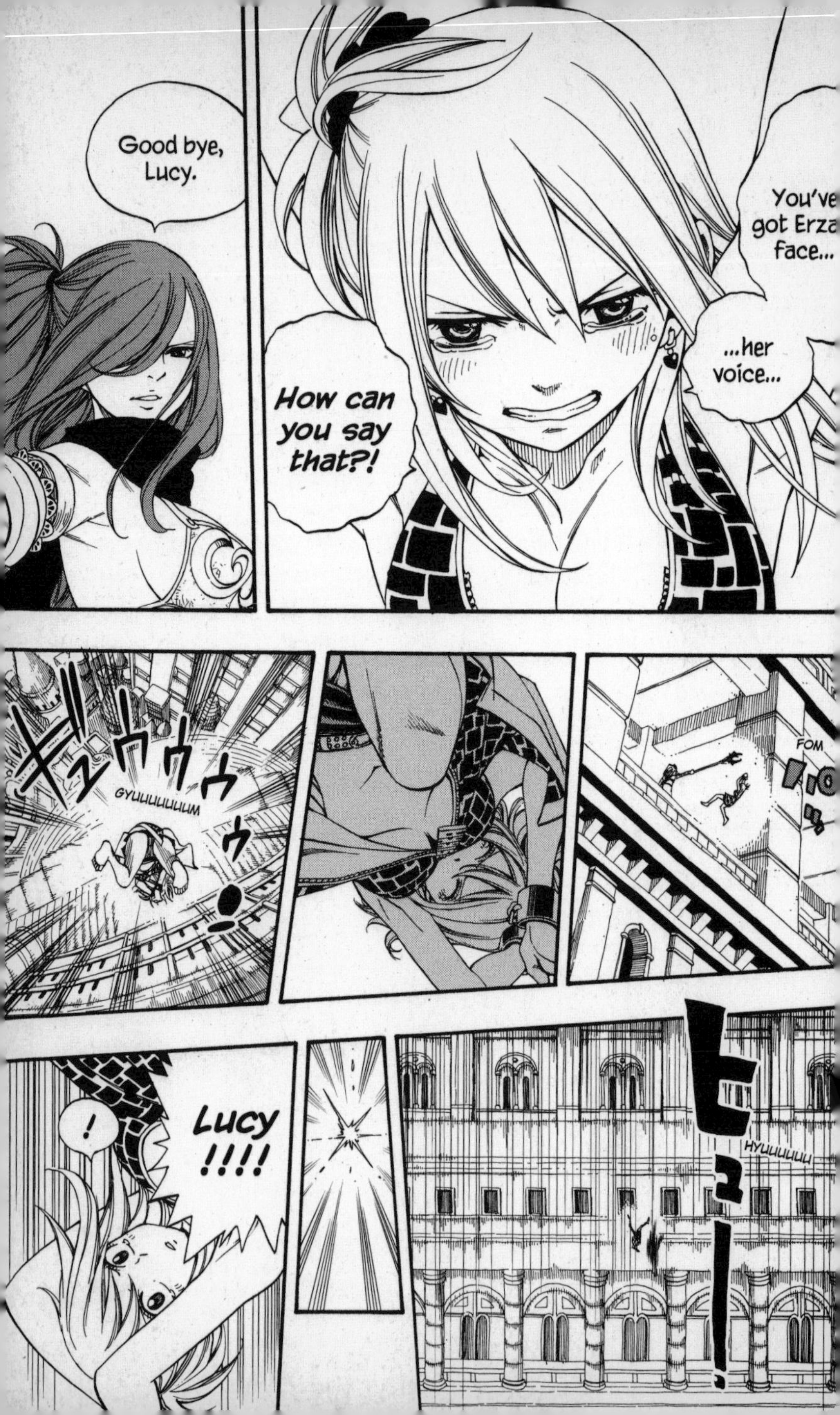

You've got Erza face...
...her voice...
How can you say that?!
Good bye, Lucy.
FOM
GYUUUUUUUM
HYUUUUUUU
!
Lucy !!!!

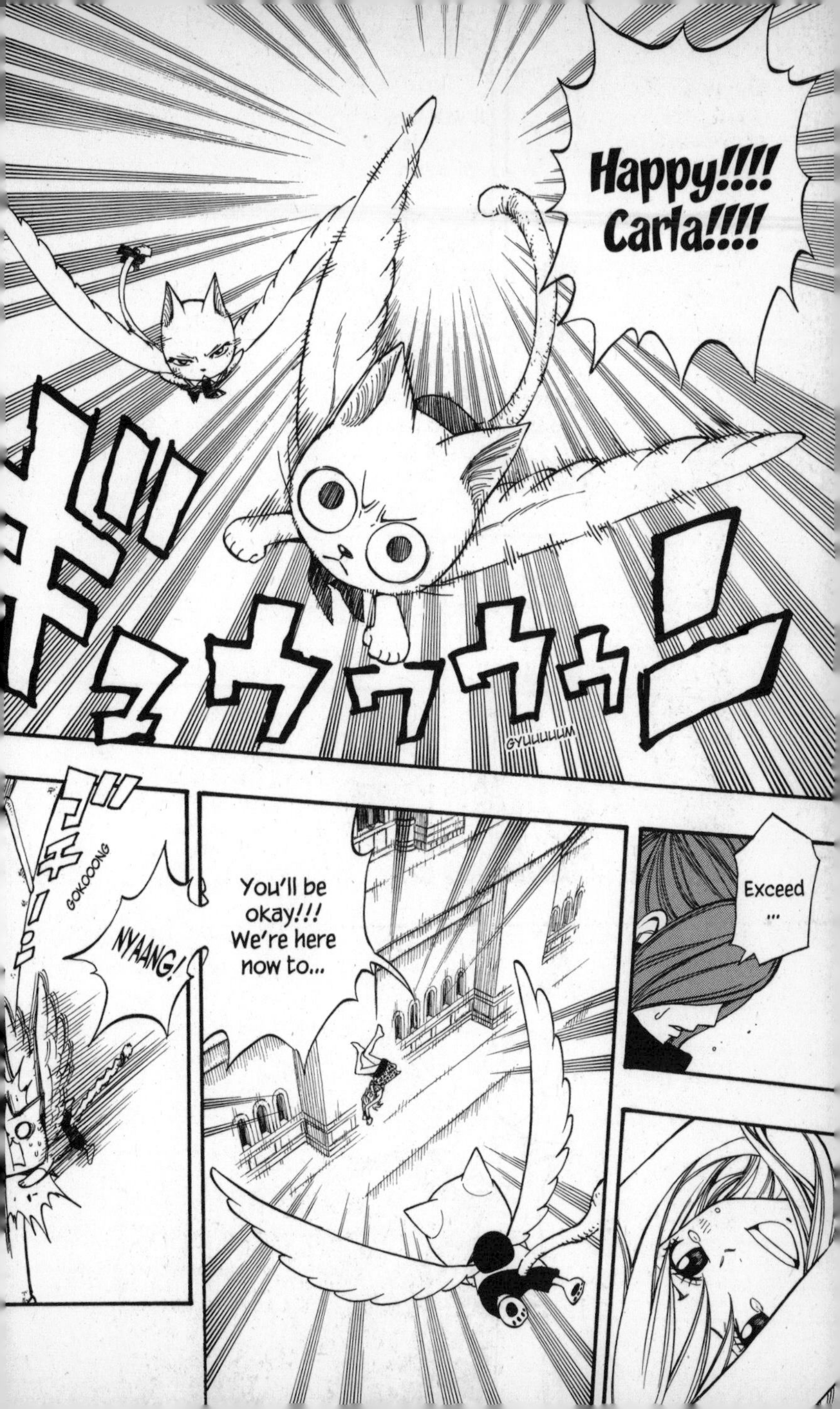
Happy!!!! Carla!!!!
GYUUUUUM
Exceed ...
You'll be okay!!! We're here now to...
NYAANG!
GOKOOONG

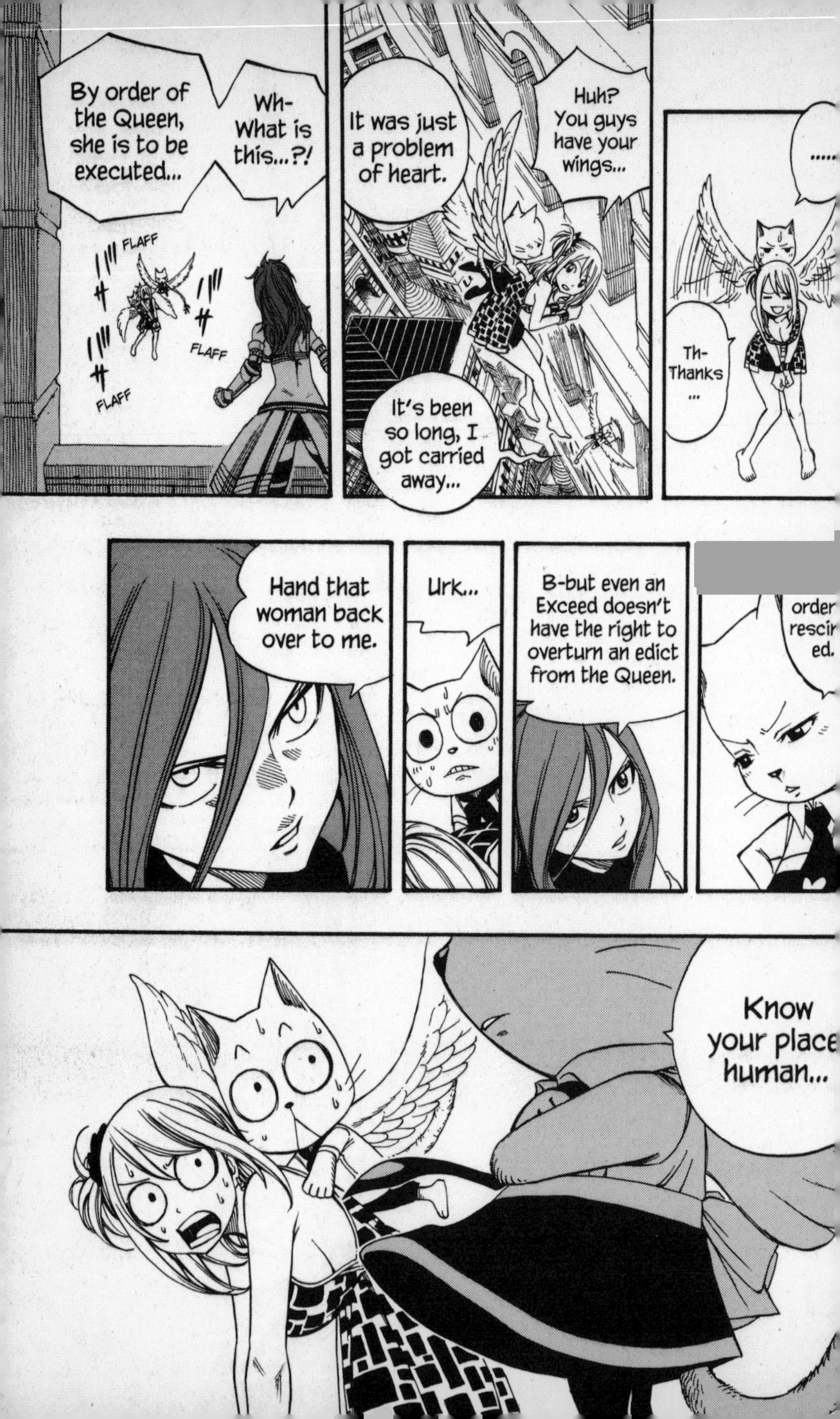
.....
Th-Thanks...
Huh? You guys have your wings...
It was just a problem of heart.
It's been so long, I got carried away...
Wh- What is this...?!
By order of the Queen, she is to be executed...
FLAFF
FLAFF
FLAFF
order resci ed.
B-but even an Exceed doesn't have the right to overturn an edict from the Queen.
Urk...
Hand that woman back over to me.
Know your place human...

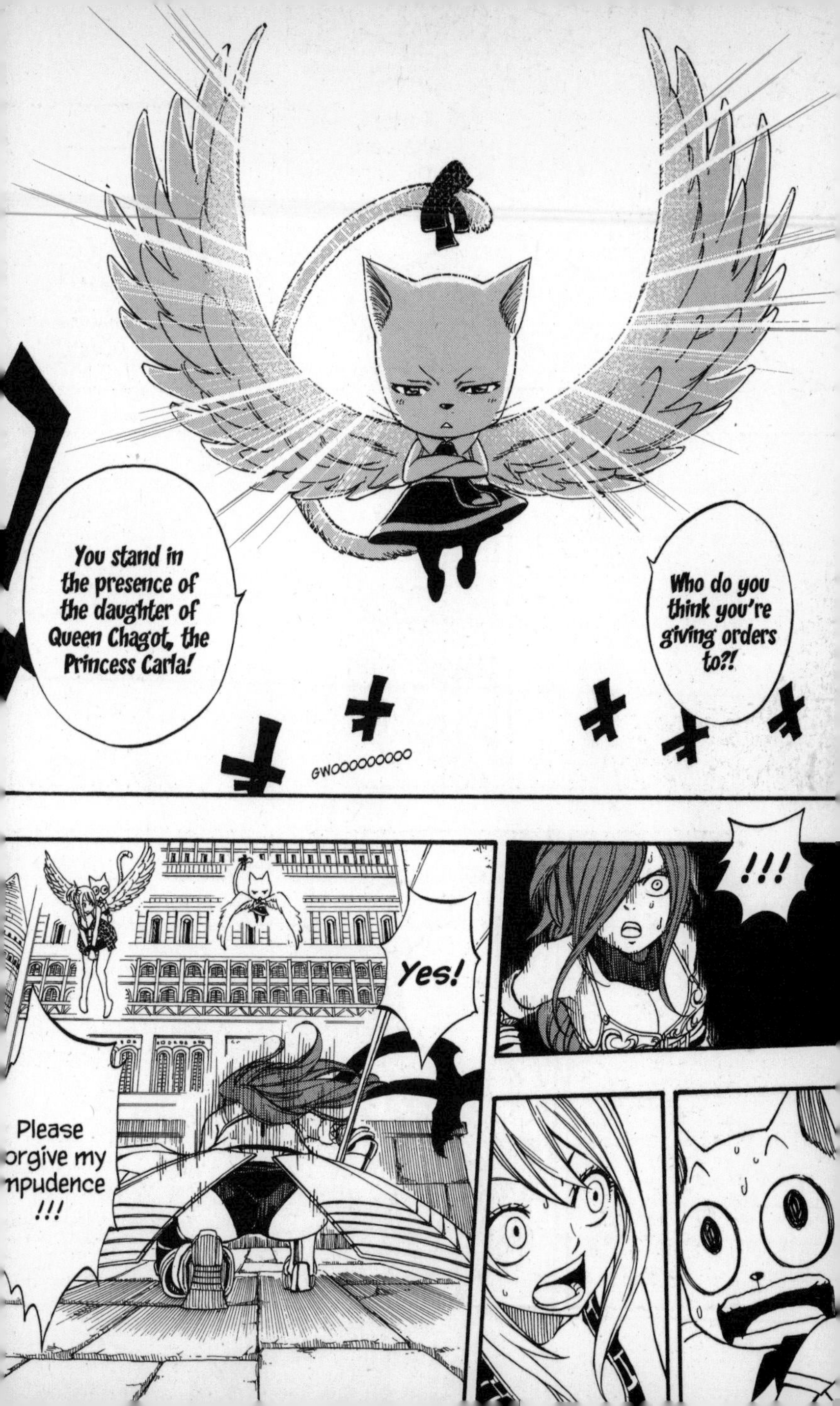
Who do you think you're giving orders to?!
You stand in the presence of the daughter of Queen Chagot, the Princess Carla!
GWOOOOOOOOO
!!!
Yes!
Please orgive my npudence !!!

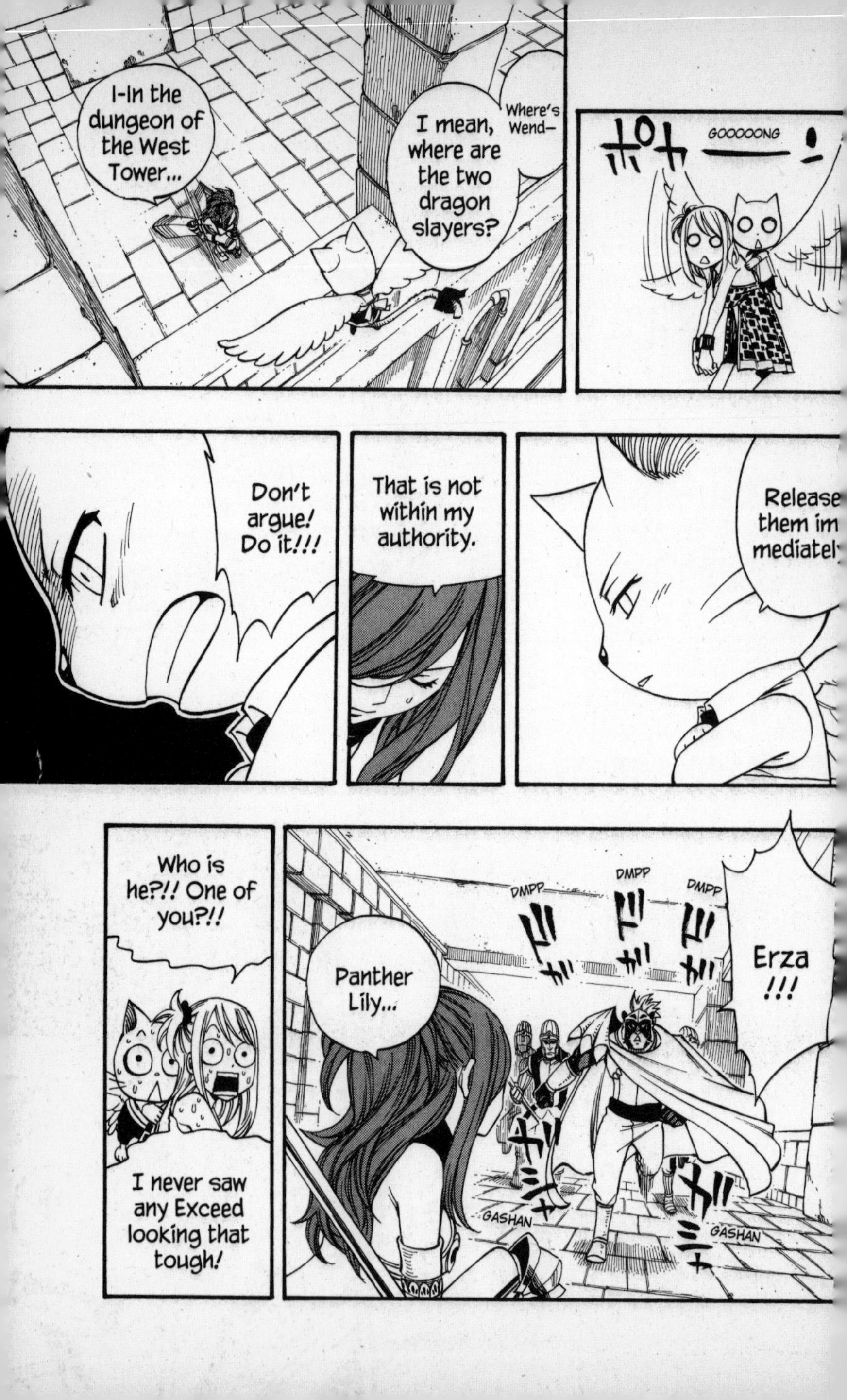
GOOOOONG
Where's Wend—
I mean, where are the two dragon slayers?
I-In the dungeon of the West Tower...
Release them immediatel
That is not within my authority.
Don't argue! Do it!!!
Erza !!!
DMPP
DMPP
DMPP
Panther Lily...
GASHAN
GASHAN
Who is he?!! One of you?!!
I never saw any Exceed looking that tough!

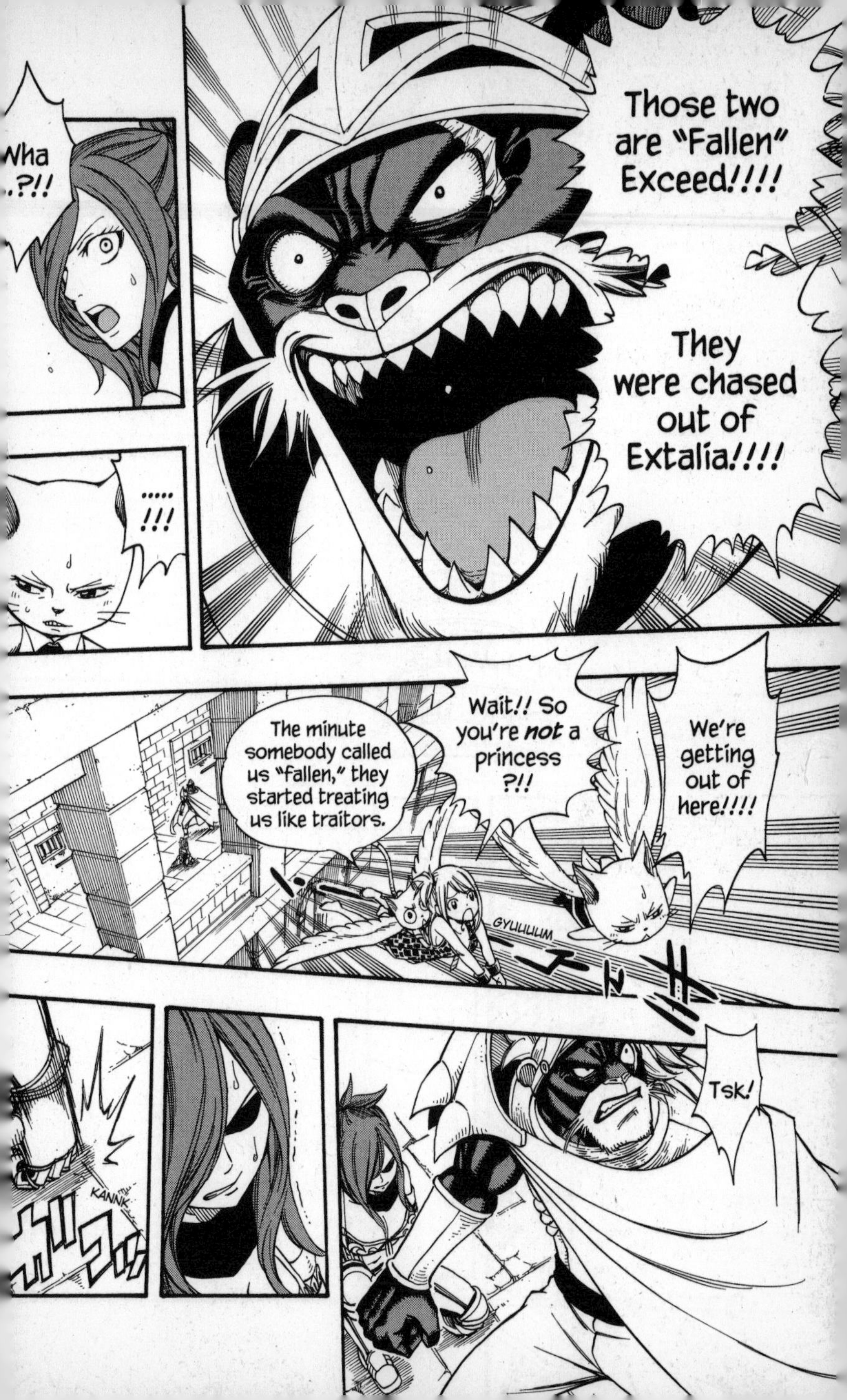
Those two are "Fallen" Exceed!!!!
They were chased out of Extalia!!!!
Wha .?!!
.....!!!
We're getting out of here!!!!
Wait!! So you're *not* a princess ?!!
The minute somebody called us "fallen," they started treating us like traitors.
GYUUUUM
Tsk!
KANNK

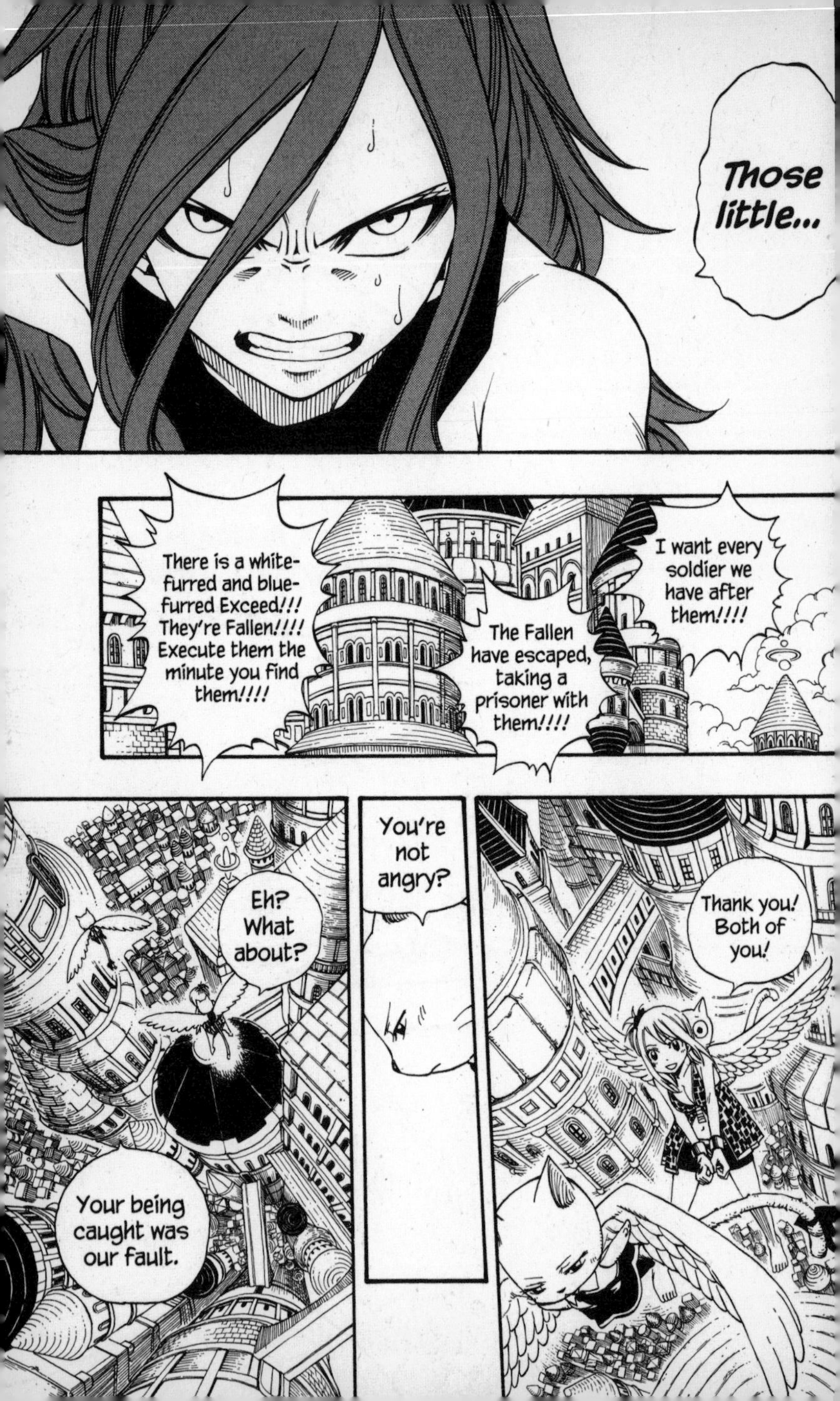

Those little...
I want every soldier we have after them!!!!
The Fallen have escaped, taking a prisoner with them!!!!
There is a white-furred and blue-furred Exceed!!! They're Fallen!!!! Execute them the minute you find them!!!!
Thank you! Both of you!
You're not angry?
Eh? What about?
Your being caught was our fault.

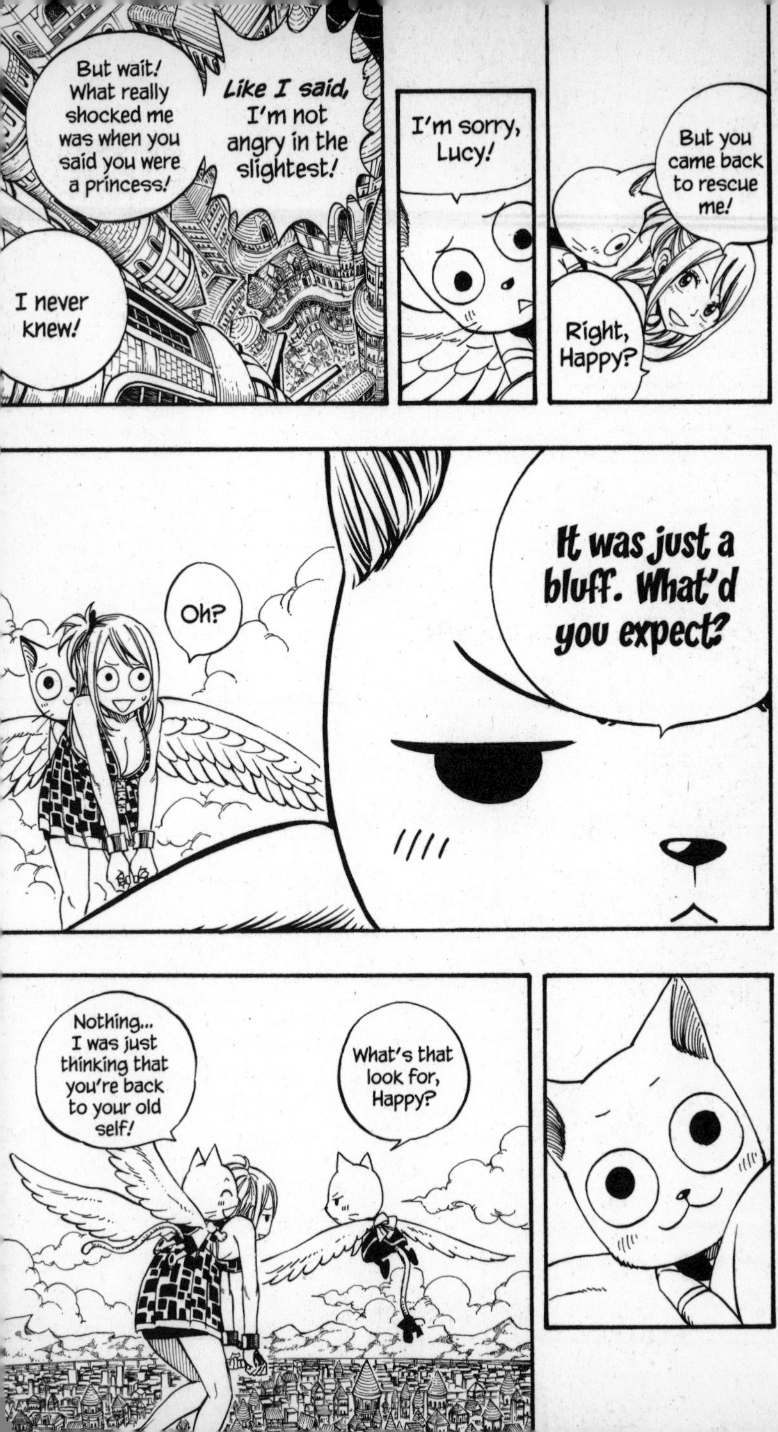
But you came back to rescue me!
Right, Happy?
I'm sorry, Lucy!
Like I said, I'm not angry in the slightest!
But wait! What really shocked me was when you said you were a princess!
I never knew!
It was just a bluff. What'd you expect?
Oh?
What's that look for, Happy?
Nothing... I was just thinking that you're back to your old self!

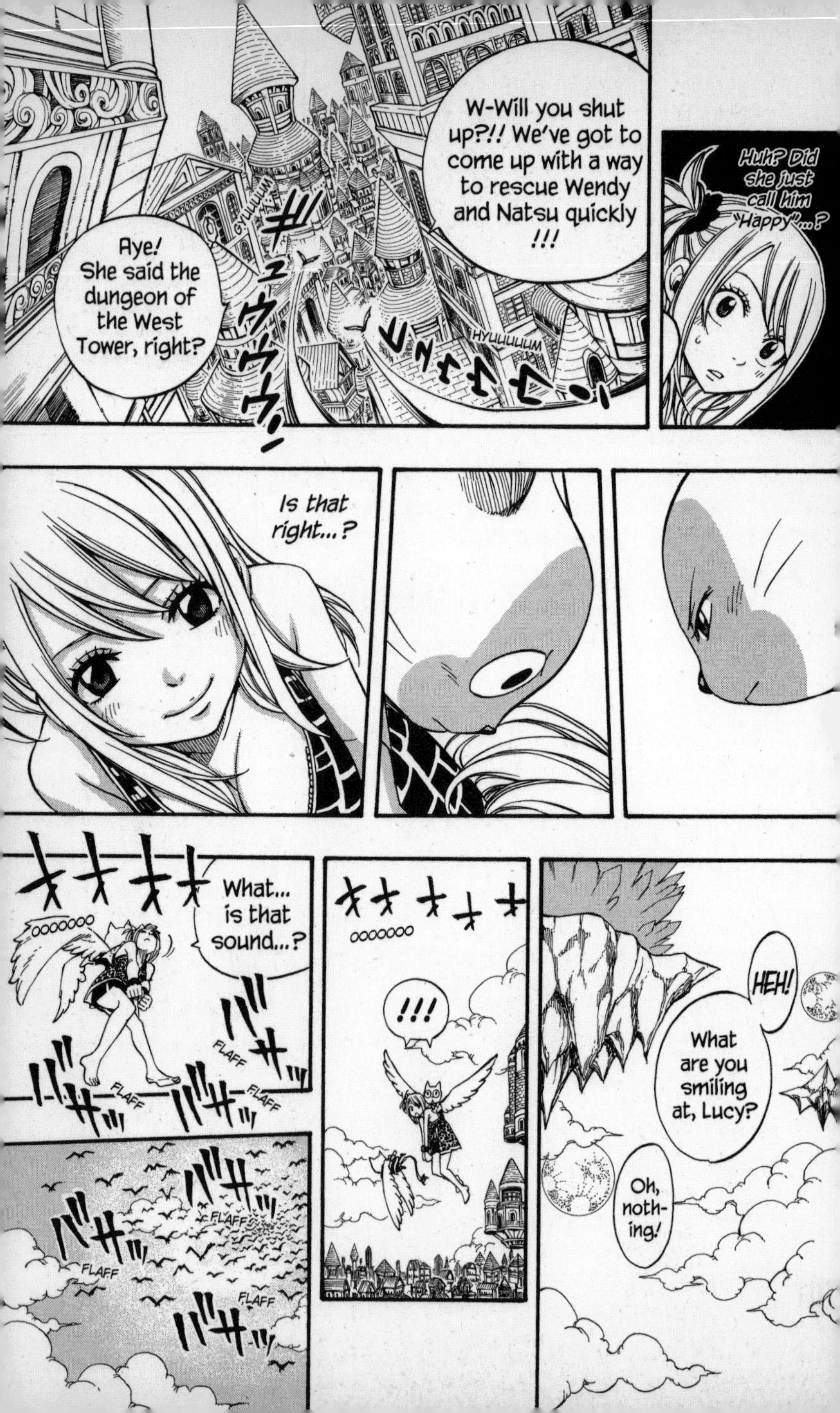
Huh? Did she just call him "Happy"...?
W-Will you shut up?!! We've got to come up with a way to rescue Wendy and Natsu quickly !!!
GYULULUM
HYUUUUUM
Aye! She said the dungeon of the West Tower, right?
Is that right...?
HEH!
What are you smiling at, Lucy?
Oh, nothing!
OOOOOOO
!!!
What... is that sound...?
OOOOOOO
FLAFF
FLAFF
FLAFF
FLAFF
FLAFF
FLAFF

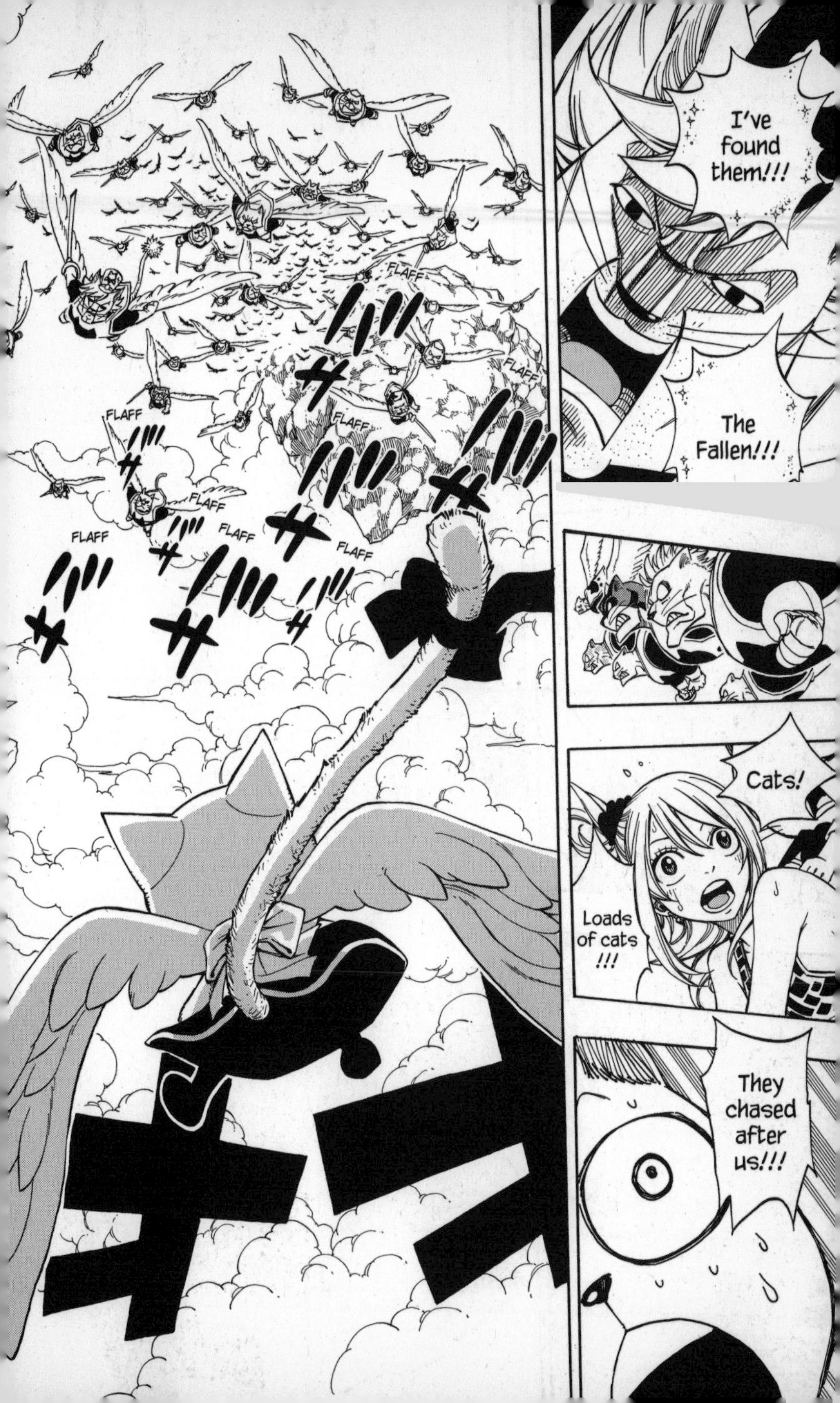
I've found them!!!
The Fallen!!!
Cats!
Loads of cats !!!
They chased after us!!!
FLAFF
FLAFF
FLAFF
FLAFF
FLAFF
FLAFF
FLAFF
FLAFF

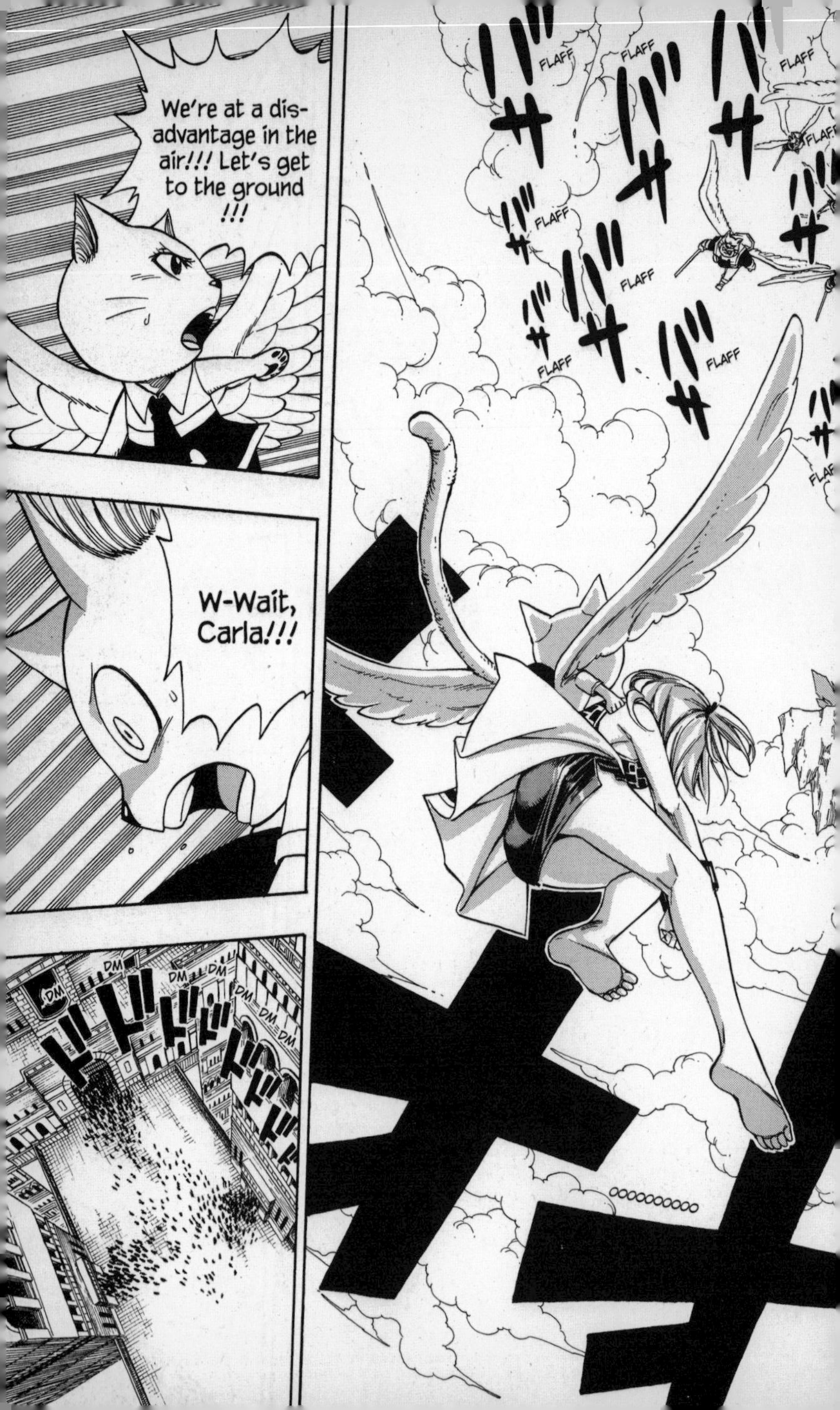
FLAFF
FLAFF
FLAFF
FLAFF
FLAFF
FLAFF
FLAFF
FLAFF
FLAFF
FLAFF
oooooooooo
We're at a dis-advantage in the air!!! Let's get to the ground !!!
W-Wait, Carla!!!
DM
DM
DM
DM
DM
DM
DM

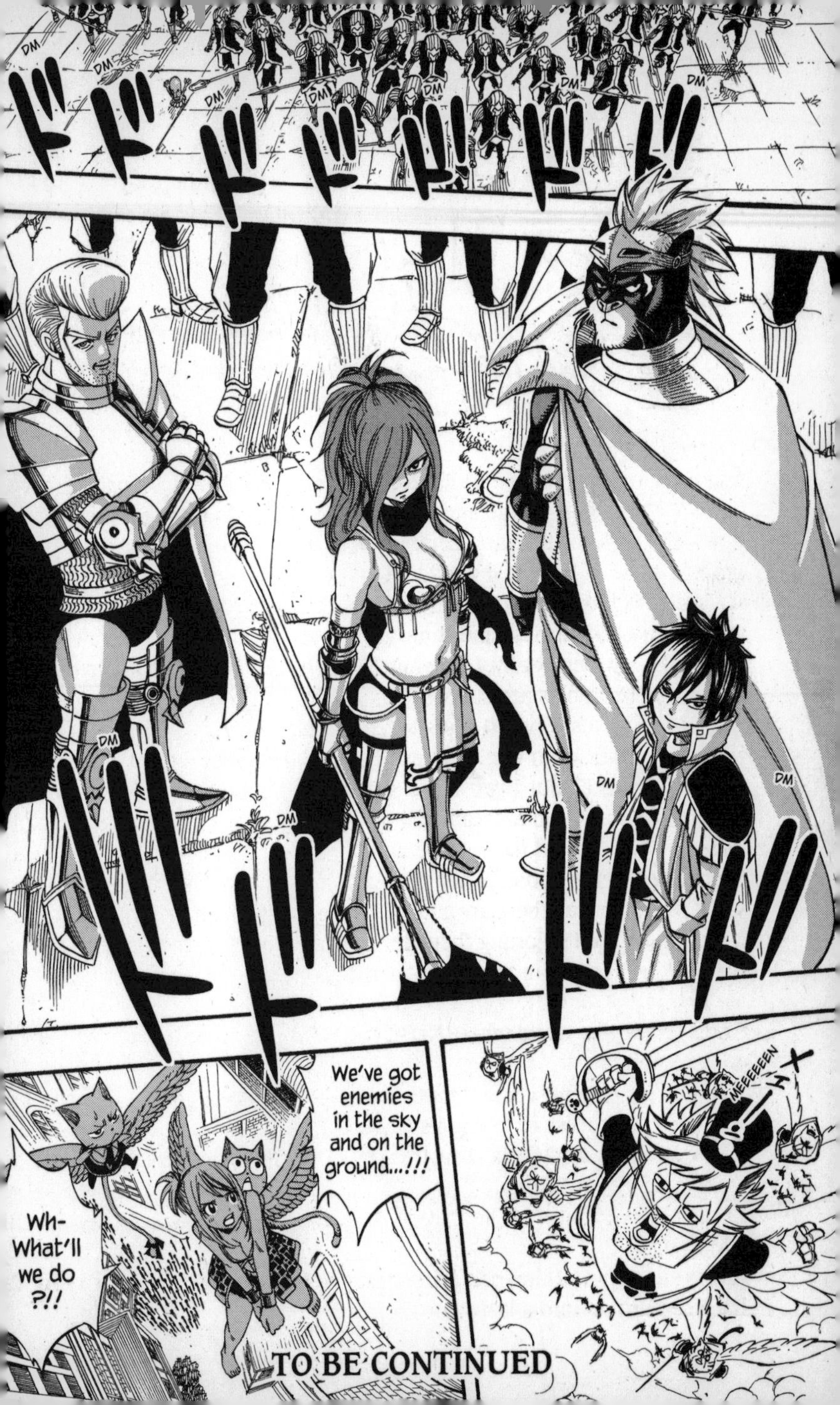
DM
DM
DM
DM
DM
DM
DM
DM
DM
DM
DM
MEEEEEEN
We've got enemies in the sky and on the ground...!!!
Wh-What'll we do ?!!

TO BE CONTINUED

Afterword

There are cats everywhere!! Especially starting on the splash page for cha[p]ter 177 all the way to the end is a steady stream of nothing but cats!!! A[nd] that's the story of this first commemorative (?) volume! Now that we're [in] the Edolas arc, I figured it would be easier to draw than the Nirvana arc th[at] we just finished, but...?!! Look at all the crowd scenes!! And now there a[re] two Natsus and Lucies, and it always takes so much time to draw Panth[er] Lily (although personally, I love him because he's so cute), and the building[s] and plants of Edolas are supposed to look like nothing you'd find on Earth[-] land, so it's such a pain!! It's suddenly turned into a series where it take[s] forever to draw even one chapter! It's been ten years since I started doin[g] this job, right...? But I can never seem to speed up the process! Ten yea[rs] ago, I thought that in a decade, I'll be drawing manga at twice the speed I'[m] doing now! I figured then I'd be able to take like three days off per wee[k!] Yeah, I remember those plans clearly... I'm so sorry, my former self of te[n] years ago! Anyway there are a lot of new terms here, and I don't want you [to] get confused, so I'm jotting them down here. Which is a good excuse becau[se] this will keep me from forgetting them too.

Earth-land: The world where Natsu and everybody live. It just means livin[g] on the Earth.
Edolas: A different world from the one Natsu and everybody live on. It's [a] world in the process of losing its magic.
Exceed: Happy and Carla. They're a race of beings that look like cats. The[y] are like angels of Edolas.
Extalia: The country of the Exceed. They have a Queen which they worshi[p] like a god.
Lacrima: A crystal that can harbor magic. Presently everyone in Fairy Ta[il] has been turned into a lacrima.

FAIRY TAIL
Bit-Part Guild Card 1

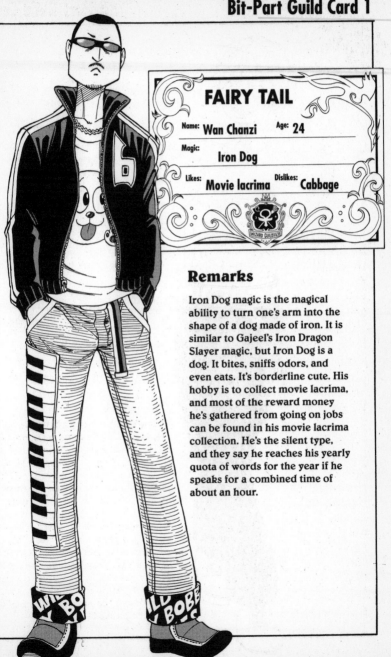

FAIRY TAIL

Name: Wan Chanzi Age: 24

Magic: Iron Dog

Likes: Movie lacrima Dislikes: Cabbage

Remarks

Iron Dog magic is the magical ability to turn one's arm into the shape of a dog made of iron. It is similar to Gajeel's Iron Dragon Slayer magic, but Iron Dog is a dog. It bites, sniffs odors, and even eats. It's borderline cute. His hobby is to collect movie lacrima, and most of the reward money he's gathered from going on jobs can be found in his movie lacrima collection. He's the silent type, and they say he reaches his yearly quota of words for the year if he speaks for a combined time of about an hour.

FAIRY TAIL
Bit-Part Guild Card

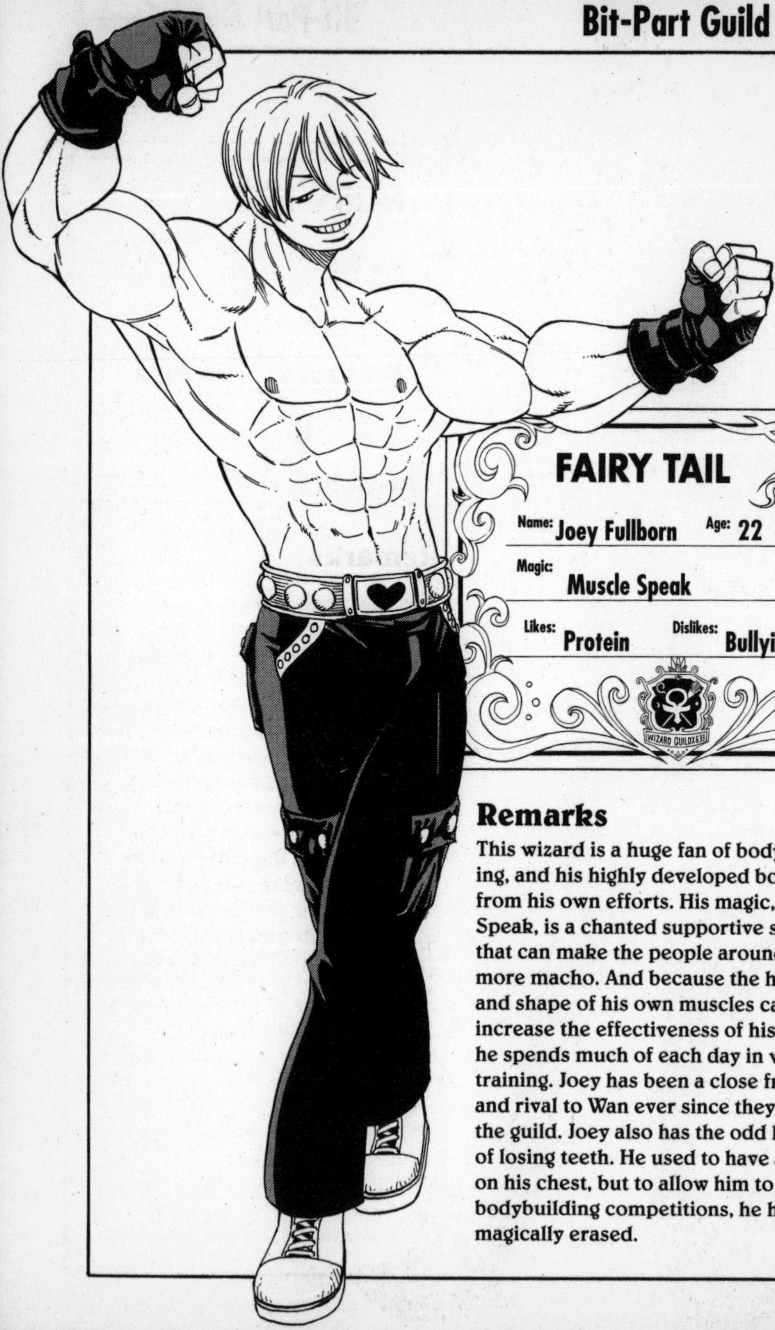

FAIRY TAIL

Name: Joey Fullborn Age: 22

Magic: Muscle Speak

Likes: Protein Dislikes: Bullying

WIZARD GUILD X633

Remarks

This wizard is a huge fan of bodybuilding, and his highly developed body is from his own efforts. His magic, Muscle Speak, is a chanted supportive spell that can make the people around him more macho. And because the health and shape of his own muscles can increase the effectiveness of his magic, he spends much of each day in weight training. Joey has been a close friend and rival to Wan ever since they entered the guild. Joey also has the odd habit (?) of losing teeth. He used to have a tattoo on his chest, but to allow him to enter bodybuilding competitions, he had it magically erased.

FAIRY TAIL
Bit-Part Guild Card 3

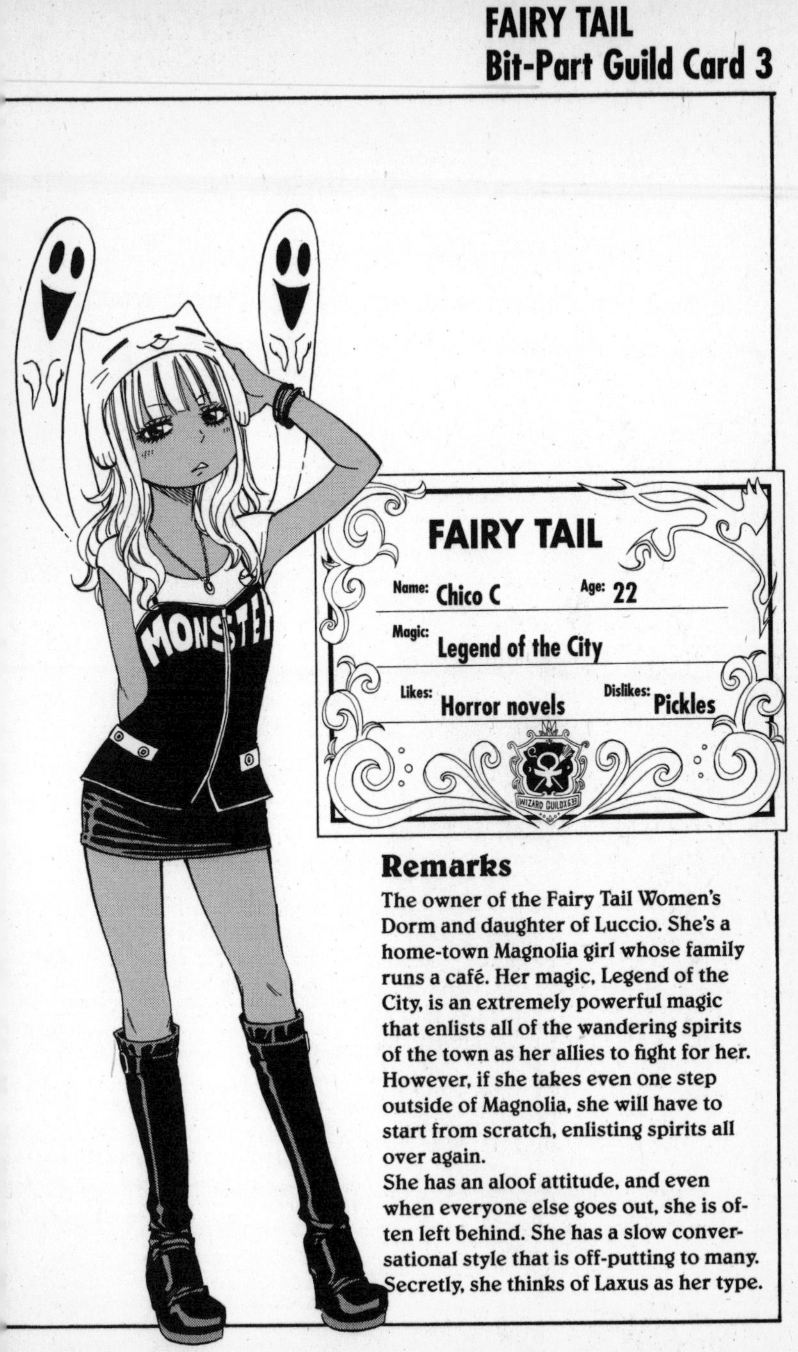

FAIRY TAIL

Name: Chico C **Age:** 22

Magic: Legend of the City

Likes: Horror novels **Dislikes:** Pickles

Remarks

The owner of the Fairy Tail Women's Dorm and daughter of Luccio. She's a home-town Magnolia girl whose family runs a café. Her magic, Legend of the City, is an extremely powerful magic that enlists all of the wandering spirits of the town as her allies to fight for her. However, if she takes even one step outside of Magnolia, she will have to start from scratch, enlisting spirits all over again.

She has an aloof attitude, and even when everyone else goes out, she is often left behind. She has a slow conversational style that is off-putting to many. Secretly, she thinks of Laxus as her type.

FAIRY TAIL
Bit-Part Guild Card

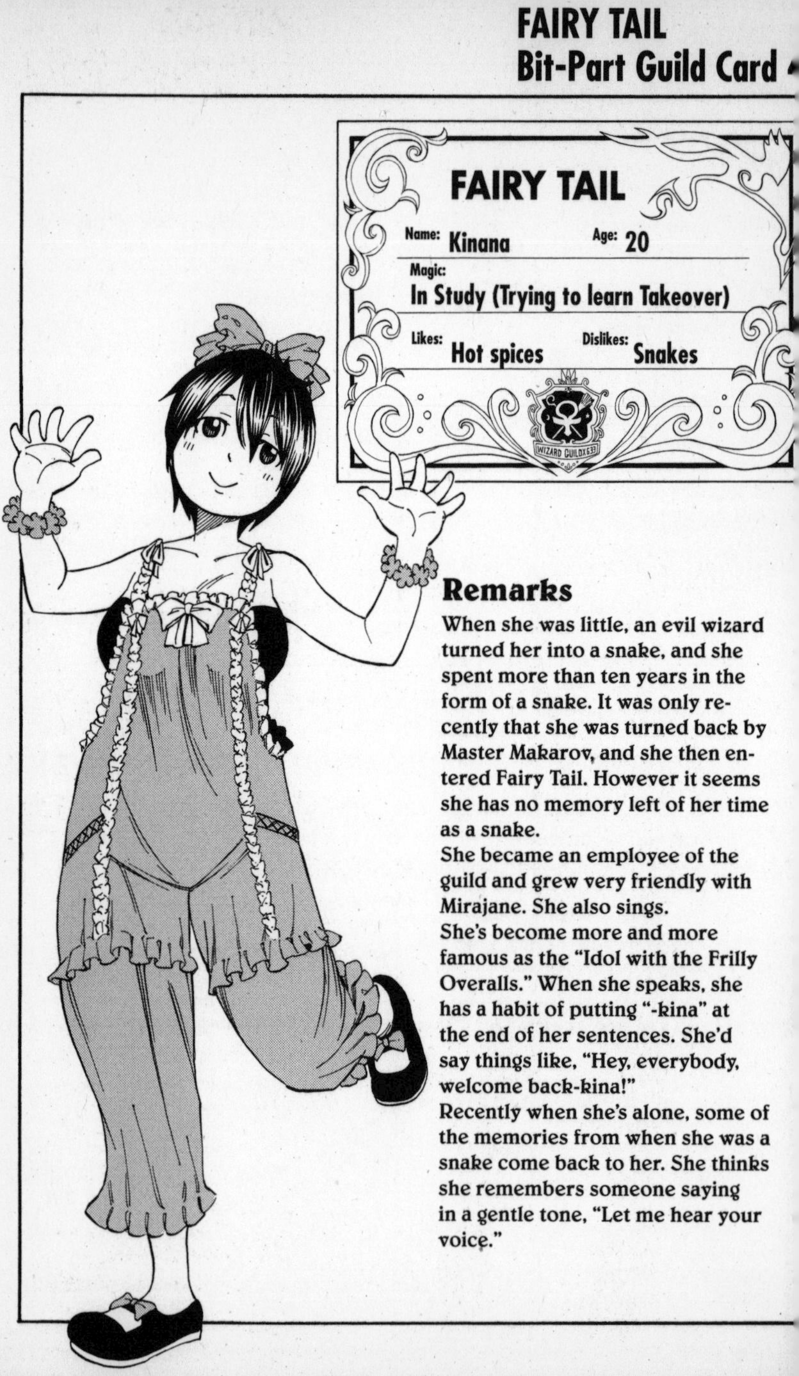

FAIRY TAIL

Name: Kinana   Age: 20

Magic:
In Study (Trying to learn Takeover)

Likes: Hot spices   Dislikes: Snakes

WIZARD GUILD×633

Remarks

When she was little, an evil wizard turned her into a snake, and she spent more than ten years in the form of a snake. It was only recently that she was turned back by Master Makarov, and she then entered Fairy Tail. However it seems she has no memory left of her time as a snake.

She became an employee of the guild and grew very friendly with Mirajane. She also sings.

She's become more and more famous as the "Idol with the Frilly Overalls." When she speaks, she has a habit of putting "-kina" at the end of her sentences. She'd say things like, "Hey, everybody, welcome back-kina!"

Recently when she's alone, some of the memories from when she was a snake come back to her. She thinks she remembers someone saying in a gentle tone, "Let me hear your voice."

Continued from the left-hand page. ↓

Mira: There are all sorts! No... Or to be more accurate, there ***were*** all sorts.

: Yeah, they were all crushed by the Kingdom...

Mira: I remember that Blue Pegasus only allowed girls to join.

Lucy: And one of my best friends, Sherry, used to be a part of Lamia Scale.

Mira: Oh, remember how Lyon-kun from that guild used to be such a big rival to Gray vying to get Juvia to just notice them?

Lucy: I ***hope*** they're all safe, but...

: Yeah...

What is Ichiya's "Meeeeen" cry all about?

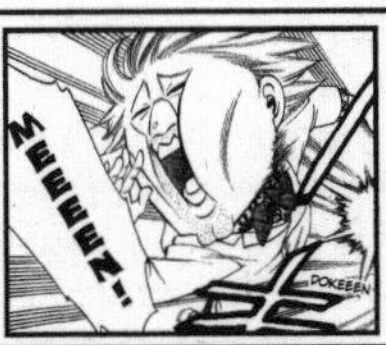
MEEEEN!
DOKEEEN

Lucy: Here's another?! Who the heck is this Ichiya guy?!

Mira: And saying, "Meeeen"...

Lucy: Isn't that a part of Kendo sword techniques? When they go for the head, the say, "Men!"

Mira: And when sheep bleat, it sounds kind of like that, right?

: Okay, then at times like this, we can just say it's this Ichiya guy's bleat!

: That's true! We have determined that, "Meeeen" is just Ichiya's way of bleating.

Lucy: Now we finally get to the last question.

Why is Mirajane the only one where the Earth-land character and her Edolas character are the same?

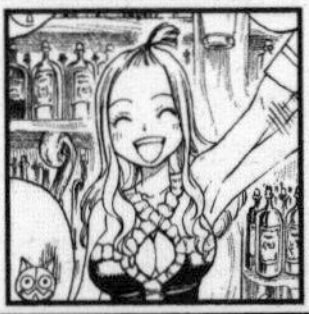

Lucy: Yeah! That's one I really want to know too!

: Hm? What are you talking about?

Lucy: Well, they say the Earth-land me is writing a novel and was raised as this little rich kid!

Mira: Really?

Lucy: And people like Gray, Cana, and Elfman are all totally different. Even their Wendy is years younger!

Mira: And I'm the same?

Lucy: According to Earth-land Natsu, there's not a single difference between you two.

: Aww... Well that's just boring, isn't it?

: I more or less think so too.

Mira: I wonder if we're exactly the same if I do ***this*** too!

: Huh...?!! What do ya think you're doing?!! Put your clothes back on!!!

Mira: Or maybe ***this***!

: Will you cut that out?!! And wait! I never met the Earth-land you anyway, so how'm I supposed to compare you two?!!!

: Well let's show the readers and let them decide...

: ***THAT IS ONE THING WE CAN'T DO!!!***
WE'LL GET IN TROUBLE WITH MASHIMA!!!

(The Earth-land Lucy has to do this every time? I don't envy her...)

Emergency Request!
Explain the Mysteries of
FAIRYTAIL

At the Edolas Fairy Tail

Lucy: You mean it's gonna be *us* this time?

Mira: That's right. They said that we should do it once in a while.

Lucy: Aww, what a friggin' pain!

Mira: No negativity. Let's give this our best!

 : (They tell me she's exactly the same no matter which world...)

Is the horse head on top of Sagittarius actually alive?

Lucy: "Sagittarius"? Who the heck is that?!

Mira: It's a Celestial Spirit that the Earth-land Lucy keeps **AS A PET.**

 : Wait! They're no "pets," right?!

Lucy: I don't know much about it, but it's just a mask, right?

Mira: I suppose... If it were alive, it'd be really scary! Let's just say it's a mask.

Anima doesn't work on Wendy, so why did Mystogan tell her to run away?

Lucy: I have no clue what this guy's talking about!

: It's probably impossible for us in Edolas to answer these kinds of questions.

: Aw, don't give me that! The word "impossible" don't apply to us!

Mira: Wow! ♡ Lucy, you're so cool!

Lucy: Here's what I figure! That he didn't know it wouldn't work on her. If you think of it that way, the rest follows, right?

Mira: Amazing! It *does* follow!

Lucy: Okay, that answers that! Hit me with another one!

Aside from Fairy Tail, what other guilds exist on Edolas?

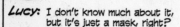

Continued on the right-hand page.

TAIL
de ART

The Fairy Tail Guild de Art is looking for illustrations! Please send in your art on a post card or at post-card size, and do it in black pen, okay? Those chosen to be published will get a signed mini poster! ♪ Make sure you write your real name and address on the back of your illustration!

▼All of the "help" of the Heartfilia Household received nice compensation packages, and they're all enjoying retirement right now.

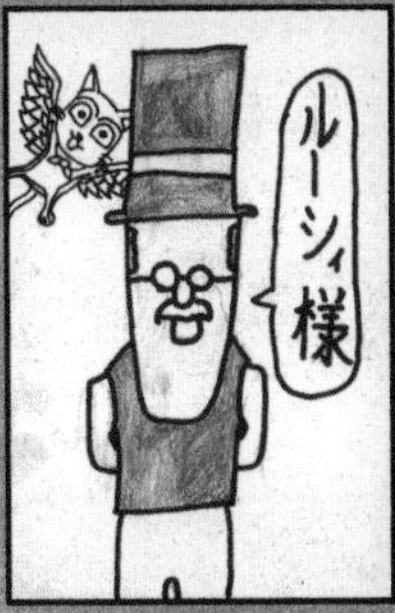
ルーシィ様

Aichi Prefecture, Kiichiro Iwata

▼I see this as a, "Right! We're headed out on a job right now!" picture.

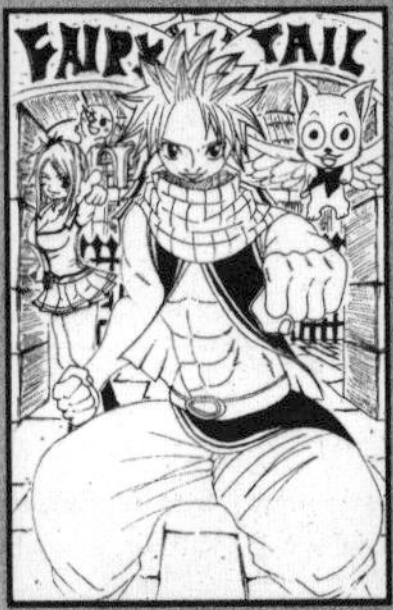
FAIRY TAIL

Tottori Prefecture, Natsuki

▼Lyon's pretty darned cool. That's what I have in mind when I draw him too.

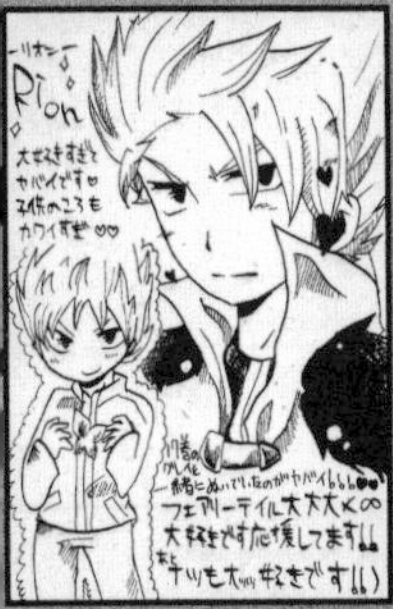
Rion

Hokkaido, Misa

▼Hey, this one's good! And really cute! You win!

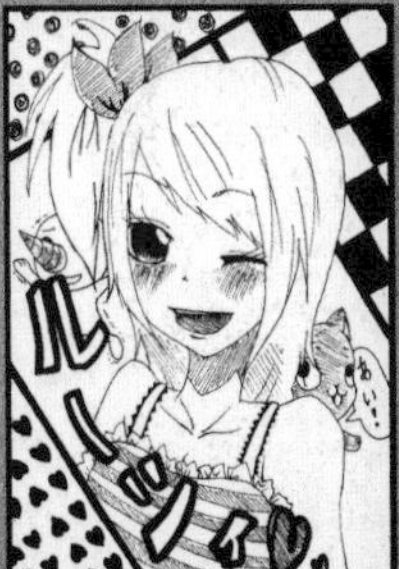

Okayama Prefecture, Natsumi Ayata

▼It's the young Mira-chan! She was always fighting with Erza.

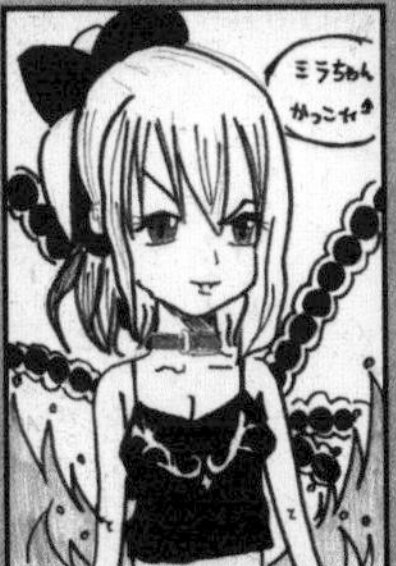
ミラちゃん かっこいい

Kochi Prefecture, Nanami Kitaoka

▼Elfman in the anime is pretty cool, huh?! Maybe I'll give him more of a part in the future.

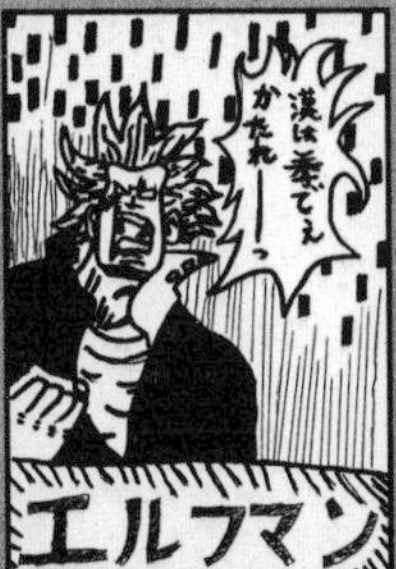
エルフマン

Oita Prefecture, Rin Kugimiya

▼Finger puppets! Happy's expression really got to me.

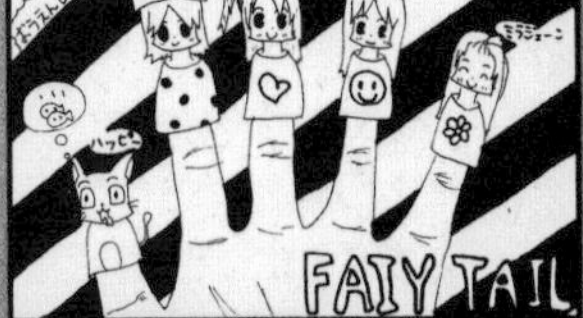
FAIY TAIL

Hokkaido, Ayano Furuya

▼Everyone's amazingly cute! It gave me an extra boost!

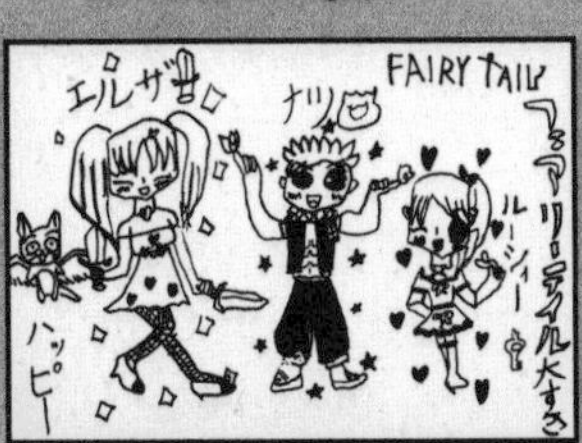
FAIRY TAIL
エルザ
ナツ
ルーシィー
ハッピー

Aichi Prefecture, Marina Miyazaki

Send to Hiro Mashima, Kodansha Comics
451 Park Ave. South, 7th Floor New York, NY 10016

FAIRY GUILD

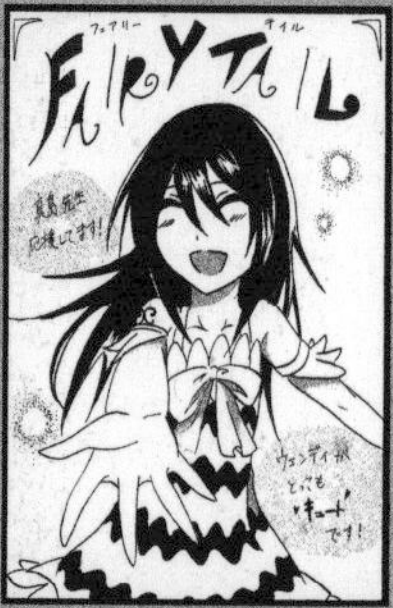
FAIRY TAIL
フェアリー テイル

Saga Prefecture, Renren

▼The smile on this one is almost too bright! I think she'll make a contribution this time!

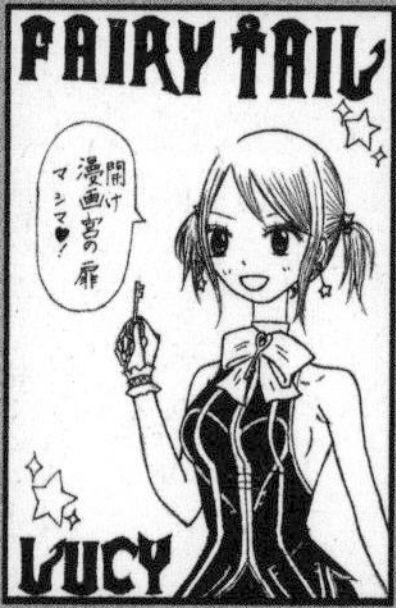
FAIRY TAIL
開け 漫画家の扉 マシマ♥!
LUCY

Gunma Prefecture, Nana Yoshizawa

▼She went and called on me! Now I have to go there!

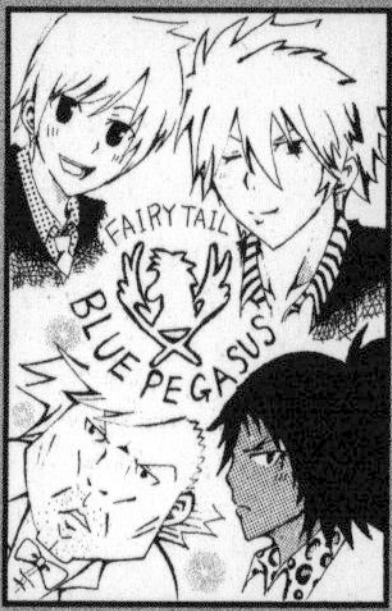
FAIRY TAIL
BLUE PEGASUS

Osaka, Suzuka Sakaguchi

And Ichiya...makes an unexpected appearance...

REJECTION CORNER

▼ I thought of questioning the meaning of this, but I've decided not to go there.

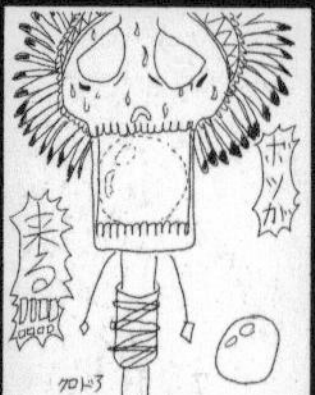

Tokyo, Ayato Nakao

▼ These two are really at the center of the action this time! I'm sure they'll play big parts next time too.

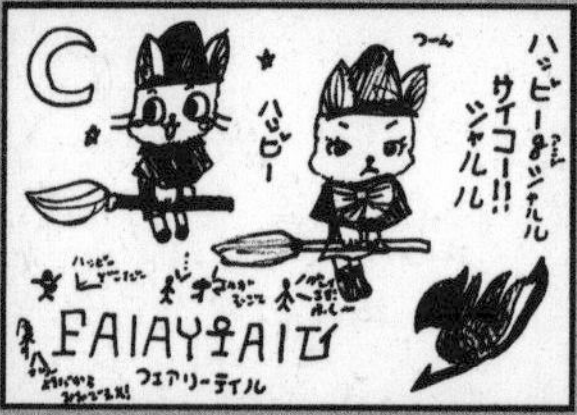
ハッピー
ハッピーおシャルル サイコー!! シャルル
FAIAYTAIL
フェアリーテイル

Tokyo, Ayumi Ichikawa

▼ The gate to Mountain-Lion-Pon was left open! Come out, come out, mountain lions!

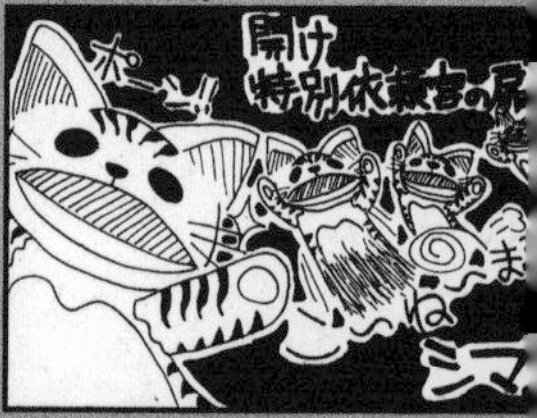
開け

Chiba Prefecture, Maccha Icecr

▼ Wow! This one's good! And everyone's got their own cool clothing style!

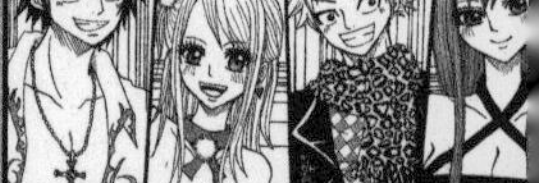
FAIRY TAIL

Yamaguchi Prefecture: Yuri Mik

Any letters and post cards you send means that your personal information such as your name, address, postal code, and other information you include will be handed over, as is, to the author. When you send mail, please keep that in mind.

Fairy Hunter
Erza Knightwalker
So you're from Earthland!
GWAAH
CHAKK

FAIRY TAIL 21

フェアリーテイル

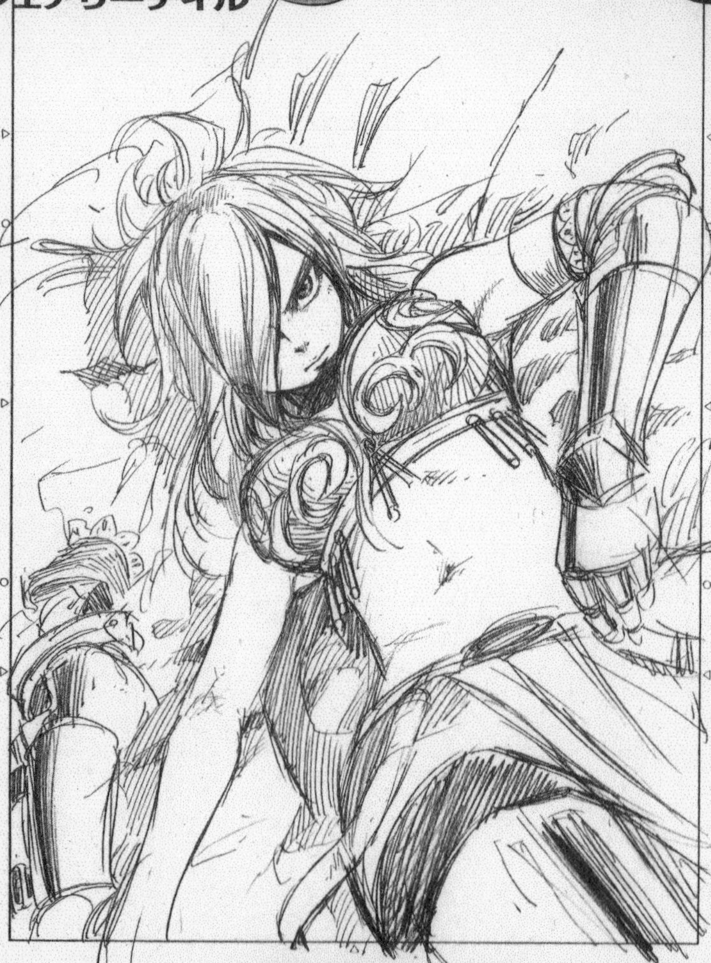

HIRO 真島ヒロ MASHIMA

Translation Notes:

Japanese is a tricky language for most Westerners, and translation is often more art than science. For your edification and reading pleasure, here are notes on some of the places where we could have gone in a different direction with our translation of the work, or where a Japanese cultural reference is used.

Page 29, -shan

Byro seems to have a speech impediment that makes his dialog a bit breathy, and "s" sounds tend to turn into "sh" sounds. That's why what would normally be Erza-san has turned into Erza-shan.

Erza-shan.
Have you not wiped out Fairy Tail yet?
Byro!

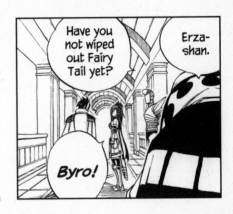

Page 36, Uriggit

The Japanese onomatopoeia (sound word) for the sound a frog makes is, "Kero-kero." But in Edolas, the frog-like creature said, "Gero-gero." This translation used a "g"-based substitution that did its best to call up the sound of a frog.

URIGGIT ...
URIGGIT ...

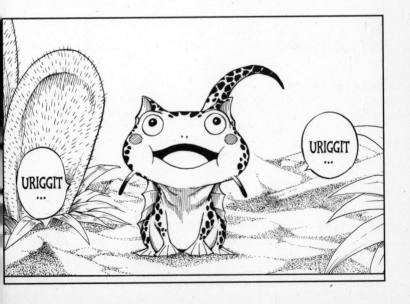

Page 66, Ebi

As noted in the notes of previous volumes, a common trait of crab characters (remember, Cancer is a crab) is to end their sentences with "-kani" which means "crab" in Japanese. Mashima decided to put a twist on this by making Cancer's sentences end in *-ebi* which means "shrimp" in Japanese.

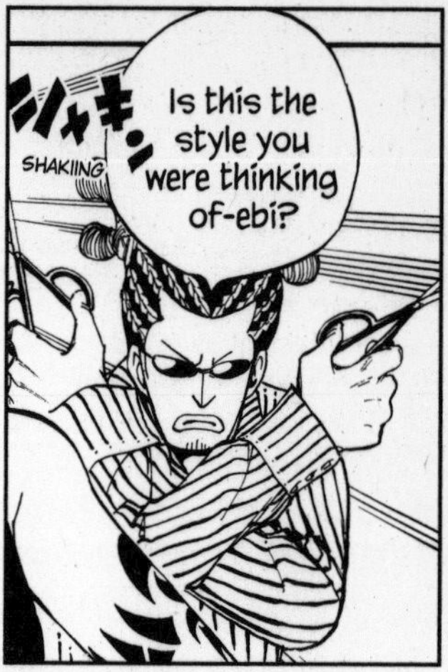
SHAKIING
Is this the style you were thinking of-ebi?

Page 71, Exceed Clan

Here, the Japanese used a word that means family or clan, but in this case, Exceed Race might be more appropriate.

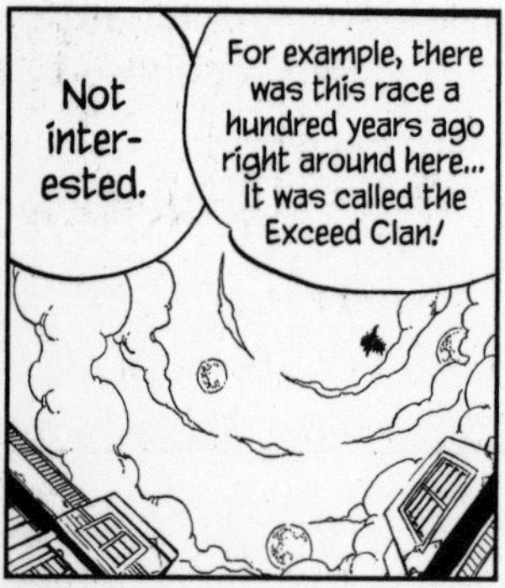
For example, there was this race a hundred years ago right around here... It was called the Exceed Clan!
Not interested.

Page 90, Butter me up

When one wants to ingratiate oneself to someone else in Japanese, one tends to use more polite honorifics than the situation might call for. In the Japanese original, Edolas Natsu called the Earth-land Natsu, Me-san, and Natsu complained since it was like calling himself -san (something not normally done).

Page 145, Fallen

In Japanese, the term for traitorous Exceed is the same term that is used for fallen angels, so this translation used the word, "Fallen."

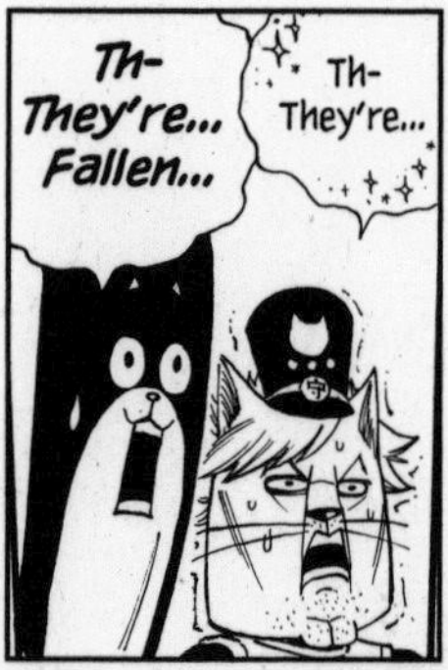
Th-They're...
Th-They're... Fallen...

Page 188, Men

In the sword-based martial art of Kendo, it is common to announce the part of the body that one is aiming for when striking. It's usually, "Chest," when aiming for the torso and, "Men," when aiming at the head or face area. One of the Japanese words that is pronounced *men* means face.

Page 188, Bleat

In Japanese, the onomatopoeia for the bleating of sheep sounds like, "Meeeeh."

Mira: And when sheep bleat, it sounds kind of like that, right?

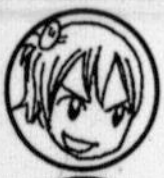

Okay, then at times like this, we can just say it's this Ichiya guy's bleat!

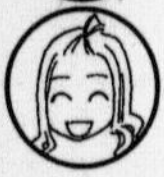

That's true! We have determined that, "Meeeen" is just Ichiya's way of bleating.

Lucy: Now we finally get to the last

Preview of *Fairy Tail*, volume 22

We're pleased to present you with a preview from Fairy Tail, volume 22. Please check our website (www.kodanshacomics.com) to see when this volume will be available.

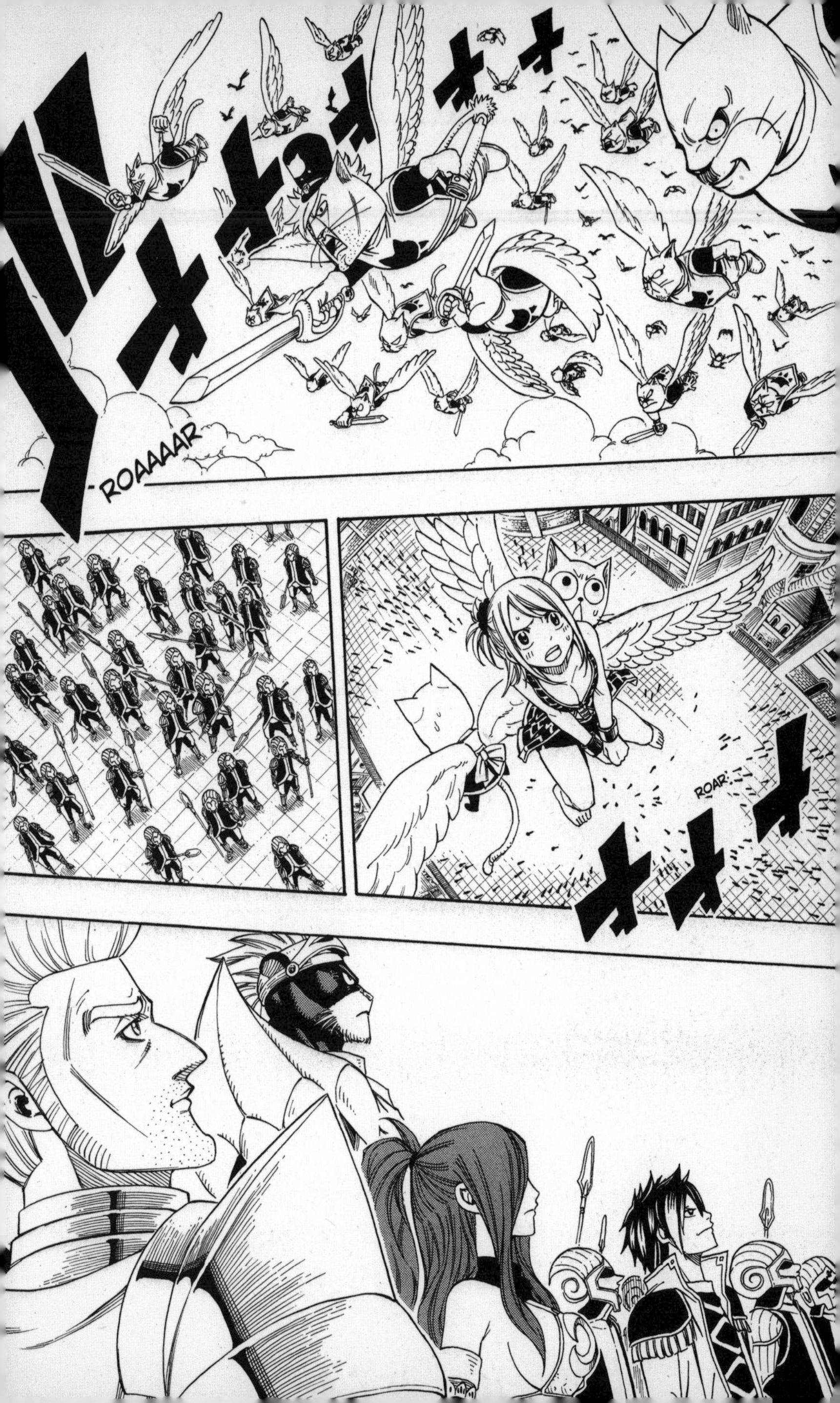
ROAAAAR
ROAR

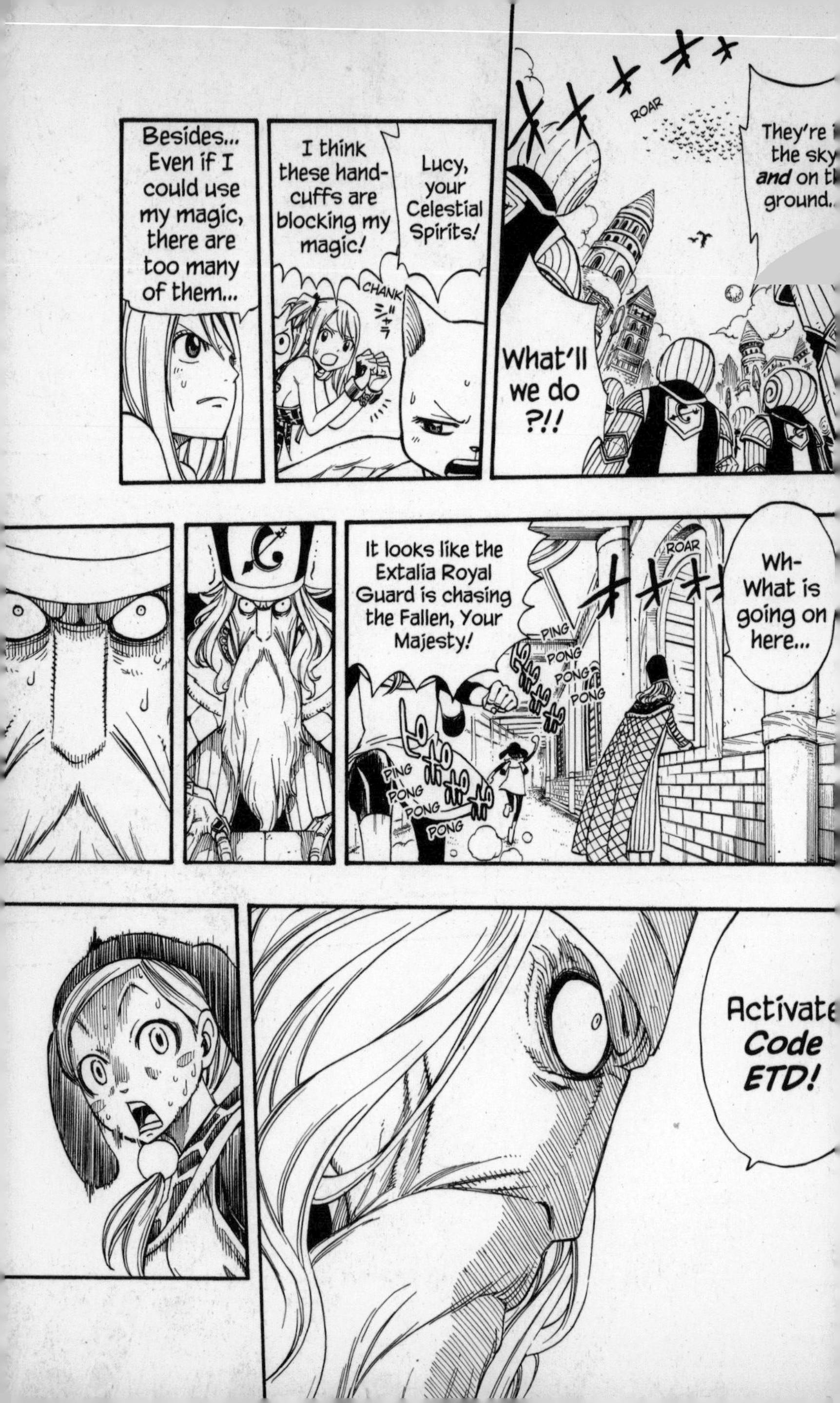

They're i the sky *and* on t ground...
ROAR
What'll we do ?!!
Lucy, your Celestial Spirits!
I think these hand-cuffs are blocking my magic!
CHANK
Besides... Even if I could use my magic, there are too many of them...
Wh- What is going on here...
ROAR
PING PONG PONG PONG
It looks like the Extalia Royal Guard is chasing the Fallen, Your Majesty!
PING PONG PONG PONG
Activate *Code ETD!*

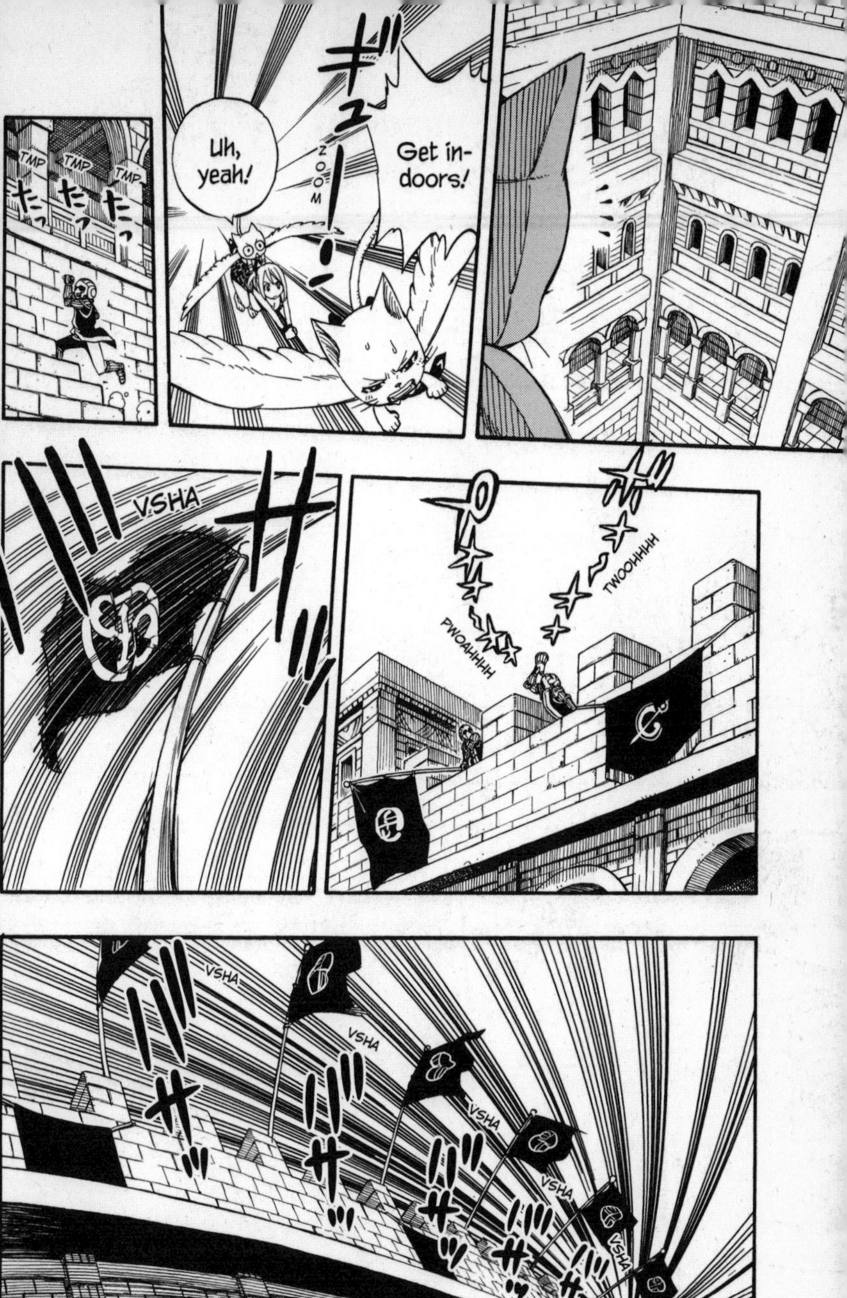
Get in-doors!
Uh, yeah!
ZOOM
TMP
TMP
TMP
TWOOHHHH
PWOAHHHH
VSHA
VSHA
VSHA
VSHA
VSHA
VSHA

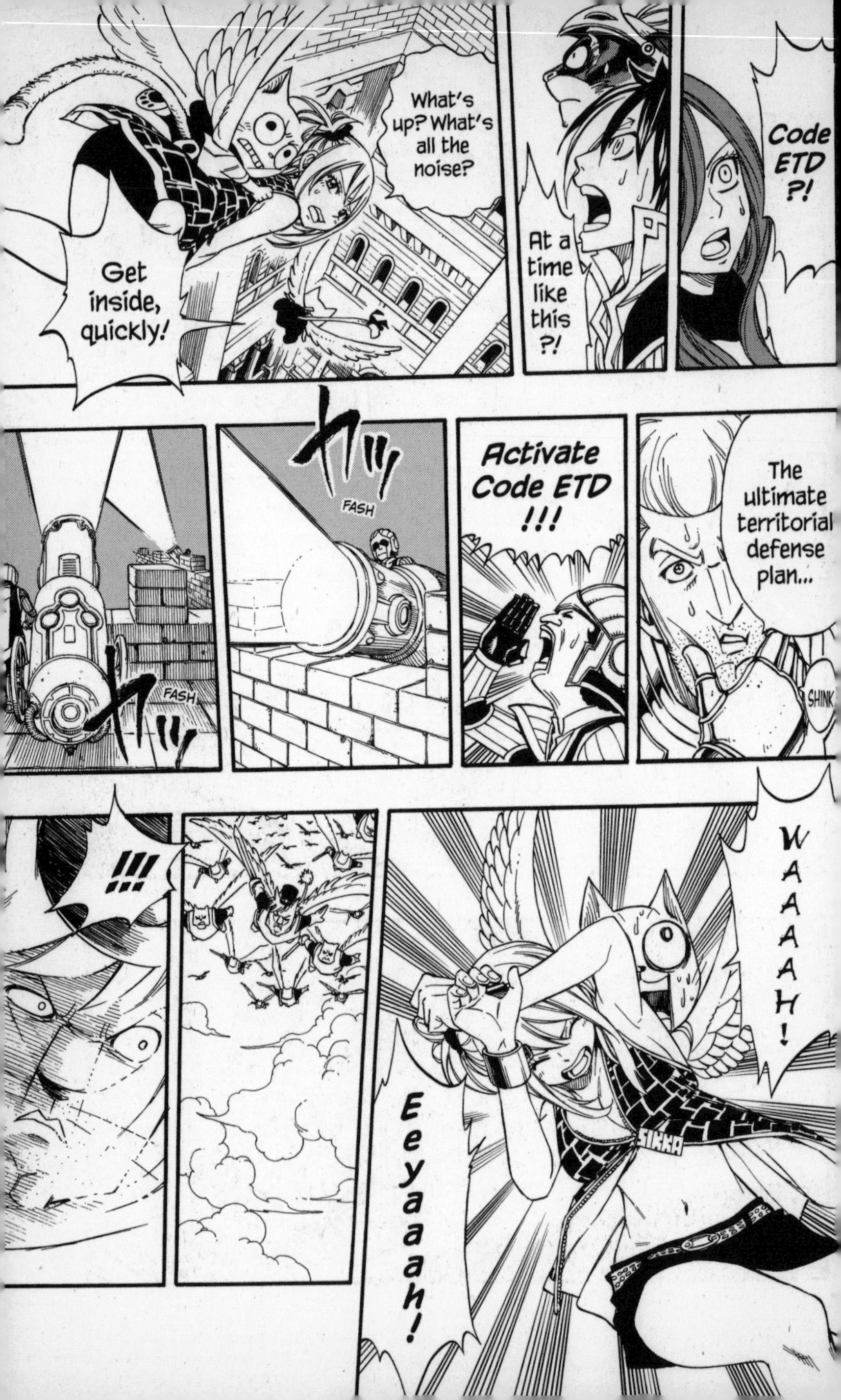
Code ETD ?!
At a time like this ?!
What's up? What's all the noise?
Get inside, quickly!
The ultimate territorial defense plan...
SHINK
Activate Code ETD !!!
FASH
FASH
WAAAAAH!
Eeyaaaah!
!!!

TOMARE!

止まれ

[STOP!]

You're going the wrong way!

Manga is a completely different type of reading experience.

To start at the *beginning*, go to the *end*!

That's right! Authentic manga is read the traditional Japanese way—from right to left, exactly the *opposite* of how American books are read. It's easy to follow: Just go to the other end of the book and read each page—and each panel—from right side to left side, starting at the top right. Now you're experiencing manga as it was meant to be!